DATE DUE

NOV 16 2011	

Sprawl, Justice, and Citizenship

Sprawl, Justice, and Citizenship

THAD WILLIAMSON

The Civic Costs of the American Way of Life

OXFORD
UNIVERSITY PRESS

2010

OXFORD
UNIVERSITY PRESS

Oxford University Press, Inc., publishes works that further
Oxford University's objective of excellence
in research, scholarship, and education.

Oxford   New York
Auckland   Cape Town   Dar es Salaam   Hong Kong   Karachi
Kuala Lumpur   Madrid   Melbourne   Mexico City   Nairobi
New Delhi   Shanghai   Taipei   Toronto

With offices in
Argentina   Austria   Brazil   Chile   Czech Republic   France   Greece
Guatemala   Hungary   Italy   Japan   Poland   Portugal   Singapore
South Korea   Switzerland   Thailand   Turkey   Ukraine   Vietnam

Copyright © 2010 by Oxford University Press, Inc.

Published by Oxford University Press, Inc.
198 Madison Avenue, New York, New York 10016

www.oup.com

Oxford is a registered trademark of Oxford University Press.

Library of Congress Cataloging-in-Publication Data
Williamson, Thad.
Sprawl, justice, and citizenship : the civic costs
of the American way of life / Thad Williamson.
p.   cm.
Includes bibliographical references and index.
ISBN 978-0-19-536943-4
1. Cities and towns—United States—Growth.
2. Social justice—United States.
3. Citizenship—United States.   I. Title.
HT384.U5W557 2010
307.760973—dc22   2009026096

1 2 3 4 5 6 7 8 9
Printed in the United States of America
on acid-free paper

For Wendell S. Dietrich,
Teacher, Mentor, and Friend

"Houses make a town,
but citizens a city."
Jean-Jacques Rousseau,
The Social Contract

ACKNOWLEDGMENTS

THIS BOOK BEGAN LIFE as a doctoral dissertation begun in 2001 and completed in 2004 in the Department of Government at Harvard University. I owe my dissertation committee—Michael J. Sandel, Robert D. Putnam, Ann Forysth, and Russell Muirhead—an enormous debt for helping conceptualize the project and eventually bring it to fruition. I especially appreciate that each committee member saw the value of combining normative and empirical inquiry and of drawing on multiple disciplines. I am grateful to Michael Sandel for consistently pushing me to bring out my own voice in this work, and I remain enormously proud to have been part of the teaching corps for his "Justice" course at Harvard, an experience that had a profound impact on the content of these pages. The opportunity to take two graduate seminars on U.S. politics and social capital with Bob Putnam as a first-year graduate student helped let me into many of the specific questions addressed in this book, and I also am extraordinarily grateful to Bob for facilitating my access to the Social Capital Community Benchmark Survey and his engagement with the details of my analysis and arguments. Ann Forsyth provided a needed planner's voice and, at times, a reality check to my thinking, and Russell Muirhead challenged and helped me translate intuitive judgments into concrete arguments. All four committee members, in addition to being outstanding scholars, have been exceptionally supportive to me throughout this project. I am proud to call all of them friends.

I also would like to thank the Multidisciplinary Program on Inequality and Social Policy at the Kennedy School of Government at Harvard University. In addition to supplying dissertation support, the program provided invaluable opportunities for early critical feedback on the first iterations of the empirical work. I am particularly grateful to Christopher Jencks, Katherine Newman, and J. Eric Oliver for their invaluable feedback at the early stages of this project, and to David Barron and Gerald Frug for allowing me to attend their yearlong seminar on cities at Harvard Law School during the 2002–03 academic year. I also would like to thank Alan Altshuler, David Luberoff, and the Taubman Center for State and Local Government at the Kennedy School of Government for additional financial support for the dissertation in addition to feedback on the work-in-progress. Thomas Sander of the Saguaro Center for Civic Engagement at the Kennedy School has helped answer my questions about the SCCBS and provided valuable comments on my analyses.

I owe a special debt to Daniel J. Hopkins, a graduate-student colleague with whom I have collaborated extensively on the analysis of the SCCBS data, particularly with respect to political participation. Dan has helped me think through the methodological issues in the analysis and sharpen the theoretical approach employed. This is a much better book because of my collaboration with Dan. I also would like to thank Christopher Adolph, Erik Craft, Crystal Hoyt, Gary King, and Byron Lutz for additional help on methodological issues.

My interest in urban and spatial issues began not in graduate school but as a research assistant for Gar Alperovitz at the Institute for Policy Studies and National Center for Economic and Security Alternatives in Washington, from 1992 to 1996. Gar helped me begin not only thinking about sprawl but also seeing it as part of a broader political–economic system that functions to reproduce inequality rather than as an isolated policy issue. One of the first people I came into contact with during that period was David Imbroscio, who has played an invaluable role since then as a mentor, coauthor, and friend. Coauthoring *Making a Place for Community* with Gar and David in many ways laid the groundwork for this book.

I also wish to acknowledge the effect on my scholarship of the community of scholars and students at Union Theological Seminary in New York City, where I earned a master's degree from 1996 to 1998. My training in social and Christian ethics there also helped paint the background for this book. In particular, I would like to thank Larry Rasmussen, a wonderful teacher and friend and a brilliant analyst of the relationship between community, sustainability, the good life, and justice; Christopher Morse, in whose course on Christianity and politics I wrote a short paper on "sprawl and political leadership," which stands as my first venture into the subject; and Beverly Harrison, a powerhouse thinker who both encouraged theologians and social ethicists to engage with the ethics of everyday life and demonstrated how ethicists can fruitfully draw on multiple paradigms.

Since coming to the University of Richmond in 2005, I have been blessed to be part of a small but wonderful community of urbanists and urban-minded folk who have helped me learn a new city and in the process sharpen and refine the arguments of this book. Douglas Hicks, Amy Howard, Glyn Hughes, Crystal Hoyt, Ana Mitrić, John Moeser, Terry Price, and Karen Zivi have engaged with my arguments and helped me strengthen them, and have also been wonderful friends. The Jepson School of Leadership Studies as a whole has been supportive of me and my work in every way imaginable for the past four years, and the opportunity to teach in a multidisciplinary setting, with the job of connecting social justice to ordinary life, has exceeded the wildest dreams of my graduate school days! Several University of Richmond students and graduates have contributed research assistance to the project, including Deanna Boyd, Kate Simma, Patrick Scanlan, and Jordan Wade.

I am grateful to numerous additional scholars and colleagues who have read and provided feedback on parts of the book and related analyses at various stages of development, including Peter Cannavó, Stephen Elkin, Archon Fung, James Gimpel, David Kitchen, Loren King, Jason Maloy, Martin O'Neill, Daniel Palazzolo, Noah Sachs, Adria Scharf, and George Williamson. I am particularly grateful to Daniel Aldrich, Susan Fainstein, Michael Harvey, Douglas Hicks, David Imbroscio, Todd Swanstrom, and Stuart White for reading the complete manuscript as it neared publication and providing very helpful comments. James DeFilippis, Stephen Macedo, and an anonymous reviewer reviewed the manuscript for Oxford and provided incisive and extremely helpful comments that have helped improve the book. Needless to say, I remain responsible for any remaining errors of fact or argument.

My editor, David McBride, at Oxford has been wonderfully supportive and patient in bringing this project to culmination. I also thank Assistant Editor Alexandra Dauler and Senior Production Editor Christine Dahlin for their hard work on the project.

Above all, I need to thank my family. My parents, Joan and Sam Williamson, have provided encouragement, love, and support all the way through this long process. My brother, George Williamson, and sister, Treeby Williamson Brown, have in different ways been invaluable confidants, and their families a source of joy and inspiration.

My wife and friend, Adria Scharf, has put up with more than she or any other reasonable person should have had to as the book has made the long journey to completion. No rational person in any original position would have readily agreed to helping me absorb the various stresses and pressures putting this book together has entailed. How fortunate it is that love conquers all! And how fortunate we both are to have our daughter, Sahara, who has provided the inspiration and motivation for the final lap. Words cannot do justice to the debt I have incurred to Adria in this process.

Finally, I wish to acknowledge an individual who does not study sprawl, political participation, or contemporary political theory, but nonetheless has had an enormous effect on my life and on the making of this book. As my undergraduate mentor at Brown University, Professor Wendell S. Dietrich challenged me intellectually and in his typically understated way helped nurture my confidence as a student and scholar. The core texts and ideas from his undergraduate seminar on religious and secular social thought in the twentieth century have remained, despite my other excursions, my core intellectual and spiritual reference points, and his example as a teacher and mentor is one I try my best to emulate in my own teaching. It is with pleasure and gratitude that I dedicate this book to him.

CONTENTS

Sprawl, Justice, and Citizenship

Introduction

Sprawl as a Moral Issue

M UST THE STRIP MALL and the eight-lane highway define twenty-first-century U.S. life?

The possibility that they might is depressing to many concerned Americans. The sight of yet another new subdivision on the fringe of a metropolitan area, the opening of another big-box store, and the prospect of another road-construction project raise little enthusiasm among either academic critics of sprawl or ordinary Americans worn out by growing traffic congestion and long automobile commutes.[1]

Yet the anti-sprawl movement, one of the most striking recent developments in both environmental and urban politics, finds itself at an impasse. Local and state initiatives aimed at combating sprawl have thus far failed to generate either political momentum or broad public consensus on behalf of sustained, comprehensive policy action. Nearly two decades after the formation of the Congress for the New Urbanism and Vice President Al Gore's failed proposal for a carbon tax, federal policy continues to promote suburbanization while Hummers and SUVs overrun the nation's roadways, doing their part (and then some) to contribute to the nation's prodigious greenhouse-gas emissions. The anti-sprawl movement has reshaped the debate and spurred some constructive policy steps at the local and state levels, and criticism of urban sprawl is a regular feature of numerous politicians' speeches on urban policy, including the current president of the United States.[2] Yet while the recent economic crisis in the United States has slowed suburban growth in many areas, decentralized, automobile-driven expansion of the metropolitan fringe remains the dominant form of urban development in the United States.[3]

Part of the difficulty is that, contrary to the rhetoric of many anti-sprawl activists, sprawl is not a black-and-white issue, but rather one involving both empirical and moral complexity of the highest order. Critiques of sprawl that are too simplistic or too sweeping are neither intellectually credible nor politically efficacious.

Indeed, as observers such as Robert Bruegmann, William Bogart, and David Brooks have argued, there *is* a powerful case to be made on sprawl's behalf.[4] Sprawl, such writers suggest, is, by and large, a good thing because it fulfills Americans' preferences for privacy and mobility and provides a spatial context in which millions of citizens can access the American dream of a comfortable private home in a safe, pleasant neighborhood.

Those are serious arguments, and it is the aim of this book to provide a serious response. The assessment of sprawl reached here is at odds both with optimistic assessments that because sprawl exists, it must be good, and with polemical portrayals of sprawl and continued suburbanization as wholly irrational. Sprawl *does* benefit millions of Americans who prefer lower-density environments and would rather not live close to the concentrated social problems characteristic of U.S. cities.

But it does so at a significant moral cost. Suburban sprawl as currently practiced is fundamentally hostile to the aspiration of achieving a society capable of meeting even modest norms of equal opportunity. Sprawl is also constituent of a way of life that prioritizes privatism and consumerism over engaged political participation and ecological sustainability. The ultimate civic cost of the U.S. way of life, as exemplified by sprawl, is a political culture characterized by weak citizen participation, a declining capacity to provide equal opportunity to citizens, and an inadequate response to the challenges posed by climate change.

Whether this civic cost is worth the benefits associated with sprawl is fundamentally a moral question. In making judgments for or against sprawl, we are necessarily making judgments about what kind of society we wish to live in.

Preliminaries I: Sprawl as Collective Choice

A fundamental contention of this book is that to debate suburban sprawl is to do nothing less than to debate how we are to live together. Counting the costs and benefits of sprawl and evaluating its economic efficiency is an essential task, but that counting exercise does not fully answer the question of whether sprawl is desirable or not, or in what respects. Evaluating who benefits from sprawl and who does not can provide us with important information concerning whether and how sprawl is linked with inequality and social injustice—but even this evaluation is incomplete. The right questions to ask are not simply whether sprawl is *efficient* or *fair* but also whether it is *good*. It is simply not possible to evaluate sprawl and its consequences without interrogating the goodness and moral worthiness of the way of life sprawl promotes.

Posing this question takes us into terrain where many a liberal political theorist fears to tread. Such theorists might remind us that just as there are multiple plausible views in contemporary societies concerning the best way of life, so, too, are there a multitude of plausible conceptions of how the arrangement of the built environment might best foster (or permit) well-lived lives. Yet unlike ideas about which diet, exercise regime, balance of work and play, choice of leisure activity, or even religious convictions best promote the "good life," competing conceptions of how space should be organized cannot be accommodated simply by permitting individuals to pursue their own ideals of a well-designed community while the state remains officially neutral.

This is the case for four key reasons: First, individual actions regarding land use and housing may generate externalities that affect one's neighbors and even the identity of a whole community. Second, and closely related, individuals may have preferences not only about their own living space but also about the character of the neighborhood they wish to inhabit. (Recognition of these first two points underlies many local zoning ordinances in addition to rules set by common-interest developments.) Third, any community involves some shared or public space that is the common concern and responsibility of all residents. Individual persons do not have individual sidewalks, streetlamps, and roads at their disposal.

Fourth, and most important, collective choices made or shaped by the state help structure the range of choices available to individuals. Residence in the outer suburbs did not become possible until governments built the roads that service such locations. As a practical matter, no process of housing development or community building in the United States can proceed without substantial public assistance and state involvement in the form of building roads, providing infrastructure and other services, hiring police to protect property, and the like. Building a public road to link a new, privately developed community to existing settlements is itself a political act, just as the notion that all built communities in the United States should be physically connected to one another via publicly accessible ground-level transportation is a political idea.

The spatial organization of communities thus necessarily represents a collective choice, mediated through politics. (Communities may collectively opt to let market forces and individual actions determine spatial development, and residents may accept the consequences; but this, too, is a political choice.) Collective political choices about how to organize communities spatially necessarily involve conceptions (stated and unstated) about what the good life is and what way of life a community wishes to promote. Inattention to this dimension of the sprawl issue leads to an inadequate, even evasive, response to the question, what is wrong with sprawl? It also yields an inadequate understanding of the consequences of the various policy choices that affect the spatial organization of communities.

Indeed, it is implausible and incoherent to suggest that government decisions that help shape land use and the organization of space could ever be "value neutral" in any meaningful sense. When localities set minimum lot-size zoning requirements for new housing developments, they are (quite often explicitly) invoking the ideal of private home ownership—and the ideal of living in a community of other private homeowners. When state planning authorities build new transportation infrastructure to accommodate automobile travel, they are both accommodating and reinforcing a vision of the good life that places high priority on individual mobility and that assumes that well-lived lives do not require that home, work, and the location of other daily activities be geographically proximate. Conversely, when New Urbanist planners seek to build neotraditional towns in which residents can access most places on foot, and ample public spaces that encourage informal social interactions, they, too, are invoking a particular conception of the good life.[5] At the local, regional, and state levels, decisions about the organization of space, the provision of transit, the establishment of building codes, and other components of the built environment are bound to reflect conceptions about what sort of life citizens will engage in on a daily basis. As the journalist Anthony Flint has succinctly put it, the ongoing public debate concerning sprawl is "uniquely revealing about who we are as a country." He adds, "It's about our politics and our culture and our ability to think collectively."[6] Failing to acknowledge this point is, at the theoretical level, a mistake. At the practical level, ignoring this point means that unspoken assumptions about what the best way of life is can often become the basis for policy, without serious public deliberation about the worthiness of that way of life.

To recognize that debates about the built environment are also debates about the good life is to lay the groundwork for a more robust, inclusive, and substantive dialogue concerning how competing normative values might best be balanced with one another in formulating and implementing spatial and transportation policies. A short list of values and goods that may plausibly be thought to be at stake in how communities are designed includes safety, privacy, convenience, mobility, beauty, order, economic efficiency, neighborliness, sense of community, civic attachment, gender equity, child-friendliness, respect for nature, tranquility, and social and economic inclusiveness.[7] Many contemporary critics (and some friends) of suburbia in general and sprawl in particular argue that contemporary spatial forms give excessive weight to certain of these values—those concerning private well-being—at the expense of those values concerning the civic and social dimensions of our communities.[8]

Explicitly identifying the variety of normative values at stake in urban planning decisions might help tilt the substance of these decisions so as to give greater weight to civic and social considerations. Equally important, the process of critically reflecting as citizens on what sort of communities we aspire to live in (and by extension, what habits and experiences of daily life we want to encourage) might deepen the legitimacy of public decisions about the built environment. Rather than conceptualizing the built environment as simply reflecting citizens' preferences and "choices," democratic theory suggests that public decisions about the built environment should reflect considered *judgments* by citizens about which competing values are to be prioritized in organizing space.[9] Such judgments are possible only after a process of public deliberation in which all competing values are put on the table, and in which citizens are compelled not only to see beyond their initial interests but also to critically reexamine their own preconceptions about what communities are for and what ways of life they wish to promote.[10]

Preliminaries II: Normative Arguments and Policy Diversity

To insist that value questions be debated openly is not, of course, to suggest that there exist universal, determinate answers to such questions. One source of skepticism toward the notion that democratic societies can conduct substantive debates about the good life is the fear that majorities could impose their conceptions of the good upon unwilling minorities.[11] This concern is especially salient in the suburban sprawl debate; some critics of the contemporary anti-sprawl movement, such as Robert Bruegmann, have portrayed critics of sprawl as high-minded elites anxious to force others to conform to their vision of the good.[12]

How might the danger of a single segment of society simply imposing its spatial preferences on others be avoided? First, it is precisely the *absence* of an explicit, values-driven debate about the shape of our built communities that has enabled the dynamics of automobile-oriented sprawl to emerge in metropolitan area after metropolitan area. Without public debate, unexamined assumptions about what constitutes a desirable community hold sway over zoning ordinances, incentive structures, infrastructure provision, and other policy mechanisms that influence the shape of urban development. Such policy measures influence the type of neighborhoods private developers are prone to build, leading developers to continue to build familiar car-centered developments rather than to attempt to offer a broader array of neighborhoods to prospective residents.[13] The all-too-familiar pattern of outward sprawl has lent a spatial monotony to the metropolitan United States that is at odds with the aim of providing a diverse set of spatial environments capable of satisfying a wide variety of individual and community preferences. Americans (with sufficient means) now can choose whether to live in cities, in near-in suburbs, or in far-flung exurbs, but (with only rare exceptions) they can't choose to live in a metropolitan area in which growth and development are systematically targeted toward maintaining a strong urban core or in which there is a rough balance of political power, economic opportunity, and educational quality between cities and suburbs.

Second, to embark upon substantive debates about the purpose of the built environment is not to assume that the goal should be to identify a one-size-fits-all balance between competing values. Different communities are likely to weigh competing values differently. It is inevitable that communities and regions with distinct cultural, geographic, demographic, and historical specificities will pursue different responses (or nonresponses) to sprawl, in terms of broad strategy and still more in policy details. It is possible and necessary to recognize this point and, at the same time, to maintain a critical perspective on such value choices, especially when there is good reason to suspect that the decision-making structures are themselves biased, flawed, or inadequate, from a democratic point of view. With more than 360 metropolitan areas in the United States, even if structures for regional decision making that met demanding conditions for democratic inclusiveness and equality of representation existed, it would be folly to suppose that deliberations about the competing values at stake in the debate on sprawl would fail to yield very diverse public decisions and policy outcomes.

Indeed, greater policy diversity at the metropolitan level might beneficially expand the range of choices citizens have concerning what kind of urban environment they want to live in. Equally important, diverse policy outcomes might help produce better-informed judgments about the effects of various policy strategies. Dozens of plausible tactics to redress urban sprawl have been proposed (and, in an increasing number of cases, implemented), ranging from regional-growth boundaries to congestion pricing to developer-impact fees.[14] In many of these cases, the relevant policies are relatively untested.[15] In this circumstance, the possibilities for "policy learning" would be expanded by having each community implement a different strategy, to one degree or another.[16] The existence of alternative strategies in one state or region may affect policy choices in another region by expanding the range of options policymakers consider plausible. As experience with such strategies grows, evidence regarding the effectiveness, shortcomings, and side effects of sprawl-containment policies will accumulate, which may in turn help citizens and officials make better-informed policy choices.

With respect to the spatial environment, policy variation at the local level is thus inevitable and also, at least arguably, desirable on normative grounds: there is little or no danger that decentralized policy experimentation addressing sprawl will lead to the undemocratic imposition of a particular urban form upon an unwilling public. Acknowledging these points is not inconsistent, however, with recognizing that sprawl is also a national issue—and that local spatial environments are quite substantially shaped by state and national policies. National policies such as mortgage deductions for homeowners, transportation infrastructure and funding, assistance to cities, parking subsidies, and federal housing-development initiatives all impinge upon local spatial environments. State policies regarding transportation, public-good provision, and assignment of municipal powers also help shape urban environments in critical ways. Such larger-order policies affecting sprawl often reflect, at least in part, the influence of material interests. But they also reflect value choices, and both the policy choices themselves and the values underlying them have too often escaped critical scrutiny.

Public debate about "sprawl" thus occurs at multiple levels of government and hence at multiple levels of generality. At the most immediate local level, localities, cities, and regional bodies are directly engaged in zoning, project-approval debates, and other forms of public planning. Very specific tradeoffs between different development possibilities occur at this level. At an intermediate level, states set transportation-planning priorities, make decisions about the disposition of state-owned land, and grant municipalities the power to engage in local-level planning. States may choose to use this influence to steer municipalities toward a particular set of spatial policies (as Maryland has done since 1997).[17] It is at these two levels of government that debate—and action—about how to deal (or not deal) with suburban sprawl has been most sustained.[18] At the national level, the federal government can steer (either coherently or haphazardly) the behavior of individuals, developers, and local governments in ways that do or do not favor particular habitation patterns.

To this extent, a national debate about whether federal policies should favor one type of built environment over another, perhaps by lending support and aid to states and metropolitan areas pursuing "smart growth"–type policies, or instead simply remain as neutral as possible and allow such decisions to be made at lower levels of government is appropriate. Indeed, much greater debate about these questions at the national level would be desirable.

To Debate Sprawl Is to Debate the Good Life

Public decision making pertaining to the spatial structure of built communities thus reflects underlying ideas about the good life: what the proper balance between private and public space is, which values a community should seek to maximize, what pitfalls communities should seek to avoid. These ideas in turn reflect and express underlying normative political philosophies: ideas about the purposes and proper scope of political association. Does the state have the right to "interfere" in market transactions (such as land deals) for the sake of efficiency, equality, or some other social value? Should communities seek to promote a particular way of life, or attempt to remain "value neutral"? Should policy be guided by a desire to maximize the private well-being of individual citizens, or should the attainment of common goods take priority in some circumstances? Such questions lie just beneath the surface of the public debate about sprawl.[19]

A principal aim of this book is to assist scholars, policymakers, and citizens in thinking through the core values at stake in the debate about suburban sprawl, and thereby enhance prospects for informed, democratic judgment about sprawl and sprawl-related policies. The book proceeds by posing four fundamental questions:

- Is sprawl efficient?
- Is sprawl fair?
- Is sprawl conducive to democratic citizenship?
- Is sprawl ecologically sustainable?

Answering these questions requires a two-fold approach. First, we must explain what we mean by terms such as "efficiency" and "fairness," and why we think such values are important. It is my contention that the practical argument about sprawl is inextricably tied to larger-order debates about politics and its purposes. What we think about sprawl will depend in large measure on what we think is important in political life, and on what we think the broad aims of public policy should be. Consequently, this book investigates and critically compares how three central strands of contemporary normative political thought—utilitarianism, liberal egalitarianism, and civic republicanism—assess sprawl as a public concern. Each of these normative views provides a critical framework for evaluating U.S. society, and taken together, these traditions have supplied much of the vocabulary of modern politics, including our conceptions of "efficiency," "fairness," and "citizenship." But each tradition offers a distinct understanding of politics, its purposes, and its possibilities—distinctions that turn out to be quite important in evaluating the phenomenon of sprawl. Consideration of these theoretical perspectives both deepens our understanding of what is at stake in the sprawl debate, and helps clarify the profound moral tradeoffs the U.S. public faces in charting a course to manage sprawl.

Second, we must consider relevant empirical evidence that will allow us to assess how well or how poorly sprawl fares when judged by these norms. My principal tool in testing key claims about sprawl's effects on social and civic well-being is detailed analysis of the Social Capital Community Benchmark Survey (SCCBS). The SCCBS is a unique survey of more than 29,700 Americans that was conducted by the Saguaro Center on Civic Engagement at the Kennedy School of Government (Harvard University) in 2000. Roughly 90 percent of the survey respondents are clustered into one of forty-one geographic communities representing all regions of the country, metropolitan areas of various sizes, and rural areas; the remaining cases consist of a representative national sample. The SCCBS contains geo-codes allowing us to match individual cases with 2000 census data on local spatial and demographic characteristics, measured at the census tract level. This rich data set enables us to systematically explore the relationship among four spatial features commonly associated with sprawl—population density, neighborhood age, automobile dependence, and suburban residence and a variety of important goods, including local quality-of-life, social trust, political ideology, and political participation.[20]

This book thus departs from a mode of political theorizing that is performed in the abstract, independent of any particular historical situation or the facts of any given case. What we wish to explore here is how three prominent public philosophies might help us think both critically and constructively about a concrete issue facing contemporary Americans; namely, whether we ought to continue with the pattern of urban development that has dominated for more than half a century or instead fashion alternatives to the continued outward expansion of our metropolitan areas, given what we know about the relationship between this pattern of development and the goods we care about. The book also departs from many conventional empirical studies, in that the empirical analyses undertaken here are explicitly driven by normative concerns, and the results of such analyses are explicitly analyzed through the lenses of those same concerns.

The Argument, in Brief

The overall empirical picture drawn in this book can be summarized this way: Sprawl appears to be ecologically unsustainable, inconsistent with democratic theories of justice, and inimical to the active practice of citizenship—yet Americans (by and large) like it anyway. Key elements of sprawl are linked to reduced levels of specifically political participation, especially more confrontational forms of political participation. But sprawl is not apolitical in the usual sense; rather, it is part and parcel of a political regime characterized by systemic social inequalities mediated in part by geography. I show how sprawl is both symptom and cause of fundamental inequalities tied to spatial location, and how suburban residence is linked to politically conservative attitudes that resist efforts to rectify those inequalities. Finally, I demonstrate how sprawl—and in particular, automobile-centered urban development—is deeply complicit in America's prodigious generation of climate-threatening greenhouse gases.

Taken together, these arguments present a powerful brief against sprawl and its consequences. But to stop here would be to present an intellectually incomplete and politically unhelpful one-sided argument. I also show that key elements of sprawl are *positively* related to two widely valued goods; namely, social trust and local quality-of-life. Sprawl—in its fundamentals, if not in every excess—does seem, on average, to satisfy the widespread desire for secure, pleasant neighborhoods.

Considering the advantages and disadvantages of sprawl reveals a profound, deep-seated tension between several core democratic ideas (equality, robust political engagement, ecological sustainability) and two fundamental features of the American way of life: the aspiration to live in a comfortable, convenient spatial environment, safely removed from social problems, and the habitual prioritization of private satisfactions over public concerns. Navigating this tension is a particularly acute challenge for versions of liberal political theory that stress the primacy of individual choice and the importance of respecting individuals' decisions about where and how to live. In this view, the state should remain as neutral as possible with respect to various ways of life. But it is difficult to see how public policy can make substantial alterations to sprawl—or secure other goals that liberals value, including equal opportunity, democratic engagement, and sustainability—without challenging the norms and lifestyle practices characteristic of life in the United States today.

Public versus Private Ideo-Logics: The Libertarian Challenge

As we shall see, there are significant differences among the utilitarian, liberal egalitarian, and civic republican approaches to politics and public policy. All three, however, might reasonably be counted among what Alan Altshuler describes as "public ideo-logics"—worldviews that stress the significance and priority of the general good over purely privatistic concerns.[21] Indeed, the differences among these positions might be regarded by some observers as intramural debates overshadowed by the more fundamental dispute between public "ideo-logics" of all types and what Altshuler terms "private ideo-logics." All three public ideo-logics considered here, for instance, provide grounds for challenging or overriding individual choices to secure other goals, in some circumstances. Private ideo-logics, in contrast, insist on the primacy of private choice and market processes in assessing public policy.

Libertarianism is the example par excellence of a private ideo-logic, and libertarian perspectives are highly influential in practical debates about land use policy. Consequently, some elaboration upon why I reject the libertarian approach to evaluating sprawl is warranted. That task will consume the remainder of this introductory chapter.

The thrust of the libertarian position is this: individuals as a general rule have strong rights to use (or not use) their private property in any way they see fit, and any limitation of these rights by the state, in the form of regulation, taxation targeted to favor some land uses rather than others, or prohibitions against certain uses of land represents an infringement upon and effective reduction of individuals' liberty. Land use policies that might affect liberty thus must meet a very high standard of public necessity. Since a defining aim of government is to protect private property, policies that unnecessarily restrict liberty for the sake of some alleged public good are an abuse of government's purposes.

As Joshua Cohen points out, libertarian thinking falls into two main camps: possessive libertarianism, which emphasizes the moral claims of property rights, and choice-based libertarianism, which stresses the desirability of maximizing the scope of individual choice.[22] It is incumbent upon partisans of any of the three public ideo-logics at the center of this inquiry to address both sorts of arguments.

POSSESSIVE LIBERTARIANISM, STRONG AND WEAK

Possessive libertarianism is based on the thesis that government is fundamentally a mechanism to defend preexisting property rights. This thesis, in turn, relies on a notion of a natural right to property. In a hypothetical state of nature prior to the formation of government, it is posited, individuals may legitimately acquire a right to a given piece of land by investing the effort to cultivate and develop the land. A prime aim of government is to protect this natural right by protecting the landowner–user from unwanted incursions, whether from persons internal or external to the community.

Acceptance of this line of reasoning, derived initially from John Locke and rearticulated in contemporary political thought by thinkers such as Robert Nozick, has profound consequences for public policymaking. It is important, however, to distinguish between strong forms of the possessive argument associated with Nozick, and the somewhat weaker version associated with Locke. The strong argument made by Nozick holds that so long as no one is actually made worse off by my taking possession of a piece of property, then I am entitled to claim full possession of that property.[23] Individuals thus can claim an individual right to property as a trump against almost all taxes and regulations, even those that would unambiguously promote the public good.[24]

The weak argument also allows for individuals to establish a moral claim to property prior to the formation of government but acknowledges that such moral claims can be outweighed by other considerations. Locke, for instance, conceives of the world as a common inheritance granted to humanity by God (not as originally unowned) and presumes that "men, once being born, have a right to their preservation," a right that limits claims to property; consequently, Locke held that those with a surplus of property have a moral obligation to assist the needy.[25] As Jeremy Waldron puts it, the "special right" to property that Locke espouses is outweighed by a "general right" of all people to subsistence.[26] Likewise, Locke places limits on the scope of just acquisition of property: for instance, no one has the right to claim a piece of property and then waste or discard its fruits, or hold the property for the sole purpose of denying others its use; individuals have no moral claim to land they do not make productive use of. Famously, Locke also argued that initial acquisitions of property in the state of nature should leave "enough and as good" resources for others to access.[27]

Thus, while Locke did envisage respect for preexisting property rights as setting boundaries on what governments can do, those rights were not absolute and were intended to be compatible with and conducive to the broader common good. One of Locke's most powerful arguments on behalf of a right to property contends that private property rights promote the general prosperity by encouraging the cultivation and rational development of land and resources.[28] More generally, Locke accepts the legitimacy within civil society of both taxation and state regulation of property aimed at advancing the public interest.[29] Whereas Locke was concerned with preventing *arbitrary* expropriation or taxation of land by unjust rulers unconcerned with the common good, Nozick was concerned with minimizing taxation and regulation as such, even when imposed by democratic publics acting for common purposes.

These are significant differences, and it is not obvious that the sorts of regulations of property accepted as morally legitimate by contemporary adherents of "public ideo-logics" of land use violate Lockean principles. But Locke's view is frequently invoked to justify a sweeping view of property rights that gives owners near-absolute rights regarding how they dispose of their property, and that obliges government to compensate property owners not just for the existing value of property but for the value of potential future uses that might be affected by public regulations.[30] Thus, there are good reasons to push further and both (1) reject even the weak possessive account of the origins of property rights and (2) question the relevance of the natural-rights account (whether in its strong or weak form) as a binding constraint on the regulation of contemporary urban property.

THE CONVENTIONALITY OF PROPERTY RIGHTS: THEORY

Consider first the case against a natural rights conception of property. As Jean-Jacques Rousseau insisted, there is a critical distinction between *possession*—the fact that one happens to occupy a particular piece of land—and *property,* which is a legally recognized and enforceable claim of an individual to a particular plot.[31] In this contrary view, property rights are not prior to, but rather the creature of, the state.

Why should we accept this alternative view? Consider the nature of property. Property rights fundamentally involve the capacity to *exclude* others from using a piece of land or a particular manmade artifact (such as a house); consequently (and ironically), they involve quite literal deprivations of liberty for those excluded. But in a hypothetical state of nature prior to the existence of government, the lucky soul who happens upon an unusually favorable piece of land and develops it can have no reasonable expectation that others will stay off that land just because he is already there. On the contrary, he can expect physically stronger people—or people with a larger private army—to periodically attempt to displace him from his favored spot.

And why not? There is no prior relationship between persons in the state of nature. That being the case, there is no reason that one individual should accept as valid another person's property claim while receiving nothing in return, particularly if an individual or group is significantly disadvantaged by that claim. It is only the existence of government that provides the landholder–user a reasonable expectation that his exclusionary claims on some particular piece of property will be respected by strangers. Put another way, it is only the *acknowledgment of the legitimacy of a rights claim by a wider community*—not the mere act of claiming a right—that establishes a binding right.[32] An explorer may claim half of a continent in the name of his king, or I may claim a particular bench in Central Park as my "special place" that no one else can use, but neither of us can reasonably expect that claim to carry any effective force or legitimacy unless or until it is accepted and acknowledged by the wider community of persons affected by the claim.[33]

The advocate of natural property rights might acknowledge that the institution of government is necessary to enforce individuals' claims to property but nonetheless insist that persons who make productive use of land have a moral claim to a property stake and that states *should* respect that claim. In short, having dismissed the notion that people can have an enforceable right in the absence of government, natural-rights claims might be reframed as a normative argument about property claims that government *should* respect. Because I work the land and mix my labor with it, the state should honor my claim to a property stake. Yet even this formulation of the natural-rights claim to property is open to serious question.

First, even granting a natural right to benefit from one's own labor, it is unclear why the combination of labor with land should give one the right not simply to the resulting product (i.e., what is grown) but to the land itself. Consider one of Locke's key arguments for allowing an individual to control this land, which is that the land has scarcely any value apart from what human labor adds to it. This assertion is, at best, an argument for allowing proprietorship of actively cultivated agricultural land, not for permitting unimpeded private control of urban land (which does have inherent economic value). Moreover, it is not clear that the argument persuasively establishes an exclusive right to property: instead of allowing the laborer total control over the relevant property, we might believe (as Waldron puts it) that "the appropriator should acquire a substantial interest in the object he has worked on, roughly proportionate in some sense to the labour he has expended on it, but that this should not be deemed to exclude altogether the common rights of other men."[34]

Second, the strong natural-rights formulation assumes that the individual's labor-based claim is the *only* morally relevant consideration in judging who should benefit from the property in question. As we have already observed, Locke specifically rejects this idea. Even Nozick (pushed sufficiently) relents on this point, acknowledging that in the case of a desert island or a catastrophe that leaves an individual in exclusive control of an essential resource, individual property claims must be superseded by the claims of a broader common good. Having conceded on the principle, it is not clear why we should regard individual property claims as automatically trumping community considerations in less dramatic cases where substantial community interests are being damaged by the existing pattern of appropriation.[35] (Communities have a legitimate moral interest, for instance, in ensuring that the land and resources of a given community do not fall into the possession of a narrow group of persons; in short, communities have a legitimate interest in not reverting to de facto feudalism, a possibility not precluded by strong Nozickean property rights.)[36] The acknowledgment that a "natural" claim to property is not absolute in all cases necessarily forces us back to the view that property claims in general gain their moral force not merely by assertion but by the recognition of such claims by the wider community of persons affected by the claim.

To put it another way, the would-be property holder is not the best judge of his own claim to a property right; judgment is reserved to the community that will enforce any claims that arise from individuals' holdings prior to the formation of political society. As Waldron points out, it seems morally odd, indeed bizarre, to hold that it is possible for a single person, via his or her own self-regarding act (that of initially acquiring property), to impose a morally binding obligation on all other persons for all time (namely, the obligation to respect both the initial owner's claim to property and the claim of all succeeding owners to whom the property may be transferred). Any such argument runs counter to the commonsense view that while we may have general moral obligations (i.e., not to cause harm to other people), and while we may freely assume further specific moral obligations (such as by the act of promising, or the act of getting married and having children), we do not have the ability to impose specific moral obligations on other people without their consent.[37]

Third, the moral intuitions about property upon which Lockean natural-rights theory trades can be satisfied much more persuasively by accounts that view property as a social convention. Locke is sometimes read as providing a *desert*-based argument for natural property rights; but if desert is to be the core moral principle undergirding a system of property rights, then there is no reason that only the labor and effort of the *first* person to work on a property, and not that of all subsequent others, should be morally privileged. Similarly, partisans of natural property rights sometimes stress the importance of respect for the legitimate expectations of owners and the importance of having security that one's rights will be honored; but there is no reason that property rights understood as a social convention whose precise content is defined by the state cannot fulfill those expectations. Indeed, doing so is the very purpose of modern property law. Fourth, as we have noted, Locke (like Nozick) stresses the connection between the establishment of property rights and the promotion of general prosperity. But if general prosperity is the most important consideration, it is not obvious that providing absolute rights to first acquirers of property, rights that the state must respect, is the best way to promote such prosperity, particularly if there is good reason to think that vast inequalities that deny many people the resources to meet their own needs is a likely result of such a system.[38] Finally, property rights are often regarded as important because of their role in promoting individual freedom and autonomy. But there is no reason that a conventionalist account of property cannot support those goals, and there is indeed good reason to think that promoting a broader, more general dispersion of property than a strict natural-rights account permits is a more plausible strategy for realizing freedom and autonomy for each and all.[39]

THE CONVENTIONALITY OF PROPERTY RIGHTS: HISTORY AND PRACTICE

In any case, the notion that absolute property-rights claims in the contemporary United States can be justified by appeal to supposed primordial natural-rights claims is wildly implausible. First, consider the obvious fact that possession of the North American continent by the United States of America was acquired through political action involving no small amount of physical force and violence.

Second, as Elizabeth Anderson and others have pointed out, numerous crucial features of capitalist economies—such as the limited-liability corporation and patent law—depend upon manifestly artificial creations of government policy.[40] With respect to urban land in particular, modern real estate markets depend fundamentally on the establishment of a public network of transportation, in addition to the establishment of government conventions regarding such matters as lending and financing rules, building and inspection standards, tenant rights, property subdivision, easements, and zoning.[41] Such rules are not hindrances upon the market; rather, they help constitute it.

Third, the value of much private property in the United States is bound up in or shaped by public goods and public activities of various kinds. This is especially true in urban land markets; holders of property located near a public park, for instance, might be expected to enjoy a boost in the value of their holdings relative to comparable property located far away from such publicly generated amenities. As Liam Murphy and Thomas Nagel have pointed out in the general case of taxation of income and wealth, it is simply illogical for such property holders to claim a right to be exempt from taxation or regulation, given that their very enjoyment of property is dependent upon the existence of such a system of taxation and regulation.[42] This point is generalizable, to the degree that all landowners benefit from the existence of government and of a stable system of property.

Modern property rights, in short, are the creation of government. Therefore, government action to limit or redefine the scope of such property rights in order to advance the public good carries a fundamental legitimacy. Why? Because property rights are not ends in themselves but rather instruments for advancing a common good. Property rights are a social creation whose fundamental purpose is to advance important public goods, such as social peace and economic productivity. To be sure, action that redefines or limits such rights must be enacted via legitimate democratic mechanisms and should not be undertaken for capricious or arbitrary reasons divorced from public benefit. But property holders have no inherent "natural" right to use their property in any way they see fit or to extract maximum economic value from such property unless or until the community at large grants such permission.

This way of understanding property assumes that that the desirability of any particular proposal to expand, alter, or reduce regulations on property must be based on the effects such action will have on the larger public good. This understanding is particularly appropriate in the case of urban land markets. Quite obviously, there is not "enough and as good" land remaining for all to enjoy in U.S. metropolitan areas; hence, even those who accept a Lockean account of just property acquisition have strong reason to accept the legitimacy of nesting property rights within a broader set of policies aimed at better securing the common good.

There can be little question that the Lockean view of property played an important part in the thinking of the framers of the United States Constitution; an explicit aim of James Madison was to defend both property, as such, and *inequality* of property. Nonetheless, as it has evolved, the constitutional law tradition in the United States has increasingly recognized that private-property rights are not absolute but are subject to limitations established by government for the sake of preserving and promoting the common good.[43] Constitutional law in the United States upholds the right of the government to tax land and regulate its use, and also to appropriate private land for public purposes, with due compensation to owners.[44]

Beyond this, as the property rights scholar Joseph Singer has illustrated in chapter-and-verse detail, law frequently must adjudicate between competing property-rights claims, as when one landowner drains a large amount of water from beneath his or her own land, with the effect of draining the local water table and affecting the value of neighbors' properties. Property law is therefore fundamentally a social and political convention, not simply the neutral application of preexisting, self-evident moral claims to property. Libertarian views of property, Singer charges, fail to take seriously the fact that property owners do not live in a vacuum but must live *with other people* and, hence, under a set of rules to adjudicate conflicting claims. Likewise, libertarianism fails to recognize that property rights are fundamentally relations between *persons,* not relationships between persons and things.[45]

Singer's assessment reflects the views of many contemporary property-rights theorists who regard property as fundamentally a social convention adopted to promote particular public goods. But the stability of this understanding of property cannot be taken for granted: libertarian activists have aggressively promoted initiatives to require governments to compensate property owners for economic losses (or future gains denied) due to regulatory requirements (even when no appropriation is involved). If successful, the "regulatory takings" (or "property rights") movement has the potential to seriously weaken the practical capacity of government to regulate property, including regulations aimed at slowing or reversing sprawl.[46]

CHOICE-BASED LIBERTARIANISM

Quite apart from the possessive argument on behalf on an inviolable right to property, libertarians also appeal to a second sort of argument, focused on the desirability of maximizing choice and freedom of action.[47] Maximizing the scope of choice available to any individual shows respect for individuals' ability to guide and direct their own life. Constraints on choice should therefore be viewed skeptically and must meet a very high threshold of necessity to be considered wise policy. Milton Friedman is an exemplar of this variety of libertarian argument; notably, the plausibility of his view does not depend upon acceptance of a natural-rights account of property but simply upon a general presumption that individual autonomy and liberty are best enhanced by unconstrained market transactions.[48] In the case of land use, choice-based libertarianism presumes that individual "privacy, mobility, and choice" is best ensured by an unfettered market.[49]

Partisans of public ideo-logics have four possible responses to this view. One response is to express general agreement with this perspective but to go on to argue that libertarian policies do not necessarily follow from a general commitment to expanding choice for each and all. Expanding choice for all might require restricting the unlimited privileges of a few, redistributing elite-controlled resources, and providing basic social goods to each and all. In short, expanding the domain of choice might require expanding what traditionally have been called "positive" freedoms.

That argument is surely an important one, but it is of limited direct relevance to questions about land use and sprawl. A second, more specific response calls into question the assumption that current socio-spatial patterns are simply a product of market forces responding to individual preferences. Instead, as Jonathan Levine has stressed, sprawl has been endemically shaped by a variety of government interventions, including subsidies at the federal level and restrictive, exclusionary zoning at the local level. In short, the practical policy choice we face is not between a supposed free market and a planned regime but between one form of planned regime and another. Consequently, a choice-based argument cannot be used to defend the policy status quo.[50]

A third possible response follows closely on the heels of the second. As already noted, there is a fundamental distinction between "choices" about land use and choices about diet or lifestyle or sexual partners. Land use and development, by their very nature, occur in time and space, and each decision about how land will or will not be developed affects not only the person making the choice but also everyone else presently in the vicinity, as well as those who will use the space in the future. Dropping a new shopping mall with a vast parking lot into a previously undeveloped rural community will fundamentally change the nature of that community. Consequently, the lifestyle—and "choices"—available to an entire community can be drastically affected by the action of a single individual, firm, or developer. It is as if one took an eight-mile jog, and each of one's neighbors got sore knees. Because individual land use decisions can impose costs on others against their will, the state is justified in regulating such decisions.

The most far-ranging critical response to the choice-oriented libertarian, however, challenges the very assumption that land should be treated primarily as a privately held commodity. As Karl Polanyi notably argued, land (like labor and money) does not fit the classical definition of a commodity—that is, an object produced *for* sale. This is true in two senses: first, land is obviously not a product of human labor; second, its fundamental purpose is not to be sold for private gain but rather to be lived upon. If extraterrestrial life forms were found, no one would regard it as legitimate for an enormously wealthy human to buy all the Earth's land and then resell it to a buyer from another planet at a profit.[51]

Consequently, persons who happen to hold title to a plot of land should be treated (and should regard themselves) as stewards of the land, rather than owners with an unrestricted right to exploit the land for private advantage. As Timothy Beatley has forcefully argued, the market-based normative paradigm dominant in U.S. land use practices is "largely economic, wrongly narrow in scope, and morally indefensible for many, if not most, land use conflicts."[52] A stewardship conception of land suggests that landowners have additional ethical responsibilities beyond refraining from harming others or the public at large. These responsibilities include protecting both the land itself and the ecosystems of the land, being mindful of the needs and interests of future generations, and not exercising control over land to deny others the means to fulfill their basic human needs. In short, neither private landowners nor the public should treat land as simply an instrument for generating economic value.[53] Rather, land use policy and practice must take into account a much broader range of ethical considerations that derive from the fact that land is not merely a commodity produced for private sale but a shared resource whose use or abuse affects the conditions of life for the entire community.[54] Hence, advocates of a public land use logic can coherently reply to choice-based libertarians as follows: choice and economic efficiency are indeed praiseworthy goods, but they are not the only goods at stake in decisions about land use and development, or in decisions about the spatial design of the built environment.

This book assumes that both possessive and choice-based libertarian arguments fail as an account of private property and the moral issues arising from its use and regulation. But to stress that choice and individual liberty are not the only goods at stake in a given policy arena is hardly to conclude that such goods are unimportant or can be safely neglected. With respect to suburban sprawl, the central moral question is this: given the interdependence implied in metropolitan forms of life, and given that the Jeffersonian dream of wholly independent landowners unbothered by one another is not a realistic aspiration in our urbanized society, how ought we live *together?*

Answering that question requires taking into account not only our commitments to liberty and freedom but a range of other aspirations, including efficiency, social justice, democratic engagement, and ecological sustainability. The primary aim of this book is to illuminate how U.S.-style suburbanization—and by extension, the American way of life itself—affects this broader set of goods, and thus to clarify the moral choices facing the U.S. public as it charts a metropolitan development path for the twenty-first century.

We begin, however, with a more mundane but absolutely essential question: what exactly is sprawl, and how can it be measured?

<table>
<tr><td>ONE</td><td>Defining, Explaining,
and Measuring Sprawl</td></tr>
</table>

THIS CHAPTER UNDERTAKES FIVE important tasks that will lay the groundwork for the rest of the book. First, I review a variety of definitions of *sprawl* and introduce the working definition used in this book. Second, I examine the question of what causes sprawl, a question that any study aiming to assess the merits and deficiencies of sprawl must consider. Third, I introduce the conceptual framework guiding this book's empirical inquiries; namely, the notion that different places have different social functions and meanings attached to them, and that these differing characteristics of place may influence individual behavior and attitudes in notable ways. Fourth, I introduce and explain the specific measures of sprawl used in this book and explain the quantitative methodology I employ in subsequent chapters. Finally, I introduce and summarize the Social Capital Community Benchmark Survey, the primary data source used in this investigation.

What Is Sprawl? Technical and Quantitative Definitions

The most straightforward available definitions of sprawl are technical. For instance, any process by which the geographical terrain claimed by a given urban area expands over time might be labeled "sprawl." In the context of continuous population growth and ongoing urbanization, this definition is too broad to be useful for most purposes. Almost every urban area on the planet could be described as "sprawling" by this understanding—even if population density within a given urban area were actually increasing.

A more specific technical definition refers to a process by which the geographic expansion of an urban area expands faster than population growth in the same area. A 2001 Brookings Institution study found that expansion of urbanized land outpaced population growth in more than 90 percent of the nation's metropolitan areas between 1982 and 1997.[1] By this measure, sprawl is the defining form of urbanization in the United States. Yet, even this seemingly straightforward definition has sparked scholarly controversy; some commentators on sprawl prefer the census definition of "urbanized areas" (places with density of at least 1,000 persons per square mile) to the Brookings study's definition of "urbanized land," which relies on the National Resources Inventory's assessments of land use.[2] Other scholars have defined the phenomenon in terms of the decentralization of employment or the amount of open space surrounding residential development.[3]

Many commentators, however, conceive of sprawl not as a single phenomenon but as a bundle of related dimensions of spatial development; hence, they have sought to develop a multidimensional definition. The best-developed definition to date of metropolitan-level sprawl has been provided by a research team led by the economist George Galster. Galster et al. define sprawl not as a *process* of development (as above), but as a "condition of land use" measured along eight distinct dimensions (quoted verbatim here):

1. *Density:* the average number of residential units per square mile of developable land in an urban area (UA).
2. *Continuity:* the degree to which developable land has been developed at urban densities in an unbroken fashion.
3. *Concentration:* the degree to which development is located in relatively few square miles of the total UA.
4. *Compactness:* the degree to which development has been "clustered" to minimize the amount of land in each square mile of developable land occupied by residential or nonresidential uses.
5. *Centrality:* the degree to which residential and/or nonresidential development is located close to the central business district of an urban area.
6. *Nuclearity:* the extent to which a UA is characterized by a mononuclear (as contrasted with a polynuclear) pattern of development.
7. *Diversity:* the degree to which two different land uses exist within the same micro-area, and the extent to which this pattern is typical of the entire UA.

8. *Proximity:* the degree to which different land uses are close to each other across a UA.[4]

Galster et al. do not specify whether a given metropolitan area must be "sprawling" (i.e., not compact, with varied land uses distant from one another) with regard to every one of these characteristics, a majority of them, or only one or two to be properly labeled "sprawling." Indeed, their intent is to move away from a dichotomous definition of places as either sprawling or not sprawling to a continuous definition in which places could be ranked as more or less sprawling. Even this goal, however, leaves open the problem of whether all eight of these factors are equally important and should be weighted equally. Interestingly, while six of these measures of sprawl refer to the geographic distribution of land use, the final two, "diversity" and "proximity," refer to the *type* of land use in a given region—an acknowledgment that observers of sprawl are concerned not just with geographic features but also with social processes.

Not all definitions of sprawl have aimed at precise quantitative measurements, however. The New Urbanist planners Andres Duany, Elizabeth Plater-Zyberk, and Jeff Speck identify five distinct "components" of suburban communities: housing developments, shopping centers, office parks, civic institutions, and roadways. Viewed in the abstract, these components might be seen as simply necessary building blocks of any community. But according to Duany et al., when these components assume the specific form characteristic of most U.S. suburbs, the cumulative result is "sprawl." What makes typical suburban-housing developments, shopping centers, and office parks part of "sprawl" is their single-use character and their separation from one another. Similarly, in suburbia civic institutions such as schools, government buildings, and churches are often located "nowhere in particular," as opposed to acting as "neighborhood focal points." Roadways contribute to sprawl by holding together the "other four dissociated components," according to Duany et al.: "Since each piece of suburbia serves only one type of activity, and since daily life involves a wide variety of activities, the residents of suburbia spend an unprecedented amount of time and money moving from one place to the next. Since most of the motion takes place in singly occupied automobiles, even a sparsely populated area can generate the traffic of a much larger traditional town."[5] For Duany et al., it is the spatial separation of the functions of everyday life (home, work, market) that constitutes "sprawl."

This definition is especially helpful in calling attention to the *character* of suburban communities as a *whole* as an important component of sprawl. Assessments of the character of a given built community necessarily focus on qualitative dimensions of local life and necessarily are at least somewhat subjective in nature. Four especially relevant qualitative dimensions of suburban communities that might be plausibly associated with sprawl can be noted here: commercialism, composition of businesses, aesthetic qualities, and spiritual resonance.

The first dimension, commercialism, concerns the degree to which communities are organized on the principle of facilitating (and indeed maximizing) private consumption of goods. Is shopping the primary activity in a community's public spaces? Do citizens most often interact with each other in the process of buying things? Are persons with no capacity or desire to buy goods welcome in publicly accessible spaces? The imaginary most often employed by critics of sprawl is the contrast between the enclosed shopping mall encompassed by a vast parking lot and an urban downtown area in which shopping areas (including mall space) are mixed in with public parks, libraries, plazas, and other spaces that permit informal socializing, random contacts between strangers, occasional political gatherings, and open access to the public, regardless of ability to pay or intention to buy.[6] The concern here is not simply with the sheer amount of public space in a community but with the character of that space—and also with the character of all publicly accessible places, whether or not they are formally defined as public or private. (One can imagine suburban communities with large amounts of public space that, perhaps by being segregated from other functions or by being accessible only to a narrow portion of the population, fail to perform the functions of prototypical urban public places.)

The second qualitative dimension often associated with sprawl relates to the character of the business enterprises offering goods and services to the public. As Oliver Gillham suggests, whether a strip mall is populated by "Denny's or diners" might make a considerable difference in one's assessment of it.[7] Shopping areas characterized by corporate chains with a large percentage of high-turnover, low-paid employees, standardized product offerings, and no particular commitment to any specific location beyond its capacity to maximize sales volume can be meaningfully distinguished from shopping areas characterized by independent, locally owned businesses with long-term owner–operators whose life savings are invested in not only the business but, by extension, the community in which the business operates.[8] The predominance of large chain operations and massive superstores is widely seen as either a substantial element of "sprawl" itself, or a closely related symptom.[9]

Aesthetics is a third qualitative dimension of place considered in the sprawl debate. Critics of sprawl (most notably the popular writer James Howard Kunstler) have consistently described sprawling places as ugly, garish eyesores marked by endless signage, vast parking lots, gridlocked intersections, and cookie-cutter housing developments.[10] The impact of "mall glut," "logo buildings," and "category killers" on the U.S. landscape has been impressively documented in aerial photography assembled by the urban historian and critic Dolores Hayden, who describes the "visual culture of sprawl" as "the material representation of a political economy organized around unsustainable growth."[11] Indeed, while defenders of sprawl have often argued that aesthetic judgments are too subjective a basis on which to build public policy, only rarely have they suggested that Kunstler-type assessments of sprawling places are substantively wrong.

The notion that aesthetics and visual attractiveness are important relates to a fourth qualitative dimension of built communities: whether or not places exude "spiritedness" such that people feel invigorated, inspired, or edified by the spatial environment they inhabit. The idea here is that "ugly" places do not simply cause displeasure to residents and visitors that can be measured on a utilitarian pain–pleasure axis but that they also have a deeper, not easily quantified effect on human beings' spirit and sense of well-being. To put it bluntly (and at the same time invoke a concept rarely appealed to in contemporary political theory), might not ugly, sprawling places deaden the human *soul*? What if it is not possible to live a coherent, meaningful life while residing in a fragmented, inhospitable, incoherent place?[12]

Lewis Mumford hinted at this sort of conclusion when he wrote, in the late 1930s, "A habitat planned so as to form a continuous background to a delicately graded scale of human feeling and values is the prime requisite of a cultivated life. Where that is lacking, men will fumble uneasily with substitutes, or starve."[13] Indeed, qualitative judgments related to the aesthetics of a built environment can sensibly pertain not simply to whether an observer regards a given place as "cute" or "ugly," finding visual pleasure or displeasure, but whether certain places may evoke much stronger feelings of nausea, emptiness, and dehumanization (as opposed to feelings of welcomeness, warmth, etc.). For at least some critics, including Mumford himself, this stronger set of negative feelings (and the sense that these are related in some way to extremely deep human needs or longings) are components of the sprawl phenomenon.[14]

———

Sprawl can thus be cogently defined in at least five distinct ways:

- As a type of land use with certain physical and geographic characteristics,
- As a type of settlement *combining* physical and geographic features with a certain type of socioeconomic composition,

- As a type of settlement with certain qualitative features that are not necessarily amenable to precise quantitative measurement,
- As a type of settlement aimed primarily at realizing a particular way of life, and, finally,
- As a *process* by which each of these end-states is created, replicated, and extended in metropolitan areas.

I believe there is value in recognizing and, indeed, maintaining the intellectual tension between relatively narrow and more expansive definitions of "sprawl." Nonetheless, it will be helpful to articulate here the working definition of sprawl employed in this book: I define sprawl as recently built suburban development characterized by low density and high reliance on automobile transportation. This definition is, quite deliberately, both as narrow and as precise as possible. Nonetheless, it should be understood that this inquiry is motivated by an interest in documenting and assessing *the way of life associated with sprawling development*. In short, we seek not just to measure sprawl but to examine how sprawl affects the way we live.

That investigation takes place at multiple geographic scales in this book. Most commonly, as in the empirical analyses in chapters 3, 5, and 7, I compare the impact of living in a *sprawling neighborhood* rather than a prototypical urban neighborhood on a range of individual behaviors and attitudes. In the discussion of sprawl and social justice in chapter 4, I focus primarily on the relationship and interaction between sprawling suburban areas and urban-core neighborhoods. Finally, in both chapter 2 (examining the efficiency of sprawl) and in chapter 8 (examining the environmental consequences of sprawl), I focus on sprawl as a metropolitan-level phenomenon. In short, while the overall aim is to assess the civic, social, and environmental consequences of sprawling development as compared to plausible alternative development patterns, the geographic scale at which the investigation proceeds varies according to the question being asked.

What Causes Sprawl?

Social scientists are likely to be suspicious of any effort to describe sprawl as an end-state, or even as a specific process of continuously falling urban densities, that does not give fundamental attention to the *causes* of sprawl. At issue is whether it is a mistake to treat sprawl as the independent variable driving certain kinds of outcomes, if one does not also treat sprawl as a dependent variable—that is, a phenomenon that itself has causes. In the parlance of contemporary social science, sprawl is endogenous to political and social processes, shaping them even as it is shaped by them.

The following section thus provides a brief overview of nine of the most frequently noted causes of sprawl. The focus of attention will be on understanding how and why sprawl emerged as the dominant form of urban development in the United States, not on explaining variations in the degree of sprawl between different metropolitan areas.[15] Understanding, in at least a rudimentary way, the causes of sprawl will further our understanding of what exactly sprawl is, helping set the stage for the remainder of this investigation.

1. *Population growth and falling household size.* The most obvious causal factor driving metropolitan expansion is population growth, combined in the United States with falling household size. Total population in the United States grew from less than 132 million people in 1940 to more than 281 million in 2000; the number of Americans living in metropolitan areas grew at an even faster clip, from 63 million in 1940 to 226 million in 2000. At the same time, average household size fell from 3.68 in 1940 to 2.59 in 2000. In short, the United States has had to accommodate an enormous increase in the number of persons and households in its metropolitan areas.[16] Two further observations are warranted: first, although rapid population growth was and is a crucial factor driving metropolitan growth, it does not, by itself, make sprawling (i.e., low-density, automobile-oriented) development inevitable. Metropolitan growth could have been accommodated by more compact development patterns. Second, U.S. metropolitan areas will continue to grow in the first half of the twenty-first century and likely beyond. Current census estimates project the U.S. population will grow from roughly 310 million in 2010 to 440 million in 2050; the overwhelming proportion of such growth will be in metropolitan areas.[17] Whether such population growth is accommodated primarily by continued, indefinite sprawl or by alternative growth strategies depends in large measure on the actions and inactions of policymakers.

2. *Private ownership of land.* Urban land is, by and large, treated as a commodity in the United States. Commercial developers design and build sites with the intention of eventually generating profit streams; to do this, they must design developments that are both desirable and financially accessible to consumers. In economically vibrant metropolitan areas, the operation of the land and housing market will tend to generate pressure to build on the fringe of cities. In such cities, standard economic models predict that land values will rise as demand for urban space increases; at a certain point, significant numbers of housing consumers will be willing to live several (and

eventually many) miles away from the city in order to access more afford-able housing.[18] In many U.S. cities, this textbook process in which increased demand for urban space leads to the development of city outskirts is aug-mented by the presence of decaying and unsafe urban neighborhoods with concentrated poverty; the existence of places in which a substantial propor-tion of consumers are unwilling to live exacerbates the pressures generating outward development.

Would something like sprawl be possible if private ownership of land were not a central institution in the United States? In any society experienc-ing urbanization and continuous population growth, the question of whether it is rational or necessary to expand metropolitan areas outward is likely to arise.[19] Yet, the specific patterns of sprawl seen in the United States would likely be quite different if, for instance, public entities owned land and then leased it to private developers and homeowners for approved uses. While property rights *are* (necessarily) constrained in important ways, and while many kinds of property development are subject to public oversight of vary-ing intensities, private landowners nonetheless occupy a privileged position in land use debates. Private landowners, in general, tend toward a set of concerns quite different from the ecological and social goals of early propo-nents of population decentralization (e.g., Sir Ebenezer Howard).[20] While some commentators argue that there is not a necessary connection between developer profit-making and specifically low-density forms of development, there is an internal connection among the creation of *new* neighborhoods, the attraction of residents to such neighborhoods, and the eventual realization of development profits.[21] Previously undeveloped suburban land presents devel-opers with a tabula rasa for new developments, leaving them free from the encumbrances that often accompany attempts to redevelop in the urban core; land and labor costs are typically lower in suburban locations, and there are fewer political or zoning complications. Given the relative ease of making a profit in suburbia, it is predictable that developers should both (1) dispro-portionately favor suburban locations as the site of new developments, and (2) stimulate efforts to get relatively affluent urban residents to move to new suburban developments.[22]

3. *The rise of the automobile.* Many urban planners and economists believe that urban form is fundamentally a consequence of transportation technology.[23] Indeed, there is widespread agreement among both critics and friends of sprawl that the outward expansion of metropolitan areas is inextri-cably linked with the emergence of the automobile. The economists Edward Glaeser and Matthew Kahn have forcefully argued that the car is *the* most fundamental cause of sprawl: In standard monocentric economic models of

urban development, reduced transportation costs associated with cars "mean that the edge of the city expands and density decreases. As commuting costs fall, the amount of land area consumed increases and the edge of the city expands.... In the polycentric model, the switch from public transportation to cars severely reduces the fixed costs of opening new employment centers [in suburbs]." These theoretical models, along with empirical evidence correlating employment deconcentration and automobile use in the United States (and in other countries), lead Glaeser and Kahn to judge that "the ultimate driver of decentralization is the private automobile and its commercial equivalents, including the truck."[24]

4. *Technological shifts permitting greater deconcentration of industry.* The explosive growth of suburbia could not have occurred if it were simply a matter of residents with jobs in the cities choosing to live outside the city's boundaries. Rather, many "primary" economic activities have relocated to suburbia, to take advantage of cheaper land, less political red tape, and, in some cases, access to a pool of skilled workers.[25] This shift in the location of economic activity has been made possible by two related phenomena: first, as just noted, the evolution of communication and transportation technologies, which have reduced the need for centralized operations in a single location, even for manufacturing firms; and second, the shift to a postindustrial economy, in which it is not as critical for firms to be adjacent to transportation hubs.[26]

5. *Urban decline and metropolitan fragmentation.* Over the past half century, shifts in the location of business activity have combined with residential suburban flight to induce population losses, reduce tax bases, and heighten economic stresses in many U.S. cities, especially heavily industrialized cities (e.g., Buffalo and Detroit).[27] At a certain point, urban decline and blight can themselves become impetuses to accelerated suburbanization.[28] Fear of crime, in particular, is often cited as a major motivation driving suburban flight. So, too, is the desire to live in a district with high-quality public schools—inadequate funding and concentrated poverty result in central cities typically having the least effective, most dysfunctional public schools in a metropolitan area.

A closely related factor is the governance arrangement of most metropolitan areas. With rare exception (e.g., Portland) local government in the United States is fragmented. That fragmentation contributes to sprawl in three important ways. First, fragmentation promotes economic segregation by allowing more-affluent citizens to sort themselves into municipalities that do not share resources with neighboring jurisdictions. The resulting inequality in public goods (some places have more-desirable schools and safer streets than others) provides an impetus for households with sufficient resources to move to jurisdictions where they will not pay big-city taxes and endure big-city problems. Second, jurisdictions compete with one another for residents, jobs, and tax base, creating incentives for municipalities to attempt to lure neighboring municipalities' businesses (and jobs), often at the expense of cities. Third, by their very nature, efforts to slow or stop sprawl require regional coordination. When independent localities operating within a fragmented metropolitan area take measures intended to "stop sprawl" (usually by preventing nearby growth), the result often is to create more sprawl (by funneling development yet further out). In fragmented systems, local governments have incentives to take measures to defend their own local interests and prerogatives, which often leads to a collectively irrational (and inequitable) result from the standpoint of the region as a whole.[29] For all these reasons, the revitalization of cities and the creation of new political mechanisms (such as metropolitan-area governments) to bring metropolitan residents under the same fiscal roof are major strategic goals of many critics of sprawl.[30]

6. *Federal and local policies that have accelerated suburbanization.* Urban scholars have repeatedly cited a smorgasbord of federal policies, many still in effect, that have tended to promote suburbanization, either directly or indirectly. Three major categories of government influence upon the pattern of metropolitan development witnessed in the United States since World War II loom large: federal and state road building and automobile subsidies, federal subsidies for new housing and homeownership, and local zoning regimes.

Roads. The notion that one ought to be able to travel by automobile from any one destination to any other with minimal inconvenience and no obligation to pay for the full social costs of one's trips strikes most Americans today as self-evident. But, as the historian Owen Gutfreund has illustrated, this fundamental notion is, in fact, a twentieth-century invention; for most of the nineteenth century, the federal government simply was not involved in road building, limiting its involvement in transportation infrastructure to railroads. Nor was there an extensive system of privately owned highways. Instead, roads were considered a local matter.[31]

All this changed with the explosive development of the automobile, which created enormous political pressure (with the automotive industry itself leading the charge) to build a new auto-based infrastructure, both within and between cities. (Gutfreund provides fascinating, detailed accounts of exactly how this played out in Denver, Colorado; Smyrna, Tennessee; and Middlebury, Vermont.)[32] In particular, the postwar expansion of freeways connecting cities to increasingly far-flung suburban locations had two tangible effects that were almost immediately felt: it facilitated auto-based commuting between suburban residences and city centers, and, in many cases, it led to the division or destruction of urban neighborhoods bisected or simply plowed through by the new highways.[33] In the long term, the development of suburban freeways also facilitated the removal of jobs to the suburbs.

The U.S. public never explicitly voted on whether to systematically favor the automobile as a mode of transportation over rail, bus, or other means of transit. But the cumulative effect of decades of public spending disproportionately favoring auto travel nevertheless produced a nation of drivers, as it produced a nation with many metropolitan areas in which there is simply no plausible alternative to car ownership for the middle and working classes. In addition to tallying money directly spent on highway construction, we must also count the cost of tax-deductible parking benefits, tax-deductible car-sales taxes, highway patrols, and an assortment of other publicly borne costs. In an unusual arrangement, the United States has long relied on a largely autonomous highway trust fund able to capitalize new expenditures with a continuous stream of gas-tax revenue and other fees; as Pietro Nivola points out, "In almost all other industrial countries . . . highway plans have been supported out of general revenue, thereby forcing these public works to compete with other priorities in national budgets."[34]

The key point here is not whether this pattern of spending was wise policy or not, but simply that extensive—indeed massive—public activity (often encouraged and shaped by private interests) was *required* to create the transportation infrastructure that makes low-density, automobile-oriented metropolitan areas possible. No less than mass transit, rapid travel by personal vehicle is a publicly constituted and publicly regulated activity that government and public policy play a vital role in sustaining. Moreover, as Gutfreund points out, the manner in which government undertook road building was itself systematically biased toward laying new roads in outlying areas; for decades, urban streets were not eligible for federal funding, and formulas for distributing highway funds favored suburban areas. Ironically, the many billions of federal dollars spent in the twentieth century on highway infrastructure never made redressing traffic congestion *within* the largest cities a major priority; the emphasis was on facilitating travel between cities and trips in and out of the center city. Examining the twentieth-century pattern of auto subsidies, Gutfreund identifies two distinctive features:

> First, they undercharged motorists by a wide margin, penalizing the nonmotoring majority while simultaneously inducing more and more Americans to adopt the automobile as the preferred mode of

transport....A study of fourteen industrialized European nations found that, on average, user fees were nearly three times the amount of direct highway costs, while in the United States they were only about half. Second, American highway legislation consistently favored construction in unpopulated areas while impeding investments in urban transportation networks.[35]

Homeownership Subsidies. Increasing the proportion of middle- and working-class families owning their own homes became a major priority of federal domestic policy in the 1930s. The principal policy mechanisms included low-interest loans from the Home Owners' Loan Corporation, especially loans guaranteed by the Federal Housing Administration (FHA) and the Veterans Administration (VA); FHA- and VA-sponsored housing accounted for nearly one-third of all private housing built in the 1950s.[36] While the primary aim of these policies was to encourage homeownership, increased suburbanization was the inevitable effect, for a number of reasons. First, federal agencies engaged in redlining to help steer new investments into more-affluent, homogeneous areas in suburban locations rather than into demographically diverse urban areas. The historian Kenneth Jackson reports that between 1934 and 1960 the FHA provided mortgage insurance in St. Louis County, Missouri, worth over six times as much on a per capita basis as insurance provided in the (legally separate) city of St. Louis over the same time period; roughly five times as much insurance per capita in both Montgomery County and Prince George's County, Maryland, as in Washington, D.C.; and over ten times as much insurance per capita in Nassau County, New York, as in both Brooklyn and the Bronx.[37] Second, sharply increased demand for single-owner homes could be much more easily accommodated by building in open suburban spaces (as in Levittown, N.Y.) rather than by erecting new homes in urban cores; moreover, neither federal loans nor private lenders were keen to finance homes in such neighborhoods. Additionally, in the immediate postwar period, the condominium form of city-center housing was not yet widespread; it was not until 1961 that buyers moving to condominiums were able to obtain federal mortgage insurance.[38] Consequently, in the decisive period of the 1940s and 1950s, becoming a first-time homeowner generally meant moving to suburbia. Third, and perhaps most important, the postwar wave of homeowner-driven suburbanization helped create a new cultural *norm* defining a healthy American life, premised on residence in a clean, spacious suburb.[39]

Subsidies to homeowners have not ended. Of greatest import, in substantive terms, is the allowance for homeowners to claim a federal-tax deduction on the interest paid on their home mortgages. Some writers, such as Robert

Bruegmann, have argued that the mortgage deduction should not really be considered a subsidy to suburbanites since it is available to homeowners in cities as well.[40] Here we must distinguish between the tax deduction's historic effect and its present one. As Michael Lewyn points out, there can be little doubt that *historically* the tax credit accelerated suburbanization, precisely by making the marginal cost of homeownership lower, given that (as noted above) in the postwar decades acquiring a new home generally meant moving to suburbs.[41]

The primary *present* effect of the subsidy is not geographic but simply regressive: it uses the tax code to effect a net transfer of wealth from poorer to wealthier residents. But this "transfer effect," in turn, reinforces inequalities between wealthier suburbs and poorer central city areas. A detailed study to determine which congressional districts claimed the highest mortgage interest subsidies in 2003 found that "fast-growing suburbs" had the highest number of taxpayers claiming the subsidy, whereas districts claiming the least subsidies both in number of taxpayers and dollar amount were located in New York City.[42] Even if we regard the inequality-reinforcing nature of the deduction as its most salient feature, this, too, has long-run consequences for the U.S. socio-spatial order: the subsidies received disproportionately by wealthy suburban homeowners make them better able to afford local public goods, further increasing the desirability of affluent suburban neighborhoods vis-à-vis neighborhoods with fewer affluent homeowners.

Zoning. Land use patterns in the United States are pervasively shaped by regulations; a 2006 Brookings Institution study of zoning practices in the nation's fifty largest metropolitan areas found that 92 percent of jurisdictions in these areas had some form of zoning regulation.[43] Some of these regulations directly contribute to sprawl by mandating low-density development; the Brookings researchers found, for instance, that some 39 percent of localities in the nation's largest metropolitan areas forbid development densities of higher than eight persons per acre, and that roughly 30 percent would forbid construction of a moderately-sized, forty-unit apartment complex. Such measures contribute directly to low-density development; they are also associated with heightened concentrations of poverty and minorities. Those metropolitan areas that eschew exclusionary zoning in favor of inclusive zoning and growth management exhibit urban–suburban poverty ratios (i.e., the proportion of poor people living in city centers compared to the proportion of poor people living in suburbs within a given metropolitan area) markedly lower than more "traditionally" zoned regions; similar patterns hold with respect to concentrations of African Americans and Hispanics.

Research by Jonathan Levine sheds additional light on the importance of local zoning in shaping development patterns. In a 2001 national survey of building developers, Levine found that 78 percent of them counted local government as a major obstacle to the construction of "alternative," higher-density residential development, while only a minority cited insufficient consumer demand as a limiting factor. Case studies by Levine have demonstrated in detail how the attitude of local planning authorities toward proposals for higher-density housing often has a decisive effect in either facilitating such plans or in forcing compromises that may dilute or eliminate the distinctive features of high-density development.[44]

Clearly, road construction, homeowner subsidies, and local zoning have had tangible effects on the U.S. pattern of metropolitan development. It is important, however, not to overstate the claim: for instance, as Robert Beauregard has argued, it is at least questionable whether federal subsidies were the primary causal factors driving urban decline (as measured by population loss) during the postwar era. Beauregard readily admits, however, that "cities and suburbs do not compete for households and investors on a level playing field." He further notes, "The federal government subsidizes decentralization and sprawl, and state governments subsidize jurisdictional fragmentation. The result is cities that cannot manage their opportunities."[45] This is the fundamental point: not that federal policies are responsible for all urban problems but that they have biased metropolitan development in a suburban direction.

It might be claimed, however, that these interventions were, in the main, very popular and reflected both the will of democratic populaces and existing market trends, not elite connivance. This claim is questionable on its own terms; Gutfreund, for instance, specifically rejects the claim that U.S. road-building policies reflected a democratic "public choice" and provides detailed evidence of the intense and sometimes misleading political pressure brought to bear on the policy process by well-organized elite groups.[46] Yet, even if the claim is accepted, it illustrates again one of our core themes: sprawl is a collective choice, shaped by public policy. Making this observation does not require a strong judgment that these policies are wrong, nor does arguing that these policies were popular when they were adopted suffice to defend their continuation in the present. The democratic process (with its manifold imperfections) generated one set of policies aimed at a specific set of goals in the past that helped produce sprawl; that same process might in the future create policies aimed at quite different ends.

7. *Affluence and preference for private space and automobiles.* Comprising a seventh causal factor driving sprawl are the preferences and tastes of U.S. consumers—and, in particular, U.S. ideas about the ideal domicile. Homeownership is a well-established ideal to which most consumers aspire

and which politicians across the political spectrum endorse; homeownership is a primary status marker in U.S. society; and homeownership has also
been promoted as the primary mechanism by which most households can
accumulate wealth over time. Among homeowners, the size and amenities
of one's home are important status symbols.[47] Indeed, the size of the average
new single-family U.S. home doubled between 1950 and 1999, partially the
result of new suburban construction, especially in the outer tier of suburbs.[48]
Rising household incomes fueled demand for more living space, a demand
most easily accommodated by new suburban developments.

If homeownership is one pillar of the dominant way of life in the United
States, automobile ownership is surely another. Cars function as systems of
transportation—and increasingly necessary systems, especially for suburban
residents lacking access to reasonable-quality mass transit. But they also act
as status markers and, even more strikingly, as instruments of freedom, permitting people to pick up and go anywhere at any time at minimal cost,
allowing teenagers to escape their parents and young men to express their
masculinity. Examining responses to the 2000 General Social Survey's questions about "freedom," Orlando Patterson reports that cars are considered a
vital source of freedom by all Americans, but especially by working-class and
minority men.[49] Cars offer Americans the promise of remarkable geographic
freedom, a capacity to treat an entire town, city, or even metropolitan region
as one's oyster on any given day, the opportunity to go where one wants,
when one wants, without (seemingly) obtaining permission from anyone or
engaging in a larger system of social cooperation. Congested urban areas are
increasingly unable to fulfill the promise of unfettered mobility (and, indeed,
can sometimes transform the car from a vehicle of freedom into a daily prison
on wheels); yet such congestion further impels additional road construction
and development on the perimeter of metropolitan communities, where dis-
tances between places may be longer but traffic less congested than in central
cities.[50]

8. *The notion of the "American Dream."* Closely related to but conceptually distinct from the American consumer's preferences are Americans'
shared ideas about what makes for a good life, what counts as success, and
what kinds of places are desirable. The widely assumed narrative trajectory of
the successful American life pivots on the critical moment when a household
is able to accumulate enough capital or credit to acquire a private home in
a comfortable environment, preferably with good public schools. (In many
areas of the country, white Americans habitually define a "comfortable environment" as one in which there are few members of other races, particularly African Americans of low socioeconomic status.) Politicians and other

commentators often take for granted that a crucial aim of public policy is to facilitate the pursuit of this ideal, whether from a conservative direction (defending the value of existing homeowners' property) or a liberal one (using government to help citizens realize their dream of homeownership). Within the context of a growing population, this ideal of private homeownership is bound to help produce pressures for outward metropolitan expansion to accommodate as many people's dreams as possible—especially in circumstances in which large parts of the existing metropolis are considered unsafe, undesirable places in which no one who could afford to live elsewhere would choose to live.

9. *Broad patterns of capitalist development.* Finally, some urban scholars in the neo-Marxian tradition have linked postwar suburbanization to broader patterns and trends in capitalism as a whole. The most well-known of these scholars is David Harvey, who has described postwar suburbanization as a "spatial fix" for U.S. capitalism: the idea is that the massive shift of Americans from cities to suburbs, and the ensuing boom in residential construction and automobile use, presented capital and capitalists with enormous opportunities for growth and hence was vigorously supported by both business groups and the political establishment. In 1973, Harvey described automobiles as the "linch-pin of the contemporary capitalist economies" and predicted that a downturn in the auto industry would lead to "severe economic and financial disruption." Harvey thus contended that "much of the expansion of GNP in capitalist societies is in fact bound up with the whole suburbanization process."[51]

An interesting restatement of this theoretical perspective has recently been provided by Jason Hackworth; he argues (and provides evidence for the proposition) that whereas in the immediate postwar period the logic of capitalist development involved a move to the metropolitan periphery (suburbanization), in the most recent period (especially since 1990) the tendency has been toward reinvestment in core downtown areas (gentrification) *in addition to* continued suburbanization. "By contrast," Hackworth writes, "the suburban housing of the Keynesian managerialist period (inner suburbs) is largely falling victim to disinvestment, as the wealthy flee for either the gentrified neighborhoods of the inner city or the gated ones of the suburbs."[52]

Accounts of this sort are more ambitious theoretically insofar as they seek to incorporate many of the specific factors noted above into a more general explanation of suburbanization. They also provide an important service by explicitly linking the evolution of spatial form to political–economic developments. Such argumentation risks lapsing into determinism if it is taken to imply that U.S.-style suburbanization was an *inevitable* feature of U.S.

capitalist development, but it is not unreasonable to suggest that achieving a substantially different form of urban development in the United States in the second half of the twentieth century would very likely have required a different set of political–economic arrangements (i.e., a different logic of capitalist development).

———

This overview of the most important causes of sprawl is hardly exhaustive. Most other factors contributing to U.S.-style suburbanization, however, can be subsumed under or related to the nine causal factors described above. There is as yet no accepted, persuasive account of the relative importance of each of these factors, and the weight assigned to each varies by discipline, with economists stressing falling transportation costs, social historians stressing the politics of race, and political scientists stressing public policy decisions. Moreover, the relative importance of these factors has surely varied across locations and time periods. In general, however, scholars tend to emphasize the "pull" factors making suburban life attractive and affordable when they explain the massive wave of suburbanization beginning in the second quarter of the twentieth century; later, "push" factors associated with urban decline and the manifest inequalities between cities and suburbs become more important.[53]

For the purposes of this book, what is important about this brief discussion is the notion that ideas about ways of life are *themselves* important parts of the story. On occasion, these ideas about the good life or the best way of living have been made quite explicit by participants in the sprawl debate; at other times, such ideas have lurked in the background as unspoken assumptions informing practical arguments.

Place, Space, Action, and Attitude: Why Place (Often) Matters

A common assumption among citizens and scholars concerned with land use is that the nature of the built environment helps shape social life in important ways. Yet many scholars have been wary of spatial determinism, for two reasons: first, one might commit the error of attributing to the built environment outcomes that are actually the product of individual attributes or actions or of demographic clustering; and second, any implication that humans are mere prisoners of their built environments is implausible.[54]

Both concerns are well placed. Nonetheless, there is good reason to believe that the character of particular built environments might be linked to individual actions and attitudes in predictable ways, although we must be careful to stress that such linkages reflect only probabilistic relationships between one factor and another rather than ironclad social laws. This book makes no claims to any *determinate* relationship—if *x,* then necessarily *y*—between a given sort of environment and a particular outcome; what we are interested in are probabilities and tendencies.

But why might we think there are any such probabilistic correspondences between certain kinds of spaces and certain kinds of attitudes and behaviors? We can usefully distinguish four mechanisms here.[55]

First, the physical design of a given area may facilitate certain kinds of activities while inhibiting or preventing others. Safe and rapid automobile travel, for instance, requires there be roads of a certain width and a system of traffic regulation. Likewise, self-directed pedestrian activity requires sidewalks and relatively calm traffic patterns; it is no accident that urbanites in Boston spend their Sundays walking along the banks of the Charles River as opposed to strolling the Route 128 loop. The quintessential urban activity celebrated by writers from Jane Jacobs to Iris Marion Young, that of unscripted, chance interactions between residents, is commonly thought to require the presence of publicly shared, accessible space that itself contains meaningful specific destinations (shops, homes, libraries, parks). A four-lane highway cannot function as this sort of urban space—nor can a privately held mansion (even if located within the boundaries of a large city), a location (such as a vacant lot, or an undeveloped marsh) that contains no specific destination likely to attract a mix of persons on a daily basis, or a place where walking is dangerous or viewed as socially unacceptable. Not all kinds of activities are equally compatible with all possible road configurations, arrangements of physical landmarks and buildings, ownership patterns, and functional uses; each combination of these features makes different sorts of behaviors and actions more or less likely.[56]

Second, particular places are often linked to—if not defined by—normative scripts about the sorts of behaviors that are acceptable in a given location. In England, hordes of young- to middle-aged men singing spirited, frequently offensive songs and chants while inebriated is socially accepted (to a degree) within the confines of a soccer stadium, but it is only on unusual occasions acceptable within other urban public spaces, and it is never acceptable on the grounds of a cathedral. Similarly, in Chapel Hill, North Carolina, virtually every local resident knows that when the North Carolina Tar Heels defeat their archrivals Duke or win a national title in basketball, it is acceptable to form a joyous mob spanning the two commercial blocks of Franklin Street between Henderson and Columbia Streets; yet on such occasions no one starts bonfires and climbs treetops in the residential neighborhoods just blocks away.

Likewise, to take an example of direct relevance to this book, some sorts of urban locations become normatively acceptable locales for the expression of political speech, whether in the form of actual demonstrations with speakers, chants, and marches, or in the form of posters, handbills, or other types of printed messages. In Richmond, Virginia, Monroe Park near the campus of Virginia Commonwealth University (VCU) is the most familiar—and indeed the most practical—location for political rallies of substantial size in the metropolitan area. The circular park can easily hold several thousand people, is accessible by foot from VCU and several neighboring residential areas, and is centrally located in the city as a whole. While not the only site of frequent political speech in the city (the streets outside the governor's mansion are another popular choice, for obvious reasons), Monroe Park is the favored outdoor space for larger gatherings. Conversely, it is almost unimaginable that activists would attempt (and be permitted) to hold a large-scale public gathering featuring strident political speech at the corner of Libbie and Grove in the city's tony West End, and any attempt to take such a rally to the green open spaces of the Country Club of Virginia's golf course would result in certain arrest. Outspoken political activism of that sort would violate the established scripts and norms governing those locations and would likely be greeted with both fierce disapproval and (when possible) legal sanction.

This is not to say that the social meanings and scripts attached to particular places are natural, permanent features; on the contrary, they are socially constructed, and they can change over time by intentional or unintentional means. But activities that violate the normative behaviors associated with a given locale are certain to be labeled as deviant and to be felt as a real offense by other users or residents of that space.

Third, and closely related, modes of social control differ from one physical location to another. The front lawns of privately owned homes are not welcome territory for strangers to lounge uninvited; if necessary, the police can be beckoned to confront those who violate this norm, but social expectations alone are generally strong enough to induce the desired behavior. That expectation, in turn, flows from the fact of ownership. Similarly, privately owned and operated malls can (and do) enforce a different code of behavior than would be possible in, say, Washington Square Park in New York City.[57] But the fact of ownership is just one factor in the regime of social control in any given location; the degree to which individual behavior is publicly observable is another. An individual walking alone through a forest with few, if any, other persons around is free to sing off-key loudly with little fear of social sanction. But a person in a very dense urban area might also feel free to engage in unconventional behavior, because there is little risk of social sanction, compared to the risk a resident of a smaller, more homogeneous community, where anything unusual is quickly noted, might face.

Fourth, each kind of place attracts a different kind of person, for different reasons. To take an obvious example, those without access to private automobiles will generally limit their travel to areas that are relatively easy to reach by public transit or foot. People with limited financial resources are less drawn to high-end coffee shops in gentrifying neighborhoods than are those who can afford to spend $5 a day on caffeine. Those who value walking their dog every day will be more likely to visit (or move near) parks or streets that facilitate this activity. In short, each kind of place, by the nature of the functions it performs, in addition to the normative scripts and particular design features it exhibits, will prove more attractive or necessary to some parts of the population than to others. This process, commonly labeled "self-selection," emphasizes the choices individuals make to inhabit or visit some places rather than others. As Jonathan Levine and others have pointed out, however, this term taken alone can be misleading: choices are made, but those choices are informed by the very real qualities of the particular places that are chosen.[58]

A central aim of this book is to test the hypothesis that these differential qualities of place are systematically related to differences in individual attitudes and behaviors. The widely held belief among urban planners and others who have studied suburban sprawl is that suburban spaces have a fundamentally different character than do prototypical urban spaces: suburban places are marked by design features, local norms, and patterns of social control that differ from those of urban places; consequently, they attract a different kind of person. As a result, suburbs are experienced as qualitatively different than urban places; and, it is hypothesized, such places encourage or induce behaviors and attitudes different from those that urban places conjure.

Perhaps the best way to summarize the point is to consider the four distinctive features of urban life posited by the political theorist Iris Marion Young. For Young, a healthy city featured "social differentiation without exclusion" (i.e., a location welcoming of diversity); "variety," said to result from the diverse uses of shared spaces; "eroticism," which involves the sense that one might always experience or encounter something new within the city; and "publicity," which involves the presence of spaces "accessible to anyone."[59] Implicit in this description of city life is the notion that prototypical suburbs do not exhibit these characteristics, at least not to the same degree: to take the obverse of Young's urban virtues, we might think of prototypical suburban space as characterized by homogeneity, sameness, predictability, and privateness.[60]

Quite obviously, any claim that cities and suburbs are so dramatically different as Young's list of virtues (and their implicit opposites) suggest would be an implausible overstatement. But looking at these lists does help clarify the conceptual basis for the empirical investigations in this book: in short, I posit first that places vary in at least four key dimensions (design, normative scripts, social control, and attractiveness to different groups), and second that in the United States urban places generally have a quite different character than do suburban places, distinct enough to cause one to believe that they may predictably be associated with differences in behaviors and attitudes.

Given the enormous diversity of both U.S. cities and U.S. suburbs, however, we should avoid overly simplistic categorizations of these places. Instead, we will want measures of place characteristics that reflect (to the degree possible) the reality that places differ among themselves along a continuum (as, for instance, either more or less pedestrian-friendly). The next section describes the measures of "sprawl" I employ for that purpose.

From Conceptualization to Measurement:
A Methodological Overview

In any public policy debate, profoundly different normative conclusions rooted in contrasting philosophical positions can be drawn from the same set of facts. When those debates involve very complex empirical phenomena, however, it cannot be taken for granted that participants are looking at the same set of facts or the same set of phenomena. Substantial empirical knowledge of the topic at hand is thus a requirement for scholars who wish to make normative assessments of a given phenomenon; it is a further requirement that such scholars identify and elucidate the set of facts and findings she or he is relying upon to draw normative conclusions. This method allows subsequent scholars to make sense of normative arguments that might seem far-fetched or unlikely without an understanding of the facts the analyst is considering; and it allows subsequent scholars to undertake independent critiques of such arguments by identifying flaws and oversights in one's normative thinking and/or in the empirical picture a scholar is examining.

Often the most normatively significant facts about a given social phenomenon can be identified through descriptive data or relatively simple analyses indicating the correlations between one phenomenon and another. Yet some questions of intense normative significance can be approached only by going beyond descriptive data and simple correlation analyses to attempt to impute causation between a given set of factors and a given outcome. Specifically, if the key question is whether sprawl is a healthy or unhealthy development in U.S. life, it will be important to measure the *effects* of sprawl. This, in turn, requires analysis of the effect of sprawl, or elements thereof, on outcomes of substantive interest.

It is impossible, of course, for any single study or source of data to assess the effect of sprawl (however measured) on all outcomes we might care about. Many of the most important outcomes relevant to sprawl concern its effect on larger-order collective outcomes, such as the quantity of carbon emissions released into the atmosphere by our motor vehicles. In this book, however, the focus is primarily on how the elements of sprawl affect a range of individual-level behaviors and attitudes, such as satisfaction with the local community, social trust, political orientation, and rates of political participation. The normative significance and theoretical expectations attached to each of these dependent variables are discussed in the relevant empirical chapters (3, 5, and 7); the purpose of the following section is simply to describe the methodological apparatus underlying the study as a whole.

DATA AND METHODS

The overall aim is to explore how differences in residential contexts correspond to differences in a variety of behaviors and outcomes with normative importance for contemporary political theorists and political scientists. Getting leverage on that question requires the use of data that (1) represent a wide range of geographic settings; (2) allow us to distinguish between community-level effects and individual-level effects; (3) allow us to distinguish community-level effects that are demographic from those that relate to spatial setting; and (4) present information about a wide range of behaviors of normative significance.

The data used in this study meet all of those criteria. The principal tools of analysis in this investigation are the restricted-use version of the Social Capital Community Benchmark Survey (SCCBS), conducted by Harvard's Saguaro Seminar and released by the Roper Center in 2001, and Summary File 3 of the 2000 United States Census. The SCCBS, conducted in the summer and fall of 2000, includes some 29,733 respondents. Ninety percent of these respondents are members of one of 41 distinct geographic areas, including 32 urban areas; about three thousand respondents are from a representative national sample.[61] The urban areas in this data set range from metropolitan areas often associated with sprawl, such as Charlotte, Atlanta, and Houston, to cities with very high density, such as San Francisco. Roughly 14 percent of the survey respondents live in rural areas, 40 percent in central cities, and 46 percent in suburbs. Most important for this research, the restricted-use version of the data includes geographic markers for some 29,140 cases at the county, zip code, census tract, and census block group level, permitting detailed analysis of the effects of community characteristics on multiple forms of civic and political participation and social attitudes.[62]

MEASURES OF SPRAWL

As we have already seen, the meaning and definition of sprawl has been debated and contested by scholars and advocates; social scientists seeking to operationalize the concept of sprawl have chosen diverse measures. Some studies have attempted to combine diverse indicators into a single sprawl index.[63]

This book, in contrast, does not attempt to create or use an index or any single determinate measure of sprawl. Instead, I contend that conceptual and analytic clarity are best served by *disaggregating* the array of community characteristics that are often grouped together under the common label of "sprawl."[64]

Consequently, this book focuses on four distinct community characteristics that can be plausibly associated with the concept of "sprawl," insofar as "sprawl" is used to indicate a particular type of residential setting (as opposed to, as described above, a particular process of urban growth). These community characteristics include a locality's status as a central city or a suburb, local population density, local transportation and commuting patterns, and neighborhood age. These measures, in turn, correspond to the working definition of sprawl offered above. Each of these measures is explained in detail below.

Central city/suburban residence. I sort places represented in the SCCBS into one of three categories: census-designated central cities (with population greater than 25,000); suburbs (within a metropolitan statistical area [MSA] but outside of central city); and rural areas (places outside of MSAs); as explained below, in analyses I often further distinguish between urbanist and non-urbanist rural locations.[65] Strictly speaking, whether one lives in a central city or a suburb is not a measure of urban design: the proportion of residents in a metropolitan area who reside in central cities varies, and in some cases neighborhoods within central cities may be more "sprawling" than those in suburban jurisdictions. Nonetheless, it is highly plausible that, independent of variations in density and neighborhood form, whether one resides within the boundaries of a central city or not may affect a range of attitudes and behaviors. Including this measure allows us to distinguish between the possible effect of *suburbanization* on Americans' behavior and the more specific characteristics of suburban communities generally connoted by "sprawl."[66]

Density. Perhaps the most commonly cited indicator in relation to "sprawl" is population density, measured in persons per square mile. I measure density using 2000 census data on the density of census tracts. Census tracts are subsets of counties; each tract typically contains three thousand to six thousand residents.[67] Census officials construct tract boundaries to correspond to locally acknowledged neighborhood boundaries or other geographic markers. The mechanisms by which density may affect social behavior and social attitudes differ markedly according to whether the dependent variable under consideration is political participation, social trust, or satisfaction with local quality of life; further discussion of these mechanisms is hence postponed to the appropriate chapters. Because the tract-density measure is highly skewed upward, I employ a natural log transformation of the raw density measure in the statistical analyses presented in this book.

Transit mode. The notion that sprawl is connected to and constituted by the hegemony of the automobile is one of the most widely agreed upon, best established points in the literature on sprawl. Nationally, more than 75 percent of all workers drive alone to work.[68] People in the workforce who are not driving alone may be using public transit, or they may be biking, walking, carpooling, or working from home. Following Lance Freeman's work on the relationship between sprawl and social ties, I use the percentage of a given census tract's workers who drive alone to work as a measure of the degree to which local transportation networks depend on the automobile.[69] Strictly speaking, this is a measure of collective behavior: this statistic captures the degree to which residents of a given neighborhood use cars to get around, which is important, in itself, given our definition of sprawl as an automobile-centered form of development. This measure thus speaks to our sociological interest in sprawl as a way of life.[70] In addition, this measure can be understood as a proxy for the degree to which local built environments accommodate the car via thoroughfares, parking lots, and related infrastructure—in addition to the degree to which infrastructure supporting alternative modes of transportation, such as walking, biking, and taking public transit, is absent from the built environment.[71]

Neighborhood age. The final sprawl-related variable is neighborhood age, measured here as the median age of the housing units in a given census tract. Neighborhood age is related to sprawl in two ways. First, as suggested by J. Eric Oliver, it can be seen as a partial proxy for neighborhood design, to the extent one believes (as most urban designers critical of sprawl do) that neighborhood design shifted substantially in the postwar era and that developers increasingly designed communities in which work and home were rigidly separated, as opposed to communities that integrated multiple functions within a single coherent place.[72] Second, as suggested by Paul Jargowsky, neighborhood age is also a proxy for the degree to which a neighborhood is a wholly new development on the fringe of a suburban area. "Sprawling" communities will tend to have much younger buildings than longer-standing developments.[73]

Both the transit mode and the neighborhood age measures are presumed to capture variations in the on-the-ground spatial layout of neighborhoods. To validate this presumption, Google Earth was used to collect photographs of hundreds of census tracts represented in the SCCBS, sorted as relatively "sprawling" (more recently built, more car-dependent) and "non-sprawling" (older, less car-dependent). Not surprisingly, the non-sprawling tracts tended to be near (or inside) central cities and to be denser than the non-sprawling locales; they also were far more likely to be organized as traditional street grids with many points of accessibility to any given location.[74] Suburban examples of older, less car-dependent places include Cicero, Illinois; Quincy, Massachusetts; and Compton, California. More-sprawling places, in contrast, were far more likely to consist of separated subdivisions, with winding, unconnected roads and many cul-de-sacs, connected to one another by large arterials. Good examples include the suburban edge of Greensboro, North Carolina; Lakeville, Minnesota (south of Minneapolis-St. Paul); and the area whose zip code is 46237, south of downtown Indianapolis within Marion County, Indiana.

Our principal concern here is with the cumulative effect of the various dimensions of sprawl. Because each of these measures is significantly correlated with the others, we must attend to the possibility that the sprawl-related variables may be jointly significant predictors of some outcomes. Generally, we will explain our results in terms of the overall effect of living in a "high-sprawl" (automobile-dependent, low-density, recently built suburb) tract compared to a "low-sprawl" (less automobile-dependent, higher-density, older urban) tract.[75] In many cases, however, only one or two of the sprawl-related variables proved to be statistically significant predictors of a given dependent variable. To ease interpretation of results and reduce the amount of "noise" in the models, in these cases I omit non-significant sprawl variables from reported findings. As we shall see, which dimensions of sprawl are significantly correlated with which measures of social and political behavior varies from case to case.[76]

LEVEL OF GEOGRAPHIC ANALYSIS

One important clarification about this approach to measuring sprawl should be noted here. These census tract–level measures of sprawl are designed to capture spatial differences among specific neighborhood-level environments; they are not intended to measure or capture the overall level of sprawl in a given metropolitan area. I believe this approach is most appropriate for gauging the effect of immediate spatial environments on *individual-level* behavior; metropolitan areas typically have enormous internal diversity, and we cannot reliably infer neighborhood spatial context from metropolitan-wide spatial attributes. (At the same time, neighborhoods within a given metropolitan area are not independent of one another; the specific attributes of any given tract are, obviously, influenced by metropolitan-level characteristics.) This is not to say, however, that metropolitan-level measures of sprawl are not useful or important tools for measuring other outcomes possibly associated with sprawl, such as total pollution generated or total land consumed in a metropolitan area.

Put another way, the primary object of this study is not to compare the possible effect of metropolitan-level sprawl upon individual-level outcomes, but rather to assess the effect of *where one lives* within a given a metropolitan area on outcomes. Many analysts are accustomed to thinking of and describing sprawl as a metropolitan-level phenomenon. In this book, the emphasis is instead on the effect of living in a *sprawling neighborhood;* that is, a neighborhood that exemplifies low-density, automobile-oriented suburban development, as opposed to a more traditional urban neighborhood (or a rural area). The underlying theoretical rationale is that if spatial characteristics are associated with individual behavior or attitudes in significant ways, that association should be most visible in the residential environments individuals inhabit: the sorts of spaces and places individuals see, use, and travel through everyday, as opposed to metropolitan-wide spatial features. Suburban golf-course communities marked by winding roads and cul-de-sacs likely exhibit a similar correspondence with individual behaviors and attitudes across metropolitan areas, regardless of whether the metropolitan area in which any particular such community is located is relatively dense or not.

ADDITIONAL VARIABLES INCLUDED IN THE ANALYSIS

Any study of the effect of sprawl-related variables upon individual behavior may yield only spurious findings if it fails to control for other, non-sprawl-related community and individual characteristics. The following two sections describe the additional community and individual characteristics I employ as control variables.

Commuting Times

The average commuting time in one's locality has often been used as a proxy for sprawl in previous studies.[77] In traditional models of the monocentric city, in which suburban residents commuted to jobs in the central city, commuting time could serve as a plausible proxy for sprawl, or a least a rough approximation of the distance between suburban homes and the metropolitan core. But we should be far less confident that long commuting times mean sprawl nowadays because this tendency is mitigated by the rise of polycentric metropolitan areas in which an increasing proportion of jobs are in the suburbs. Moreover, some very large cities with extensive public transit also have long average commuting times—yet no one would suggest that Manhattan exhibits sprawl. Put another way, a measurement of *time* is not a very sound criterion from which to infer *distance* (i.e., the distance between a suburb and an employment center).

Nonetheless, commuting patterns continue to be important in categorizing communities. If most residents in a given neighborhood spend a long amount of time traveling to and from work, it is highly plausible that that fact might have significance for other areas of social life. I employ two distinct measures of commuting patterns in this study. First, I use information provided in the SCCBS itself about individuals' personal commuting time.[78] Second, I use census data on the average length of commutes in one's census tract, because living in a place where the commutes are long may affect individual outcomes, independent of whether one personally has a long commute.

City Size

Another factor social scientists commonly use to categorize communities and distinguish them from one another is size. It is plausible to suppose that individuals living in a tiny hamlet might have a different relationship to their community (especially as a political entity) than might a resident of a huge city; research by J. Eric Oliver reiterates the connection between smaller city size and enhanced civic participation.[79] Consequently, when examining the relationship of sprawl to political participation, the possible effect of city size must be considered alongside the effect of more specific sprawl-related variables. To this end, I constructed a measure of city size that distinguishes (1) between communities with less than one hundred thousand people and those with more than one hundred thousand people, and (2) among larger cities themselves; this measure is included in analyses reported in chapter 7.[80]

Residential Stability

Stable neighborhoods with many long-term residents may have a quite different social character than less stable neighborhoods dominated by those who have recently moved in; consequently, it is desirable to control for local residential stability as a possible confounding effect. Residential stability is measured here as the proportion of residents within a given census tract who lived in their current residence five years previously (excluding children under 5).

Sprawl-Related Individual Variables

Two individual-level variables are of particular substantive interest for these analyses, insofar as both are broadly related to suburbanization, mobility, and sprawl. The first is whether or not an individual is a homeowner. Homeownership is a well-known predictor of enhanced social and civic engagement and is also substantially correlated with suburban residence.[81] In comparing the effect of living in suburbs versus central cities, it is important to note the effect of homeownership at the individual level alongside the possible effect of community-level variables.

The second key individual-level variable is years lived in the same community. Long community tenure is also well established as a strong predictor of civic engagement.[82] Traditional models of suburbanization portray a process in which residents of central cities and inner suburbs are persuaded to move farther out onto the metropolitan perimeter, leaving behind accumulated social capital. Indeed, the high geographic mobility of Americans can be seen as a factor contributing to growth pressures in metropolitan areas and, in turn, to sprawl—especially since such mobility often takes the form of net regional migrations, with some cities losing residents and others gaining them.[83] Analysts of suburban sprawl thus have a particular interest in weighing the effect of stable community tenure on individual's behavior, alongside the effect of sprawl-related contextual variables.

Additional Contextual Variables: Measures of Socioeconomic Composition

In addition to the sprawl-related contextual variables, I include as controls three measures pertaining to the socioeconomic composition of the census tracts in which each respondent lives: neighborhood income level, neighborhood-level racial diversity, and average educational level. Each of these variables has been included in recent scholarly work on the effect of community characteristics upon various forms of social capital.[84] Neighborhood-level racial diversity is measured by use of the Herfindahl index of dissimilarity, measured at the tract level. Neighborhood income is generally measured by median household income in the census tract; however, because neighborhood income levels sometimes have a curvilinear relationship to outcomes of interest, instead of using the conventional measure of median neighborhood income, in some cases I employ two separate income measures: proportion of households in the tract earning less than $25,000, and proportion of households in the tract earning more than $75,000. Employing this alternative measure is useful in illustrating curvilinear relationships between neighborhood income levels and certain individual-level outcomes.[85] Neighborhood educational level is measured as the proportion of adults in the census tract who are college graduates. In addition, in some models I include controls for proportion of African Americans and proportion of Hispanics living in the census tract, when these prove statistically significant.

Finally, I control for whether one lives in a rural area and for which region of the country one lives in. Two distinct control variables for rural residents are included: a variable counting persons considered to live in a rural town (classified here as a person living outside a metropolitan area in a census tract that is at least 50 percent urbanized where at least half of residents work and live in the same community), and a variable counting persons living in non-urbanized sectors outside of metropolitan areas. Making this distinction among rural residents helps account for the fact that some places outside metropolitan areas have urban qualities.[86] I also employ a set of regional controls based on the census's four regional categories: Northeast, South, Midwest, and West.[87]

INDIVIDUAL CHARACTERISTICS

The final major set of control variables included pertain to individual characteristics that may affect civic engagement and other outcomes: race, gender, age, household income, education level, marital status, employment status, number of children in household, language the survey was conducted in, and (in most models) citizenship status. Some models also include controls for the number of adults in the household, when this proves significant. More details on the measurement of each variable are contained in appendix I.

Not all of the control variables measured here have statistically important relationships with each of the dependent variables analyzed in this book. In general, I treat individual-level behavior and outcomes as a function of five explanatory factors: individual demographic features (who one is); individual attachment to one's locality (how long one has lived in a community, plus homeownership status and commuting time); community demographic features; community spatial features; and broad regional differences. In the reported models, except as noted I always include each of the core individual-level controls, in addition to the two most important and consistent community demographic features, neighborhood-level education and neighborhood-level income.

Each of the remaining contextual and regional factors, including the sprawl-related variables, is tested in each multivariate analysis. Those factors that have a substantial, theoretically plausible relationship with the given dependent variable are included in the final reported models.

Statistical Method

For the most part, the dependent variables considered in this study take the form of categorical rather than continuous data. The categorical shape of this data makes traditional OLS regression an inappropriate tool of analysis; instead I employ logit and ordered logit analyses (in most cases), models specifically developed to analyze categorical data.[88] To facilitate substantive interpretation of findings, I employ the computer program Clarify, which uses simulation analysis to generate estimates of the substantive effects implied by multivariate models.[89]

The data used in this book are clustered, consisting of individuals nested within census tracts, within community sub-samples. Consequently, I reported standard errors corrected for clustering at the community-sample level. Employing this technique takes account of the fact that the data do not consist of twenty-nine-thousand-plus independent observations at the individual level. Because neighboring census tracts are not independent of one another and the data were collected so as to form representative samples within each community, I report robust standard errors corrected for clustering at the community sub-sample level.[90]

Substantive Overview of the Communities Included in the SCCBS Data

The SCCBS is an exceedingly rich resource permitting researchers to draw detailed pictures of the social universe of particular metropolitan areas or even particular neighborhoods and census tracts. Such detailed descriptive analysis is not a central aim of this book. Rather, the empirical analyses in chapters 3, 5, and 7 focus on the complex relationships between the components of sprawl and the variety of outcome variables examined, with little attention given to specific neighborhoods or cities. Nonetheless, it is important for readers to have some sense of the character of the communities included in this data set. This section thus provides a brief overview of the forty-one regional areas that serve as the principal focal point in the empirical analyses to follow. Table 1.1 illustrates the spatial contours of each metropolitan area at the tract level, focusing on the measures of sprawl noted above; table 1.2 presents information on other basic demographic characteristics of these regions. In each case, the reported data reflect the unweighted average for each variable among respondents to the SCCBS.

TABLE 1.1. Spatial Characteristics of the SCCBS Communities

	Density (Persons/Sq. Mile)	Solo Drivers (% of All Workers)	Year Median Home Built
Atlanta, GA	2,761	73.9%	1977
Baton Rouge, LA	2,383	81.7%	1973
Birmingham, AL	1,792	83.6%	1971
Bismarck, ND	2,319	83.3%	1971
Boston, MA	20,081	45.0%	1944
Boulder, CO	3,656	69.6%	1975
Charlotte, NC	1,360	80.8%	1977
Chicago, IL	10,162	67.9%	1961
Cincinnati, OH	3,214	80.3%	1964
Cleveland, OH	6,282	75.9%	1953
Denver, CO	7,737	67.3%	1955
Detroit, MI	4,513	81.6%	1962
Grand Rapids, MI	5,459	79.6%	1952
Greensboro, NC	2,204	80.5%	1973
Houston, TX	4,947	74.6%	1974
Kalamazoo, MI	1,997	84.3%	1966
Lewiston, ME	2,025	77.1%	1961
Los Angeles, CA	12,732	69.9%	1962
Minneapolis, MN	8,359	65.7%	1947
N. Minneapolis, MN	9,347	59.4%	1942
Oakland, CA	14,481	52.3%	1949
Phoenix, AZ	4,839	74.3%	1980
Rochester, NY	3,828	79.3%	1957
St. Paul, MN	3,416	79.4%	1969
San Diego, CA	6,888	74.2%	1972
San Francisco, CA	30,162	39.0%	1945

(*continued*)

TABLE 1.1. (continued)

	Density (Persons/Sq. Mile)	Solo Drivers (% of All Workers)	Year Median Home Built
San Jose, CA	7,932	75.8%	1965
Seattle, WA	8,349	60.7%	1958
Syracuse, NY	3,602	77.9%	1958
Winston-Salem, NC	1,408	81.6%	1973
Yakima, WA	2,356	76.6%	1967
York, PA	2,501	83.6%	1965
Delaware	2,626	78.1%	1971
Fremont, MI	207	79.0%	1970
Indiana	1,818	81.9%	1965
Montana	1,258	74.0%	1967
New Hampshire	1,266	80.5%	1966
Central Oregon	788	73.1%	1980
Rural South Dakota	16	68.1%	1939
East Tenn.	823	83.1%	1974
Kanawha, WV	1,376	79.1%	1965
National	6,238	74.0%	1967

Sources: SCCBS; 2000 U.S. Census.

TABLE 1.2. Social Characteristics of the SCCBS Communities

% Central City	Residents in Sample	Median Tract Income %	Nonwhite in Tract
Atlanta, GA	19.0%	$54,364	44.8%
Baton Rouge, LA	53.9%	$42,517	37.3%
Birmingham, AL	27.8%	$44,039	31.9%
Bismarck, ND	51.3%	$41,049	4.8%
Boston, MA	93.9%	$43,185	44.3%
Boulder, CO	63.2%	$56,891	11.6%
Charlotte, NC	38.5%	$46,978	26.1%
Chicago, IL	34.5%	$56,195	30.7%
Cincinnati, OH	26.8%	$47,810	16.0%
Cleveland, OH	35.8%	$41,809	30.8%
Denver, CO	90.9%	$41,725	34.0%
Detroit, MI	24.6%	$51,110	29.9%
Grand Rapids, MI	77.7%	$41,822	28.3%
Greensboro, NC	76.6%	$44,953	36.0%
Houston, TX	54.8%	$47,544	41.1%
Kalamazoo, MI	29.1%	$44,252	14.3%
Lewiston, ME	35.7%	$37,585	3.2%
Los Angeles, CA	44.6%	$47,030	48.2%
Minneapolis, MN	80.2%	$44,496	27.0%

N. Minneapolis, MN	98.5%	$35,142	63.8%
Oakland, CA	88.0%	$47,830	59.0%
Phoenix, AZ	50.3%	$48,915	21.3%
Rochester, NY	30.8%	$43,092	21.9%
St. Paul, MN	24.1%	$57,101	13.0%
San Diego, CA	46.9%	$48,776	31.9%
San Francisco, CA	97.3%	$57,394	47.4%
San Jose, CA	31.1%	$76,547	39.8%
Seattle, WA	68.1%	$49,435	25.3%
Syracuse, NY	35.6%	$42,896	14.3%
Winston-Salem, NC	62.7%	$46,065	28.3%
Yakima, WA	33.3%	$36.419	30.9%
York, PA	11.0%	$45,105	7.0%
Delaware	21.2%	$49,012	25.0%
Fremont, MI	0.3%	$36,974	5.5%
Indiana	29.5%	$42,976	11.4%
Montana	26.2%	$33,377	8.3%
New Hampshire	16.4%	$48,941	3.7%
Central Oregon	0.0%	$39,242	9.5%
Rural South Dakota	0.3%	$29,899	0.9%
East Tenn.	20.6%	$34,187	7.1%
Kanawha, WV	24.5%	$35,317	7.6%
National	30.5%	$43,350	25.9%

Sources: SCCBS; 2000 U.S. Census.

Tables 1.1 and 1.2 show that the SCCBS contains several very large traditional urban areas—high-density regions in which older neighborhoods
are prevalent and transit alternatives to the automobile are heavily used; San
Francisco, Boston, Minneapolis, Chicago, Denver, Seattle, and Los Angeles
all fall into this category. A second category consists of mid-density urban
areas with moderate overall density, more automobile dependence, and a
mix of older and newer neighborhoods; such areas include Detroit, Syracuse,
Grand Rapids, and St. Paul. Sprawling larger cities comprise a larger category: these are larger metropolitan areas that have low to moderate overall
density and are highly automobile dependent. Charlotte and Houston both
fit this category, most closely matching popular conceptions of "sprawl." A
fourth identifiable group consists of smaller mid-density cities with relatively young neighborhoods. Such places include Kalamazoo, Baton Rouge,
Greensboro, and Birmingham, where solo drivers make at least 80 percent
of the daily commutes. The data set also includes several small low-density cities with moderately aged neighborhoods, such as York, Yakima, and

Lewiston. Finally, the data include rural and predominantly rural areas such as southeastern South Dakota and rural Oregon. Obviously, numerous other places in the data set (such as the San José region) exhibit a mix of these traits and do not fit easily into a single category. With the exception of Delaware and, to a lesser extent, Indiana, nonmetropolitan areas included in the SCCBS tend to have suburban-level densities.

The SCCBS thus contains a wide variety of U.S. communities, including large, relatively compact metropolitan areas; large, relatively sprawling metropolitan areas; smaller and medium-sized cities; rural areas; very racially homogeneous places, such as Bismarck; and veritable melting pots, such as Los Angeles. The spatial, regional, and demographic diversity of the data set makes it an excellent tool for exploring how various socio-spatial characteristics affect a range of outcomes of keen interest to scholars and ordinary citizens alike.

TWO

Counting Costs and Benefits

Is Sprawl Efficient?

WHAT OUGHT TO BE the guiding aspiration of public policy? The utilitarian tradition gives a straightforward answer to that question: to maximize the aggregate benefits accruing to society's members while minimizing the costs they bear. No utilitarian can take an a priori position on the goodness of sprawl or any other public policy issue: evidence speaking to the costs and benefits of a given phenomenon is required. The utilitarian-minded analyst thus asks, does sprawl in fact produce the greatest good, compared to plausible alternatives? The pursuit of an answer to that question has led economists, geographers, and social scientists to seek ever more precise measurements of sprawl and its effects, both positive and negative.

This chapter begins by examining utilitarianism's plausibility as a public philosophy and reviewing how notions of the "public good" have motivated urban planning and policy evaluation in the United States and Britain. We then examine research that has attempted to evaluate sprawl's costs and benefits both from the standpoint of the state (in its role as tax collector and provider of infrastructure and services) and from a "global" perspective (taking into account both public *and* private costs and benefits). Finally, we take up the question of whether utilitarians should aim simply to satisfy citizens' *existing* preferences, or whether, in certain circumstances, there might be compelling justifications for utilitarian policymakers to override or reshape such preferences.

Previous research on the costs and benefits of sprawl suggests that the financial inefficiencies associated with sprawl may be modest. Moreover, from a utilitarian perspective, analyses of the financial costs associated with sprawl are only the first step in a comprehensive reckoning of sprawl's goodness: utilitarians also need to know how much "satisfaction" sprawl provides, and whether people living in sprawling areas are happier, healthier, and more pleased with their communities than are other Americans. Evidence on this question is introduced in chapter 3—but even that information is insufficient to allow the utilitarian analyst or critic to rest confident in her judgments about sprawl. One would also need to know whether sprawl increases total utility compared to plausibly available alternative patterns of metropolitan development—such as a development pattern that systematically stabilized and improved the quality of life of central cities such that there were no neighborhoods within the metropolitan region likely to be regarded by middle-class citizens as "undesirable."

Here I argue that the methodological tools available to policy analysts are unable to provide the knowledge utilitarians need to apply their own principles. Any effort to compare sprawl's costs and benefits with those that would be produced by an utterly different policy regime must be speculative in nature—particularly since it is often hypothesized that a different land use and development-policy regime in the United States would substantially alter Americans' preferences vis-à-vis the built environment. How well Americans' preferences might be satisfied under an entirely different policy regime cannot be plausibly inferred from studies of their *existing* preferences, if we have reason to think that those preferences might well be quite different under an alternative regime.[1] In short, empirical analyses of sprawl may succeed in illuminating specific costs and benefits associated with existing development patterns and may also shed light on which sorts of built environments best satisfy Americans' existing preferences, but they provide inadequate answers to the larger question of whether sprawl is or is not, over the long run, the best form of metropolitan development from a utility-maximizing point of view.

In the course of developing this argument, we also consider more common criticisms of utilitarianism and cost–benefit analysis. These include the difficulty utilitarians have when considering the costs of environmental damage, and the broader problematic associated with assuming that goods are commensurable and interchangeable along a single axis of value. At the same time, we aim to take utilitarianism's claims seriously by reviewing evidence relevant to the costs and benefits of sprawl in a manner that should be of interest to both utilitarians and non-utilitarians. Crudely applied cost–benefit analysis may appear to some critics to be an overly simplistic approach to public policy, and, as already suggested, there are good reasons to think that the capacity of cost–benefit analysis to speak meaningfully to certain larger-order social questions is, at best, limited. Nonetheless, a proper appreciation of utilitarianism should yield respect for both its capacity to critically interrogate the policies and institutional regimes under which we live and for the impetus it provides to policy analysts to examine and attempt to measure the effects of various policy approaches.

––––––

Utilitarianism's first key premise is that the moral worth of an action must be judged with respect to its consequences, not the intentions of the actor. The goodness of a given act is ultimately judged by its results, and the actor herself must undertake a thorough assessment of an act's likely results and use that assessment as a guide to action. For the utilitarian, good will is not enough—good calculations are needed, too.

The second key premise of utilitarianism is that there is a single identifiable standard for assessing the consequences of an action; namely, the degree to which it promotes, or indeed maximizes, "utility," or, as John Stuart Mill more explicitly put it, "happiness." Mill's use of the term "happiness" was intended as a clarification to and improvement upon Jeremy Bentham's earlier formulation of utilitarianism as maximizing "pleasure" and minimizing pain; the word "pleasure," Mill noted, could easily be construed as emphasizing bodily pleasures rather than the full range of satisfactions of which human beings are capable. Mill's account of utilitarianism insists that "happiness" is the one good beyond all others to which human beings aspire and, hence, is the natural measuring stick for assessing the desirability of actions. Moreover, Mill suggested that there is a range of identifiable goods with which happiness is closely and determinately linked—including having health, being intelligent, being active, having companionship with and concern for others, and possessing and exercising virtue, prudence, and wisdom. For Mill, happiness is not "a life of rapture," but rather,

> moments of such in an existence made up of few and transitory pains, many and various pleasures, with a decided predominance of the active over the passive, and having as the foundation of the whole, not to expect more from life than it is capable of bestowing. A life thus composed, to those who have been fortunate enough to obtain it, has always appeared worthy of the name of happiness.... The present wretched education, and wretched social arrangements, are the only real hindrance to its being attainable by almost all.[2]

The egalitarian emphasis in this passage from Mill reflects a third key presumption of utilitarianism: each person's utility is to be weighed equally. Policymakers should aim to rank alternative courses of action based on their expected effect on the sum of each person's utilities, counting each person for one. This principle provides utilitarianism with critical leverage for assessing "wretched social arrangements" that deprive large numbers of people of the possibility of attaining happiness.

Utilitarianism thus rests, or can rest, on a rich, insightful, and even inspiring view of the human situation, of the possibilities for human flourishing afforded by modern societies and the obstacles that remain to such flourishing.[3] But the critical focus of Millian utilitarianism extends beyond questions of individual morality and individual decisions about how to live to debates over institutional arrangements, including the structure of politics and the organization of the economy.[4] Mill's brand of utilitarianism does not assume that we are already living in the best of all possible worlds, or under the best possible institutions. Nor need it assume that the actually existing preferences of human beings are those that are most admirable and that should be promoted or endorsed by public policy. Instead, Millian utilitarianism provides a warrant and a mandate to reform and on occasion revolutionize flawed institutions, and to promote decisively those habits of mind and conduct that are most conducive to the realization of happiness and the progress of humanity. (Mill believed that the latter goal was generally best served by promoting a culture of individual liberty and rejecting stultifying conformism.)[5] Moreover, while Mill's blunt judgmentalism with respect to "higher" and "lower" pleasures remains controversial, it is far less so with respect to social institutions and political and economic arrangements.[6] Bentham and Mill disagreed on whether the children's game pushpin could be judged a more worthwhile pursuit than poetry, but not on whether a standard of utility could be used to critique and reform existing political and economic arrangements.

All this is very different from libertarianism, or any public philosophy that celebrates the outcome of market processes as in themselves good (no matter what they are), or that endows individuals with permanent and unalterable rights (such as near-absolute rights to property) upon which society cannot intrude, no matter the costs. It is no surprise then, that utilitarianism has been historically adopted by many urban planners and government agencies as a justification for intervening in the processes of market operations in advanced capitalist societies. As noted in the introduction, utilitarianism is most frequently associated with what Alan Altshuler terms the "public ideo-logic" of land use debate, an ideology that insists on the importance of public goods and "provides a rationale for frequent government intervention to correct market failures," over and against a "private ideo-logic" that "stresses individual freedom to own property and choose one's associates, the efficiency of market allocation, and the perverse effects of big government."[7] Utilitarianism provides a potentially powerful justification for intervening in markets, precisely by insisting that if market operations fail to maximize utility, they should be altered or corrected via public intervention.

But the notion of a "public interest" realizable by good planning has attracted serious criticism from various directions. First, as Heather Campbell and Robert Marshall note, friendly critics of the public interest model have called on practitioners to be more self-aware, and worried that the professionalization of planning could lead to a process of fossilization in which the public good became equated with the professional interests of planners. Second, some critics of planning have argued that real-life plans tend to reflect power struggles, or at best compromises with power (i.e., between the state and powerful private actors, such as developers and landowners), rather than the realization of some neutral public interest.[8] Third, and perhaps most troubling, are postmodern critiques that attempt to problematize the very notion of a unitary public interest. A mild critique along these lines focuses on the experiences of persons and groups whose perspective is typically excluded or marginalized in the policy process; a stronger critique challenges the idea that there is any "public interest" at all that transcends the highly specific experiences of diverse groups and persons. From this perspective, the public interest is a "universalizing, homogenizing concept which carries with it the danger that difference and heterogeneity will be masked," and hence, "a potentially oppressive idea."[9]

Nonetheless, Campbell and Marshall argue that planning theory and practice require a concept of the public interest. It is impossible to escape the necessity of making public judgments about the best course of action, even in cases where interests, preferences, and ideologies conflict. The utilitarian aim of maximizing the well-being of all provides a plausible yardstick for measuring the public interest (although as Campbell and Marshall also note, there are other ways the concept can be grounded).[10]

This line of thought highlights the aspect of utilitarianism that will be emphasized in this chapter: its relevance as a *public philosophy* that purports to offer a baseline standard for evaluating the goodness of our institutions, practices, and policies, rather than its plausibility as a comprehensive guide to all moral action. Perhaps the most common generic criticism of utilitarianism is that the pursuit of maximal utility may lead to actions that seem at odds with or repugnant to commonly held moral intuitions about proper conduct. Few would readily praise a parent who sold his child into slavery and then used the proceeds to save the lives of a hundred starving children, though such a course of action might very plausibly increase utility.

Such doubts have led one prominent contemporary utilitarian, Robert Goodin, to retreat from understanding utilitarianism as a guide to personal ethics at all. Goodin argues that some of the most unattractive features of utilitarianism—its impersonality (refusing to privilege the health of one's mother over the health of millions of others one does not know), its emphasis on calculation (as Goodin notes, "Among intimates it would be extremely hurtful to think of every kind gesture as being contrived to produce some particular effect"), and its consequentialism (which implies that no action—not even killing—is wrong in and of itself)—are in fact attractive virtues *when applied to the public sphere*. While we would not admire Olympian disinterestedness in personal relationships, we would admire a public official for being disinterested when considering the competing claims of two constituents (particularly if there is reason to suspect that one disputant has a more favorable social, economic, or political status than the other and we know the official has conscientiously avoided being swayed by this status in her deliberations). We do not want friends to calculate the exact minimum of our bad jokes or self-indulgent stories they must listen to in order to retain our companionship, but we do want Social Security administrators to calculate quite precisely the amount of Social Security paid to the retired in a given year so as to meet their needs without bankrupting the system. It is in this public sphere of decision making that utilitarianism is most attractive and most appropriate, Goodin argues; he approvingly cites J. S. Mill's observation that Bentham's philosophy had provided "the means of organizing and regulating the merely business part of the social arrangements" of society, but had little to say to humanity's "spiritual interests."[11]

Goodin's theoretical move rescues utilitarianism from obvious objections based on counter-examples taken from daily life and the sphere of individual ethics, and hence presents utilitarianism in its most plausible form. As the subject matter of this investigation concerns public policy and the manner in which competing normative theories treat a concrete problem in public policy, we will follow Goodin's lead and consider utilitarianism (to the extent possible) in this most plausible form, as a theory of government, law, policy, and economics, not as a theory of personal ethics. As we shall see, the complications and difficulties of utilitarianism as a public philosophy as they emerge in relation to the debate about suburban sprawl are in themselves quite substantial.

———

These initial observations already suggest that there is a substantial gap between philosophical accounts of utilitarianism, which permit or even require taking a very broad look at social institutions and can assume that nothing that exists is in itself good, and the often quite narrow perspective of cost–benefit analysis practiced by economists and other public policy scholars. Economists generally employ one of two normative standards in evaluating policies. The first is the minimalist standard of Pareto optimality, in which the aim is to reach a state of affairs in which no one's situation can be improved without hurting anyone else. If steps can be taken to improve someone's situation without hurting anyone else, this is an efficiency gain to which no one can reasonably object. The second is the Kaldor-Hicks test, in which the aim is to identify *potential* Pareto optimalities. Potential Pareto-optimizing policies might in fact impose costs on some parties, but if the overall benefits gained are sufficiently large, losers from the policy could in principle be compensated for their losses, leading to a Pareto improvement. This looser standard amounts, in effect, to a test of whether net benefits outweigh net costs.[12]

Marginal analysis of particular changes or particular policies is the most frequent mode in which utilitarian ideas are operationalized in contemporary debates about suburban sprawl, not holistic analysis in which entire policy and institutional structures are critically interrogated by the principle of utility. In this sense, contrary to the politically radical implications of the Benthamite and Millian formulations of utilitarianism in the nineteenth century, utilitarianism as cost–benefit analysis is an inherently less ambitious and more conservative enterprise: rather than asking what institutional structure or distribution of goods would best maximize utility, such analysis typically takes the status quo and the existing distribution of benefits as the appropriate starting point, then asks what the utility-maximizing next step is, given that starting point.[13] As we shall see, this narrowing of focus is not entirely an accident: strong reasons internal to the methodology of the cost–benefit framework drive much policy work to marginal analysis.

To What Are We Comparing Sprawl?

To make meaningful statements about sprawl's goodness—that is, the costs and benefits of sprawl—policymakers must compare sprawl to some other possible alternative. The theoretical range of alternatives to sprawl is almost limitless; for instance, we might compare the conditions of economic and population growth that have helped drive the process of sprawl to an alternative scenario in which the economy had remained entirely static for the past sixty years and both population and average household size had remained stable, thereby reducing growth pressures in metropolitan America. Or we might compare suburban sprawl with a far more thorough and more intentional dispersal of urban centers, in which every American returned to the land and lived in rural settings, with each family of four allocated ten acres of land, a small farmhouse, two cows, and a dozen chickens. Or we might compare suburban sprawl with proposals to relocate the population into enclosed arcologies, or to create island–cities at sea, or to ban permanent homes altogether and require citizens to live nomadic existences.

Such fanciful comparisons are of little practical use to policymakers: comparing one policy or institutional structure to another requires placing bounds on the range of alternatives that can be considered.[14] Drawing the boundary too loosely might lead to absurd comparisons, such as those suggested above, but drawing the boundary too tightly might lead to excessively narrow thinking that does not do justice to the possible courses of action a polity might reasonably pursue. The most reasonable standard for drawing the boundary, then, is to compare a given policy to the other plausible and achievable alternatives available at a given historical moment. With respect to suburban sprawl, the most commonly cited plausible alternatives are, first, attempts to stop or slow the pace of suburbanization and to strengthen central cities, with the overall goal of keeping metropolitan regions as geographically compact as possible (call this strategy "urban revitalization" or "smart growth"), and second, attempts to alter the spatial layout of suburbs themselves (call this strategy "New Urbanism"). These two basic strategies (which are not mutually exclusive) are those against which sprawl is most commonly compared in contemporary public debates.[15]

This study follows that convention. Throughout this book, comparisons are drawn between the effect of living in a prototypical sprawling community and that of living in a more traditional urbanist neighborhood, on the view that this comparison might tell us something useful about the likely effects of using policy to encourage and strengthen traditional urban neighborhoods rather than to promote low-density suburban communities. As discussed in chapter 1, however, we make the further move of disaggregating sprawl into four distinct components whose effects can be measured and compared individually (suburban residence, population density, transportation patterns, neighborhood age). Nonetheless, for simplicity's sake, we will continue to refer to "sprawl" as a unified phenomenon in the following section, as we go on to specify just what sorts of costs and what sorts of benefits a thorough utilitarian analysis must account for.

The costs commonly associated with sprawl can be grouped into three major categories: infrastructure costs, social and economic costs, and environmental costs. The benefits produced by sprawl can be described even more compactly: first, the degree to which sprawl produces economic benefits for developers, businesses, and residents; and second, the degree to which suburban sprawl provides satisfaction to the residents of sprawling areas, both in subjective and objective terms. Often such satisfaction is interpreted as the degree to which the built environment responds to the *preferences* of citizens, although as we will see, the issue of whether policy should aim to maximize the satisfaction of citizens' existing preferences is not straightforward (even on utilitarianism's own terms).

Infrastructure Costs

A critique of sprawl based on a strict concern with public costs and being frugal with public resources need not lead to the conclusion that comprehensive anti-sprawl policies would be desirable.[16] So long as buyers of housing are willing to pay (in the form of increased housing costs) for the increased public costs associated with fringe suburban housing, there is no basis to complain about sprawl from a public fiscal perspective. A policy perspective on sprawl that takes the costs borne by the public as its benchmark has no basis for critiquing outward development on the suburban fringe if it can be shown that either (a) such development is not more expensive to the public than development closer to the metropolitan core, or (b) effective policy mechanisms to compensate the public for any such cost differences can be identified and implemented.[17]

In short, from a public fiscal perspective, if consumers are willing to pay the true costs associated with new development, then they should be free to buy, and developers free to develop, on the suburban fringe—or anywhere else. Fiscally speaking, there is no more reason to be concerned about a citizen willing to pay an extra $10,000 to live in a house in the suburbs (if that is what must be paid to compensate the public for the public costs associated with this new house) than there is to be concerned about a consumer who pays an extra $5,000 for a fancier car.

Reams of literature involving ever more sophisticated studies have been published on the topic of the infrastructure costs of sprawl. The most ambitious recent attempt at a comprehensive reckoning of sprawl's costs and benefits is that of a research team led by Robert Burchell and Anthony Downs, based on research for their massive volume *The Costs of Sprawl–2000*. Burchell et al. compare various costs associated with two possible urban-growth scenarios over the 2000–2025 time period, one labeled "sprawl growth," the other "compact growth." The sprawl-growth scenario projects a continuation of current trends out to 2025; the compact-growth scenario assumes the implementation of two kinds of restrictions on growth. First, growth is to be directed toward existing urbanized counties rather than into currently rural areas abutting the metropolitan core; second, growth is also to be directed toward the already urbanized sectors *within* partially urbanized counties. Essentially, Burchell et al. ask, what would happen if every metropolitan area in the country implemented the equivalent of an urban-growth boundary?

In both scenarios, it is assumed that roughly 53 million new development units, residential and nonresidential, will be added to the nation's metropolitan areas over the 2000–2025 time period, and that nearly 48.5 million new adult residents will need to be accommodated. In the unrestricted-growth scenario, 63.3 percent of the new building units and 61.9 percent of the new residents would be channeled into existing urban and suburban centers or nonmetropolitan counties with an urbanized center. In the compact-growth scenario, 69.9 percent of new building units and 67.3 percent of new residents would be located in existing in urban and suburban centers. Put another way, the compact-growth scenario would increase the proportion of growth directed to existing areas by some 9 percent (around 3 million units) and increase the population of such areas by roughly 2.6 million people compared to the unrestrained-growth scenario.

If the compact-growth scenario were implemented, Burchell et al. estimate, there would be moderate but significant savings in a variety of areas, including land preserved from development, water and sewer infrastructure costs, road-construction costs, overall residential-construction costs, and the fiscal costs of providing public services. These estimated costs, projected over the entire 2000–2025 time period, are summarized in table 2.1.[18]

Estimates calculated by Burchell et al. suggest that the total financial costs associated with sprawl (public and private) will total some $870 billion (in 2000 dollars) over a twenty-five-year period, or nearly $35 billion a year; additionally, they suggest, sprawl will consume more land and may generate greater ecological costs than will compact development. These findings are consistent with the estimates of a 5–10 percent savings associated with carefully planned growth (compared to sprawl) provided by other experts, such as Alan Altshuler and José Gómez-Ibáñez.[19]

While this is a significant cost difference, it alone is insufficient evidence that Americans should abandon sprawl. If sprawl-type development satisfies Americans' preferences and desires much better than more-compact development, than perhaps 5–10 percent extra is a small price to pay. Cost–benefit analysis asks that we compare the costs borne by governments to the benefits that may accrue to private actors; if total utility is

TABLE 2.1. Savings Achieved under Burchell, Downs, McCann, and Mukherji's Compact-Development Scenario, 2000–2025, Compared to Continued Unchecked Growth

Agricultural Land	1.5 million acres
Environmentally Fragile Land	1.5 million acres
Other Lands	1 million acres
Total Land	**4 million acres**
New Water and Sewer Laterals	4.6 million (10% fewer)
Water and Sewer Infrastructure Costs	$12.6 billion (6.6% savings)
Road Construction	188,000 miles (9% fewer)
Road Construction Costs	$109.7 billion (12% savings)
Total Infrastructure Costs	**$126 billion (11% savings)**
Per Unit Property Development Costs (Residential)	$13,003 (7.8% savings)
Per Unit Property Development Costs (Nonresidential)	$865 (1.1% savings)
Aggregate Property Development Costs (Residential)	$384 billion (8.2% savings)
Aggregate Property Development Costs (Nonresidential)	$36 billion (1.9% savings)
Total Property Development Costs	**$420 billion (6.6% savings)**
Annual Net Fiscal Savings (National)	$4.205 billion (**9.7% savings**)
Total Fiscal Savings (National), 2000–2025	**$105.1 billion***
Daily Travel Costs	$24 million (2.4% savings)
Total Travel Costs	**$219 billion**
Total Financial Costs, 2000–2025	**$870 billion ($34.8 billion annually)**

Source: Burchell, Downs, McCann, and Mukherji, Sprawl Costs. *All amounts expressed in 2000 dollars. *Total fiscal savings estimate based on annual savings expected at full build-out of projected development.*

increased by public subsidies of private actors, the utilitarian cannot, in principle, object.

Utilitarians persuaded by the theory of diminishing returns—the notion that the rich derive less utility from additional money than do the poor—might be concerned, however, if the nature of this redistribution from public to private actors had the effect of widening inequalities, such that the benefits of sprawl were claimed primarily by the well-off. This would be especially true if sprawl benefited mostly the super-rich, for whom additional money produces very little utility. On the other hand, the possible inequities generated by suburbanization might not (on utilitarianism's own account) be a very compelling concern if the beneficiaries were not a narrow class of the super-rich but rather a much wider class of people (say, upper-middle-class suburbanites), for whom more money can provide very real utility benefits.[20]

Social and Economic Costs

Many critics of sprawl argue that the process of outward suburban development imposes social and/or economic costs on residents of central cities and older suburbs, especially in the form of jobs lost and investment redirected. The counter-factual scenario these analysts have in mind is a policy in which public and private investments are systematically directed toward shoring up established neighborhoods rather than building new communities on the suburban fringe. More specifically, the utilitarian critic of sprawl must show that the costs borne by central cities and inner suburbs when they lose jobs and investment exceed the benefits accruing to outer suburbs (or that the disutility experienced by central cities so closely matches the utility gained in the suburbs that any utility gain is outweighed by the costs of moving itself). One way of arguing this point is to claim that systematic economic disinvestment in an urban community produces a trigger effect with long-term social consequences far exceeding the initial costs of the jobs and income denied an urban neighborhood when jobs move to the suburbs. The well-known account of urban decline developed by William Julius Wilson links low marriage rates, family breakdowns, and related social disorders to joblessness (especially concentrated joblessness) in urban neighborhoods. As a result, poor neighborhoods are not just poor, they are also undesirable, unhealthy, and unsafe places to live.[21] Job loss in economically weak or threatened neighborhoods thus may have a higher "multiplier" effect on total utility lost than investment and jobs lost in relatively well-off neighborhoods—or in suburban fringe green-field areas where no community would exist at all if economic investments were systematically directed toward the metropolitan core.[22] If accepted as empirically valid, an argument of this sort would provide a solid utilitarian justification for ensuring that socio-spatial policies not push some communities past a tipping point at which negative consequences begin to snowball at an accelerated rate.

Other social costs commonly cited by critics of sprawl include health costs related to air pollution and traffic accidents, and loss of open space. The standard approach urban economists use to assess these problems is to ask whether there are market failures at work helping produce "excess" sprawl. The assumption here is generally that sprawl (understood here as a process) is in itself benign if it is simply the product of market forces, but that it may become "excessive" if it arises from the failure of the market to price goods properly or to impose appropriate costs. In such cases, smarter, more efficient policies might improve Pareto optimality.[23] As Brendan O'Flaherty argues, what is important is not whether metropolitan areas are relatively dense or relatively sprawling, but whether observed urban form is the product of efficient policies or not. Within this paradigm, O'Flaherty builds a strong case for the proposition that Americans drive too much (resulting in decentralizing urban form), presenting evidence that drivers do not fully pay for the externalities they produce in the form of air pollution and, especially, injuries and deaths from accidents: "U.S. motorists pay for only a small portion of the costs they impose with every mile of driving. They pay about two cents a mile in gas taxes but cause three to five cents in pollution costs and about ten cents in accident costs. Trucks cause an additional three cents or so of road damage costs."[24] In a similar vein, O'Flaherty identifies a range of policies that likely contribute to "excess" sprawl, including (among others) the pricing of sewers' use, parking subsidies, and the tax treatment of residential land and garage space.

Environmental Costs

The third major category of potential costs associated with sprawl is environmental damage and natural resource consumption. Taking environmental damage seriously raises the controversial question of how cost–benefit analyses can account for the value of goods not ordinarily considered commodities. Economists have tried to solve this problem by inferring the value of human life or of ecological amenities from surveys indicating how much citizens would be willing to pay to avoid certain risks or to preserve the environment. As Elizabeth Anderson and Mark Sagoff have each pointed out, this technique is highly problematic: Anderson argues that the results of such survey questions are unreliable because people are being asked to convert into dollar terms the worth of goods whose essential value is nonmonetary. Anderson notes that in some surveys respondents have often rejected the very terms of such questions, indicating (in her view) that most people regard some goods as simply not amenable to monetary calculation.[25]

Cost–benefit analyses of sprawl that attempt to assign a monetary value to the environment should be regarded with suspicion, particularly when there is reason to think that the environmental goods in question would not be regarded by most people as goods that might be straightforwardly traded for other goods. Some types of environmental goods—such as the amount of air pollution generated in a locality—do lend themselves fairly plausibly to trade-offs. Given that existing transportation technologies ensure that pristine, completely pure air is not an attainable goal in urban centers, one can easily imagine environmentalists being willing to balance limitations on air pollution with other social goals, without thinking that such a trade-off undermines the good of clean air. Consider a hypothetical cost–benefit analysis demonstrating that in a given city it would be, say, three times more expensive for the public to arrange the built environment and related transportation technology so as to limit pollution to 2.0 tons a day, compared to what it would take to reduce pollution to 2.2 tons a day. In this scenario, even fervent clean-air advocates would likely conclude that they should settle (for now) for the 2.2-ton mark.[26]

It is possible, of course, to imagine a hard-core green position that would essentially place lexical priority on ecological protection over all other human goods. The logical conclusion of such a philosophy is that modern societies should seek to minimize or even dismantle their existing industrial mechanisms and return to a way of life that minimizes not only energy use but also the use of natural resources and the generation of pollution. While it remains an open question whether ecological limitations might someday impose quite drastic changes on existing economies as a matter of necessity, the notion that ecological well-being in general is the sole or even the most important good to be maximized is alien to the existing practices of modern industrial societies. Implicit in our current methods of production and habits of consumption is the view that at least some damage to the environment can be legitimately inflicted in order to satisfy other human desires. In short, unless we are willing to renounce industrial society itself, at least some types of ecological goods can be reasonably thought of as tradable against other goods; in daily life, modern societies presume such trade-offs.

What does this mean for utilitarian analyses of suburban sprawl? Three central points need to be made: First, utilitarians need to take into account the costs of environmental damage when constructing a cost–benefit analysis. Second, actually doing so is quite difficult; to convert the value of clean air into a monetary value that, in turn, can be traded against other goods requires guesswork and debatable assumptions. Third, from an environmentalist point of view, even if one could establish credible procedures for quantifying the value (in financial terms) that most people assign ecological goods, there remain strong philosophical reasons to object to defining environmental concerns simply as inputs into a cost–benefit analysis: at least some environmental goods are non-commodifiable; they cannot be assigned a monetary value without doing serious injustice to their worth. Put another way, nature itself cannot simply be regarded as a commodity with no value other than that which humans assign it in the market.[27]

As we shall see in chapter 8, environmental concerns present perhaps *the* most compelling reason to critique suburban sprawl as a pattern of spatial development. The most sophisticated cost–benefit analyses of sprawl now attempt to systematically take account of these concerns, but the inherent difficulties (both practical and philosophical) of translating concern for ecological damage into a counting exercise ensure that environmentalists will quite properly be suspicious of such analyses, no matter how conscientiously executed.

Tallying up the Totals: Toward a Comprehensive Cost-Benefit Analysis of Sprawl

It is not necessary to believe that cost–benefit analyses should be the ultimate standard for comparing different sorts of policies to recognize that such analyses can be a useful tool. Even so sharp a critic of utilitarianism as Elizabeth Anderson acknowledges that "any rational evaluation of policies must take account of their costs and benefits."[28] To be sure, there is a considerable difference between using a technocratic application of a cost–benefit analysis to guide or even determine appropriate public policy—the approach invited by utilitarianism—and using the results of such analysis as just one important consideration among many in democratic deliberation about public policy.[29] But the results of cost–benefit analyses properly remain a subject of interest in evaluating suburban sprawl, for both friends and critics of utilitarianism. Cost–benefit analyses can be and often are undertaken from a particular point of view. For instance, when a corporation makes decisions about where to locate a factory, it can construct a matrix to compare total costs borne by the corporation versus total expected benefits reaped by the company. Such analyses routinely ignore the costs or benefits that the corporation's activity might impose on other parties. Conversely, a fiscal watchdog group might choose to evaluate two housing-development proposals strictly by considering which proposal will most benefit the public coffers by maximizing new tax revenue while minimizing new public-infrastructure costs, without considering the private benefits that may be at stake.

From the standpoint of the impartial utilitarian spectator, the most relevant type of cost–benefit comparison is analysis taken from a "global" point of view: total benefits incurred (no matter who receives them) should be weighed against the total costs generated (no matter who bears them). An instructive, thorough example of such a global analysis with respect to suburban sprawl has been presented by the urban economists Joseph Persky and Wim Wiewel.[30]

Persky and Wiewel try to ascertain the net benefit of locating a new electrical-equipment factory employing one thousand workers in a greenfield location on the fringes of the Chicago metropolitan area, and to compare it with the net benefit of locating the same factory within Chicago itself. They begin by tallying the costs of the externalities generated by private actors (but borne by other private and public actors) in the course of building this factory. These externalities include costs associated with traffic congestion, traffic accidents, air pollution, lost open space, the waste of existing housing in city centers, and the implications of the distance between suburban jobs and central city residents who cannot access those jobs or jobs of comparable quality. Persky and Wiewel then go on to consider the direct fiscal costs associated with a new development, showing that the positive fiscal impact of new middle-class households locating in central city areas is far stronger than the effect of locating such households in suburbs. Combining the externality costs of a greenfield site with the public-sector costs, Persky and Wiewel estimate that building the new thousand-employee electrical-equipment plant in a greenfield will produce $2.67 million a year more in social costs than would siting it in a central city location (see table 2.2 for details).

Persky and Wiewel then go on to estimate the *benefits* corresponding with each site. These benefits consist principally of (1) increased rents and land values for suburban and rural landowners, who see the value of their property rise as suburban development proceeds (although Persky and Wiewel argue that this gain is illusory and estimate that private landowners in the city would benefit from the proposed plant's relocation to their community *more* than would their suburban counterparts); (2) reduced wage costs for the suburban employer; and (3) reduced land, construction, and tax costs for the employer. Persky and Wiewel estimate the additional *private* benefits of locating a new plant in the outer suburbs compared to siting it in the central city to be $2.6 million a year.[31]

The authors thus conclude that "the costs and benefits associated with the continuing deconcentration of manufacturing are of the same order of magnitude."[32] In short, their analysis suggests that a utilitarian case against

TABLE 2.2. Estimated Comparative Costs and Benefits per Year of Locating a 1,000-Employee
Electrical Equipment Plant in a Greenfield vs. Urban Location in the Chicago MSA

	Difference between Greenfield and Urban Scenarios (i.e., Greenfield benefits - Urban benefits)
COSTS	
Externalities:	
Traffic Congestion	–$493,000
Accidents	–$105,000
Air Pollution	–$18,000
Open Space Lost	–$68,000
Waste of Housing	–$46,000
Spatial Mismatch (Lost Income)	–$426,000
Avoided Externalities	$63,000
Total Externalities:	–$1,121,000
Net Fiscal Impact:	
Local Government	–$925,000
Federal Government	–$623,000
Total Fiscal Impact:	–$1,548,000
Total Costs: (Fiscal Impact and Externalities)	–$2,669,000
BENEFITS	
Benefits to Residents	–$362,000
Abandonment Avoided	–$58,000
Reduced Wage Costs	$1,902,000
Reduced Land Costs	$616,000
Reduced Business Taxes	$499,000
Total Benefits:	$2,597,000
BOTTOM LINE	–$72,000

Source: Persky and Wiewel, When Corporations Leave Town. *All amounts expressed in 1995 dollars.*

sprawl based simply on comparing total costs and total benefits may be rather weak. Arguments against sprawl that portray it as a wholly irrational form of development—much the tone adopted by the initial wave of research in the 1970s on the costs of sprawl—appear to be mistaken or, at a minimum, overblown, at least with respect to industrial development.

Obviously, Persky and Wiewel's conclusions, drawn from a single hypothetical example in a single metropolitan area, depend heavily on several key (but necessary) operational assumptions, especially with regard to environmental costs, the proper magnitude of which remains (as the authors readily acknowledge) amorphous. Moreover, in some cases, suburban sprawl may involve deadweight losses—as when usable central city public or private facilities are abandoned at the same time new facilities are built on the fringes of the same metropolitan area.[33]

Even so, Persky and Wiewel's analysis strongly suggests that although sprawl does generate higher fiscal costs and increases in the most common externalities associated with development, suburban sprawl does not represent massive financial irrationality in a transparently obvious sense; sprawl also yields increased benefits to private actors, largely offsetting these costs. These findings are, for the most part, consistent with a literature review and analysis of the costs and benefits of sprawl (understood as employment decentralization) by the economists Edward L. Glaeser and Matthew Kahn. Glaeser and Kahn considered potential costs associated with congestion, environmental consequences, infrastructure costs, productivity losses, social consequences, and suburban zoning policies. They argue that congestion-related costs can be treated without reversing "sprawl" by congestion fees and other schemes, that environmental costs of land and forest loss are minimal, that pollution costs associated with more driving are being offset by cleaner car technology, that any infrastructure costs not being adequately paid by developers can be offset by better application of impact fees, and that functional sprawling areas should be able to achieve the same agglomerative productivity benefits as traditional high-density cities.[34] These authors acknowledge that suburban zoning powers may lead to an artificial scarcity of housing, but they contend that, from a cost–benefit perspective, the problems wrought by sprawl can be handled with specific measures far short of trying to reverse sprawl itself.[35]

As Persky and Wiewel suggest (and Glaeser and Kahn partially acknowledge), deconcentration of employment and population often involves a substantial redistribution of benefits to higher-income households and away from lower-income, central city residents (see chapter 4 for further elaboration). This redistributive effect, however, is only a second-order concern for utilitarians.

Sprawl, the Market, and the Question of Preferences

In the preceding analysis, we have looked in some detail at the question of whether sprawl is a beneficial or wasteful proposition in monetary terms. What cost–benefit analysis has not told us, however, is whether sprawl promotes *happiness*. Indeed, the monetary costs of sprawl can best be viewed as the denominator of a utility function: even if the size of this denominator is very large (i.e., sprawl is very expensive in economic terms), we cannot judge whether sprawl enhances utility or not until we know what is in the numerator of the utility function—that is, just how much well-being is being purchased, and at what cost. Utilitarians will not be alarmed just because sprawl may be somewhat more expensive than the alternatives; they will be alarmed only if sprawl fails to return good value in terms of the happiness and human flourishing achieved by this somewhat more expensive method of building communities. As Glaeser and Kahn observe, the square footage of U.S. private homes has grown rapidly in the past forty years, precisely in the suburbs, and private space in the United States is very large, by international standards; perhaps (as Glaeser and Kahn seem to assume) this more expansive living space makes for happier, more satisfied people.[36]

Indeed, a common assumption among economists is that because suburban sprawl exists—because Americans have bought homes on the perimeter of metropolitan areas in such vast numbers while shunning (in relative terms) urban areas and many older suburbs—it must reflect the preferences of consumers. If life in the outer suburbs were not desirable, why would so many people move there? Surely, investments of families' life savings can be taken as a fair indication that families buying homes in suburbia really do want to live there and must value the kind of life it provides. According to orthodox economic theory, people's preferences are revealed in their buying decisions; because homes in suburbia are popular, suburbia must have some intrinsic qualities that make it more desirable than other locations. Whatever complaints residents may have about suburbia, we should expect that since its residences are generally the most *desired* within U.S. metropolitan regions (as measured by consumer demand), they must also, in fact, be in the best places to live. This is the end of the story as far as most land and real estate economists are concerned: whether or not desirability really makes something intrinsically *good* is not a topic with which many economists are preoccupied, concluding either that such an equation is not problematic at all, or more plausibly, that no one but the consumer herself can be the judge of what is good, and that those judgments are, in fact, reflected in actual buying decisions.

Good public policy with respect to housing development, most mainstream economists would urge, should have as its aim to permit developers to respond to consumers' preferences, operating on a level playing field (that is, without public funds being used to disproportionately or preferentially subsidize any particular kind of place). Given diverse housing preferences—some people want to walk to museums and five-star restaurants, whereas some people want three-acre yards—it is to be expected that an unfettered market will produce a variety of urban forms.

The built environment can thus be plausibly viewed as a product of people's preferences, and if consumers show a taste for suburban or exurban living arrangements as opposed to urban life or high-density developments, this is no more objectionable than an ice cream parlor's adding some flavors, as demand for them emerges, and discontinuing those that have failed to generate or sustain consumer interest. According to this view, developers of the built environment ultimately provide what people want. Indeed, there is ample evidence that developers *do* think of their work in precisely these terms: the journalist Joel Garreau's acclaimed work on "edge cities" stresses that developers of the new exurbs "[view] themselves as utterly egalitarian observers, giving people what they repeatedly demonstrated they desired, as measured by that most reliable of gauges: their willingness to pay for it."[37] A Houston-area developer explained Americans' preference for a sub-urban lifestyle, saying, "People in the United States are not going to live the way people in Paris live. They will not live in a thousand-square-foot apartment and raise a family and go out and get the loaf of bread and the jug of wine and walk down the street and live their whole lives within one square mile. That is not the way Americans live. They have a different level of freedom, a different level of expectations."[38]

Recent journalistic portrayals of life in U.S. metropolises continue to examine urban form in terms of consumer and lifestyle preferences: David Brooks argues that young, cool hipsters choose to live in the cities; liberal families with young children populate "crunchy" inner suburbs; and bar-becue-grill dads flock to outer suburbs with easy access to Home Depot.[39] Should the utilitarian be satisfied with a type of metropolitan development in which different types of communities emerge in response to different kinds of preferences?

The answer is not as obvious as it may seem. We now consider three broad challenges to the notion that housing and land use policy should simply aim to maximize the satisfaction of existing preferences. The first challenge questions whether the existing preference of Americans for suburbs, as opposed to cities, reflects constrained choices rather than a "true" preference. The second challenge raises the issue of whether even "true" preferences might be morally objectionable in some circumstances, and the third challenge questions whether "neighborhoods" ought properly to be treated as commodities at all.

CONSTRAINED CHOICES AND DISTORTED PREFERENCES?

Constraining preferences for the sake of some specific way of life (a theological vision, or a strong communitarian vision) would not be sanctioned by most recognizable versions of utilitarianism; even constraints on preferences adopted for the sake of encouraging habits amenable to political democracy or maintaining a particular system of distributive justice would be acceptable only if it could be persuasively shown that such constraints would increase total utility. Yet utilitarianism as such does not necessarily validate people's existing preferences as inviolate in the same way that, for instance, libertarian thinking does, or that many economists and other practitioners of cost–benefit analysis seem to assume it does. Goodin thus specifies five distinct utilitarian justifications for "laundering preferences"—allowing the state to take actions at odds with a population's current preferences—each of which (he contends) are consistent with the view that the state should, in general, respect people's preferences.

First, people's actual preferences may not be revealed in choices, especially if such choices are made under duress, with incomplete information, or in ignorance of the alternatives; thus, Mill supposed that only persons exposed in equal measure to the pleasures of pushpin and poetry would be competent to choose between them.[40] Second, citizens may agree, or *on reflection* might agree, that abstaining from certain individual preferences in expectation that others will do the same would increase collective utility (as in an apartment building where residents all agree to abstain from indulging their preference for occasionally playing loud music late at night). Third, individuals, on reflection, may have what Goodin terms "preferences for preferences" (i.e., a rational desire to be guided by moral principles, social ideals, healthy lifestyle habits, etc.). But, in practice, individuals often need help or additional steering to actually live by these higher-order desires; thus, Goodin remarks that "if someone finds that one set of preferences is actually guiding his behavior, when he dearly wishes another would instead, then we can justify laundering his preferences as a simple case of respecting his own preferences for preferences." Fourth, Goodin argues that such "preferences for preferences" need not be explicitly acknowledged by an agent to exist; they can be inferred from existing patterns of preferences. Hence, everyone can be supposed to have a strong interest in their personal health, even if this is not reflected in their behavior, and the state may thus be justified in regulating health-averse behaviors. Fifth, Goodin argues that certain types of preferences—those at odds with the overall goals of the social-decision process (such as sadistic preferences)—can be properly ignored by public policy.[41]

To this list we can add a sixth, obvious observation: that people's preferences are shaped by the nature of the choices presented to them. This, in turn, raises the possibility that Americans' existing choices and preferences with respect to living environments may be distorted in some systematic sense.[42] A utilitarian analyst of sprawl may suspect that people's actions in the housing market today cannot be understood as their genuine preferences, because anti-urban public policies of various kinds and the unnecessary concentration of adverse social circumstances in cities biases people's choices in a suburban direction. Developers of new suburban housing commonly claim that they are simply meeting consumers' desires to live in safe neighborhoods. It goes almost without saying that relatively unsafe places are poorer, less attractive, and have fewer amenities—and that in the United States, such unsafe places are overwhelmingly found within cities. In short, Americans are typically not asked to choose between living in a clean, safe suburb with effective public institutions and living in a clean, safe city with effective public institutions, making the choice on the basis of whether one prefers the inherent qualities of low-density, car-dominated suburbs or the inherent qualities of high-density, pedestrian-friendly cities.

Much more typically, Americans are asked to choose between living in a clean, safe suburb with relatively effective public institutions and living in a potentially unsafe city with at least some rundown areas and public institutions of dubious effectiveness. It might be hypothesized that if existing cities, through reinvestment, local reforms, or other efforts, were able to rectify these negative features such that middle-class parents would have no reason to suspect that their child would be better off (educationally or safety-wise) in a suburban environment as opposed to a central city, then suburbanization in the United States would be slowed or even reversed.

Empirical evidence in support of this train of thought has recently been supplied by Isaac Bayoh, Elena Irwin, and Timothy Haab in a study of intrametropolitan moves among seventeen school districts in the Columbus, Ohio, metropolitan area in 1995. Bayoh et al. found that per-capita income in the school district and good school-district quality were a significant positive predictor of choice of residence among the 824 moving households surveyed, while higher crime and property taxes were negative predictors (as was commuting time) of choice of destination. Strikingly, these results hold even when controlling for neighborhood age (residents were less likely to move to areas with a higher proportion of housing built before 1970). In short, these movers systematically chose areas with better schools and higher income levels, while avoiding older neighborhoods with more crime and higher property taxes. Further, Bayoh et al. found that the likelihood of a household choosing to live within the city of Columbus declined substantially if it included a school-age child. School quality is shown to have a particularly powerful effect; it is estimated that a 1 percent improvement in average test scores in the Columbus city school district would lead to a 3.68 percent increase in the likelihood of a household choosing to live in that district; a 1 percent increase in per-capita income in the city would lead to a further 2.09 percent increase in the likelihood of a household living there. This evidence led the researchers to conclude that "flight from blight" is a powerful motivating force in locational choice within a metropolitan area; when mobile households choose suburbs, they are choosing better schools and more affluent neighborhoods than can be found in city centers.[43]

Given this set of observations, ought not utilitarian analysts consider the question of whether total utility could be enhanced by undertaking reforms in the spatial distribution of goods that might ultimately significantly alter individuals' preferences—even if this requires enacting policies that are at odds with most people's *current* preferences?

The logic of what might be termed fully-informed-and-rational-preference utilitarianism strongly suggests that the answer to that question must be yes. The notion that consumers' observed choices are constrained by the social reality that many places in the United States are regarded as undesirable places to live is a potentially powerful objection to the economist's assumption that choices reveal preferences in a straightforward way. Nonetheless, this objection should not be allowed to disguise the fact that there are *inherent* differences between cities and suburbs (or more precisely, between high-density and low-density places) that would remain, even if U.S. cities tended to look more like Paris than Camden. Even from a sophisticated utilitarian standpoint, individuals' choices about where to live based on their preferring the particular attributes of suburban settings over those of urban environments are unobjectionable as long as such choices are not distorted by the concentration of social problems or pathologies in one particular setting rather than another, or by the disproportionate public subsidy of one kind of place rather than another.

THE CORRUPTIBILITY OF PREFERENCES

Another line of criticism of markets as efficient responses to individual preferences critically interrogates the *sources* of such preferences. Where do people's tastes come from? On the one hand, the claim that individual preferences are purely *determined* by social forces or cultural currents is demonstrably false; on the other hand, it is demonstrably true that many preferences are *shaped* and influenced by social and cultural norms. Once it is acknowledged that preferences are not fully exogenous products of individuals living in a vacuum, the possibility, frequently highlighted by critics of neoclassical economic theory, that producers themselves can help shape—or even create—individual preferences (primarily through advertising) presents itself.[44] This possibility is quite relevant to the analysis of housing patterns in the United States, given the historic role of housing developers and the real estate industry in not only building but also marketing suburbia as a desirable place to live.[45] It is difficult to gauge the precise effect that such advertisements may have had on housing consumers' thinking about where to live. However, it should be noted that housing developers are far from the only advertisers—and probably not even the most important—to affect Americans' thinking about the relative desirability of suburban places. Countless ads aimed at *selling other products* have shaped the view that owning a home in the suburbs, owning two cars, and driving to work is the U.S. norm and, implicitly, is the most desirable way of life.[46] Consequently, the behavior of consumers reflects culturally specific preferences that have, in turn, been largely conditioned (and, on occasion, created) by private parties who have a profit stake in consumers' coming to prefer their products. Yet, even if these points are acknowledged, it is not clear that this recognition forms an adequate basis for critiquing the operations of the housing market. While acknowledging the possible influence of producers and other factors on consumers is important to modifying the notion of the sovereign, autonomous consumer, it does not necessarily follow that the heteronomously determined preferences of consumers should not have weight in shaping our built environment.

Not, that is, unless a far more reaching critique of market operations is offered; namely, one that argues explicitly that individual preferences (even if autonomously generated) should *not* necessarily be ratified as the primary determinant of how built communities are shaped. A weak version of this objection, echoing Goodin, would simply claim that giving individual preferences free play is not an automatic guarantee that the collective result will be desirable. For instance, individuals may desire to live away from the hustle and bustle of the city and the headaches of traffic a little ways out into the countryside, on a lot with a wide-ranging view of the sky and plenty of open space to enjoy. The arrival of neighbors with similar preferences would mean more traffic, more nearby strip malls, and less open space. The result would be a situation in which no one wants sprawl but everyone gets it as a result of each individual seeking to fulfill his or her own preferences. In such a case, then, there would be a strong utilitarian justification for using the state or other collective mechanisms as a complement to private housing markets to ensure that widely desired goods that no one can obtain individually (such as close access to open space) be made available. Many current policies aimed at modifying, containing, or mitigating sprawl have precisely this sort of justification; for instance, the idea that the government can mandate preserving public space or a portion of a region's land or forests from development is widely accepted. These sorts of policies can be (and commonly are) endorsed, precisely on utilitarian grounds, as a superior way to meet the full range of people's preferences and thereby maximize utility. Observing that the unimpeded market does not always maximize utility and requires complementary public action in no way signifies a retreat from utilitarian ideas—or from the idea that the aim of policy is to fulfill people's preferences.

A much stronger critique of that core utilitarian idea contends that even if residents' true preferences could be deduced they should not necessarily be the ultimate benchmark for evaluating the desirability of a given pattern of housing arrangements. Before endorsing a society's preferences, this perspective urges, we should critically examine the motives underlying such preferences and ask whether such motives serve morally praiseworthy or morally problematic ends. Experience teaches that preferences can be corrupted and directed to unworthy ends, ends that may be at odds with genuine human flourishing. In contemporary media-saturated societies in which professional advertisers use the broadcast media to shape the preferences and desires of children from their earliest years, there is special reason to suspect the worthiness of uninterrogated preferences.[47] Those uninterrogated preferences may reflect years of social and cultural conditioning aimed at producing people who equate utility with consumption and whose decisions are affected by social pressures equating consumption (especially of cars and houses) with high social status.

Consider, to update slightly Robert Nozick's famous thought experiment, the case of a society so addicted to virtual-reality helmets that citizens' first thought upon waking in the morning was how quickly they could enjoy the blissful experiences such helmets might provide. Such addiction might be critiqued by theorists holding a substantive view that the good life necessarily involves active effort and participation in human endeavors rather than passive consumption of pleasant experiences. Or critical theorists might argue that a well-ordered human community should be one capable of generating creativity and innovation—a new song, a new work of art—from as many directions as possible rather than one in which experiences are preprogrammed.[48] Still other theorists might critique such a society as, in principle, wrong because it is based on individuals' being consumed with their own private imaginative worlds rather than being engaged with one another, which, in turn, is bound to lead to a deterioration of the human capacity to relate to one another and, hence, to the degradation of the human species. Finally, such theorists might argue that the citizen addicted to the virtual-reality helmet is unlikely to be an actively engaged one, who vigilantly seeks to hold political and economic power to account. None of these arguments rests, in the end, on an appeal to utility, but rather on substantive, non-instrumental claims about the worth of democratic self-governance, the meaning of human freedom, and the nature of the good life.

Utilitarianism is quite capable of developing convoluted explanations about why a virtual reality–addicted society that appears to produce happiness may, in fact, fail to do so, but it cannot reject out of hand the *possibility* that the virtual reality–addicted way of life is the utility-maximizing one. Nor, it should be noted, is this hypothetical example so implausible that it can be dismissed as fantastic or fanciful. Utilitarians committed to maximizing the satisfaction of preferences cannot appeal to moral intuitions, specific conceptions of the good life, or specific conceptions of what any particular political system requires, when judging the worthiness of the virtual-reality society—or for that matter, the worthiness of any particular way of life. Arguments that the way of life associated with sprawl may be intrinsically objectionable are not readily available to the preference utilitarian.[49]

VALUING THINGS FOR THEIR OWN SAKE,
NOT FOR THEIR USEFULNESS

A third critique of preference satisfaction as a guide to policy directly challenges the notion that preference fulfillment provides the only or most relevant form of human value. Elizabeth Anderson has mounted a powerful critique of utilitarian theories of value, arguing that our everyday manner of valuing things, people, and practices reflect a pluralist theory of human goods; that is, in daily life, we intuitively recognize that goods differ from one another in kind, such that not all goods can be traded for one another, nor can they be interpreted along a single, common continuum of value (such as monetary worth or utility itself). In what Anderson terms an "expressive" theory of value, the *object* of a person's positive regard is the source of value, not the fulfillment of an individual's preferences for that thing. To take an example relevant to the ecological consequences of urban development, the value of a majestic mountain is the mountain itself, not the feelings of pleasure that humans derive from it, or people's preferences for having mountains around. Suppose oil were found near Mount Rainier in Washington State and drilling required the total destruction of the mountain to fully exploit. It would not adequately satisfy the concerns of Seattle-area residents who value the mountain if the government promised to force the oil-drilling companies to pay for an enormous, virtual rendering of the mountain that would be just as beautiful as the one people in Seattle had seen through their windows. Put another way, usefulness is not the only relevant "mode of valuation" we employ in our everyday lives; so, too—to cite Anderson's list—are respect, appreciation, consideration, honor, admiration, reverence, and love.[50]

The notion that goods differ in kind and that not all human goods can be reduced to a single standard of value leads directly to a critique of the indiscriminate commodification of human goods. Anderson argues that we must examine the internal logic of various goods to determine whether they can be treated as commodities to be bought and sold without doing violence to the goods themselves. For example, Anderson argues that paid surrogate-motherhood arrangements undermine the good of parental love and that it would be damaging to our social practice of motherhood to permit freely consenting adults to openly treat childbirth and related functions as commodities. Other goods, such as health care, are mixed in nature, requiring partial but not complete commodification if the internal practice of care is to be upheld within the context of scarce resources. And still other goods, such as ice cream cones, are best regarded and treated as simply commodities. Indeed, Anderson strongly argues for the value of permitting private, personalized consumption spheres in which people are free to consume goods simply because they want them.[51]

Anderson's approach to valuing goods can be usefully applied to the sprawl debate by inquiring into the logic of the goods provided by neighborhoods. Chapter 6 assumes this task, suggesting that one important good that neighborhoods provide is the opportunity for self-governance; it further suggests that the public-choice account of how neighborhoods and localities reflect individual preferences sees residents only as consumers, not as citizens.[52] Unlike an ice cream cone, the built environment is, at least in part, a public good, and, hence, is the proper subject of public deliberation. The process of such deliberation, of course, is very likely to reflect the preferences of the individuals who live in a given society—and from a democratic standpoint, it is entirely possible that a society may, on reflection, decide that the sorts of housing arrangements now produced by the market are, in fact, the most desirable. But it is also possible that individuals' preferences may *change* during the process of deliberation in response to new evidence or in response to hearing and recognizing claims made by other persons. The possibility of such change is a key reason that theorists of deliberative democracy believe that policymaking ought not be seen as a simple matter of aggregating individuals' existing preferences.[53]

———

Even if we reject the view that satisfying current preferences is the sole important consideration in formulating public policy, those preferences must be taken into account, one way or another. Existing preferences should be understood as neither sovereign nor irrelevant. Put another way, the higher-order question of whether utilitarians ought (or ought not) regard the satisfaction of people's preferences for various kinds of spatial environments as paramount in shaping spatial policies can be brought into proper focus only once we know something—empirically—about the lower-order question of how spatial characteristics actually correlate with subjective well-being, taking people (and their preferences) as they are. I address that empirical question in chapter 3.

THREE

Do People Like Sprawl (and So What If They Do)?

I T IS NOT NECESSARY to regard preference satisfaction as the supreme aim of public policy to believe that people's existing preferences are important considerations in judging whether the U.S. pattern of suburbanization is on balance healthy or defective. It would be difficult to imagine a political philosophy consistent with democratic norms that held that it simply makes no difference what people like or enjoy, and that the state (or the professional planners) should plan towns, cities, and suburbs according to what they consider best, with no reference to citizens' preferences. Even if there is reason to believe that a particular set of preferences is distorted, or reflects an impoverished view of life, or simply fails to meet the Millian test of being the product of people with the capacity and experience to adequately judge the worth of different kinds of goods, a long tradition in Western political thought urges that the cultural norms and mores of particular societies, once set upon a particular trajectory, are not subsequently infinitely malleable: Institutions and practices that might function very well indeed in one cultural setting may utterly fail in another if they take no heed of the established habits and desires of the population.[1]

We thus now turn more directly to the question of whether "sprawl" or its components are systematically related to Americans' subjective well-being. As we have noted, existing studies of the "costs of sprawl" have focused most thoroughly on the financial implications of sprawl; less explored is whether living in low-density, highly automobile-dependent communities actually promotes human well-being (both subjectively and objectively measured). Treating for the moment people's preferences as given, immutable, and beyond normative critique, do low-density suburban communities do a better job than cities of facilitating a high quality of life and contributing to individual happiness? The answer to this question is critical for utilitarian analyses of sprawl: sprawling development may be more expensive to the public and generate greater social costs than do more-compact development patterns, but if the communities it produces are vastly superior places to live, sprawl may well be worth the cost.

The following discussion focuses first on three key measures of individual well-being and satisfaction with local community life as measured by the Social Capital Community Benchmark Survey (SCCBS): personal happiness, personal health, and satisfaction with the quality of life in one's community. The first two indicators (happiness and health) relate to utility in obvious ways; the third indicator provides evidence regarding how individuals view the communities in which they live.[2] We then examine whether sprawl is systematically related to levels of "social capital," as measured by informal socializing, membership in organizations, and participation in a religious congregation. Social capital of this type has been extensively linked to a wide range of positive community and individual level outcomes, and its relationship to sprawl will be of interest to utilitarians (and others).[3]

We thus ask how well the following four characteristics of the census tract in which an individual lives—central city status, density, transportation patterns, and neighborhood age—help predict individuals' personal well-being, health, and satisfaction with community life, in addition to their level of formal and informal social engagement. Each of these analyses controls for a standard range of individual demographic characteristics (age, education, income, race, gender, years lived in one's community, homeownership status). I also test for the possible effects of several non-sprawl-related community characteristics (measured at the census tract level), including racial diversity, economic diversity, neighborhood residential stability, median neighborhood income, and neighborhood educational attainment. Finally, in this chapter we pay particular attention to the effects of commuting time on well-being. (See chapter 1 for an overview.)

Theoretical Expectations

Why exactly might we think sprawl-related variables matter at all with respect to subjective and objective well-being? Much research regarding what kinds of places Americans prefer to live has been based on simple survey questions asking respondents whether they would prefer to live, for instance, in a small town, a big city, or a rural environment. Such research has also typically focused on city size as the key variable of interest, as opposed to the richer set of sprawl-related characteristics explored here.[4] Because Americans' tastes are diverse and we observe many kinds of communities, we might believe that Americans tend to sort themselves into the kinds of communities they prefer to live in, and hence that there should be no systematic relationship between spatial characteristics and satisfaction with one's community. This argument assumes, however, that all residents have equal capacities to move wherever they like; it also assumes that residents have perfect information about the effects of their residential environment on their own well-being and that the universe of actually existing places adequately satisfies the range of preferences held by Americans. Each of those assumptions can be challenged on theoretical grounds. But if our empirical inquiry reveals that there is little or no systematic correspondence between local community characteristics and the distribution of well-being, economic theory suggests a ready-made explanation: that individuals tend, on their own, to sort themselves into the kinds of places they prefer to live.

Early twentieth-century sociological literature, however, posited that metropolitan residence had potentially powerful effects on residents' well-being. Georg Simmel and, later, Louis Wirth linked urban living to social isolation, "friction," "irritation," and "nervous tensions," albeit on the basis of limited empirical evidence.[5] More recently, and most directly relevant to this study, J. Eric Oliver has examined the relationship between suburban characteristics and mental health. Using census-defined "places" (i.e., towns or cities) as the unit of analysis, Oliver examined the relationship between municipal characteristics taken from the 1990 Census and measures of subjective well-being derived from the 1986 Americans' Changing Lives Survey. Oliver found that city size, density, median building age, and percentage of out-of-town commuters in the locality failed to predict self-efficacy or self-esteem in any way. However, he found statistically significant relationships between higher density and greater life dissatisfaction, feeling unsatisfied with one's neighborhood, and feeling unsafe; he also found a significant relationship between living in an older city and general life dissatisfaction, and between the percentage of out-of-town commuters in one's locality and feeling dissatisfied with the neighborhood. As well, he found greater city size to be significantly connected to both feeling unsatisfied with and feeling unsafe in one's neighborhood.[6]

Existing literature thus suggests that population density, central city residence, older neighborhood age, and city size might all be linked with reduced well-being, for two broad kinds of reasons: the first being the objective characteristics of dense, older neighborhoods (congestion, crime, noise, psychological effects of crowding, fewer amenities, less private space), which tend to cause unhappiness, and second, Americans' subjective tastes for living

TABLE 3.1. Self-Reported Happiness by Place of Residence

Percentage of residents describing themselves as "very happy."

Central City Residents	34.5%
Suburban Residents	39.9%
Rural Town Residents	45.3%
Rural Nontown Residents	41.9%
High-Density Tract Residents (>8,000 persons/mile)	30.9%
Low-Density Tract Residents (<2,000 persons/mile)	41.4%
Residents of Older Neighborhoods (built prior to 1950)	33.2%
Residents of Newer Neighborhoods (built 1980 or later)	42.9%
Solo Commuting by Car in Tract <65%	30.6%
Solo Commuting by Car in Tract >85%	42.5%
Tracts with Average Commutes <18 Minutes	40.5%
Tracts with Average Commutes >30 Minutes	36.0%

Sources: SCCBS; 2000 U.S. Census.

in low-density, more recently built areas. Another variable not considered in Oliver's study, commuting time, can also be straightforwardly linked to well-being: common sense suggests that most people regard longer personal commuting time as an annoyance (even if it is likely that individuals differ among themselves substantially in their aversion to commuting). We might also suspect that community-wide patterns of commuting might have some relationship, if not to personal happiness, then to individuals' subjective evaluation of their communities as places to live.

Who Is Happiest in the Contemporary Metropolis?

The SCCBS asked respondents to describe themselves as "very happy," "happy," "not very happy," or "not happy at all." As table 3.1 indicates, when we compare self-reported personal happiness among residents in various spatial settings, a suggestive pattern emerges: residents of central cities, higher-density tracts, less car-dependent tracts, and tracts with longer commutes are less likely to be highly satisfied with their personal lives.[7] Initial appearances can be deceiving, however; these observed differences might simply be a result of the demographic differences between residents of high-density central cities and low-density suburbs (residents of the latter tending to have higher incomes, an important predictor of subjective well-being).

TABLE 3.2. Effect of Sprawl-Related Variables on Personal Happiness

Predicted personal happiness.

Residence in Younger Neighborhood	.0041 (.0009)***
Individual Commuting Time	−.0024 (.0005)***
Commuting Time in Tract	−.0043 (.0020)*
Racial Homogeneity in Tract	.288 (.065)***
Educational Level in Tract	.523 (.112)***
Homeownership	.165 (.039)***
Years Lived in Community	.0030 (.0009)***

Sources: SCCBS, 2000 U.S. Census. n = 28,554. Ordered logistic regression.
As with other regression tables presented in this book, reported figures are regression
coefficients, with standard errors in parentheses.
* indicates p < .05; ** indicates p < .01; *** indicates p < .001. See appendix II
for full regression table.

Ordered logistic regression analysis (table 3.2) shows that residence in a newer neighborhood is a predictor of increased personal happiness. None of the other sprawl-related variables have a significant effect on happiness, individually or jointly; these variables are dropped from the reported results.[8] Long individual commutes, in addition to residence in a census tract with long average commutes are, unsurprisingly, significant predictors of decreased personal happiness. Residence in better-educated and racially homogeneous tracts are both linked to higher levels of happiness.[9] Finally, homeownership and years lived in the community are strong positive predictors of personal happiness.

What do these findings mean in real-world terms? If longer individual commuting time predicts reduced happiness, how much happiness payoff might we expect from a sharp decrease in individual commuting times? To answer this question, I use *Clarify,* a computer program written by Michael Tomz, Jason Wittenberg, and Gary King to facilitate substantive interpretations of multivariate analyses.[10] *Clarify* allows analysts to make predictions about the likelihood a given outcome will change when one (or more) independent variables are altered. The estimates provided below can be best understood as conveying a sense of the order of magnitude of the effects involved in each instance, in addition to the relative importance of various contextual factors identified as significant in shaping individual-level outcomes.[11]

In this case, if we are interested in the substantive impact of the length of a worker's commute on the likelihood he or she will claim to be very happy, we can set *all other* independent variables at their means, then ask what the likelihood is that a hypothetical "average" worker will be "very happy" if he or she happens to have a forty-five-minute commute and live in a tract with an average commute of thirty minutes and compare this with the likelihood that the worker will be "very happy" if he or she happens to have a fifteen-minute commute and live in a tract where fifteen-minute commutes are the average. In short, the length of the individual commute and neighborhood commuting times are the only moving parts in the analysis; all other variables (both at the individual and at the community level) are held constant.[12]

Clarify's simulation analysis suggests that the substantive impact of long commutes on individuals' well-being, taken in itself, is modest: moving from a situation in which you commute just fifteen minutes to work and the average employee in your neighborhood commutes fifteen minutes, to a situation in which you commute forty-five minutes and the average employee in your neighborhood commutes thirty minutes reduces one's likelihood of being "very happy" from 38.1 percent (37.1%, 39.2%) to 35.0 percent (33.8%, 36.1%). (Ninety-five percent confidence intervals are listed in parentheses.)[13] Marginal changes in commuting patterns would produce much smaller differences in predicted subjective well-being. What about the finding that persons living in newer neighborhoods tend to be happier than persons living in older neighborhoods (after controlling for a range of individual and contextual factors)? Holding other things equal, a resident of a neighborhood built in 1980 is predicted to have a 38.4 percent (37.7%, 39.1%) chance of saying she is "very happy," compared to 35.6 percent (34.6%, 36.5%) for a resident of a neighborhood in which 1950 is the median date of home construction. The most straightforward interpretation is that living in a relatively recently built neighborhood is perceived as—and may in fact be—a "good" thing by most Americans. Newer neighborhoods might have better amenities, might be better maintained, might contain fewer eyesores, or might have a higher degree of social esteem attached to them than older neighborhoods, or they might simply be less stressful places to live. Moreover, as noted above, private living space per capita is greater in recently built suburbs than in older cities; this might, in turn, correspond to higher local quality of life.[14]

Spatial Characteristics and Self-Reported Health

J. S. Mill described disease as "that most intractable of enemies" and made clear that progress in medical science and public health must be central to any utilitarian program.[15] Several recent studies have presented evidence of a link between "sprawl" and obesity, a finding that naturally raises the question of whether sprawl might be systematically linked to health outcomes among adults.[16] Sprawling environments are thought to be associated with much less daily walking and physical activity, and, consequently, with poorer health.

The SCCBS can provide only inconclusive evidence regarding this claim (see table 3.3.). Individual commuting time is a statistically significant negative predictor of self-reported health, although the substantive effect is quite small: moving from a forty-five-minute down to a fifteen-minute commute is predicted to raise's one likelihood of reporting "excellent" health from 23.3 percent (22.4%, 24.2%) to 24.6 percent (23.8%, 25.3%), a marginal gain. Among the sprawl-related variables, higher tract density is a statistically significant predictor of reduced health; none of the other sprawl-related variables are statistically significant.[17] (See appendix II for full regression table.) Consequently, the self-reported health of a resident of a denser neighborhood, controlling for other factors, is predicted to be very slightly lower than the health of a resident of a low-density tract.[18] From a health standpoint, it seems that the *worst* setting would be residence in a dense neighborhood requiring a long commute to one's job.

Obviously, the SCCBS's measure of self-reported health is an imprecise instrument for exploring the possible relationships between sprawl and health, and the inconclusive findings noted here should not be taken as an indictment of the growing body of work linking various measures of sprawl

TABLE 3.3. Self-Reported Health by Place of Residence

Percentage of residents who rate their personal health as "excellent."

Central City Residents	24.0%
Suburban Residents	25.2%
Rural Town Residents	27.0%
Rural Nontown Residents	22.1%
High-Density Tract Residents (>8,000 persons/mile)	23.4%
Low-Density Tract Residents (<2,000 persons/mile)	24.4%
Residents of Older Neighborhoods (built prior to 1950)	23.3%
Residents of Newer Neighborhoods (built 1980 or later)	26.7%
Solo Commuting by Car in Tract <65%	23.6%
Solo Commuting by Car in Tract >85%	25.5%
Tracts with Average Commutes <18 Minutes	26.5%
Tracts with Average Commutes >30 Minutes	23.3%
Individual Commute >30 Minutes (Workers Only)	25.6%
Individual Commute <15 Minutes (Workers Only)	29.4%

Sources: SCCBS; 2000 U.S. Census.

(generally, indices at the metropolitan statistical area or county level) to specific health outcomes such as obesity (although self-selection may be a key factor driving that linkage).[19] Also relevant from a broad utilitarian standpoint are studies linking sprawl to higher rates of death in auto accidents, illnesses from air pollution, and increased costs related to these problems. More-specific research is needed to test the possible relationship between neighborhood-level (as opposed to metropolitan statistical area or countywide) measures of spatial context and specific human health outcomes.

Spatial Characteristics and Community Quality of Life

We now consider the ways in which neighborhood context affects how individuals assess their own localities as places to live. Subjective quality-of-life ratings are just that—subjective: any given individual might base them on the quality of the local schools, whether the garbage gets picked up on time, whether the community is visually and aesthetically attractive, or any number of other factors.[20] Table 3.4 provides preliminary evidence that the effect of community characteristics on community quality-of-life ratings is substantial. Residents of central cities have a substantially lower opinion of their own communities than do residents of suburbs and rural areas: so, too, do residents of higher-density communities, residents of tracts in which public transit and pedestrian activity is more common, and residents of older

TABLE 3.4.   Community Satisfaction by Place of Residence

Percentage of residents who rate their community as an "excellent" place to live.

Central City Residents	31.7%
Suburban Residents	45.4%
Rural Town Residents	49.4%
Rural Nontown Residents	45.2%
High-Density Tract Residents (>8,000 persons/mile)	26.3%
Low-Density Tract Residents (<2,000 persons/mile)	46.5%
Residents of Older Neighborhoods (built prior to 1950)	31.3%
Residents of Newer Neighborhoods (built 1980 or later)	47.4%
Solo Commuting by Car in Tract <65%	25.5%
Solo Commuting by Car in Tract >85%	49.8%
Tracts with Average Commutes <18 Minutes	43.4%
Tracts with Average Commutes >30 Minutes	35.0%

Sources: SCCBS; 2000 U.S. Census.

neighborhoods. Again, we must ask: do these observed differences in quality-of-life ratings across communities hold up after controlling for other individual and contextual-level variables?

Yes, and emphatically so. The SCCBS asked respondents "Overall, how would you rate your community as a place to live—excellent, good, only fair, or poor?" Central city residence, living in an older neighborhood, and living in a dense neighborhood are each significant predictors of lower quality-of-life assessments. (The proportion of commuters driving alone in one's tract is also positively correlated with high quality of life but not at a significant level, and hence is dropped from the reported model.) These relationships remain significant even after adding controls for violent and nonviolent county-level crime and for proportion of renters living in the tract. Individual and neighborhood commuting times are negatively related to quality of life, but this relationship is surprisingly weak. Just as many defenders of sprawl have insisted, Americans, taken collectively, have a strong preference for suburban communities in which several of the key constitutive elements of sprawl (low density, heavy reliance on the car, recently built housing units) are present.

In substantive terms, a person living in a low-density (1,000 persons/mile) neighborhood that is outside a central city and where 1980 is the median date of home construction is predicted to have a 42.0 percent (40.0%, 43.9%) likelihood of regarding his or her community as "excellent," compared to 32.3 percent (30.5%, 34.1%) for a demographically identical individual living in a central city with a density of eight thousand persons per mile, and

TABLE 3.5. Impact of Sprawl-Related Variables on Community Quality of Life

	Community Quality of Life
Central City Residence	−.146 (.044)***
Tract Density (ln)	−.037 (.012)**
Younger Neighborhood	.0065 (.0018)***
Racial Homogeneity in Tract	.419 (.114)***
% African American in Tract	−.602 (.114)***
% Hispanic in Tract	−.562 (.187)**
Educational Level in Tract	1.95 (.195)***
Residential Stability in Tract	.658 (.207)***
Homeownership	.442 (.038)***
Years Lived in Community	.0024 (.0009)**

Sources: SCCBS; 2000 U.S. Census. n = 28,618. Ordered logistic regression.
* indicates p < .05; ** indicates p < .01; *** indicates p < .001. See appendix II for full regression table.

where 1950 is the median date of home construction.[21] This gap widens still further (to 43.2% vs. 29.6%) if we assume that racial diversity levels and the proportion of African Americans and Hispanics in one's tract matches the central city and suburban average in each scenario: tract-level racial diversity and African American and Hispanic presence are higher in central cities; all three measures are themselves negative predictors of residents' satisfaction with local quality of life.[22]

Spatial Characteristics and Social Capital: The Importance of Commuting

For decades, the stereotype of U.S. suburbs has been that of lonely, isolated people utterly disconnected from one another. But many academics have long been skeptical of the stereotype, instead asking, where exactly is the evidence that suburbs produce social isolation?

Academic research on this topic has yielded mixed results. On the one hand, there have been several case-study comparisons of sprawling and non-sprawling communities that suggested that less sprawling places may generate a stronger sense of place and community in addition to forging stronger neighborhood ties. A notable study by Lance Freeman, for instance, found that in three U.S. cities, living in more multimodal-transportation settings was associated with stronger community ties, measured as the likelihood one will name a neighbor when listing persons with whom one has discussed an "important matter" in the previous six months.[23] Kevin Leyden's detailed study of the relationship between the built environment and social capital in Ireland also concludes that walkable, mixed-use neighborhoods are more conducive to social-capital generation than are sprawling areas.[24] Large-scale survey research, too, suggests an inverse relationship between longer commuting time and common forms of social participation.[25] But the economists Edward Glaeser and Joshua Gottlieb caution that such research has yet to show a strong relationship between various forms of social capital and more-specific urban characteristics (such as residence in central cities). In an analysis of DDB Needham Life Style data (the core data set underpinning Putnam's *Bowling Alone*), Glaeser and Gottlieb found that central city residents were less likely to participate in several types of civic participation (registering to vote, joining a church, working on a community project, and contacting a public official) than were small-town residents, and were no more likely to participate in such activities than suburbanites. (Central city residents were more likely to write a letter to the editor than either suburbanites or small-town residents.). In addition, Glaeser and Gottlieb found a negative relationship between metropolitan-level densities and social capital.[26] Finally, Jan Brueckner and Ann Largey's analysis of the SCCBS found that among residents of urbanized areas tract density did not have a significant effect on group membership or interaction with neighbors. (Brueckner and Largey did not look at the possible effect of sprawl-related variables besides density, such as automobile dependence.)[27]

Evidence from the SCCBS largely vindicates this skepticism. Simply put, if we examine the relationship among density, automobile dependence, neighborhood age, and central city residence, on the one hand, and common measures of informal social capital and nonpolitical social activities, on the other, we find no consistent pattern of connection between the two. There is no statistically significant relationship between any of those measures of sprawl and an index of the following informal social activities: attending parades or artistic events, having a club membership, playing cards, playing team sports, or hanging out with friends.[28] Nor do those spatial characteristics substantially affect one's likelihood of having many friend or confidants.[29]

TABLE 3.6. Informal Social Connections and Group Membership by Place of Residence

Informal connections refer to number of times in previous year respondents did any of the following: attended a club meeting, played cards with friends, attended an artistic event, attended a parade or community event, played a team sport, hung out with friends in a public place. Memberships refer to total group membership, excluding church membership, membership in labor organizations, and membership in a political organization.

	Informal Connections	Memberships
Central City Residents	55.1	3.00
Suburban Residents	53.5	2.94
Rural Town Residents	59.4	3.06
Rural Nontown Residents	51.1	2.76
High-Density Tract Residents (>8,000 persons/mile)	54.0	2.81
Low-Density Tract Residents (<2,000 persons/mile)	52.3	2.92
Residents of Older Neighborhoods (built prior to 1950)	56.4	2.93
Residents of Newer Neighborhoods (built 1980 or later)	54.2	3.13
Solo Commuting by Car in Tract <65%	54.9	2.85
Solo Commuting by Car in Tract >85%	55.0	3.10
Tracts with Average Commutes >18 Minutes	59.5	3.05
Tracts with Average Commutes <30 Minutes	50.2	2.85

(continued)

TABLE 3.6. (continued)

	Informal Connections	Memberships
Individual Commute <15 Minutes (Workers Only)	60.6	3.17
Individual Commute >30 Minutes (Workers Only)	54.4	3.02

Sources: SCCBS; 2000 U.S. Census.

Spatial characteristics also have little net effect on overall membership in sixteen kinds of non-religious, nonpolitical organizations; tract density is a slight predictor of reduced membership in these organizations, but the net effect is negligible.[30] The effect of sprawl on volunteering is mixed: living in a more automobile-oriented neighborhood, for instance, is associated with less volunteering for neighborhood organizations and arts groups but has no effect on several other forms of volunteerism (such as work with youth groups or health and human service agencies) and is positively associated with blood donation.[31] Finally, there is a positive relationship between living in a car-dependent neighborhood and belonging to a religious congregation, though the effect is modest.[32] In general, suburbs—even sprawling suburbs—appear to be doing minimally, if at all, worse than cities in producing these *general* forms of social capital.[33] As we shall see in chapter 7, the relationship between sprawl and specifically political activity is another matter entirely.

Consistent with much previous research, however, the SCCBS shows commuting time to be inversely related to various forms of social capital. Longer individual commutes are a negative predictor of the number of friends and confidants one has, and the number of groups one belongs to. Longer average commuting time in one's tract is also a negative predictor of an index of informal social activity. In rough terms, a worker with a forty-five-minute commute living in a census tract where the average commute takes thirty minutes is predicted to be about 10 percent less involved in informal social activities than a worker with a ten-minute commute living in a census tract where the average commute is just fifteen minutes.[34] (See appendix II for regression tables.)

Summary of Empirical Findings

The hypothesis that the spatial characteristics of U.S. communities affect both core measures of individual well-being and the way Americans regard their communities was rigorously tested in the preceding section. From the standpoint of utilitarianism, the operative null hypothesis can be summarized as follows: if spatial characteristics do not systematically impact individuals' utility, then we have no problem (or, more accurately, no specific problem deriving from sprawl). If the variety of spatial characteristics present in U.S. communities does not affect well-being in a clear-cut way such that it is obvious that one type of community produces more utility than another, then there is no basis for concluding that, other things being equal, public policy ought to seek to alter the variety of built environments in the United States by promoting certain environments while discouraging others.

Three of the four sprawl-related factors considered here—density, central city residence, neighborhood age, and transit patterns—have little consistent effect on *individual* level measures of utility (happiness and health). The one clear exception is the observed connection between living in a newer neighborhood and having higher personal happiness. Nor does the SCCBS provide compelling evidence of a strong connection between specific spatial features and generalized forms of social capital. A welfare utilitarian concerned with maximizing objectively measurable qualities such as health, reported well-being, and social participation will find little in the evidence examined here to conclude that grave questions of human welfare are at stake in debates and decisions about what specific form our built communities take. (As noted, other researchers have drawn links between some elements of sprawl and more-specific health-related outcomes, such as obesity and auto-related injuries and deaths.)

A quite different story emerges with respect to neighborhood quality-of-life evaluations, however: Sprawl-related factors do affect individuals' assessments of what kind of community they live in and how much they like it: the evidence presented here suggests that even if Americans may not think highly of "sprawl" itself, they do prefer to live in low-density, automobile-intensive, recently built suburbs—if they can. Economic theory predicts that in a world in which everyone has the same economic resources and capacity to move, and in which households have a range of living situations from which to choose, no person or group of persons should be stuck for long in a neighborhood context that does not align with their preferences. The very existence of negative neighborhood effects in high-density, public transit–oriented, central city areas indicates that the United States does not presently represent such a world.[35]

Sprawling places, then, seem to satisfy Americans' preferences better than non-sprawling places, while imposing only limited costs in the form of reduced individual welfare or social connection. But there is one potentially important exception to this generalization, which must be considered, and that is the negative link between long commuting times and a range of important outcomes, including health, happiness, many forms of social participation, and, to a lesser extent, community quality-of-life evaluations.

Few can doubt that, other things being equal, it would be highly desirable if U.S. communities had shorter commuting times. But the practical significance of this observation for the sprawl debate is uncertain. First, to reiterate, long commuting time in itself is not a very reliable proxy for "sprawl." For example, among SCCBS respondents, average neighborhood commuting times in suburban locations are only one minute longer than in central city locations, and central city residents are slightly more likely than suburban residents to live in a tract with average commuting times longer than thirty minutes. The reason for this is straightforward: taking the bus or subway generally makes for a longer (if, in some cases, more convenient) commute than driving to work. In the short term, at least, the quickest way to reduce commuting times in any one community might involve building *more* communities on the suburban fringe, or moving more jobs from urban to suburban locations.[36]

Second, even if we made the systematic reduction of commuting times a high priority, it would require a truly massive shift in the structure of urban economies to reduce commuting to a degree likely to generate substantial improvement in the measures of utility considered here. Cutting the average commuting time from twenty-five minutes to, say, fifteen minutes, for instance, would be a truly daunting challenge: even if an expert panel of urban planners were given absolute power to reshape metropolitan regions to reduce commuting, a reduction on that scale is extremely difficult to imagine.

These findings establishing a link between long commuting time and reduced well-being are not strong enough, from a utilitarian point of view, to allow us to conclude that we, as a society, should actually embark on such an ambitious project. Even if a plausible strategy capable of reducing commuting times to such a degree as to yield tangible welfare benefits could be devised, we would need to have a sense of the costs of such a project. More difficult still, we would need to have some way of knowing at what rate we should trade off goods such as increased individual well-being and satisfaction with quality of life for the good of money (i.e., the costs of changing our existing approach)—or, for that matter, any number of goods with which the goal of reducing commuting times might come into tension. To be sure, the knowledge that longer commutes are undesirable might motivate efforts to ensure that commutes not increase and might cause us to look skeptically upon new neighborhoods that require very long commutes. But this knowledge, in itself, does not suggest that a fundamental reconfiguration of spatial patterns of living and working in the United States would yield substantial welfare benefits.[37]

Putting It All Together: A Utilitarian Analysis of Sprawl

Utilitarian-informed policy analysis must take account of a complex array of factors in evaluating a large-scale phenomenon such as suburban sprawl. Chapters 3 and 4 have suggested that utilitarian concerns with sprawl—or with the evaluation of built communities in general—can best be organized around the metaphor of a utility/cost fraction, in which the efficiency of a policy is judged by how much human well-being it secures for a given financial cost, compared to plausible policy alternatives. In the denominator of the fraction stands the sum total of the quantifiable costs described by Persky and Wiewel (i.e., the sum of the financial costs of sprawl minus the sum of its financial benefits). To estimate this denominator, we need to know about the financial benefits gained from sprawl (profits for developers, reduced wage costs for employers, cheaper housing for consumers), in addition to the financial costs generated by sprawl (increased infrastructure costs paid by public bodies, costs associated with increases in transportation and road travel, environmental externalities, including costs deferred to the future, costs borne by residents of central cities experiencing disinvestments, etc.). Estimating this denominator alone is an extremely formidable task; the data requirements for making such an estimate are overwhelming. In practice, selected case study approaches are the most plausible method for at least roughly gauging the costs and benefits of sprawl compared to alternative development patterns. Persky and Wiewel's case study (described in chapter 2) compared the scenario of private factory investment in a greenfield versus factory investment in an existing urban location; other possible studies might compare the costs and benefits of locating public facilities in central cities versus in suburban fringes, or of locating a housing development in an urban brownfield site compared to a greenfield site, or any number of other possibilities.

To recall, Persky and Wiewel concluded that the costs and benefits of job sprawl are of the "same order of magnitude."[38] To be sure, this conclusion itself is based on several assumptions, particularly with respect to environmental issues, which bear critical scrutiny and which non-utilitarian analysts may reject. Indeed, Persky and Wiewel conclude that sprawl *is* a mild negative in cost–benefit terms. But critics of sprawl attempting to argue that development on the suburban fringe is a massive form of financial irrationality need far more evidence to make that claim credible. As it stands, Persky and Wiewel's judgment stands as a reasonable approximation of academic consensus on the issue of the costs and benefits of sprawl; to recall, the recent exhaustive study of financial costs associated with sprawl conducted by Burchell et al. estimates that compact forms of growth could yield long-run financial savings across the board on the order of 5–10 percent, compared to continued unchecked sprawl.

The issue of calculating the "denominator" of financial costs and benefits is quite obviously complicated enough. But there are even more vexing difficulties when looking at the "numerator" of the utility fraction. This numerator consists of the subjective satisfaction—utility—actually derived by individuals from a particular organization of space. In this chapter, it has been measured in terms of subjective well-being and satisfaction with one's community, as well as in terms of health and social capital.

Yet four crucial difficulties remain when one attempts to move from these specific findings to a more generalized statement on the question of whether sprawl maximizes utility. The first is the commensurability problem—the question of how differing goods (health, social capital, subjective happiness) are to be weighed against one another when measuring overall utility. Even if this problem could be satisfactorily resolved, a second problem would present itself: the question of how to trade off the good of utility or preference satisfaction against the good of money. Is a way of life that is more expensive than plausible alternatives worth paying for if it better satisfies people's preferences? Practitioners of cost–benefit analysts have attempted to find ways to answer that question by, for instance, examining the trade-offs made in actual markets; but even economists who, in theory, endorse the idea of this sort of cost–benefit analysis concede that "many of the methods used by cost–benefit analysts generate systematically biased prescriptions" (such as undervaluing future costs and benefits relative to the present).[39] Other scholars, such as Henry Richardson, reject cost–benefit analysis entirely, favoring an iterative deliberative process aimed at working out "reasonable compromises" among competing values. According to this view, the best the utilitarian analyst can hope to do is to gain some sense of the scale of the trade-offs between money and subjective satisfaction as a starting point for what Richardson terms "intelligent public deliberation."[40]

The third difficulty is the question of whether utilitarianism should aim to maximize objective measures of human welfare or instead focus on the satisfaction of preferences (and, if so, whether even poorly informed or irrational preferences should be respected). "Welfare utilitarianism" or "fully informed and rational utilitarianism" holds an obvious appeal for utilitarians who, like J. S. Mill, want to avoid equating utility maximization with the indiscriminate satisfaction of people's preferences. Yet, quite obviously, to attempt to specify and measure the elements of *objective* human welfare is a vastly complicated and inherently controversial enterprise; so, too, are efforts to deduce what preferences "fully informed and rational" persons might have in any particular context.

There is one further difficulty as well. Suppose the utilitarian were to dispense with efforts to calculate and quantify welfare, or the content of fully informed preferences, and set the more modest goal of satisfying individuals' existing preferences, whatever they are. Clearly, Americans, in the aggregate, currently regard low-density, car-friendly environments in suburbs as better places to live than central cities. But how do we know that the fit between Americans' preferences and the neighborhoods they live in would not improve if a wider range of functional community types—for instance, more places with short commutes—were available? Or that the fit would not improve if U.S. cities became objectively more livable places, so that people who really love the city could live there comfortably? Or that Americans' current set of preferences would not change if such policies to make cities more livable were pursued?

These are not merely rhetorical questions. The strong finding that Americans who live in suburbs are better satisfied with their local quality of life does not necessarily imply either that sprawl is unproblematic or that efforts to create alternatives to sprawl would lead to sharp reductions in overall quality of life. Three points loom large here. First, as noted above, the fact that quality-of-life evaluations vary systematically across spatial settings can be interpreted not simply as a story of suburban success, but rather more pessimistically as a story of metropolitan-level failure: Some neighborhoods in the metropolitan area are widely considered to be worse places than others, yet people persist in living there anyway (by choice or necessity). Put another way, the sharp inequalities in quality-of-life evaluations between central city and suburban residents may indicate the presence of systematic social injustices within the metropolitan area: some people get to enjoy pleasant neighborhoods; others do not. (I consider this topic more fully in chapter 4.)

Second, individuals have diverse tastes and preferences; just because many people are content to live in sprawling places does not mean everyone is. For this very reason, Burchell and Downs suggest that a "compact-growth" scenario over the 2000–2025 period should not lead to any effective loss of quality of life compared to their "unrestrained-growth" scenario: both scenarios permit individuals to access a variety of residential settings.[41]

Jonathan Levine goes further, presenting evidence that there is now unmet consumer demand for higher-density residential development because of zoning restrictions and other public policies that, in effect, mandate sprawl. Levine compares the Atlanta and Boston metropolitan areas' ability to satisfy the diverse preferences of its residents and finds that less sprawling Boston does a better job than Atlanta. In Boston, the larger number of pedestrian-oriented environments means that residents who would prefer to live in such a neighborhood are more likely to do so. Levine's research found that 83 percent of Boston residents in the top decile of preferences for transit and pedestrian-friendly environments lived either in the central city or in an inner suburb; in Atlanta only 48 percent of those with strong preferences for transit and pedestrian-oriented neighborhoods lived in such areas. The natural conclusion of this research is that even if quality-of-life evaluations tend to be higher in sprawling areas, at least in some metropolitan areas preferences for more compact, less sprawling living arrangements are not being satisfied.[42]

The third major point is that sprawl-reform strategies need not involve forcibly removing residents from existing sprawling areas; far more plausibly, they will involve attempting to influence *future* growth and residential location decisions, and/or efforts to improve the quality of life in central city and older neighborhoods so as to make such locations more attractive residential environments. Put another way, insofar as alternatives to sprawl involve *improving* quality of life in substandard areas, it is difficult to see how such strategies would necessitate *worsening* overall quality of life in the metropolitan area, even if it involved the modest redistribution of resources from richer to poorer neighborhoods.[43]

Nonetheless, it remains the case that attempts to modify or reform sprawl necessarily must be modest in scope so long as Americans (collectively) retain a strong preference for suburban living arrangements. Yet we have seen that this preference is likely, at least in part, to be a function of the choices offered to Americans (healthy suburb or decaying city). The question of whether overall utility might increase if these preferences could be reshaped so as to make a traditional urban way of life much more attractive to Americans is a front-burner issue in the sprawl debate. This is a question with which utilitarian policy analysis cannot easily cope: if policy can induce a change in preferences—Frank Hahn gives the example of more education changing an individual's preference from watching television to reading—how can policy alternatives that produce different sets of preferences be ranked against one another?[44] We may feel confident that Americans' existing preferences would best be satisfied by discouraging the creation of very dense places, but how do we know that if more Americans were somehow persuaded to live in Paris-style densities (perhaps by making such places more attractive), they would not, in fact, develop a different set of preferences, and in turn acquire an appreciation for the virtues of dense city living that is now lacking? This is not a far-fetched question—in fact, it is a question raised by numerous critics of suburban sprawl, who argue that Americans' distaste for density is based on the mistaken acceptance of "myths" regarding density's effects, and that if more Americans recognized that high density is required to sustain walkable places they would adopt different attitudes.[45]

Important work by the social theorist Jon Elster on the notion of "adaptive preferences" can help us specify the question further: perhaps Americans' taste for suburbs is, in part, an adaptation to the reality that, for many citizens, the virtues of urban life—the eroticism and excitement described by Iris Marion Young—are simply unavailable, or even unknown. Perhaps Americans have resigned themselves to the view that the joys of easy car access to shopping malls are superior to the joys of walking through an open pedestrian plaza on an everyday basis because they know that they cannot attain the latter—and also send their kids to decent schools. In this circumstance, continued suburbanization might better satisfy existing preferences than resettling cities; but if improving and resettling cities changed the content of Americans' preferences, then the city-strengthening policy regime might satisfy Americans' *new* preferences better than continued suburbanization. If this were the case, which policy path would utilitarians recommend?[46]

It is not clear by what method or by what set of calculations utilitarian analysis can adequately answer that question—even though in many respects that is precisely *the* question at the heart of the ongoing debate about suburban sprawl in the United States. Indeed, the problem of how to choose between alternative social states in which preferences are variable illustrates a broader difficulty facing utilitarianism. In its relentless reliance on empirical evidence to test the goodness of things, utilitarianism must either retreat into silence or resort to highly questionable guesswork in making judgments about matters for which there is no solid empirical data. This is likely to be the case when data is simply unavailable, or when data of the kind required (i.e., full information on the effects of far-reaching policy changes that alter people's very preferences and conceptions of who they are) cannot even in principle exist, or when the problem at hand is not resolvable (except in a deeply unsatisfactory way) by appeals to evidence. (Can empirical evidence tell us what the monetary worth of a human life is?)

Some utilitarian-informed policy analysts have simply despaired of ever being able to make meaningful judgments about widely different social states or institutional arrangements. For example, David Braybrooke and Charles Lindblom's influential text on policy analysis actively discourages policy scholars from attempting too-ambitious comparisons involving either nonincremental shifts in policies or an examination of all the possible consequences of a policy: "[W]hile one can speculate on nonincremental alternatives, an analyst is often without adequate information, theory, or any other organized way of dealing systematically with nonincremental alternatives.... They cannot be very rationally explored, therefore, even if one wished to try."[47] Instead, Braybrooke and Lindblom urge that clarity of analysis is best served by limiting the scope of inquiry (with respect to both scenarios considered and the range of consequences to be studied), which, in short, means marginal analysis.

Braybrooke and Lindblom may well have been correct on the methodological requirements of utilitarian policy analysis. But if they were, this illustrates only the inadequacy of cost–benefit approaches for analyzing a large-scale phenomenon such as sprawl, in which not just marginal changes but *entire ways of life* are ultimately being debated: marginal analysis would restrict the debate on sprawl to questions about whether, given existing preferences and existing socio-spatial structures, it would be more advantageous to build this or that factory, sewer, school, or park in this location rather than another, while setting aside questions of whether the social-spatial structure itself (and the way of life that goes with it) is really that most conducive to human flourishing. Such a demarcation of the question cuts the heart out of Mill's highest aspirations for utilitarianism as a public philosophy capable of inspiring sustained critical inquiry into the nature of our social institutions and social life, by assuming that the fundamental questions have already been solved and that all that remains is to tinker along the edges, making marginal improvements here and there. As Charles Taylor argues, this type of utilitarianism can ask only what it would be good to *do* (in policy terms, what the next marginal step should be, given where we are), not what it is good to *be* (i.e., is it really good to be a suburban, SUV-driving society?).[48]

Defining the question so narrowly also fails to do justice to the actually available range of alternative long-term policy directions concerning sprawl: on the one hand, the normal process of replacing existing infrastructure and buildings will give Americans the opportunity to very substantially reshape the existing built environment in the coming decades; on the other hand, expected increases in population growth will place new pressures on existing metropolitan regions, thereby necessitating public choices about how to accommodate the newcomers.[49] In short, whether the twenty-first century involves continued outward growth on the suburban fringe, a systematic resettlement of urban cores, the creation of entirely new communities, or some other combination of policies—each of which is likely to have significant implications for the character of U.S. life and the preferences and habits of its citizens—is very much an open question. To the extent that marginal analysis's inherent limitations make comparison of these very different future possibilities difficult or impossible, its ability to speak to the central questions in the sprawl debate are limited. As Elster remarks, "[An adequate] theory of justice or of social choice . . . should not tell us that some alternatives are non-comparable, nor [should it] try to overcome this problem by stipulating that society is indifferent between all non-comparable alternatives."[50]

Contrary to Braybrooke and Lindblom, however, Robert Goodin has argued that a broadly utilitarian approach to policymaking need not be reduced to "incrementalism." Goodin argues that if policymakers have strong theoretical reasons for predicting the ability of policy changes to affect welfare and satisfy (future) preferences, then they may be justified in pursuing nonincremental policies.[51] According to this view, it might be possible, in the case of suburban sprawl, to build a utilitarian argument for dramatic changes to the built environment if there were very strong evidence that shifting from sprawl to Smart Growth, New Urbanism, or some combination thereof would satisfy citizen's future preferences better than continuing the current arrangements. But such certainty is not warranted, based on the evidence presented here; and as a practical political matter, an argument based on the proposition that social planners *could know* exactly (or even roughly) how preferences would change under a different metropolitan regime would probably be rejected as unwarranted social engineering.

———

Apart from these considerations, the actual policy environment in which utilitarian ideas must be applied is one in which there is no clarity or consensus about which elements of human well-being we should be most concerned with maximizing and no credible method for trading off subjective human well-being against the good of money; further, in this environment, the wide variety of costs and benefits associated with sprawl, in many cases, have yet to be fully specified. In this climate, policy research functions to specify one particular cost or benefit and to draw attention to it; thus, a 2001 study concluded that suburban sprawl may be helpful to first-time minority buyers of homes by reducing housing costs,[52] while other studies have reported a link between county or metropolitan sprawl and obesity. Yet from neither finding is it possible to come to a defensible policy conclusion that takes account of all the costs and benefits associated with sprawl; nor is there a sense of how competing goods ought to be weighed against one another; nor is there a widely accepted framework or procedure (i.e., one to which all participants in the policy process assent) for rationally conducting policy evaluation. Instead, policy research makes a series of isolated observations about sprawl as a social phenomenon (e.g., it pushes down housing costs, it contributes to obesity), and participants in the public debate pick and choose those observations that reinforce their own viewpoints; what they do not do is attempt to reach a consensus on how these competing findings ought to be weighed against one another in deliberating how to maximize total utility. In short, the debate about suburban sprawl belongs to the messy terrain of democracy, not to a clinical examination of total costs and benefits aimed at arriving at a comprehensive view of what makes for maximizing utility and how different kinds of considerations ought to be weighed against one another.

Deliberative models of utilitarian politics that envisage common acceptance of utility maximization as a shared public goal, reasoned debate about the pros and cons of various actions, and, finally, democratically made social choices, depend on the notion that citizens are capable of understanding the big-picture consequences of various policies and considering the good of the entire society when judging those policies.[53] Otherwise, utilitarian politics would simply collapse into interest-group clashes. Yet, there is strong reason to doubt whether, especially on very complex issues, there is a "big picture" that could be commonly and objectively recognized by most citizens; in the case of sprawl, there are dozens of potentially relevant considerations to weigh, and often no clear-cut way to balance or trade off the competing goods at stake. Moreover, substantial private interests are affected by land use policy. In this circumstance, even if, in theory, the common yardstick of maximizing utility were accepted, politics, in practice, is likely to consist of distinct interest groups that use their resources to marshal evidence that supports their point of view and to discredit evidence supporting the opposition's view. The lack of a coherent method to trade off competing goods or obtain a truly holistic view of the *total* costs and benefits at stake means that policy will likely—at best—be swayed by whichever side of the argument seems to have the most studies on its side, the most identified positive-utility effects.[54] Because science itself is not a neutral social practice, however, the ability of groups holding distinct points of view to marshal evidence on their own behalf is likely to be strongly affected by the resources available to the various actors in a political debate. As critics of too-facile notions of the "public interest" have long insisted, utilitarianism, in this mode, can all too easily slide into interest-group politics by another name.[55]

Detailed considerations of this kind—concerning how utilitarians treat preferences, compare the worth of very different goods, compare two substantively different states of affairs, and the like—would not be necessary if it could be shown that sprawl is an unambiguously good or an unambiguously bad form of spatial development. That is not the case, however. Sprawl may be slightly more expensive fiscally than more-compact development, but Americans seem to regard neighborhoods with sprawl-like characteristics as substantially better places to live. Low-density, car-dominated developments may have relatively little effect on the personal well-being of residents, but they generate environmental and social costs that are difficult to measure in cost–benefit analyses and that many citizens think should not be converted to dollar terms at all. Long commuting times associated with the contemporary U.S. metropolis may be bad for individual well-being, but it is far from clear how we might even plausibly calculate whether the financial costs of rebuilding that metropolis in ways that minimized commuting would be worth the hedonic benefit it would presumably bring. Nor is it clear how utilitarian policy analysts can be sure that preferences are being better satisfied under the current policy regime than under any other, given that alternative policy regimes would likely (whether by accident or design) induce alterations in the content of those preferences.

This does not mean that the utilitarian analyst has nothing at all to say about sprawl. First, while strong confidence that a program of improving central cities and older suburbs might alter Americans' overall preferences (given sufficient time) is not warranted, the claim is plausible enough to justify policy experimentation at the state and regional level to gauge how citizens' preferences respond to policy changes. Such experimentation might generate useful knowledge that could inform subsequent policymaking. Second, there might be other utilitarian justifications for favoring some of the policies supported by advocates of promoting smart growth and reversing sprawl; for instance, improving urban living conditions and limiting carbon emissions might be good utility-enhancing things to do, independently of whether such policies affect citizens' future residential preferences or have a substantial effect on sprawling growth patterns. What utilitarianism cannot do, however, is provide strong, objective reasons for judging existing metropolitan-development patterns as, on balance, better or worse than plausible, widely discussed alternatives. Whether a more-compact, urban-oriented version of the U.S. way of life would be an improvement over the current sprawling version is not a question that utilitarian modes of analysis can persuasively answer.[56]

Some utilitarians might respond by stating that this is the wrong question to ask and that we should be content with marginal analyses aimed at identifying particular inefficiencies. But this approach cannot succeed either (other than as an academic exercise) so long as it ignores political obstacles to correcting such inefficiencies (such as the unwillingness of suburban municipalities to end exclusionary zoning policies that have the effect of producing more sprawl than would be efficient). To address those obstacles, in turn, requires launching an inquiry into the distribution of resources and of political influence in the United States, in addition to an inquiry into questions of institutional design and distribution of powers among various levels of government. Utilitarians can remain content with marginal analysis and abstain from the need to make larger-order comparisons among very different kinds of social arrangements (and the preference structures they produce) only by assuming that the existing political structures through which policy decisions are made are themselves *already* utility-maximizing—a highly doubtful assumption that writers such as J. S. Mill would have soundly rejected.[57]

Utilitarian thinking thus emerges as a tremendous stimulus to generating new empirical knowledge, but, at least in very complex cases, as an inadequate prism for synthesizing such knowledge and forming practical judgments. This inadequacy is partly rooted in the lack of sufficiently sophisticated tools to perform the truly comprehensive calculations that utilitarianism requires, but even more so in inherent problems in the utilitarian method—problems such as the reduction of all goods to a single marker of value, the difficulty of accounting for changes in preferences when estimating the likely consequences of various courses of actions, and the difficulty of comparing widely differing states of affairs using only utility as a barometer.

In a broad sense, however, Mill was correct to argue that we are all, to a considerable degree, utilitarians; that is, all secular political philosophies do hold the advancement of human welfare as a prime goal and are (or should be) centrally concerned with the practical consequences of public action.[58] Utilitarians are also correct to note that making trade-offs between different goods is an inevitable feature of policymaking.[59] But competing public philosophies offer different answers than does utilitarianism to questions such as whether there is a single irreducible human good, how conflicts among competing goods should be adjudicated, and whether specific forms of governance or specific ways of life might be good for their own sake. Most importantly, competing public philosophies propose that controversial public topics must be debated and resolved with reference to substantive moral values, with complex calculations of costs and benefits playing a subordinate (though at times vital) role in the decision process.

Our examination of suburban sprawl through a utilitarian lens has hardly been fruitless, however. At a minimum, we have considered strong evidence for rejecting the view that the simple fact of living in a car-dependent, low-density, relatively new suburban neighborhood depresses either individual well-being or neighborhood satisfaction. Sprawling neighborhoods appear (on aggregate) to satisfy Americans' existing preferences significantly better than the presently available alternatives. As we have noted, however, the wide gap in neighborhood satisfaction between sprawling and urbanist locales we have observed can also be taken as a troubling indictment of the U.S. metropolis as a whole. Why aren't urban neighborhoods delivering as much satisfaction as suburban areas, and why are so many Americans apparently stuck in relatively worse-off neighborhoods?

That question, in turn, raises fundamental questions about the *fairness* of U.S. society, in addition to the underlying question of what a "fair arrangement" of social institutions would look like. To address that set of concerns, in chapters 4 and 5, we examine suburban sprawl through the lens of Rawlsian liberal egalitarianism, a normative political philosophy that demands that we ask not just whether sprawl is efficient or satisfies preferences, but whether it is consistent with and supportive of the institutional arrangements of a just society.

FOUR

Is Sprawl Fair?

Liberal Egalitarianism and Sprawl

Is sprawl fair? Consider two contrasting approaches to the question. The first approach takes as given the background inequalities of life in the United States, then tries to isolate the marginal contribution of sprawl to increasing or reducing such inequalities of race and class. Given existing inequalities, does one additional unit of "sprawl" produce one additional unit of inequality? A good example of this approach is the work of Anthony Downs, who has explored the relationship between a number of indicators of metropolitan-level sprawl and central city decline. Downs found that while important aspects of suburbanization are indeed connected to central city decline, the specific spatial configurations associated with sprawl (as he defines it) have no additional impact above and beyond this general suburbanization effect.[1]

A second approach focuses less on the marginal contribution of sprawl to exacerbating inequalities than on the role the overall spatial configuration of the metropolitan United States plays in *constructing* and *reproducing* the fundamental *background* inequalities of opportunity that characterize life here. In this approach, the aim is to illustrate the connection between the socio-spatial structure of metropolitan areas as a whole—including not just "sprawl," but the overall relationship between central cities, older suburbs, and newer suburbs—and the structure of opportunity in the United States. What is of interest to this approach is the way that inequality of opportunity in the United States is codified in and reproduced by the spatial configuration of our metropolitan areas.

A crucial methodological difference between these two approaches is that the former examines the fairness of sprawl only by considering sprawl as an independent variable—an independent factor that contributes to social inequality, net of all other factors. The latter approach, in contrast, examines sprawl as both a possible cause and a possible *effect* of systemic unfairness—and openly admits that with respect to the relationship between sprawl and the social order writ large, it may be difficult or impossible to make meaningful distinctions between sprawl as an independent and sprawl as a dependent variable. This latter approach conceptualizes sprawl not necessarily as the primary *driver* of fundamental social inequalities but as an important *vehicle* by which inequalities get reproduced and extended over time, and as an important *product* of fundamental social inequalities.

The contrast between these two approaches to the question of sprawl and fairness maps neatly onto the difference between cost-benefit and liberal egalitarian approaches to inequality and fairness as such. Simply put, the former approach takes the existing socioeconomic structure of society as given, and the latter does not. Marginalist analysis (whether aimed at maximizing utility, or at Pareto optimality) presumes the legitimacy of existing social relationships and distributions of power and opportunity, then inquires into the effect of marginal changes on such distributions. A structural approach, in contrast, begins by critically assessing the legitimacy of the existing social structure and then asks what sorts of institutional arrangements might produce a more just structure.

To think of justice and fairness in terms of fundamental social structures is perhaps the primary contribution of John Rawls to contemporary political thought. Rawls was interested in specifying the basic structure of a social system that could be regarded as just and fair by *both* the best and the least well off. Such a society would, Rawls argued, provide each of its members a substantively equal opportunity to develop their capacities and to pursue positions of authority and prestige, with none disadvantaged by arbitrary social factors. Such arbitrary factors include race, gender, and class and might also include one's place of birth or residence. For Rawls, a just society must be one in which where you happened to live as a child would have minimal material effect on how your life would likely go, and, especially, what your likely social status as an adult would be. Few, if any, serious observers believe that the United States lives up to this standard of geographic social justice today.

_____

Within a Rawlsian framework, the relationship between urban spatial forms and justice raises two broad concerns. The first is whether or not a given spatial arrangement of community life is intrinsically unjust; that is, whether it is wrong because its very existence means that people do not get their due. Justice, however, involves relationships between people, not the relationship between humans and the built environment. Consequently, what makes an unjust spatial arrangement unjust is not the organization of space per se, but the way spatial patterns are placed in the service of unjust social arrangements.[2]

For instance, the existence of a housing development that is physically separated from the rest of the urban community by water and a large moat and offers only one road in and out of the development, a road that can be blocked at any time, cannot necessarily be labeled *unjust* (though its isolation might thwart achievement of other important values). Perhaps the development is, in fact, a tourist attraction, consisting of vacation houses that could, in theory, be accessed by anyone with the ability to pay; or perhaps the development is a monastery housing those with a commitment to a particular way of life that is best realized in a communal setting, physically detached from the wider, secular society. In these hypothetical cases, the developments are not obviously unjust. But if the development is a ghetto into which all residents of a certain ethnicity within a given city are required to live, the development would be regarded as morally objectionable according to virtually any contemporary conception of justice.[3] This is an example of the first sense in which a particular spatial configuration might be regarded as unjust: any built community designed for the purpose of mandating or extending involuntary segregation by ascriptive characteristics is *in itself* wrong. A striking recent example of such flagrant injustice is the South African township of the apartheid era, in which blacks were forced to live physically segregated from other groups.[4]

The decisive factor in critically evaluating whether a particular socio-spatial configuration is just or unjust is not the spatial layout of a given community but the purposes for which it is built and the nature of the social relations it tends to promote. It is possible, of course, to imagine spatial arrangements that just societies (societies predicated on freedom and equality) would be very unlikely to adopt; for instance, Fritz Lang's classic 1927 film *Metropolis* portrays a city where workers in slave-like conditions live and toil far underground while the elite live in tall buildings amid the clouds. But even in such extreme cases, the built environment can be properly viewed as effect rather than a cause of fundamentally unjust relations.

There is a second, less obvious justice-related concern that is also at stake in evaluating our built environments; namely, whether a particular social-spatial pattern tends to *undermine* the realization of a just society. For instance, if a development is a wealthy gated community, which de facto excludes residents below a certain income threshold, serious questions can be raised about whether such a community is compatible with a democratic society—even though the development may not be as obviously unjust as an apartheid-era South African township. No one is being forced to live in this neighborhood, and no one can legally be excluded by ascriptive characteristics. Yet, if this self-segregation by the rich has negative effects on the rest of the community, or if the physical separation of classes undermines the sense of social solidarity required to sustain just social relations and ensure that each and every citizen receives her due, then these built communities, too, can be reasonably described as "unjust," or more precisely, as "contributing to injustice."

But what do we mean by "justice"? Discussion on this point has been dominated in the past generation by liberal social contract approaches, deriving especially from the landmark work of Rawls. A common problem of many conceptions of justice, historically, is that they reflect, consciously or unconsciously, the social class and/or the underlying assumptions of a given writer. As Karl Marx pointedly argued, dominant normative ideas about how goods should be distributed have often reflected, in fact, the material and class position of particular groups.[5] The genius of Rawls's thought is that it suggests a mechanism for trying to think impartially about justice, independent of the biases that inevitably shape particular individuals' outlook on life, the world, and the organization of society.

Rawls asks us to conceive of a thought experiment involving rational persons possessing first, a reasonable regard for their own self-interest and an interest in obtaining those basic social goods that are the precondition for carrying out rational life projects, and second, a reasonable knowledge of basic principles of social cooperation.[6] These persons, conceived of as distinct individuals, are then asked to set aside knowledge of their own position in the world, in addition to their own preferences, interests, particular vision of the best way of life, and religious and ethical commitments. Behind this "veil of ignorance," these rational persons, who are well informed as to how societies work but ignorant of their own personal circumstances, assume the task of constructing principles for ordering social and political institutions, with a view to producing regulative social and political institutions corresponding to a conception of ourselves as free equals. The results of this deliberation, Rawls postulates, would be principles of justice adequate to modern societies: broad principles that people in very different life situations and with very different commitments can affirm as valid.

Rawls argues that the two principles of justice likely to be derived from this "original position" are, first, a commitment to securing "basic" liberties and to making such liberties equally available to all, and second, a commitment to both providing substantive equality of opportunity to all and to distributing material goods in such a fashion that the well-being of the *least* well off in the society is maximized. Rawls further argues that the first principle should be considered "lexically prior" to the second. Rawls believes that these two principles of social order provide a far more solid grounding than utilitarian thought for securing respect for individuals and ensuring that all persons are treated fairly. Each principle is fundamentally rooted not in contingent utilitarian calculations but in explicit ethical conceptions—in particular, the idea that people should not be treated as means to ends, that we regard ourselves and one another as free equals, and that society ought to be seen "as a scheme of cooperation for reciprocal advantage regulated by principles which persons would choose in an initial situation that is fair."[7]

The following two chapters examine suburban sprawl through the critical lens offered by Rawlsian liberal egalitarianism. (The core of this analysis should also be of interest to adherents of other variants of liberal egalitarianism, such as the social-insurance model of justice advocated by Ronald Dworkin.)[8] We begin in this chapter with a theoretical discussion of the ways in which socio-spatial patterns might be thought to be intrinsically unjust from a Rawlsian point of view; then we go on to consider more-specific evidence implicating the broad pattern of suburbanization in the United States in continued patterns of socioeconomic and racial segregation and in the violation of fairness norms involving equal opportunity. As we shall see, a contested issue is whether *sprawl,* understood as a particular form of suburbanization involving low-density, automobile-oriented development on the perimeter of metropolitan areas, is linked to violations of fairness norms in a manner distinct from the broader pattern of suburbanization. (This is the question of whether sprawl can be specifically linked to marginal *increases* in social inequality, noted above.) Our primary concern here, however, is with the larger question of the role the overall spatial configuration of U.S. metropolitan areas plays in *reproducing* unjust social inequalities.

Socio-Spatial Arrangements and Injustice:
A Brief Taxonomy

We begin by examining in further detail what sorts of socio-spatial arrangements liberal egalitarianism is likely to regard as unjust (and why). The following discussion explicates five central categories of spatial injustice:

direct constraints on human liberty in socio-spatial arrangements, socio-spatial arrangements that conflict with the notion of substantive equality of opportunity, socio-spatial arrangements that limit the kinds of communities people may choose to live in, socio-spatial arrangements that conflict with the Rawlsian commitment to ensuring inequalities benefit the least well-off (the "difference principle"), and socio-spatial arrangements that undercut the sense of solidarity required to sustain egalitarian polities.[9]

I. DIRECT CONSTRAINTS ON LIBERTY

Forced Segregation and the Denial of Choice

Perhaps the most straightforward manner in which a socio-spatial arrangement can violate liberal norms of justice is by making residence in a particular place compulsory. Rawls counts "freedom of the person" as one of the "basic liberties" to be established by a system of justice.[10] Freedom of the person appears to refer primarily to freedom from wrongful imprisonment in addition to wrongful intrusions upon either the bodies or minds (via "psychological oppression") of human beings. It can easily be extended to derive a concept of "freedom of movement" that would more explicitly stipulate that citizens have the right to live and travel where they please within the polity, unobstructed by arbitrary constraints.[11] As with all basic liberties, Rawlsian justice requires that freedom of the person and, in turn, freedom of movement be *equally* available to all. Thus, socio-spatial schemes that permit some racial or ethnic groups to move freely but constrict others to certain locations would be considered unjust, both in extreme cases, such as that of South African apartheid, and milder cases, such as those involving the use of state power to reinforce involuntary racial segregation (as in the common practice of "redlining" undertaken by the Federal Housing Administration between the 1930s and 1960s, in which federal housing loans were systematically steered away from neighborhoods with African American residents).[12] Also at odds with basic freedom of movement are schemes that require citizens to carry "internal passports" to travel, or forbid citizens from moving from one city or region to another, or use state power to *discourage* certain kinds of people from visiting or moving to a given location (i.e., systematic police harassment of black youths walking through predominantly white neighborhoods).

The injustice of schemes of forced segregation based on ascriptive status is widely recognized by not only Rawlsian liberals but also utilitarians, civic republicans, and others who endorse the notion of basic personal liberties.

Much more disputed are two closely related questions: First, if involuntary residential segregation is wrong, does this mean that integrated, racially diverse neighborhoods ought to be the goal of policy? Second, what if *equal* liberty of movement is constrained not legally, by ascriptive characteristics, but in a de facto manner, by disparities of wealth that block some people from moving? As we shall see, how we answer each of these questions has practical bearing on the suburban sprawl debate.

The Harm of Segregation: Two Views

The debate over integration as a social ideal can be usefully illustrated by contrasting the positions of two nominally "liberal" thinkers, the legal scholar Owen Fiss and the late political theorist Iris Marion Young.[13] Fiss argues that the existence of urban black ghettoes in U.S. urban areas constitutes a systemic injustice that the state has the responsibility to redress. The continuing disproportionate black presence in decaying urban neighborhoods leads to the degradation of African American life, Fiss argues, as too many blacks are compelled to live in areas in which social problems are highly concentrated and access to mainstream society has been all but cut off. This, in turn, leads many Americans to link conditions of poverty, crime, and drug use with race, perpetuating racial stigmas that negatively affect all African Americans (including those who are middle-class suburban residents).[14] Fiss thus advocates federal programs to systematically abolish black ghettoes in central cities and to resettle residents in suburban locations or in racially integrated areas of the city—even though such a program might worsen prospects for ghetto residents who choose to remain.[15] Fiss's agenda presupposes a positive reply to the question of whether the state should compensate those hurt by past socio-spatial policies that violate norms of justice (although Fiss links present-day racial segregation not simply to policies that are socio-spatially specific but to the larger history of slavery and discrimination against African Americans in the United States).

This sort of view is rejected by Young, who urges a distinction between compulsory and voluntary racial segregation. While opposed to restrictions on liberty of movement, Young argues that the harm of segregation consists not in persons of the same skin tone or ethnicity living in close proximity, but rather in the way that segregation constrains individual choice, reproduces "structures of privilege and disadvantage," and impedes "political communication." Voluntary residential "clustering" of ethnic, racial, or other social groups provides several important goods to residents, Young argues; among these are a more welcome setting for people who do not fit into mainstream society, a setting for preserving and institutionalizing particular cultural norms, and greater opportunities to be in close contact with people who have similar experiences or backgrounds. Many integration schemes, Young would argue, fail to recognize the positive goods provided by voluntary racial and ethnic clustering and violate norms of choice (by eliminating the option to live in a vibrant community characterized by such clustering). Extending Young's view, we might believe that redressing the consequences of past socio-spatial injustices should take the form not of subsidized mobility but rather of increased resources to support neighborhoods (especially ghettoized central city areas) damaged or neglected by previous policy choices.[16]

Formal Equality and Unequal Mobility

A second issue related to freedom of movement concerns whether such freedom is violated when there are sharply unequal capacities to move, not because of formal discrimination, but because of monetary inequalities. Rawls himself deliberately avoids taking sides in the well-known debate between "positive" and "negative" conceptions of liberty. Instead, Rawls describes practical constraints on the capacity of some to exercise liberties (such as resource limitations) as "affecting the worth of liberty" but not as violating liberty itself. Rawls then turns to the "difference principle" as the mechanism for reconciling liberty and equality:

> Freedom as equal liberty is the same for all; the question of compensating for a lesser than equal liberty does not arise. But the worth of liberty is not the same for everyone. Some have greater authority and wealth, and therefore greater means to achieve their aims. The lesser worth of liberty is, however, compensated for, since the capacity of the less fortunate members of society to achieve their aims would be even less were they not to accept the existing inequalities whenever the difference principle is satisfied. But compensating for the lesser worth of freedom is not to be confused with making good an unequal liberty. Taking the two principles together, the basic structure is to be arranged to maximize the worth to the least advantaged of the complete scheme of equal liberty shared by all.[17]

It follows that, for Rawls, there is no injustice involved in citizens having unequal capacities to exercise freedom of movement with respect to preferred living arrangements—so long as the background conditions of distributive justice have been established. Central among those conditions is the notion of equal opportunity.

II. SOCIO-SPATIAL ARRANGEMENTS AND FAIR EQUALITY OF OPPORTUNITY

"Equal opportunity" is often defined in popular conversation as simply open access of anyone to any career or any public position: no citizen should be blocked from any public office for any arbitrary reason, nor prohibited from taking any job. In speaking of "fair equality of opportunity," Rawls meant this popular definition, but he also meant much more: "The thought is that positions are to be not only open in a formal sense, but that all should have a fair chance to attain them." Rawls went on to specify that "social class" should not substantively affect citizens' "prospects of culture and achievement," and even specified certain policy parameters that this principle implied, including "preventing excessive accumulations of property and wealth" and "maintaining equal opportunities of education for all." In particular, he noted, "the school system, whether public or private, should be designed to even out class barriers."[18] This conception of equal opportunity, which Rawls labeled the "liberal interpretation," already provides a fairly stringent normative basis for criticizing many existing market societies, even without considering Rawls's further enumeration of the difference principle.

Spatial Inequalities and Education

How might socio-spatial arrangements affect the provision of equality of opportunity? Rawls's attention to education provides the most straightforward way into this question. Clearly, if in a single, national polity, residents in one area of the country—say, the North—have educational opportunities vastly superior to those of residents in another area of the country—say, the South—then the principle of equality of opportunity is being violated. Discrimination by virtue of geographic residence is no more morally acceptable than discrimination on the basis of ascriptive personal characteristics, according to the logic of Rawls's framework. This being the case, it is also true that if, *within* specific metropolitan regions, residents of some parts of the region enjoy educational opportunities vastly superior to those of residents in other parts, then norms of equality of opportunity are being violated.

There is widespread consensus among education and urban scholars that suburban public schools tend to be safer, better-managed, better-maintained, and better-staffed institutions than public schools in central cities.[19] As elaborated below, severe inequalities between neighborhoods will likely be regarded as unjust from a Rawlsian standpoint, particularly when we consider that mobility between neighborhoods is neither costless, nor, in some circumstances, possible. Yet, it is not initially obvious that the spatial pattern of *sprawl* itself can be implicated in such injustice; instead, the injustice might be thought to reside in the system of funding for public education in the United States, in which more than two-fifths of school expenditures are funded by local property taxes.[20] This system virtually ensures that wealthier localities will have more resources (especially relative to need) than will poor localities and will hence provide greater substantive opportunity to its residents. In theory, efforts to change this system of funding need not make any explicit attempt to reverse sprawl, although it is likely that drastic improvements in urban schools might, as a byproduct, lead to reduced demand for more sprawl.

Beyond Education: The Incompatibility of Concentrated Poverty and Equality of Opportunity

Simply equalizing educational resources across spatial environments is unlikely, taken alone, to be an adequate response to the reality of unequal opportunity within U.S. metropolitan areas, from a Rawlsian point of view. This is because the substance of unequal opportunity does not simply consist in unequal public schooling but in a host of interrelated social problems concentrated in some specific geographic areas and largely absent from others. Even if public schools in impoverished areas were equivalent in quality to suburban schools, residents of such environments would face numerous other handicaps with a substantive negative impact on their opportunities either to develop their own capabilities or to strive for certain careers or positions. In short, the very *existence* of neighborhoods with highly concentrated social problems is likely to be seen as unjustly denying equality of opportunity to its residents by any Rawlsian liberal familiar with these "social facts."

Iris Marion Young provides an eloquent description of the harms involved when systematic inequalities are embodied and reinforced by socio-spatial patterns. Whereas much research on urban poverty focuses primarily or exclusively on the harms done to poor neighborhoods, or debates strategies for improving living conditions and life prospects for residents of such neighborhoods, Young stresses that from the point of view of *justice,* the issue is not simply that of poverty, but of *inequality.* Scholars describing the poverty of disadvantaged neighborhoods, Young charges, "often fail to highlight the correlative privilege of those in predominantly white neighborhoods and communities that attends these same facts." After describing some of the advantages enjoyed by relatively affluent neighborhoods, Young goes on to make the critical empirical claim that "at least to a certain extent, the predominantly white neighborhoods and communities often *have* such amenities *because* the segregated neighborhoods do not. If city or regional economies often can support only a certain number of grocery stores, theaters, coffee-houses, and so on, then the choice of their location has a critical distributive effect. Presumably a city government has limited funds for garbage pick-up or fire protection. Thus if some neighborhoods have the privilege of excellent service, it is likely at the expense of other neighborhoods where service is poor."[21]

As stated, Young's empirical claim is highly contentious. Basic amenities of the sort Young describes tend to be absent from depressed neighborhoods not because there is a fixed number of such amenities available in any given urban economy, but because doing business in certain areas has often been perceived as excessively risky; contrary to this perception, many community-development efforts and some private entrepreneurs have had substantial success bringing just such amenities to urban neighborhoods.[22] But Young's larger proposition, that the existence of highly privileged neighborhoods whose privileges are intimately linked to the existence of severely deprived neighborhoods represents a *fundamentally unjust* form of inequality, would likely be accepted by Rawlsian liberals. Importantly, far more persuasive demonstrations of a causal link between the emergence of affluent suburbs and the deterioration of central cities than the claims ventured by Young can easily be specified (see below).

Note again, however, that the injustice of socio-spatial arrangements that provide very different life opportunities to residents of middle-class suburbs and residents of poor central city neighborhoods consists primarily in the social composition of these neighborhoods, not in their spatial layout per se. One might imagine a socio-spatial layout with degrees of racial and economic segregation comparable to those found in the contemporary United States but in which privileged, better-off residents were concentrated near the center of the city and poorer residents inhabited the metropolitan fringes. Indeed, such a socio-spatial pattern has frequently recurred in the history of Western cities.[23] The important point to keep in mind, for the sake of this discussion, is that while the historically specific phenomenon of urban sprawl in the United States may exemplify a socio-spatial relationship that unjustly hurts the life opportunities of residents of certain areas within the metropolitan region, very different spatial configurations (even those advocated by many contemporary critics of sprawl) could, at least in theory, yield the same injustices.

III. SPRAWL AND CONSTRAINED CHOICES

Socio-spatial arrangements also might become problematic for liberal egalitarians if the available human settlements in a given community (or society) are so similar in nature that the choices available to citizens about where to live are effectively limited. Traditionally, metropolitan fragmentation has been thought to increase citizens' ability to choose among a variety of community settings.[24] More recently, however, some critics have charged that the recurring pattern of sprawl development has introduced monotony and extinguished meaningful local differences in human settlements from one metropolitan area to the next, that sprawl is erasing the distinction between urban and rural life (harming those who favor a rural way of life), and that, because of the condition of U.S. cities, individuals who might prefer city life are compelled to live in suburbs simply to secure such basic goods as public safety. The green political theorist Peter Cannavó thus writes, "Contemporary development demonstrates little visual or spatial connection with its surroundings, whether built or natural. Instead, there is mass production and repetition of the same kinds of structures, architectural styles, landscaping and land uses from place to place, with little or no connection to local culture, history, or natural environment."[25] Loren King adds that "prevailing incentives for residential and commercial locations impose rigid constraints on ways of life in and around the city (for example, in many cities, a pedestrian-based lifestyle is restrictive and outright hazardous) and these incentives are in part sustained by local, state, and federal laws and government subsidies."[26] In a similar vein, David Imbroscio argues that mobility-based social policies that focus on relocating poor citizens from central cities to suburban locations undermine the freedom of citizens to live in a (healthy) central city environment.[27]

Rawlsian liberalism is capable of recognizing the force of such claims but would not describe "limitation of choice" as a violation of the two principles of justice per se. Such claims would be categorized by Rawls as pertaining to the "worth of liberty" but not to liberty itself; Rawls's principles of justice thus leave no reason to regard a situation in which the only type of housing unit available to a given society is a two-bedroom apartment in an apartment tower (or a small adobe brick house, or an igloo, or a tent) as fundamentally *unjust,* so long as it is produced by a political process that is itself just.[28] But Rawlsian liberals might regard the question of providing a variety of human settlements to citizens as relevant to efforts to maximize welfare—utility—within the framework of the principles of justice. Rawls tends to presume that promoting welfare is the default goal of social and economic policy, once the principles of justice have been realized.[29] If it could be shown that altering a society's socio-spatial arrangements would give citizens with different tastes greater scope for choice among living arrangements, and thereby increase utility, then Rawlsian liberals would likely favor such changes—but only as a matter of pragmatic utility maximization, not fundamental principle.[30]

IV. IS THE DIFFERENCE PRINCIPLE RELEVANT?

The Rawlsian seeking to apply principles of justice to the case of suburban sprawl might be tempted to proceed by asking, what sort of socio-spatial arrangements would a person in the original position adopt? Putting the matter this way, at one level, seems deeply inadequate: how could people in the original position possibly decide whether they wanted a society of high-density cities, low-density suburbs, or wholly rural areas with no information whatsoever about their own preferences or own way of life? But the proper way to apply Rawlsian ideas of justice to existing socio-spatial patterns is not to ask what sorts of communities Rawls's paper-thin hypothetical citizens would build if placed in the original position. The better method is rather to assume that these citizens would adopt the difference principle of distributive justice; having adopted this principle, they could then look at the actual social world (including their own preferences), and reason together to make informed decisions about how to apply the principle in practice.[31]

In thinking through what sort of socio-spatial arrangements distributive justice requires, Rawlsians might conceptualize neighborhoods as possessing bundles of resources and amenities and then proceed to make both qualitative and quantitative judgments about whether one neighborhood or locality possessed more-desirable bundles than another. These resources and amenities include public goods of all kinds—public educational institutions, transportation systems, usable public space, recreational facilities, public hygiene, police and fire protection, and law and order. The Rawlsian then might say that insofar as these resources and amenities contribute to the total consumption of resources by private individuals they ought to be subject to the difference principle in the same way that private income and wealth are. In short, any inequalities in the public amenities and resources available in different neighborhoods can be justified only if such inequalities can be understood as plausibly contributing to the well-being of the least well off. The most obvious way such an inequality in neighborhood resources could be justified is in the case where neighborhoods housing those with lower private incomes actually have *greater* publicly provided amenities than neighborhoods housing those with high private incomes.

The opposite scenario—in which neighborhoods housing the most affluent people also have the best public amenities—is, of course, far more common in contemporary U.S. society. The acceptance of *any* economic inequality among individuals under Rawls's theory of justice rests on the judgment that providing higher material rewards to certain individuals has positive economic and social effects: people will be more motivated to work harder, innovate, take risks, and so on.[32] The notion that those inequalities should carry over from the private realm into the realm of public goods has no such rationale. Indeed, we might think that providing equal opportunity virtually requires that the public amenities in each neighborhood be as equal as possible. The reasons are obvious, with respect to education, as discussed above. But they also apply to recreational facilities, parks, gardens, libraries, and other goods. Does a child who grows up without access to decent recreational facilities and public spaces have the same opportunity to develop himself or herself as one who has such access? How exactly do residents of a neighborhood that is unsafe, dirty, and lacks usable public space benefit from the fact that residents of other areas in the metropolitan region enjoy an abundance of safe, clean, usable public space?

I raise these questions simply to point out that the feature of Rawlsian distributive justice that has attracted the most scholarly attention and controversy—the difference principle—has only secondary relevance with regard to the *direct* evaluation of socio-spatial arrangements; the principles of equal opportunity and equal liberty are themselves an adequate basis from which to mount a powerful critique of large-scale place-based inequalities. Where the difference principle is of greater import in the sprawl debate is in the question of whether a given political culture is capable of generating and sustaining the social solidarity needed to implement the broader set of inequality-narrowing policies that the difference principle requires.

V. SEGREGATION AND SOLIDARITY: DOES SUBURBAN SPRAWL MAKE LIBERAL EGALITARIANISM IMPOSSIBLE?

Proposed solutions to the problem of achieving equality of opportunity in metropolitan regions, such as equalizing public funding throughout a region's schools, often fail to fully confront the deeper *political* reality created by the dominant socio-spatial pattern of U.S. metropolitan areas, which is that suburban constituencies in metropolitan regions are generally hostile to providing aid to central cities, or to sharing their tax base with such cities for the sake of equalizing structures of opportunity within U.S. society. Indeed, research by Juliet Gainsborough indicates that suburban residence is *in itself* a strong predictor of more-conservative views on social policy and hostility toward public aid for urban constituents (such as African Americans and food-stamp recipients)—even after controlling for a host of demographic variables.[33] As has been increasingly recognized and documented, suburban voters now form roughly one-half of the U.S. electorate, making political prospects for realizing equality of opportunity within current socio-spatial regimes even more daunting.

This observation points to the second major way in which suburban sprawl—or any socio-spatial complex—might be at odds with the requirements of Rawlsian justice: sprawl may help create a society that is incapable of realizing solidarity of the type that is *required* (by Rawls's own account) to realize liberal principles of justice. A central feature of Rawls's theory of justice is that each member of society must regard him or herself as participating in a common enterprise, the task of securing the principles and procedures of a just society. In this sense, Rawls agrees (explicitly) with thinkers such as Aristotle who criticized the view that the state is simply a mutual-protection pact (as suggested by Hobbes) or a mechanism for securing material advantage to society's members in an efficient way. For Rawls, while the just state does perform just those functions, there is a specifically moral quality to political association as well. Unlike Aristotle, Rawls does not think it possible or desirable for states to be founded upon a comprehensive moral consensus about what the best way of life is; but he does think it possible and desirable for states to achieve a moral consensus regarding principles of justice. Implementing such principles of justice in appropriate ways would, in turn, allow for a society in which individuals have equal freedom, or as much equal freedom as practicable, to pursue their own definitions of the good life.

Indeed, often overlooked in the various liberal-communitarian debates is the extent to which Rawls's theory, on its own terms, requires a sense of community and solidarity—even though *A Theory of Justice* could not be more explicit on this point.[34] Rawls describes and rejects versions of contract theory based on the ideal of "private society," in which "the persons comprising it, whether they are human individuals or associations, have their own private ends which are either competing or independent, but not in any case complementary." He writes,

> Institutions are not thought to have any value in themselves, the activity of engaging in them not being counted as a good but if anything a burden. Thus each person assesses social arrangements solely as a means to his private aims. No one takes account of the good of others, or what they possess; rather everyone prefers the most efficient scheme that gives him the largest share of assets.[35]

Rawls neatly summarizes, "Private society is not held together by a public conviction that basic arrangements are just and good in themselves, but by the calculations of everyone, or of sufficiently many to maintain the scheme, that any practicable changes would reduce the stock of means whereby they pursue their personal ends."[36]

Rawls does not want to tie his version of contract theory to such a bleak moral vision of actors wholly motivated by self-interest and viewing institutions purely instrumentally, as a mechanism for advancing that self-interest. Instead, Rawls develops the notion of the "social union," which involves humans joining together in a shared activity with a shared end in mind. Rawls likens a social union to a game in which all players agree to abide by a certain set of rules for the sake of increasing the enjoyment and satisfaction of all.[37] Likewise, in the well-ordered society, citizens must "have the common aim of cooperating together to realize their own and another's nature in ways allowed by the principles of justice. This collective intention is the consequence of everyone's having an effective sense of justice."[38]

Under what conditions might citizens in fact have this common aim? For Rawls, the fundamental point is that individuals intellectually assent to the principles of justice; that is, that they regard "the collective activity of justice [as] the preeminent form of human flourishing" and understand that by "maintaining these public arrangements...persons best express their nature and achieve the widest regulative excellences of which each is capable."[39]

This is an extremely demanding principle. Consider what specific features a society based upon such an all-encompassing social union must exhibit: First, citizens must not be motivated solely by self-interest but must be morally capable of having fair regard for the needs and interests of others, including people they do not know. Second, they must regard existing institutions as morally legitimate both in structure and practice. Third, groups within society must not believe themselves entitled to a share of society's benefits greater than that to which other groups are entitled, and they must not regard any other groups as unworthy of fully sharing such benefits. Fourth, the more privileged members of society must be willing to forgo certain benefits that a more privatistic conception of the social contract might allow them to attain, and they must be so committed to the principles of justice as a morally regulative ideal that they do not seek to exploit their advantages in ways that might subvert the system of justice. For instance, privileged groups must refrain from using wealth to exert disproportionate influence on the political process with the aim of securing some private end unlikely to be attained or fully attained in a fully realized just society. Well-designed institutions might help minimize such distortions but cannot eliminate them if privileged groups—including not just the wealthy, but the best educated, the most clever, the most attractive, and so on—are not themselves motivated in public action by respect for the principles of justice.

Each of these specific features is demanding in its own right; what Rawls is pointing to is a society capable of producing norms of justice so powerful that each member internalizes them and grows in the habit of situating his or her own legitimate interests and aspirations within the framework of the larger, common enterprise. To the question of "how might principles of justice come to be accepted?" the most powerful reply available to Rawls is, "in their very operation."[40] Institutions and practices do, in fact, help inculcate moral and social norms: popularly held ideas concerning what degree of income inequality represents unfairness, what the proper role of the state in the economy is, what a just system of voting entails, and whether or not citizens are entitled to guaranteed health care are all demonstrably variable among societies and across historical periods.[41] Just as Americans now have come to regard voting rights for all races and for both genders—a dramatic change in the past century—as a binding moral norm, with much greater support for universal suffrage than existed before its institution, and just as most conservatives in the United States now accept a mammoth government-run pension plan (Social Security) as morally legitimate, despite strong principled opposition to the scheme before its implementation, so it is that Rawls can plausibly theorize that citizens habituated to living in a society in which liberal principles of justice were realized would come in time to embrace such principles as binding moral norms.[42]

But Rawlsian thought risks lapsing into irrelevancy or sheer utopianism if it can be applied only to ideal, hypothetical societies, not existing societies with actual histories; and Rawls is serious in his intention that the principles of justice be realized in at least approximate form by contemporary Western democracies—even if none have so far. Within this frame, the sociological question of what sorts of societies might best be able to reach a moral consensus upon the principles of justice and then implement them naturally arises. It is perfectly reasonable to suggest that some kinds of institutional *and* cultural configurations may be more amenable to the principles of justice being realized than others. Rawls acknowledges this but, when considering the question, presupposes a society in which "favorable circumstances" are present. Some of these "circumstances" can be taken as simply historical givens, such as geography, history, racial composition, and other factors described by Tocqueville as "circumstances unconnected with human volition."[43]

But other "circumstances" are amenable to human adjustment or self-conscious alteration. These include, first, the specific characteristics of the institutions created to implement the principles of justice ("laws," in Tocqueville's usage), such as whether the political system is parliamentary in nature, how authority is divided among local or state as opposed to national units, how the executive and the judiciary are organized, what the voting rules (proportional representation or winner-take-all) are, and so forth.

A second circumstance potentially alterable by human volition involves the content of a nation's cultural norms (Tocqueville's "customs"). As Rawls recognized, public activity shapes the cultural norms (and diversity thereof) in a given society in countless ways. While Rawls (and more broadly, "neutralist" liberals) have argued that the state should not adjudicate among competing "comprehensive" worldviews (such as religious and ethical orientations), many contemporary liberals allow that the state must take a constructive interest in fostering virtues conducive to a liberal regime.[44]

A third set of "circumstances" potentially amenable to conscious human alteration through political processes is the organization of the "public sphere" itself, understanding "public sphere" in the Habermasian sense as publicly responsive institutions in which substantive debates concerning public matters take place. The public sphere thus includes the mass media but also smaller-circulation magazines and journals, local newspapers, some academic journals, and the Internet, in addition to lectures, speeches, public debates, and other forms of face-to-face communication.[45] The shape and general characteristics of this public sphere is one of the central elements defining any political regime, and most versions of liberalism can easily justify ongoing public regulation and oversight of the structure of the public sphere to help secure the good of free, democratic speech.

Finally, it can plausibly be suggested that the *organization of public, commercial, and residential space*—the spatial layout of communities—should be regarded as a fourth potentially alterable "circumstance" affecting prospects for Rawlsian liberal democracy, and that, consequently, Rawlsian liberalism should take an interest in which sorts of spatial and socio-spatial arrangements would best support the sort of public culture required by a just society. The political theorist Susan Bickford thus argues for "expand[ing] our focus on the public sphere to encompass the built environment that helps constitute that 'sphere'" and for understanding the built environment as "a space of attention orientation, a space that shapes citizens' sense of what people, perspectives, and problems are present in the democratic public."[46]

In particular, spatial arrangements may affect citizens' capacity to develop and express solidarity with one another. Loren King thus urges that "the political imagination of affluent citizens" should not "be constrained in ways harmful to democratic aspirations: if there are few visceral and enduring experiences of public life beyond carefully policed urban and suburban enclaves, then there is unlikely to be much willingness on the part of affluent citizens to imagine citizenship as requiring more than occasional fleeting acts of engagement across a variety of personal differences and spatial scales."[47] In short, socio-spatial contexts might plausibly structure the way citizens understand social reality and the way they do or do not regard one another as equal citizens worthy of equal moral concern. As Bickford argues, political theorists (especially theorists with egalitarian aspirations) need to pay attention to "how the built environment can cultivate or eradicate that specific stranger-like recognition that is central to the possibility of democratic politics in a diverse and unequal polity."[48] Rawlsians thus have excellent reason to interrogate sprawl as a social "circumstance" that may well be "unfavorable" to prospects for a just society.

Sprawl and Justice: What Does the Evidence Say?

This chapter has discussed several ways in which socio-spatial arrangements in general, and suburban sprawl in particular, might come into tension with the demands of Rawlsian justice. But what does the evidence say?

As an empirical matter, the notion that some places in the United States have more public amenities than others and provide better opportunities to its citizens than others is not a matter of serious doubt. Nor is it controversial to claim that suburbs, in general, are likely to provide more resources and more opportunities to citizens than depressed neighborhoods in large cities do. Neither of these widely accepted propositions, in themselves, necessitates a view that *sprawl* is exacerbating unjust inequalities among places, however. To make that claim persuasive, evidence on at least four further points is required.

First, we must have a sense of the *scale* of the inequality between affluent suburbs and less affluent central cities and older suburbs. In a partially decentralized political system, incidental inequalities between places are inevitable and may not be a matter of serious concern, especially if they do not substantially affect the life prospects of citizens.

Second, we must have reason to believe that there is a causal connection between suburban affluence and central city decay; in theory, at least, these could be unrelated phenomena, such that it would be a mistake to think that disproportionate suburban growth has actually made people in central cities worse off.

Third, we must have reason to think that "sprawl," a specific form of suburbanization that involves the continual growth of low-density, automobile-oriented development on the perimeters of metropolitan areas, has a negative effect distinct from the effects of suburbanization in general. As previously noted, Anthony Downs has made the contrary claim that sprawl contributes little, if anything, to the problems facing central cities beyond the general effects of suburbanization.

Fourth, we must have reason to think that plausibly available policy alternatives to sprawl might do a better job of realizing the principles of Rawlsian justice. It is not hard to imagine policies adopted under the banner of stopping sprawl negatively affecting the life chances and general well-being of the least well-off Americans, whether intentionally or not. The Rawlsian concerned with possible alternatives to sprawl thus needs to know how such effects can be avoided or mitigated.

A review of academic work on the causes and effects of socio-spatial inequalities in the United States indicates that the first two of these claims are not particularly controversial. Even so, it will be helpful to review briefly some of the most important evidence documenting those claims, before turning our attention to the more contentious third point. Finally, we will briefly address the fourth point by discussing how Rawlsians might weigh the charge that anti-sprawl policies will engender gentrification, with effects that might be as damaging to the realization of justice as sprawl itself.

SPATIAL INEQUALITY IN THE UNITED STATES:
HOW MUCH AND HOW SERIOUS?

Of what order of magnitude are the inequalities between suburban areas and central cities in the United States? Among urbanized metropolitan-area census tracts, median household income in 1999 in those census tracts with above-median density was $43,638, compared to $53,330 in tracts with below-median density (weighting for the number of households in a tract). To put it another way, residents of the newest neighborhoods(those built since 1985)—which tend to be located on the outer ring of metropolitan areas—lived in census tracts with (weighted) median household income averaging $62,730, compared to $39,764 for residents of neighborhoods in which the median date of home construction was in the 1940s or earlier.[49] This general picture is confirmed by Paul Jargowsky's thorough study of census tract–level income as reported in census data, which notes that, as of 1990, household income in areas built in the 1980s averaged more than $49,000, compared to a little more than $35,000 for tracts built in the 1940s.[50]

These broad differences in the economic status of suburban as compared to urban areas are important to keep in mind, yet in themselves may not cause serious alarm from a liberal egalitarian point of view. Income ratios on the order of 1.2 or 1.6 (for low-density areas) to 1 (for high-density areas), or income disparities between newer and older neighborhoods, might be seen as fairly incidental differences, especially if one could be confident that the residents of each sort of neighborhood had access to comparable public goods and services.

Much critical academic attention has thus focused on three additional issues: First, relatively modest *average* disparities between central cities and suburbs mask the much wider gap between residents of the richest suburbs and those of the poorest urban areas.[51] Taking the SCCBS data as a reference point, among metropolitan residents in the year 2000, 2,053 respondents (some 8.2 percent of metropolitan residents) lived in tracts with median household income under $25,000, with 90 percent of these residents living in central cities; the average such resident lived in a neighborhood in which 1953 was the median year in which the homes were constructed. On the other hand, some 2,417 metropolitan respondents lived in tracts where the median income exceeded $75,000. Just 31 percent of these respondents lived in central cities, in neighborhoods where the median home was built in 1971. In 2000, tract median household income (weighted by number of households) in the richest decile of urbanized metropolitan tracts in the U.S. Census as a whole averaged $93,976, compared to $20,186 in the poorest decile of such tracts.[52] This income ratio of more than 4.6 to 1 will properly cause much more alarm among liberal egalitarians; unless there were a very strong and active public sphere providing residents of the poorer areas with many amenities, one would naturally suspect that residents of the richest neighborhoods enjoyed amenities and a quality of life far superior to those of the poorest neighborhoods. This superiority would be very difficult to justify in terms of the principle of substantive equal opportunity.

This suspicion leads directly to the second issue frequently raised in scholarly analyses of the socio-spatial order in the United States: the existence of neighborhoods with concentrated poverty, and the particularly adverse effect that living in these neighborhoods is thought to have on individuals. As noted in chapter 2, William Julius Wilson's influential work on the relationship between economic decline and the emergence and perpetuation of urban underclasses argues that concentrated poverty tends to encourage isolation from mainstream society (and alienation from social norms and values) in addition to perpetuating social ills such as crime, drug trafficking, gang activity, and the like, all of which are additional disadvantages to children growing up in such neighborhoods, beyond the (already substantial) disadvantages that they are likely to be poor and that their neighbors are likely to be poor.[53] Scholars have identified substantial negative effects attributable to high concentrations of poverty in neighborhoods: Low-income residents of such areas are more likely to be unemployed than are poor persons living in areas where poverty is not concentrated; poorer students attending schools in well-off areas typically perform better than middle-class students attending mostly poor schools; drug and crime problems are more severe in schools in more impoverished areas.[54] As john powell stresses, "Concentrated poverty is best understood in terms of cumulative causation rather than in terms of a single indicator. The sorting process that generates concentrated poverty creates a web of opportunity-denying structures that limit the capacity of low-income minorities."[55]

The third prominent dimension of socio-spatial inequalities to consider is the fact that public goods and services are typically not of equal worth in richer and poorer neighborhoods. The case of public education is of marked interest to Rawlsians, especially given that Rawls specifically mentions equal educational opportunity as a sine qua non of the just society.[56] As already noted, a high concentration of poverty is linked to increased social problems in schools; not only are these problems bad in themselves, they also disrupt learning and force teachers to become babysitters and cops rather than purveyors of knowledge. A huge body of evidence demonstrates that, as Myron Orfield puts it, "monolithically poor central-city and inner-suburban schools sweep children toward failure on undercurrents that reinforce antisocial behavior, drifting, teenage pregnancy, and dropping out."[57]

Public schools in poorer areas can also be disadvantaged by inadequate funding. Because roughly 44 percent of local public education is financed locally there is generally a direct correlation between the size of a locality's tax base and the degree to which its public schools are well funded.[58] The Education Trust estimates that, after adjusting for differences in the cost of living across localities, average per-pupil public school expenditures undertaken by states and localities in 2004–5 were $938 higher in the quartile of all schools with the least poverty, compared to the quartile of schools with the highest proportion of impoverished students. (The report identified wide variations in the disparity from state to state, however, with the largest gaps found in New York, Illinois, Pennsylvania, Delaware, Michigan, and New Hampshire.) The average gap in spending between the quartile of districts with the highest proportion of racial minorities and the quartile of districts with the lowest proportion of minorities totaled $877, again with wide variation among states.[59] Most credible studies in recent years indicate that such funding disparities have important effects on student achievement, although per-pupil spending is just one factor among many determinants of student success.[60]

To be sure, low funding of urban (versus suburban) schools is *not* a universal phenomenon in U.S. metropolitan areas. Myron Orfield has shown that in the Twin Cities region, for instance, urban spending per student is higher than in suburban schools in the Minneapolis–St. Paul area; this general pattern of higher spending holds in more than half of the nation's twenty-five largest metropolitan areas.[61] Similarly, the Education Trust identifies four states in which spending in poorer districts is at least $1,000 higher per student than in richer districts (Alaska, Massachusetts, Minnesota, and New Jersey). Equal or even higher spending, however, does not mean that urban schools, especially those with high levels of poverty and racial segregation, actually provide equivalent educational experiences: the additional spending in areas such as Minneapolis–St. Paul tends to be more than offset by the negative effects of concentrated poverty. (As well, older urban schools often have higher infrastructure and deferred maintenance costs.) As Orfield observes, middle-class families have not been anxious to move back into urban school districts just because (at least in the Twin Cities) such districts have spent up to 15 percent more per pupil than have suburban districts in the area. He notes that, instead, "the existing level of poverty and student diversity are overriding deflectors."[62] The Education Trust points out that if we assume that children growing up in poverty need 40 percent more resources devoted to them to offset their initial disadvantages, then the effective national gap between per-pupil spending in the poorest quartile of school districts and in the wealthiest quartile rises to more than $1,500, a disparity of roughly 20 percent.[63]

Table 4.1 summarizes evidence of the disparity between urban and suburban schools. High-poverty schools with a large portion of students receiving free lunches report less-positive student attitudes, more disruptive behavior, and more faculty turnover than do low-poverty schools. Such schools are far more likely to be located in central cities, just as low-poverty schools are far more likely to be found in the suburbs. Central city schools consequently have more serious difficulties than do their suburban counterparts on a range of social indicators, such as student preparedness, absenteeism, and physical conflict.

From a Rawlsian perspective, policy thus can either increase per-student expenditure in poor areas to the extent that the serious educational difficulties associated with concentrated social problems are offset—likely an impossible task—or find ways to ensure that no public school is overloaded with very poor children likely to have serious problems that disrupt learning. Rawlsian-inspired policy analysts are likely to conclude that the underlying issue is the very existence of concentrated high-poverty neighborhoods, which impedes the realization of substantive equality of opportunity, beyond the disadvantages associated with growing up in a poor household.[64]

TABLE 4.1. Inequality in Public Schools

High poverty vs. low poverty schools; elementary schools, 2000.

	High Free Lunch (>75%)	Low Free Lunch (<10 %)
Average Student in School Has a "Very Positive" Attitude	28.5%	79.5%
Fighting a Serious or Moderate Problem in School	22.0%	2.3%
Likelihood of at Least 1% of Teachers Leaving School before End of Academic Year	35.8%	5.9%

Urban vs. suburban schools, secondary schools, 1999–2000.

	Urban Schools	Suburban Schools
Students Unprepared to Learn a Serious Issue	42.3%	27.8%
Student Apathy a Serious Issue	36.9%	28.8%
Student Tardiness a Serious Issue	25.9%	14.0%
Student Absenteeism a Serious Issue	35.1%	19.2%
Students Dropping Out a Serious Issue	18.5%	6.9%
Physical Conflicts a Serious Issue	6.4%	2.5%
Student Alcohol Use a Serious Issue	15.2%	18.4%
Student Drug Abuse a Serious Issue	14.9%	14.1%

Enrollment in low and high poverty schools by geography and race, 2006–7.

Proportion Students Attending School With:	High Free Lunch (>75%)	Low Free Lunch (<10%)
Urban (All)	32.2%	7.6%
—Whites (Non-Hispanic)	9.8%	12.9%
—Blacks	45.7%	2.0%
Suburban (All)	9.7%	23.5%
—Whites (Non-Hispanic)	2.4%	32.6%
—Blacks	18.3%	6.7%

Sources: National Center for Education Statistics, Condition of Education 2003, tables 12-2, 30-2. Urban-suburban comparison based on surveys of secondary school teachers' perception of obstacles to learning in public schools in 1999–2000 school year. Suburban category includes schools in larger towns located outside metropolitan areas. National Center for Education Statistics, Condition of Education 2009, table A-25-1. Public elementary and secondary schools, 2006–7.

To be sure, even critics of the ill effects of concentrated poverty allow that it is still possible for some people growing up in very poor areas to "succeed" in terms of the conventional measures of educational accomplishment and economic advancement; but what Rawlsian egalitarians are concerned with is "equal opportunity," in the substantive sense. No serious urban scholar in the United States today argues that residents, particularly children, living in areas marked by high concentrations of poverty enjoy anything like equal opportunity compared to residents of typical middle-class suburban neighborhoods (to say nothing of the opportunities available in the nation's richest areas).

THE LINK BETWEEN SUBURBAN AFFLUENCE
AND URBAN POVERTY

But is suburbanization to blame for these inequalities, and for the existence of high-poverty neighborhoods? Urban scholars have linked the U.S. pattern of suburbanization with the concentration of poverty in urban areas in at least six ways. First, historians of suburbanization such as Robert Fishman trace the origins of suburbs in eighteenth- and nineteenth-century England to an explicit desire by affluent classes to separate themselves spatially from working- and lower-class life.[65] As cities became centers of industry in addition to home to large working-class populations, suburbs became an attractive alternative for bourgeoisie seeking to distance themselves not only from the noise, pollution, and other externalities associated with industrial activity but also from the workers themselves. Notably, Fishman observes that the flight of the well-to-do to suburban environments in nineteenth-century England was more thorough and more extensive in those cities (such as Manchester) that were most thoroughly industrialized and had the worst living conditions for working classes.[66] (The historian Robert Fogelson describes how a similar process unfolded in the United States when suburbs initially emerged between 1870 and 1930.)[67] Equally important, Fishman takes pains to argue that this desire for spatial separation by class was a necessary but *not* sufficient condition for suburbanization; in other European countries, such as France, elites found ways to achieve the desired separation *within* urban areas.[68]

In the case of both England and the United States, suburbanization became the desired mechanism for creating middle- and upper-middle-class neighborhoods divorced from industrial processes and industrial working classes, and, more to the point, from poor people.[69] In the case of the United States, the causal connection between urban stress and the relocation of affluent classes to suburban communities could not be clearer: if upper-middle-class people can move to jurisdictions sufficiently far from central cities, then their property cannot be taxed to help pay for urban infrastructure, social programs, and the like. Local governments in the United States are far more dependent on locally generated revenues (over three-fifths of local government expenditure is self-funded) than are local governments in most

European nations, meaning the consequences of middle-class exit for urban fiscal health are particularly severe.[70] As Myron Orfield has argued at length, in recent decades older, inner-ring suburbs have also fallen victim to the outward movement of affluent populations and, in some cases, are actually worse off than urban areas (which still generally tend to maintain fairly stable cores of business activity and some affluent citizens, leading to stronger tax bases than can be found in decaying older suburbs).[71]

A second causal connection between suburban growth and urban decline concerns the location of jobs. As the economist Edward Glaeser has stressed, the declining importance of rail- and port-based transportation hubs in the U.S. industrial economy, combined with the rising importance of cars and trucks, opened up dramatic new possibilities for the decentralization of employment, even in the manufacturing sector. With less compelling need to be near a shipyard or some other major transport outlet, firms could move to suburbs or elsewhere, taking advantage of cheaper land prices. Recent innovations in communications technology have further hastened the wholesale shift of jobs to suburbs. Such employment decentralization has had a severe effect on numerous U.S. cities, many of which have struggled to replace the jobs (and tax base) that moved away. This trend continues undiminished: a 2009 study published by the Brookings Institution reported that employment decentralization characterized 17 of 18 industries studied in some 98 metropolitan areas during the 1998–2006 period. In these metropolitan areas, 45 percent of employees worked at least ten miles away from the central business district; just 21 percent worked within three miles of downtown.[72]

A third causal connection between suburban affluence and urban stress, emphasized strongly by the urban scholar Anthony Downs and many other analysts, is the prevalence of exclusionary zoning practices in suburban areas, which make it more difficult, if not impossible, for low-income people to find affordable housing in suburban areas. "Many middle-income and upper-income households establish independent jurisdictions to pass local zoning, building, subdivision, and other regulations that raise the costs of housing high enough to exclude low-income people," notes Downs. "It is much easier for middle- and upper-middle-income residents to exert enough local political control to engage in exclusionary zoning if they live in small, relatively homogenous localities."[73] Such districts may, for instance, require lots to be a certain size, thereby mandating single-family houses and eliminating the possibility of row houses or other, more dense forms, or they may place strict restrictions on rental housing. In addition, affluent suburban communities typically staunchly resist efforts to locate public housing within their communities.[74] The material incentives behind such exclusionary policies are powerful; because, for most Americans, family net worth (and long-term retirement plans) is intimately connected with the value of their homes, no one wants to see changes that could adversely affect property values.[75] Poor people and the problems they are thought to bring (crime, etc.), in addition to minority groups, especially African Americans, are seen as direct threats to local property values. State and federal courts have upheld many forms of exclusionary zoning that are not explicitly racial, on grounds that local communities have the right to shape their environment to produce a desired quality of life.[76]

A fourth mechanism by which suburban affluence can be linked to urban stress is the disproportionate share of public subsidies that suburban areas receive, particularly from the federal government. In fiscal year 2008, for instance, the expected value of the tax deduction offered on home-mortgage interest payments—claimed disproportionately by suburbanites—was projected to be nearly $95 billion, compared to $16 billion in Section VIII subsidies for low-income renters. (Total discretionary spending by the Department of Housing and Urban Development, which primarily flows to central city areas, is estimated to total roughly $38.5 billion.)[77] While central city homeowners are also offered the mortgage deductions, the benefits disproportionately flow to residents of suburban communities. Other subsidies take the form of highway-construction spending, low fuel taxes (compared to other rich nations), subsidies for parking fees and widespread provision of free parking, and highway-patrol spending in automobile-heavy areas.[78] Importantly, such subsidies to suburban residents are rarely publicly scrutinized or challenged by mainstream politicians; in contrast, direct spending on urban needs and attention to urban issues often reflects current political tides. Federal aid constituted some 15 percent of city budgets in 1977; today the figure is 3 percent.[79] As Bruce Katz and Joel Rogers have noted, such shifts "lower the costs to individuals and firms of living and working outside or on the outer fringes of metropolitan areas, and increase the costs of living and working in the core."[80] Thus, when making the case for a causal connection between suburban affluence and urban distress, it may be contentious to claim, as Iris Marion Young did, that there is a fixed amount of urban amenities and businesses in any given metropolitan area, but such a claim would be far more valid with regard to the expenditure of public resources. Suburban subsidies are larger than commonly understood and are nearly untouchable politically, but federal resources available to urban communities are limited, both in total financial terms and, even more so, relative to existing needs, and are politically vulnerable.

A fifth connection between suburbanization and metropolitan-level inequality concerns the distribution of the costs and benefits associated with the relocation of development from established urban areas to greenfields. Here the work of Persky and Wiewel is of particular importance. As noted in chapter 2, Persky and Wiewel's comparison of the costs and benefits associated with opening a new factory in a greenfield location as opposed to in a central city identified only a slight efficiency cost associated with sprawl. But Perksy and Wiewel's subsequent analysis of the distributional consequences of job sprawl produced striking findings.

First, low-income households (those earning less than $25,000 a year) bear 40 percent of the private externalities associated with sprawl, compared to just 27 percent for households earning over $75,000 annually. This discrepancy is driven by the fact that lower-income households overwhelmingly bear the costs associated with job–spatial mismatch.[81] Conversely, 90 percent of the *benefits* of job sprawl accrue to households earning more than $75,000 a year; this is because such benefits consist largely of the lower wage and tax rates associated with suburban development. Economic theory predicts that suburban workers with shorter commutes to a suburban employer will accept lower wages than those with longer commutes into the city. For example, in the Chicago area, Persky and Wiewel find that suburban wages are markedly lower among highly skilled women who place a high premium upon maintaining a short commute (these women accept a lower wage to work near their suburban residence rather than travel all the way into the city). Benefits from these lower suburban wages largely accrue to the owners of capital, and capital ownership is disproportionately held by affluent households. Finally, public-sector costs associated with job sprawl must be taken into account; these are paid largely (52 percent) by middle-income households (those earning between $25,000 and $50,000/year), although affluent households bear a higher share (33 percent) than do low-income households (15 percent). Taking these three categories together, locating a one hundred–employee factory in a greenfield rather than in a central city results in net annual costs of $636,000 for low-income households, but net annual gains of $1,534,000 for residents of more-affluent households. In short, Persky and Wiewel's work illustrates how, by transferring benefits from workers and taxpayers to owners of capital, job decentralization produces a strikingly regressive shift in the distribution of income. This shift also has a clear geographic component: while the biggest gainers in this income shift are shareholders living outside the metropolitan area, the biggest losers are central city residents.[82]

Finally, it should be noted that suburban flight contributes to what scholars of urban political economy term the "economic dependence" of cities—that is, the degree to which local government is dependent on highly mobile business (and highly mobile wealthy citizens) as a source of tax revenue. This dependence gives both business and the well-off a privileged position in local urban politics, weakening citizens' capacity to substantively affect policy through concerted action and taking certain kinds of political outcomes (such as aggressive redistributive efforts) effectively off the table at the local level.[83] Suburbanization exacerbates this dependence: not only must central cities compete with other cities within (and, to some degree, outside) the United States to attract investment, but they must also compete with their own suburbs. Public choice theorists such as James Buchanan have pointed out that, in this situation, it becomes rational for local government—acting in the majority interest—to offer special incentives to the rich to stay in town, even when this requires policies that exacerbate inequalities.[84] In short, the reality of suburban flight contributes not only to inter-jurisdictional inequalities between residents of affluent suburbs and those of struggling cities but also to intra-jurisdictional political and social inequalities within cities themselves.

BUT IS "SPRAWL" ITSELF LINKED TO METROPOLITAN INEQUALITIES?

The consensus among urban scholars upholds the twin proposition that inequalities among spatial locations in the United States are substantial and seriously affect citizens' life chances and that suburban growth and affluence are causally linked in at least five fundamental ways to the pressures on central cities and on their residents. Such pressures are caused by fiscal strains on cities resulting from the relocation of households to suburbs; fiscal strains and wage losses associated with the relocation of jobs from central cities to suburbs; exclusionary suburban zoning; a disproportionate flow of public subsidies to suburban residents; and the exacerbation of political inequality within cities, as their fiscal and economic position weakens. To return to the distinction made at the outset of this chapter, the social and demographic *structure* of U.S. metropolitan regions—who lives where, and who has access to what resources—is clearly deeply intertwined with the process of suburbanization that has unfolded in the United States over the past sixty years. The more difficult question is whether, apart from these general suburbanization effects, the specific *spatial* attributes associated with sprawl distinctively worsen socio-spatial inequalities.

One straightforward way in which sprawl, understood in this more specific sense, tends to harm low-income residents is by, in effect, requiring metropolitan residents to own or have consistent access to cars to be full economic citizens. Several studies have identified lack of access to automobiles as a major disadvantage to poorer citizens in U.S. metropolitan areas, a disadvantage that is obviously exacerbated by the degree to which urban areas are designed around the automobile. Amy Helling argues that personal mobility is essential to take advantage of economic opportunities within contemporary metropolitan regions but notes that families with low per-capita incomes (less than $10,000 per year) are twice as likely as the average household with children not to own a car, according to the 1995–96 Nationwide Personal Transportation Survey.[85] Stephen Raphael and Michael Stoll studied the effect of access to a car on metropolitan employment patterns and found that raising car-ownership rates among African Americans to the same level as whites would reduce the employment gap between blacks and whites by (depending on how car ownership is measured) 21 to 43 percent.[86] In a related finding, Stoll has also shown that decentralization of jobs within metropolitan areas is strongly linked to spatial–job mismatch among African Americans, even when controlling for size of the metropolitan area.[87] These findings, in turn, inform Glaeser and Kahn's judgment that "the primary social problem associated with sprawl is the fact that some people are left behind because they do not earn enough to afford the cars that this form of living requires."[88] Glaeser and Kahn are not persuaded that this problem is so severe that sprawl itself should be reversed; instead, they suggest that this effect can be offset simply by increasing subsidies for private transportation for poor people.[89]

Other scholars have attempted to link specific aspects of sprawl more ambitiously with concomitant urban *decline*. Anthony Downs's study, one of the first noteworthy studies addressing this relationship, concludes that "sprawl" is not responsible for exacerbating harms to central city areas within metropolitan regions. Downs constructed two indices—one measuring sprawl, and one measuring urban decline in the 1980s—and tested the relationship between the two measures in 162 metropolitan areas. Included in this index of sprawl were the percentage of workers in a metropolitan area who drive to work, population density outside of a metropolitan area, percentage of metropolitan-area residents living outside an urbanized area's boundaries, the number of municipal governments per hundred thousand residents in each metropolitan area, percentage of metropolitan-area residents living outside a central city, total physical urbanized area in a metropolitan region, ratio of central city density to fringe-area density, and ratio of central city poverty rate to suburban poverty rate. Included in the index of urban decline were the change in the population of central cities between 1980 and 1990, per-capita income in the city, change in central city population between 1990 and 1994, high school dropout rate, proportion of high school graduates, percentage of housing units built before 1940, violent crime rate, and unemployment and poverty rates.

Downs found a modest positive correlation between a high sprawl-index score and his index of urban decline, but upon further investigation concluded that just three factors—the city–suburban poverty ratio, the percentage of metropolitan-area residents in the central city, and fragmentation of local government—were the driving forces behind this finding. On their own, Downs argued, density, transit patterns, overall land area, and percentage of population on the metropolitan fringe had little effect on urban decline. This led Downs to conclude that exclusionary zoning, not the purely spatial features of sprawl, has the most impact on urban decline.[90] Downs thus concludes that reducing low-density development alone is unlikely to benefit urban centers, unless steps are simultaneously taken to reduce exclusionary zoning, better subsidize low-income housing, and remove obstacles to development in central cities.[91]

At first glance, these findings appear to support libertarian-minded arguments that suburban sprawl is not fundamentally linked to urban decline.[92] That conclusion should be resisted, however. First, those are not the conclusions Downs himself draws; Downs argues that the dominant pattern of suburbanization has hurt central cities, but that the crucial mechanism is the socially exclusionary practices of suburban communities, not their spatial design.[93] Indeed, Downs's findings are fully consonant with a key theme of this chapter: what is decisive for social justice is less the organization of space per se than the set of social arrangements that that organization serves. Second, Downs's own definition of sprawl has been sharply criticized by other researchers for combining social and spatial factors for reasons that are not always clear. It is not clear, for instance, why the proportion of older neighborhoods in a given metropolitan area should be included as an indicator of urban decline rather than as an indicator of (lack of) sprawl.[94]

Third, and most importantly, the dependent variable in Downs's study—urban decline—is analytically distinct from *inequalities* between urban and suburban areas. Indeed, it is striking that Downs counts the city-to-suburban poverty ratio as part of the *definition* of sprawl. Yet, from a liberal egalitarian point of view, it is the level of inequality between cities and suburbs (not marginal changes in central city health over time) that is of fundamental interest. Rawlsian egalitarians will want to know whether the particular spatial features associated with "sprawl" are connected to the effective disparity in income (and presumably, life chances) between richer and poorer parts of our metropolitan areas. That is a question that Downs's study cannot (quite literally by design) help us answer.

Other researchers, however, have shed some light on Rawls's question by examining the relationship between socioeconomic *segregation* and spatial patterns. Paul Jargowsky, for instance, uses a relatively simple measure of sprawl—neighborhood age—to study the relationship between suburban growth patterns and economic segregation. Jargowsky examines the 1990 U.S. Census and concludes that the most recently built census tracts (overwhelmingly on the suburban fringe) are as a group more economically homogeneous (as measured by the normalized standard deviation of household income) than older neighborhoods. Jargowsky notes the standard deviation of median household income in newer neighborhoods is, relative to average median income in such neighborhoods, smaller than in older neighborhoods. Jargowsky thus concludes that sprawl can be linked with the spatial separation of economic classes, which, in turn, has negative effects on central cities.[95]

In more recent work, Jargowsky and Rebecca Yang conclude that several features of suburbanization (measured at the metropolitan statistical area [MSA] level) continue to be linked to economic segregation, even though concentrated poverty dissipated substantially during the 1990s due to strong economic growth and other factors. Cross-sectional analysis indicates that metropolitan areas in which newer neighborhoods are more economically homogeneous and in which central city residents' commuting times are longer (an indication that jobs have moved farther from the center) are more likely to be segregated economically; MSAs with more homogeneous new neighborhoods were also more likely to experience increases in levels of economic segregation over the 1990s.[96]

Additionally, a related study by Rolf Pendall and John Carruthers found that metropolitan areas with a higher proportion of older neighborhoods (measured as housing built prior to 1939) have lower levels of economic segregation; their study found that the physical expanse of the metropolitan area is also associated with greater segregation, net of other factors. Notably, however, Pendall and Carruthers also found that increased metropolitan-wide density is often associated with *greater* economic segregation; higher densities entail greater competition for shared space and hence more extensive sorting. Very dense metropolitan areas, however, can actually decrease income segregation by creating what the authors term a "fishbowl" effect, as groups are compelled to live in closer proximity with one another. Hence, the relationship between density as such and income segregation within the metropolis is context-dependent.[97]

To be sure, many other factors contribute to metropolitan-wide segregation. In particular, metropolitan areas with higher per capita incomes and greater inequalities in household income will tend to have a more thorough spatial sorting of households by income, and metropolitan areas with larger proportions of African American or Hispanic households also exhibit greater degrees of income segregation.[98] The effect of purely spatial factors compared to these broader demographic considerations appears to be modest. It is certainly reasonable to conclude that metropolitan-wide development patterns marked by continual growth of new, economically homogeneous and auto-dependent neighborhoods spatially separated from the poor will contribute to greater between-neighborhood inequality and economic segregation. But the literature to date suggests that an analyst with a Rawlsian lens should be preoccupied primarily not with the marginal contribution that metropolitan-wide spatial factors make to the exacerbation of inequality, but with the fact that a spatially marked pattern of wide inequalities is evident in virtually every U.S. metropolitan area.

The nature of the relationship between spatial characteristics and income becomes evident when we turn back to the census tract level. Using 2000 U.S. Census data, I examine the relationship between two key spatial characteristics associated with sprawl—transit patterns and neighborhood age—and both income and racial segregation. Tables 4.2 through 4.6 report, first, the descriptive relationship between spatial characteristics and economic and racial diversity.

TABLE 4.2. Socioeconomic Characteristics of Urban Census Tracts, Sorted by Neighborhood Age (Median Year Housing Unit Built)

	% White	Median Inc.	Poverty Rate	% Affluent	CV
Prior to 1940	66.8%	$39,936	18.1%	19.0%	.548
1940s	56.1%	$38,970	18.3%	18.3%	.482
1950s	64.5%	$43,949	14.8%	21.6%	.490
1960s	68.5%	$46,182	13.9%	23.4%	.478
1970s	74.9%	$48,747	11.1%	25.3%	.409
1980s	79.1%	$55,956	8.0%	30.9%	.367
1990s	80.9%	$66,743	5.6%	40.2%	.325

Source: 2000 U.S. Census, Summary File 3, author's analysis. n = 45,492 metropolitan tracts, totaling 201 million people. Percent affluent refers to percentage of households earning greater than $75,000/year. CV (coefficient of variation) refers to the standard deviation of neighborhood income divided by mean neighborhood income within each category. Higher values indicate higher levels of economic diversity. Proportion white includes white Hispanics. Census tracts less than 50% urbanized excluded; reported results weighted by tract population.

TABLE 4.3. Socioeconomic Characteristics of Urban Census Tracts, Sorted by Automobile Reliance (Proportion of Solo Automobile Commuters in Tract)

	% White	Median Inc.	Poverty Rate	% Affluent	CV
Less than 50%	41.9%	$33,481	27.1%	15.8%	.559
50–60%	44.3%	$35,525	23.9%	15.5%	.595
60–70%	54.8%	$39,765	19.2%	18.3%	.537
70–80%	70.3%	$47,557	12.0%	24.0%	.452
80–90%	84.9%	$56,225	6.4%	31.1%	.353
More than 90%	91.7%	$60,315	4.2%	35.0%	.297

Source: 2000 U.S. Census, Summary File 3, author's analysis. n = 45,474 metropolitan census tracts, totaling 201 million people. Percent affluent refers to percentage of households earning greater than $75,000/year. CV (coefficient of variation) refers to the standard deviation of neighborhood income divided by mean neighborhood income within each category. Proportion white includes white Hispanics. Census tracts less than 50% urbanized or with no workers excluded; reported results weighted by tract population.

Tables 4.2 and 4.3 show that as a descriptive matter, race and income are substantially correlated with neighborhood spatial characteristics. Poverty rates are highest in older neighborhoods and in neighborhoods less dependent on automobiles; median income and proportion of residents in the top quartile of income are highest in new, more car-intensive neighborhoods. Race is also correlated with neighborhood age and, to a striking degree, automobile reliance. Finally, newer and more automobile-dependent neighborhoods, as a group, are more homogeneous economically than older, less car-dependent

TABLE 4.4. Concentrations of Poverty and Wealth

	% Solo Drivers	Median Year Home Built	% Out-of-Town Commuters
Greater Than 40% of Persons Live in Poverty (1)	46.1%	1959	35.0%
Greater Than 40% of Households Earn >$100k (2)	77.6%	1973	76.4%
Greater Than 40% of Households Earn between $100k and $200k (3)	81.3%	1983	79.9%

Source: 2000 U.S. Census, Summary File 3, author's analysis. Metropolitan tracts at least 50% urbanized only. Weighted by tract population. (1) 2,186 tracts, totaling 6,972,000 people; (2) 2,776 tracts, totaling 12,612,000 people; (3) 503 tracts, totaling 2,389,000 people.

TABLE 4.5.   Black-Only and White-Only Neighborhoods

	% Solo Drivers	Median Year Home Built	% Out-of-Town Commuters
Greater Than 98% of Tract Is White (1)	83.8%	1966	82.0%
Greater Than 90% of Tract Is Black (2)	56.1%	1954	38.8%

Source: 2000 U.S. Census, Summary File 3, author's analysis. Metropolitan tracts at least 50% urbanized only. Weighted by tract population. (1) 1,496 tracts, totaling 5,760,000 people, includes white Hispanics; (2) 2,010 tracts, totaling 6,123,000 people, includes black Hispanics.

neighborhoods. (Following Jargowsky, economic diversity is measured as the standard deviation of neighborhood incomes divided by mean neighborhood income within each category.) Those neighborhoods most recently built (since 1980) and most auto-dependent (with more than 80 percent solo commuting) are particularly homogeneous. In short, even though it is the case that poverty rates have increased in recent years in some suburbs (in 2005, the total number of poor people living in suburbs exceeded, for the first time, the number of poor people living in central cities),[99] racial minorities and the poor continue to be disproportionately located in prototypical urban neighborhoods.

Tables 4.4 and 4.5 use a slightly different method to tell a similar story. Here we see that neighborhoods with very high poverty (greater than 40 percent impoverishment) tend to be in moderately old neighborhoods with a lower proportion of cars, in a central city environment. Neighborhoods with a high proportion of affluent people are located in more recently built areas with suburban commuting patterns and heavy automobile dependence. (Interestingly, the correspondence between affluence and suburban location becomes more pronounced if we exclude the very rich—those able to live in central cities at a very high living standard—and confine analysis to those earning between $100,000 and $200,000.) A similar pattern is evident with race. Census tracts that are virtually whites-only are likely to be located in suburban tracts that rely heavily on cars; census tracts that are overwhelmingly African American tend to be in central city areas with fewer cars.

Finally, table 4.6 addresses the issue a slightly different way by looking at which neighborhoods have the highest levels of internal economic diversity. There is far more likely to be a substantial proportion of poverty (greater than 6 percent) in affluent urban neighborhoods than in affluent suburban neighborhoods.

TABLE 4.6.   Spatial Distribution of Economically Segregated and Integrated Affluent Neighborhoods

Neighborhoods in which more than 30% of households earn at least $100,000 a year.

	% Solo Drivers	Median Year Home Built	% Out-of-Town Commuters
Fewer than 1% of persons live in poverty (1)	82.6%	1978	82.3%
Greater than 6% of persons live in poverty (2)	63.9%	1964	56.0%

Source: 2000 U.S. Census, Summary File 3, author's analysis. Metropolitan tracts only. Weighted by tract population. (1) 497 tracts; total population of 2,016,000; (2) 609 tracts; total population of 2,453,000.

It is important to stress that in the case of neither economic diversity nor racial diversity can we draw any conclusions about causality in this analysis; that is, we cannot say that sprawl *causes* the formation of economically and racially homogeneous neighborhoods. As we have already seen, there is good reason to think that it may often be quite the other way around, that the desire to achieve economic and racial homogeneity often stimulates development patterns recognizable as "sprawl."

When paired with our observations about the relationship between MSA-level indicators of sprawl and between-neighborhood inequalities, a portrait of sprawl as both cause and effect of social inequalities emerges. The desire to live in a neighborhood with strong public goods and away from concentrated social problems stimulates a process in which those with the means to do so move into economically privileged neighborhoods; these are often relatively new, highly car-dependent neighborhoods. In this sense, sprawl is simply the result of a sorting process; from a Rawlsian point of view it is the sorting process itself that is most objectionable, not the fact that in the U.S. context it has frequently led to metropolitan decentralization. Once established, however, sprawling spatial patterns often exacerbate place-based inequalities: not only are poor central city residents shut out of access to the superior public goods available in more affluent suburbs, lack of transportation and other obstacles damage their ability to access suburban employment opportunities, thus reinforcing their economically marginal position.

Looking forward, the distinction made here between "suburbanization" and "sprawl" may tend to diminish in importance as time goes on. Downs (and others) portray suburbanization as fundamentally a mechanism by which the well-to-do seek to separate themselves from the poor and establish havens of desirable living.[100] In the absence of substantial motivational changes in the behavior of middle-class Americans seeking a nice home in a nice community, the suburbanization process is likely to continue, at least among the middle-class and affluent families with children. But this, in turn, implies yet more building on the perimeter of metropolitan areas and continued spatial expansion of metropolitan areas in general (especially as older, closer-in suburbs both decay economically and become more diverse ethnically, motivating those who can afford it to move even farther away from the central city). In short, in the absence of very substantial policy changes or very substantial, long-term changes in the price of key inputs (e.g., gasoline), future waves of suburbanization are likely to take the form of what is now descriptively called "sprawl."

Going forward, then, the more useful analytic distinction is likely not between suburbanization and sprawl but between the spatial and social dimensions of sprawl. To reiterate, it is the socially exclusionary dimensions of suburbanization and sprawl—the way spatial arrangements facilitate unjust *social* relationships—that should command the primary attention of concerned normative theorists. Nonetheless, it also appears to be the case that, at least in the United States, certain metropolitan spatial patterns are *more conducive* to social exclusion than others, in particular, spatial patterns marked by growth on the suburban fringe that involve the creation of new, distinct communities beyond the reach (and taxing authority) of existing metropolitan municipalities, and spatial patterns that deny carless poor people access to large segments of the metropolis.

One useful way, then, of clarifying the nature of the relationship between sprawl and inequality of opportunity encoded in geography is to ask, which sprawl-related dimensions of the existing metropolitan pattern would need to be altered to markedly redress such inequality? Seven key features of the existing pattern stand out:

1. the practice of exclusionary suburban zoning, which shuts off access to proximate suburbs to working-class and poor people;
2. the high degree of automobile dependency, which makes suburban locations unlivable for those without cars and which puts many suburban employment opportunities out of the reach of central city residents;
3. the tendency to funnel new housing construction into economically homogeneous new developments rather than into existing neighborhoods, facilitating a more thorough spatial sorting of the affluent from the poor;

4. the manner in which deconcentration of employment ("job sprawl") creates spatial-mismatch costs borne by lower-income central city residents while also (via lower wages) increasing returns to owners of capital;

5. the unequal provision of public goods between poorer urban areas and more-affluent suburban areas, particularly with respect to public education and public safety;

6. the isolation of neighborhoods of concentrated poverty from the resource base of the more affluent parts of the metropolitan area, which makes it possible for more-affluent residents to live in largely self-contained neighborhoods without being asked to contribute to the well-being of poor neighborhoods in dire straits; and

7. the very presence of an "exit option" in the outer suburbs for middle-class or affluent citizens who wish to continue to access the benefits of living in a metropolitan area while separating themselves from the costs and problems associated with poverty and other urban ills. This ever-present possibility of middle-class and affluent flight contributes to *internal* inequality within cities, as city politicians feel compelled (in order to hold on to what's left of the tax base) to enact policies disproportionately favoring relatively affluent residents (to the degree this is possible) and policies favoring business interests.

Taken together, these seven features of U.S. metropolitan areas act as an inequality-reproducing machine.[101] Few of these features are directly tied to specific spatial characteristics; but all seven are related to the ongoing decentering of our metropolitan areas and the ways in which low-density development on the metropolitan fringe permits and encourages the separation of more-affluent residents from poor residents. While it would be a mistake to think that simply increasing metropolitan densities would automatically produce more-equitable social relations, any serious strategy for moving toward a metropolis in which where you live is only incidentally related to how your life goes must challenge the socio-spatial organization of U.S. cities and suburbs, in both its physical and, more importantly, its political dimensions.

BUT MIGHT NOT ALTERNATIVES TO SPRAWL ALSO BE PROBLEMATIC?

One key question remains, however. Might not policy alternatives to sprawl *also* have problematic consequences from the standpoint of justice? As we have seen, Rawlsian liberals have good reason to be concerned about the

U.S. pattern of suburbanization and the way that geographic separation by income and race undermines the possibility of substantive equal opportunity. But, like the utilitarian, the Rawlsian will also want to know what sprawl is bad in comparison to. For instance, what if the only plausible alternative to sprawl were a re-densification of U.S. metropolitan areas that took the form of extremely crowded tenement houses for low-wage workers and the poor, combined with gated communities for the rich *within* cities, complete with armed guards to fend off the rabble? In this nightmarish scenario, reversing sprawl might lead to the creation of urban conditions reminiscent of turn-of-the-century Manhattan—or modern-day mega-cities in the global south.[102]

It should not require detailed argumentation to suggest that sprawl is almost certainly better from the point of view of the least well-off than would be a form of re-densification that led to dramatic worsening of living conditions in urban environments. Sprawl, then, is almost certainly *not* the worst possible spatial formation from a Rawlsian perspective. But the more plausible result of efforts to systematically contain sprawl would not be a return of the old-style tenement house, but quite the opposite phenomenon: gentrification, as middle-class persons of means returned to the city, raising land values and rents and gradually pricing many long-term residents from working-class or poor backgrounds out of their own neighborhoods. Given the social and psychological benefits of residential stability, the financial costs of moving, and the general principle that people should be able to reasonably expect that they will not be involuntarily forced out of their neighborhoods by forces beyond their control, how can we be sure that gentrification might not be even more damaging than sprawl to the least well-off?[103]

In traditional capitalist land markets, this tension between the competing goals of avoiding sprawl on the one hand and slowing or cushioning gentrification may be unavoidable. From a Rawlsian point of view, however, the sprawl versus gentrification debate can be understood to rest on a false dichotomy, once we call into question two assumptions commonly made by urban-policy analysts.

The first assumption has to do with the background inequalities of U.S. society—the vast differences in income, wealth, and life prospects among citizens, especially between the top 20 percent of persons and the bottom 80 percent. We have stressed from the outset of this chapter that what makes socio-spatial patterns just or unjust is not (or is only very rarely) the organization of space itself but the way that spatial organization expresses and/or reinforces just or unjust social arrangements. This being the case, it might be reasonably concluded that, even in theory, there is no possibility for establishing a socio-spatial pattern fully consistent with and reinforcing of Rawlsian principles of justice without first altering the background inequalities of U.S. life. In short, perhaps urban gentrification—combined with urban, gated communities housing the rich—might be the best outcome to which policy can reasonably aspire, given this society's background inequalities. The first task of a Rawlsian analyst, then, is to critique the notion that these observed background inequalities are natural or inevitable.

We might think, however, that efforts to redress background inequalities and efforts to alter our socio-spatial arrangements must go hand in hand. How then is the Rawlsian policymaker to weigh the possible benefits of reversing economic segregation against the costs of gentrification? Answering this question requires challenging a second assumption; namely, that housing arrangements must be left entirely to the market. A variety of institutional mechanisms for securing affordable housing within urban neighborhoods have developed in the past twenty to thirty years, in addition to traditional public housing, including, most prominently, community land trusts and limited-equity cooperatives. Land trusts offer residents long-term leases on housing units owned by a trust, or even the option to buy the housing unit (but not the underlying land); upon selling the property, residents may claim a capital gain limited to a specified amount. By limiting the price of resold property, both land trust and limited-equity coops can forestall gentrification and slow the rise of housing prices—even in areas experiencing economic revivals.[104] Similarly, local governments can take steps to encourage and facilitate the production of denser housing development, thereby offsetting price pressures associated with growth boundaries.[105] In short, so long as Rawlsian liberals are willing to intervene in private housing markets in a substantial way, there is potential to alleviate or offset the expected impact of anti-sprawl strategies upon urban housing prices and minimize the social dislocation associated with gentrification.[106]

Conclusion

There is strong reason to believe that economic opportunity and class privilege correlate with—indeed, are encoded in—the social-spatial patterns that characterize U.S. metropolitan areas in ways that liberal egalitarians should find disturbing, even if there is still room for debate about the extent to which the specifically spatial elements of sprawl (as opposed to more-general processes of suburbanization and spatial sorting) are implicated in this relationship. Yet this conclusion may not be enough to persuade many liberals that dramatic policies to alter the built environment are needed to institutionalize

Rawlsian ideals of justice. If sprawl disproportionately hurts the poor, why cannot we, as economists like Glaeser and Kahn suggest, simply compensate those who lose from sprawl?[107]

Appealing as this approach may be to economists (and perhaps utilitarians, more generally), it misses two deeper points about the connection between socio-spatial realities and the possibility of egalitarian politics (and hence, egalitarian social policies) noted above. The first is that Rawlsian justice is not concerned with simply ensuring that the marginal effects of policy shifts do not fall mainly on the poor. Rather, it asks why there should be any poor to begin with, and calls our attention to the *structural* features of distributive arrangements operative in a given society. A government check to help the poor buy a car and get a job in the suburbs may indeed help recipients' life prospects in badly needed ways, but it will not provide anything like "equal opportunity" to an individual who has grown up in a dangerous neighborhood with substandard public schools, high poverty, and concentrated social problems.

The second point is that even this modest correction to the inequalities encoded in our socio-spatial structure may be—and probably is—unachievable, given the context of U.S. politics and its general aversion to redistributive efforts, and that sprawl itself may reinforce that aversion. What if sprawl, in fact, by virtue of economic segregation or other mechanisms, tends to undercut political support for policies capable of compensating "losers" from sprawl—in addition to sapping support for policies that would realize the conception of equal opportunity so central to Rawls's theory of justice? Might sprawl impede the possibility of realizing Rawls's principle of justice, precisely by undercutting the bonds of solidarity needed to bring these principles to life? We shall return to those questions in chapter 5, as we move to consider the ways in which sprawl does (or does not) contribute to the maintenance of a polity committed to liberty and equality.

FIVE

Liberal Egalitarianism in a Cul-de-Sac?

Sprawl, Liberal Virtue, and Social Solidarity

F ROM THE STANDPOINT OF Rawlsian justice, our discussion in chapter 4 placed "sprawl" under heavy suspicion. But we should not too quickly discount the ways sprawl might comport well with Rawls's framework. Rawls's theory of justice is a liberal theory, and it is characteristic of liberalism to invest individuals with certain rights and dignities upon which the state cannot intrude and to insist that individuals be allowed to live their lives without undue interference from public authority. In Constant's famous phrasing, modern liberty has typically been conceived by liberals as consisting in "peaceful enjoyment and private independence." Prominent twentieth-century liberals such as Isaiah Berlin similarly described liberty as primarily a matter of noninterference by the state in individuals' decisions.[1] Although Rawls's view of the basic liberties and their priority is importantly different from Berlin's account, his conception of the basic structure of society, too, assumes that individuals will have their private aims and particular conceptions of what to do with their lives, which the state should respect.

Given this concern with preserving and protecting the space in which individuals can conduct their personal lives as they see fit, there are at least two distinct reasons that many versions of liberalism would be likely, at least initially, to confer approval on the characteristic U.S. ideal of private homeownership with which sprawl is closely linked: First, liberalism harbors a strong bias against intervening in individuals' private choices about how to live, including choices about where and in what sort of domicile one will live. In the case of sprawl, liberalism might entertain the possibility that suburban biases in contemporary public policymaking ought to be corrected—no small qualification—but the default stance will likely be an ideal of a non-paternalist state that allows people to live where and as they choose, according to their preferences.

Beyond this general orientation toward respecting individuals' preferences, there is also a more specific historical connection between the development of liberalism as a political philosophy in Anglo-American thought and the cultural ideal of private, single-family homes. Both the notion of "private independence" and the concept of a "private sphere" beyond the scope of public intervention are intimately intertwined with the institution of private property, and, in particular, the private family home. As Robert Fishman has shown, the initial impulses toward suburbanization as we know it were rooted in the desires of relatively affluent middle-class persons to establish a space, away from both the poor and industrial activity, which would be the site of "peaceful enjoyment" and private family life, with each home serving as a private empire untouched by outside intrusions. Here, life would be governed according to the norms of familial relationships and reigning cultural practices.[2]

Fishman properly associates this ideal with the historic rise of bourgeois, patriarchal family units organized around the principle that "a man's home is his castle." But the basic concept of private personal space embodied in privately owned domiciles today retains an appeal not only to traditional nuclear families but to many other groups as well. Consider, for instance, gay couples who rely on the privacy of the home to sustain their lifestyle, fundamentalist Christians who homeschool their children in an effort to counter the dominant strains of mass culture, or any number of private projects (some of which have public relevance) that are made possible by private ownership of homes and the assumed sanctity of private home space. Given the close connection between the practice of political liberalism and the historical institution of the private home, liberals can plausibly view private control of domestic space not merely as a cultural practice to be tolerated but as a positive good that appears to be an indispensable institution within existing liberal societies. Moreover, although some advanced liberal democracies (such as Sweden) rely far more on rental units or upon multifamily-type housing than does the United States,[3] liberals can cite an additional compelling reason for favoring the more specific ideal of private home *ownership,* which is that property ownership gives citizens a positive stake in the political regime while also conferring on them a substantial degree of independence from both public and private masters.[4]

Liberal approval of the ideal of private homeownership can be plausibly extended to sympathy for suburbanization, insofar as suburbanization is a mechanism for extending (and making more affordable) the availability of private homes to the wider public. This is not to say that philosophical liberalism in itself points to any conclusion that *sprawl* is admirable, but only that liberals are likely to recognize the value of private homeownership in neighborhoods of one's choosing as a positive good in the liberal way of life and would be wary of policy shifts that significantly infringe on this ideal.

In short, while a rigorous examination of the distributive consequences of contemporary social-spatial patterns seems to push liberal egalitarians toward a critical evaluation of suburban sprawl as likely inconsistent with the demands of justice, or, more specifically, the second principle of justice, the commitment to liberty may very plausibly push Rawlsian liberals in the opposite direction: toward a cautious approach to intervening in private choices, especially in a sphere of life so closely associated with personal freedom as residential patterns. To recall, for Rawls the structure of justice is intended to secure the conditions under which individuals can equitably pursue their plans of life and private ends. For many Americans today, a peaceful life in the suburbs may *be* the end to which they aspire, or alternatively, an important good instrumental to other private goals (such as writing poetry, tending gardens, or coaching youth soccer teams). Recall also that Rawls's theory is deliberately structured to prioritize liberty over equality. It is only with the greatest reluctance that a Rawlsian liberal would advocate interventions of the kind that might substantially affect how Americans pursued their private ends. In the conclusion of this chapter, we will return to the question of how this apparent tension between the egalitarian face and the liberal face of Rawls's theory of justice might (or might not) be resolved in coming to terms with the practical question of sprawl.

Sprawl and Liberal Virtue

Liberals are generally reluctant to interfere with people's choices about how to live their lives. But interventions into private decisions might be acceptable to liberals if they were persuaded that goods vital to the liberal polity itself were at stake. We thus now turn to the question of whether sprawl is a help or hindrance to the nurturance of what might be termed "liberal virtues"—those basic qualities that liberal theorists typically acknowledge that citizens need to possess if liberal orders are to endure, let alone flourish. Numerous liberal political theorists in the last two decades, responding to a variety of critiques of Rawls's version of liberalism, have paid renewed attention to the positive qualities citizens ought to possess to help bolster a liberal state and have suggested that public policy should, when possible, promote such virtues. For such theorists, it is natural to ask whether sprawl is helpful or antithetical to the realization of those liberal virtues that make for good citizens and a healthy polity.

The relationship between philosophical liberalism and the promotion of virtue requires some additional elaboration. A common critique of liberalism from civic republican and communitarian-minded critics targets the image of the neutral state, utterly indifferent to the habits of its citizens. Such lack of concern with "civic virtue" in the long run harms the very prospects of sustaining liberal polities by creating people who may be capable of tolerating those different from themselves so long as they are themselves not bothered, and capable of obeying the law, but who view politics and public affairs as merely a necessary evil, a distraction from the real life of private commitments.[5] Such people are likely to adopt precisely the bleak attitude toward politics that Rawls himself described and rejected (see chapter 4); that is, seeing political life as instrumental to their own private purposes rather than as a common enterprise with which their own good is identified. The result is a weakened public sphere and common life, in addition to a kind of politics that comes to be defined by battles between competing self-interests. In this vein, Philip Pettit distinguishes between two conceptions of civic virtue: a strong kind, associated with Aristotelian thought, which values active participation in civic life as a good in itself and a necessary part of a well-lived human life that exercises the species' distinctive capacities for shared deliberation, and a weaker, less ambitious kind, associated with Machiavellian and neo-Roman thought, which recommends civic virtue as instrumental to the maintenance of well-governed polities.[6] An increasing number of philosophical liberals have come to embrace some form of this second, weaker conception of civic virtue as an important component of a healthy liberal polity.[7]

Commonly mentioned liberal virtues include social trust, tolerance, respect for diversity, and at least some minimal identification with the good of the whole polity; in Rawls, as we have already seen, the need for citizens to endorse the normative ideals of the regime of justice and to view themselves as members of a common enterprise is stated explicitly. More recently, Ronald Dworkin has endorsed the idea of "civic republicanism in the liberal mode," by which he means that individuals ought to regard their private lives as integrated with the public life of the society to which they belong (understood by Dworkin to be strictly limited to its formal political life). Such an "integrated liberal" will "count his own life as diminished—a less good life than he might have had—if he lives in an unjust community, no matter how hard he has tried to make it just." Dworkin argues that such integration has two positive consequences. First, a society in which everyone "accepts that the value of his own life depends on the success of his community in treating everyone with equal concern" will enjoy greater stability by virtue of possessing a "powerful bond underlying even the most heated argument over particular policies and principles."[8] Political deliberation in such a society is less likely to be poisoned by suspicion of bad motives (such as the advancement of narrow, self-interested claims) on the part of those with whom one disagrees.

Second, Dworkin argues that a society in which justice was realized would allow individuals to live their private lives with a better conscience: within unjust, unequal societies, there is often a tension or contradiction between moral responsibilities in one's private life (which impel individuals to give disproportionate attention and resources to those nearby) and the public ideal of providing equal resources (Dworkin's standard of justice) to all. For instance, under conditions of injustice, some conscientious middle-class persons might struggle with the problem of whether it is acceptable to spend thousands and thousands of dollars attending to every need of one's elderly mother in full knowledge that that same money might do more good if given directly to the very needy.[9] In a just society, individuals would be free to devote themselves to their nearest and dearest, confident that society had provided equal resources to others to do the same, and for this reason their lives would be better. Dworkin thus identifies a private (albeit moral) benefit for individuals identifying strongly with the public life of the community.

Some liberals, such as William Galston, include in their conceptions of civic virtue minimal expectations regarding private conduct; namely, taking responsibility for one's own actions, and a general commitment to, in Bill Clinton's phrasing, "working hard and playing by the rules," which can be interpreted as a general injunction to individuals to at least try to better their own lot and take care of their dependents so as to become self-supporting and not willingly become a burden upon society. The programmatic recommendations of virtue-minded liberals are generally (and self-consciously) quite modest; thus, Galston expresses skepticism that modern states can really promote higher ideals such as "the development of autonomy and critical reflection." He writes, "I for one would be satisfied if citizens obeyed the law, did what they could to support themselves and their families, contributed their fair share to the support of our basic institutions, and refrained from violence and coercion as means of promulgating their vision of the good life."[10]

Other "virtue liberals," such as Stephen Macedo and Rogers Smith, have been somewhat more expansive in describing the kinds of virtues that liberal polities should be reasonably concerned with promoting. Marc Stier, drawing on this literature, has enumerated the "liberal virtues" in some detail, noting that "the liberal ideal is a person...who is capable of choosing his or her own path in life while furthering the institutions and practices of liberalism." Such persons must, among other things, be capable of critical self-reflection, tolerant "of the widest range of human visions of the good," informed about public life and committed to public debate about public affairs, and "loathe to use coercion rather than persuasion against those with whom they disagree." Additionally, good liberal citizens should be "moderate in their pursuit of their own vision of the good and open to reasonable compromises with others."[11]

To this list of liberal virtues, Rawlsians can add the concept of social solidarity as a public virtue. To reiterate, each group of citizens must regard all other citizens as worthy of access to equal opportunity and the fairest possible share of the community's economic product. In the context of diverse societies, political liberalism also has reason to place high value on social cohesion, especially across demographic differences; more generally, echoing Galston, liberal polities have an interest in nurturing people who do not seek to manipulate, deceive, or dominate others; that is, people who are trustworthy. A contested issue is the degree to which direct participation in politics is required by liberalism; as Stier notes, remaining informed about political affairs and at least some minimal degree of participation (such as voting) would seem to be required by liberal citizenship, but most contemporary versions of liberalism do not require direct participation in self-governance in the sense associated with stronger forms of civic republicanism. Virtue liberals such as Galston generally represent political activism (or at least moderate forms thereof) as a good thing but do not claim that one must be a political activist to be a good person or even a tolerably good citizen.[12]

Given this set of virtues, which liberal political thinkers increasingly regard as important and legitimate for the state to promote, we now turn more directly to the empirical issue of whether the spatial organization of communities has any effect on the presence or absence of such virtues in the citizenry. The answer to that question will be an important consideration for liberals (in particular, liberal egalitarians) as they evaluate the phenomenon of sprawl.

Does Sprawl Inhibit Liberal Virtue?
A Turn to the Evidence

Any attempt to move from theoretical description of a concept such as virtue to operationalization in the form of concrete empirical measures inevitably involves some slippage; approximations are unavoidable. I thus operationalize the liberal virtues by examining two citizen characteristics widely thought to be important to maintaining liberal polities: trust and tolerance. I then turn to discussion of the relationship between sprawl and overall ideological orientation, a topic that will be of special interest to liberal egalitarians; I treat self-described political conservatism as a reasonable proxy for likely opposition or hostility to the "difference principle" and treat ideological liberalism as a reasonable proxy for support for redistributive policies of the type implicit in Rawlsian thought.[13]

SPRAWL, TRUST, AND TOLERANCE

We first consider the relationships between spatial context and trust, trustworthiness, and tolerance. That trust is treated here as a liberal virtue is not without irony; the historical evolution of social contract theory was strongly informed by assumptions of mutual distrust between individuals, from Hobbes's unflattering account of humanity in the state of nature to Kant's concern with developing a state fit even for a "race of devils." Yet achieving a measure of trust between rulers and the ruled was a central goal of, for instance, Lockean accounts of the social contract. Without insisting that strong bonds of trust among all members of society are possible under modern conditions, modern liberals follow Locke's lead in stressing that reciprocal relations of trust among citizens are helpful (often critically so) to the operations of liberal democracies. This claim has been expressed both by liberal theorists (including Galston) and by social scientists such as Robert Putnam, who has found strong empirical relationships between the climate of trust operative in particular cultures and the functional effectiveness of democratic governments.[14]

A long tradition of urban sociology dating to Georg Simmel and Louis Wirth suggests a connection between urban life and anomie: residence in dense cities is thought to compel individuals to retreat into private spaces and to adopt a wary attitude toward strangers.[15] This line of thought implies that there may be a systemic connection between urbanism and distrust: people living in high-density areas must take a more cautious attitude toward others than must persons living in quieter, low-density areas.

Similarly, individuals living in newer, car-dependent neighborhoods may exhibit higher levels of trust precisely *because* of the privatistic qualities of such areas: residents of such neighborhoods can be expected to have fewer involuntary, unwanted social interactions with others that require them to adopt a more wary outlook toward other people in general. M. P. Baumgartner's classic study of suburban life observes that the lack of public space and street life in suburbia "keeps unacquainted people away from one another to a degree not seen in cities, reducing the sorts of friction likely to arise in face-to-face encounters." Residents of Baumgartner's suburb make tending to one's own knitting a normative principle of public order. Baumgartner goes on to add that "the ease with which people can withdraw into their own private enclaves, leaving problems with strangers behind them, is a dimension of life in suburbia which its residents appreciate greatly."[16] The very fact that residents of this kind of suburb can largely avoid dealing with people they do not want to deal with, and the fact that there is a lack of public commotion or other unmonitored activity in public space might lead suburbanites to regard their neighbors and others as more trustworthy than urban residents regard theirs. Finally, long commuting time may also be a predictor of reduced social trust. Living in a neighborhood with long average commutes, or simply having a long commute personally, may cause individuals to regard other people as less trustworthy. Spending significant amounts of time each day fighting traffic is unlikely to raise one's estimate of human nature, and neighborhoods in which people must spend more time and energy getting to work and back are likely to have less time left over for building social capital.

The following section explores how spatial characteristics affect both overall social trust and the likelihood of trusting one's neighbors. It should be emphasized that what is of interest here is not whether individuals in various spatial contexts are more or less trusting (or, pejoratively, gullible), but the degree to which they *perceive others as being trustworthy*. In short, what we are interested in here is not the psychological attributes of individuals but rather the information their responses to these trust-related questions provide about the trustworthiness of people with whom they interact. Indeed, from a sophisticated liberal point of view, trust is not just meaningless but perverse in the absence of trustworthiness.

Table 5.1 reports on individuals' overall levels of social trust; this measure of trust is an index derived from answers to six distinct trust-related questions posed to Social Capital Community Benchmark Survey (SCCBS) respondents, permitting respondents to be grouped into three categories—high, medium, or low social trust.[17] The table also reports individuals' likelihood of trusting their neighbors. As can be clearly seen, residents of suburbs, lower-density areas, and car-dependent areas (quite often the same locations) are much more likely to exhibit high levels of trust; residents of areas with longer commuting times also report being warier of others.

The multivariate analysis presented in table 5.2 confirms that there is a substantial connection between three of these spatial variables and overall

TABLE 5.1. Social Trust by Place of Residence

Likelihood of being placed in the "high trust" category on an index of social trust, and likelihood of trusting one's neighbors "a lot."

	Very Trusting	Trust Neighbors a Lot
Central City Residents	28.5%	37.4%
Suburban Residents	38.0%	53.6%
Rural Nontown Residents	45.0%	61.4%
Rural Town Residents	46.2%	58.9%
High-Density Tract Residents (>8,000 persons/mile)	24.2%	29.4%
Low-Density Tract Residents (<2,000 persons/mile)	40.4%	57.3%
Residents of Older Neighborhoods (built prior to 1950)	30.7%	37.5%
Residents of Newer Neighborhoods (built 1980 or later)	37.9%	53.6%
Solo Commuting by Car in Tract <65%	22.4%	27.6%
Solo Commuting by Car in Tract >85%	41.4%	58.8%
Tracts with Average Commutes <18 Minutes	45.0%	55.5%
Tracts with Average Commutes >30 Minutes	27.9%	40.7%

Sources: SCCBS; 2000 U.S. Census.

TABLE 5.2.   Effect of Sprawl-Related Variables on Social Trust

	Overall Trust	Trust of Neighbors
Central City Residence	−.085 (.033)**	−.143 (.027)***
Tract Density (ln)	−.068 (.018)***	−.085 (.014)***
% Driving Solo in Tract	—	.404 (.169)*
Commuting Time in Tract	−.015 (.0039)***	−.010 (.0035)**
Residential Stability in Tract	—	.614 (.163)***
Educational Level in Tract	.996 (.134)***	1.365 (.154)***
Racial Homogeneity in Tract	.231 (.086)**	.368 (.081)***
% African American in Tract	−.196 (.082)*	−.223 (.094)*
Homeownership	.208 (.032)***	.592 (.030)***
	n = 28,565	n = 27,930

*Sources: SCCBS; 2000 U.S. Census. Ordered logistic regressions. * indicates $p < .05$; ** indicates $p < .01$; *** indicates $p < .001$. See appendix II for full regression table.*

trust, after controlling for other individual and community characteristics. Living in a high-density area or a central city depresses overall levels of trust, as does living in an area with long average commuting times. (Long individual commuting times are also inversely related to trust levels.) High car dependence and neighborhood age are not significant predictors of trust, however.[18] These results remain robust even when controlling for county-level crime rates. In substantive terms (without controlling for crime), a worker with a fifteen-minute commute living in a tract with a fifteen-minute average commute is predicted to be over 20 percent more likely (35.9% vs. 29.5%) to report high levels of trust than a person with a forty five-minute commute living in a tract with average commuting time of thirty minutes.[19] The combined negative effect of high density and central city residence on trust is of a similar magnitude to the commuting effect: moving from a relatively high-density (8,000 persons/sq. mile) urban tract to a lower-density (1,000 persons/sq. mile) suburban tract predicts roughly a 17 percent increase (from 27.6% to 32.4%) in one's likelihood of being in the most trusting group.[20]

Similar results obtain when we consider a more specific measure of trust, the likelihood of trusting one's neighbors. Again, long commuting times are associated strongly with reduced trust, but so too is central city residence in high-density areas and low rates of automobile use in one's tract. Holding other factors equal, residents of a low-density, suburban tract in which 85 percent of workers drive alone to work are predicted to have a 49.4 percent (48.0%, 50.9%) likelihood of saying they trust their neighbors a lot, compared to 39.6 percent (38.0%, 41.1%) for residents of a high-density central city tract in which 65 percent of workers are solo auto commuters.

Notably, these results hold even if we add to the analysis a control for individuals' subjective evaluation of their community's quality of life. This is important because we might think that, given the relationship between high density and lower quality of life, as established in chapter 4, the observed relationship between higher density and reduced trust of neighbors may simply be a function of high-density residents regarding their communities as less pleasant places. Even after accounting for these subjective evaluations, however, high density remains a strongly significant negative predictor of both measures of trust, and central city residence remains a significant negative predictor of trusting one's neighbors (though not of overall trust). Long commuting time also remains a strong predictor of reduced trust, even with this additional control. Put another way, it appears that both living in a high-density area and having a longer commuting time have important specific effects on trust, over and above the general impact each variable has upon the overall community's quality of life.

The story these data tell is at odds with received wisdom regarding the relationship between trust and sprawl: research conducted by Wendy Rahn and colleagues posits an inverse relationship between sprawl and trust, based on the finding that people in communities with a larger proportion of workers undertaking long commutes tend to be less trusting.[21] This relationship between long commuting time and distrust is confirmed by the SCCBS, but the more complex conception of "sprawl" employed here leads us to examine the relationship between reduced levels of trust and increased density, central city residence, and, to a lesser degree, greater reliance on public transit. Persons living in lower-density, car-dependent suburbs regard their neighbors as substantially more trustworthy than do persons living in dense, transit-intensive cities. In short, prominent aspects of sprawl appear to be *good* for trustworthiness. If we believe that the more than twenty-nine thousand respondents to the SCCBS have collectively produced a reasonably accurate assessment of the trustworthiness of their neighbors, it follows that people living in low-density, car-friendly areas *are,* in fact, more trustworthy and more honest than people living in denser environments. More cautiously, we might simply conclude that people are *perceived* to be more trustworthy in lower-density, suburban environments, but it is the perception that counts in generating the positive social benefits that flow from higher levels of social trust. In either interpretation, the apparent link between heightened trust and lower density should count as a significant point in favor of sprawl, especially from the point of view of liberal theorists, such as Galston, who stress fundamental private virtues such as honesty.

On the other hand, critical theorists such as Susan Bickford might be less impressed with a positive link between trust and sprawl if it were, at bottom, connected to inegalitarian spatial practices that "produce the illusion of safety for some at the expense of actual danger and discomfort for others."[22] The thought here is that being able to leave the doors unlocked when you leave home may be a nice thing but not if it is achieved through exclusionary practices that lock out or make invisible marginal persons whom one might be tempted to mistrust. We thus turn to the question of whether sprawl helps or hinders broad social tolerance.

Sprawl, Diversity, and Social Tolerance

Liberal political theorists have a strong interest in promoting social and political tolerance as widespread values. We thus consider the relationship between sprawl and three distinct measures of such tolerance: the likelihood that one is friends with a gay or lesbian person, an African American, a Hispanic person, or an Asian person; the degree of hostility one has toward immigrants; and whether one supports censorship of objectionable books. Many liberals have a particular interest in what Putnam terms "bridging" social capital—relationships and networks established across racial and class divides—and hence are interested in the prevalence of cross-racial friendships. Likewise, attitudes towards gays and immigrants are obviously hot-button issues in contemporary U.S. politics, and while liberal theorists may reasonably disagree among themselves regarding the specifics of policy questions such as marriage laws and immigration law enforcement, there is little, if any, warrant within recognizable forms of liberal political theory for hostility toward either group. Nor can much support be found within mainstream liberal political theory for intellectual censorship of any kind.

As a descriptive matter, white Americans who live in prototypical urban areas are substantially more likely to have a gay, Asian, or Hispanic friend. Obviously, this propensity largely reflects the fact that these populations are themselves more concentrated in non-sprawling areas. Nonetheless, it is interesting and significant that members of majority groups who live in a

TABLE 5.3.   Guess Who's Coming to Dinner?

Likelihood of having at least one personal friend who is gay or lesbian (among all respondents); African American; Asian; or Hispanic (among whites).

	Gay	Black	Asian	Hispanic
Central City Residents	47.8%	65.9%	44.5%	50.5%
Suburban Residents	40.5%	61.3%	36.6%	42.9%
Rural Town Residents	38.1%	45.5%	32.9%	39.2%
Rural Nontown Residents	29.0%	45.8%	23.8%	35.9%
High-Density Tract Residents (>8,000 persons/mile)	52.2%	67.7%	55.0%	61.0%
Low-Density Tract Residents (<2,000 persons/mile)	36.6%	56.6%	30.5%	38.4%
Residents of Older Neighborhoods (built prior to 1950)	49.5%	60.8%	40.9%	46.6%
Residents of Newer Neighborhoods (built 1980 or later)	39.6%	63.9%	38.6%	45.0%
Solo Commuting by Car in Tract <65%	51.2%	67.9%	54.3%	58.6%
Solo Commuting by Car in Tract >85%	39.1%	62.4%	32.3%	37.3%

Sources: SCCBS; 2000 U.S. Census.

TABLE 5.4. Immigrants and Censorship

Likelihood of agreeing "somewhat" or "strongly" with statements that immigrants have become too pushy in demanding rights, and that offensive books should be removed from public libraries.

	Anti-Immigrant	Pro-Censorship
Central City Residents	31.8%	20.9%
Suburban Residents	35.7%	22.2%
Rural Town Residents	34.8%	21.5%
Rural Nontown Residents	40.8%	27.9%
High-Density Tract Residents (>8,000 persons/mile)	31.7%	21.0%
Low-Density Tract Residents (<2,000 persons/mile)	37.2%	24.2%
Residents of Older Neighborhoods (built prior to 1950)	30.6%	19.8%
Residents of Newer Neighborhoods (built 1980 or later)	35.3%	21.1%
Solo Commuting by Car in Tract <65%	31.6%	22.2%
Solo Commuting by Car in Tract >85%	33.8%	21.6%
Tracts with Average Commutes <18 Minutes	32.7%	21.4%
Tracts with Average Commutes >30 Minutes	36.3%	25.0%

Sources: SCCBS; 2000 U.S. Census.

more traditional urban environment in the United States are more likely to come into contact with and form positive social relationships with minority populations, at least to a modest degree. Moreover, the fact that minorities (including gays and lesbians) tend to congregate in urban areas is itself not accidental. As suggested by Iris Marion Young and others, urban settings provide a more welcoming environment for the emergence of minority subgroups while also affording individuals greater anonymity and privacy.[23]

We now turn to two measures of what might be termed "liberal tolerance"— attitudes toward immigrants and censorship. Table 5.5 shows that residents of more-sprawling places appear to be more likely to harbor less urbane social attitudes with respect to immigrant rights and freedom of expression. As one moves away from central city environments, opposition to immigration rights and support for removal of offensive books from public libraries increases. Multivariate analysis confirms that among respondents who are white and/or a college graduate (some 79% of the sample), residence in newer neighborhoods and residence in more car-dependent areas are each strong predictors of increased hostility to immigrant rights.[24] Those effects are further strengthened when we additionally control for the proportion of residents in a tract who are Hispanic. (As the proportion of Hispanics in a neighborhood rises,

TABLE 5.5. Effect of Sprawl-Related Variables on Support for Censorship and Hostility toward Immigrants

	Support Censorship	Think Immigrants Are Too Pushy
% Driving Solo in Tract	—	.980 (.225)***
Younger Neighborhood	.0057 (.0011)***	.0054 (.0012)***
Educational Level in Tract	-.892 (.152)***	-1.258 (.144)***
Proportion of Hispanics in Tract	—	.488 (.181)**
	$n = 28{,}063$	$n = 21{,}536$ (whites and/or college graduates only)

*Sources: SCCBS; 2000 U.S. Census. Ordered logistic regressions. * indicates p < .05; ** indicates p < .01; *** indicates p < .001. See appendix II for full regression table.*

hostility toward immigrants' rights increases.) Among whites and/or college graduates, a resident of a census tract built in 1950 in which 65 percent of workers drive alone to work is predicted to have a 26.5 percent (24.6%, 28.6%) likelihood of agreeing or strongly agreeing with the notion that immigrants are too pushy, compared to the 34.1 percent (32.1%, 36.1%) likelihood of a demographically identical individual living in a tract built in 1980 in which 85 percent of workers solo commute by car thinking so.

Living in a newer neighborhood is also a strong predictor of increased support for censoring books (among all respondents). In substantive terms, a resident of a low-density neighborhood built in 1980 is roughly 15 percent more likely to support book censorship than is a resident of a higher-density neighborhood built in 1950, holding other things equal.[25] This relationship remains strongly significant if we add further controls for individuals' religious orientation and congregation membership status.

These findings suggest two prominent explanations. The first is that perhaps persons who are hostile to immigrants or have relatively constricted views of free speech systematically congregate in newer, car-dominated areas (although, if this is the case, we must ask why). The second is that there may be something about the experience of living in a prototypically sprawling area that *generates* social attitudes seemingly at odds with core liberal principles. To recall, a long tradition of urban theorists has suggested that city life fosters a sense of tolerance and acceptance of difference and novelty. In any case, it should be a matter of interest and concern to liberal political theorists that sprawl is linked to anti-immigrant and pro-censorship attitudes in ways that cannot be readily explained by either individual or community-level demographic variables. Indeed, these findings suggest a still broader question: might sprawl inhibit the generation and perpetuation of the sort of social solidarity that Rawlsian-style egalitarian liberalism requires? We now consider that possibility.

Sprawl and Political Orientation

It is now common knowledge among political professionals and journalists that U.S. suburbs, especially outer suburbs, are more congenial settings for Republican candidates for office than traditional urban areas. The political significance of the socio-spatial formations that characterize U.S. metropolitan regions has likewise received growing attention from both political theorists and empirical political scientists in recent years.

Susan Bickford, for instance, forwards several interesting hypotheses about the effects of space on the formation of political consciousness. Contending that "the architecture of our urban and suburban lives provides a hostile environment for the development of democratic imagination and participation," Bickford argues that the demographics, spatial orientation, and institutional setting of U.S. suburbs have created quasi-privatized environments that "attempt to root out from the lived experiences of the privileged both multiplicity and its attendant uncontrollability."[26] Whereas traditional urban spaces consist of a "outside togetherness," in which strangers necessarily commingle, suburban environments are designed to limit the free flow of strangers in and out of places and limit experiences of "fear, discomfort, or uncertainty," using techniques designed to "screen and partition in a fairly thorough way some citizens from others." Bickford cites gated communities, common-interest developments (CIDS), private shopping malls, and upscale gentrified urban areas as examples of spaces designed to maximize "seclusion and control." Older urban neighborhoods, in contrast, are said to be more "fuzzy and permeable."[27] Bickford argues that life and work in this new suburban architecture has significant political effects:

> The meaning and experience of "being in public" changes quite significantly in such a context. We are no longer moving with and negotiating around diverse strangers in a shared material world, but rather within a certain kind of bounded space that determines who and what we perceive. And who we "happen" to see regularly as we move through the world has an influence on who we think of as citizens and who we think to engage with as citizens—in other words, whose perspectives

must be taken into account when making political decisions. Thus, we endanger the possibility of democratic politics when we settle in these enclosures, particularly when we become so accustomed to the walls that we forget that they are there, for then we begin to imagine that "the world" consists only of those inside our gates.[28]

In practical political terms, Bickford's assessment leads to the prediction that such suburban and quasi-suburban spaces tend to generate politically conservative outlooks—that is, outlooks not predominantly motivated by overturning the "inegalitarian" and exclusionary features of contemporary metropolitan areas that Bickford deplores. Notably, in Bickford's account, what is important is not simply the demographics of suburbia—such as the fact that suburbs are generally less racially diverse than cities—but the organization of space itself. Space can be organized in such a way as to highlight the distinction between insiders and outsiders, to limit interactions among strangers, to constrain incursions from "outsiders," and to discourage unscripted, spontaneous activity. According to this view, it is the interaction between the demographics of suburbia and its spatial construction that produces politically significant effects.

In a similar vein, the political scientist Margaret Kohn argues:

It is difficult to feel solidarity with strangers if we never inhabit places that are shared with people who are different. The privatization of public space gradually undermines the feeling that people of different classes and cultures live in the same world. It separates citizens from each other and decreases the opportunities for recognizing commonalities and accepting differences. Public space is made up of more than parks, plazas, and sidewalks; it is a shared world where individuals can identify with one another and see themselves through the eyes of others. Seeing oneself through the other's eyes may be a first step towards recognizing one's own privilege and, perhaps, criticizing structures of systematic privilege and deprivation.[29]

Such theoretical arguments have been bolstered and largely vindicated by the anthropologist Setha Low's case study work on social attitudes in U.S. gated communities. Low's fieldwork in six such communities suggested that fear of others, in particular racial minorities, and a desire to maintain spaces of cultural "whiteness" motivated many residents to choose to move to gated communities; she further found that the structure of such communities themselves reinforced a sharp difference between insiders and outsiders and a sense of fearfulness toward the outside world. Noting that "architecture and the layout of towns and suburbs provide concrete, anchoring points of people's everyday life" that "reinforce our ideas about society as large," Low concluded that "the gated community contributes to a geography of social relations that produces fear and anxiety simply by locating a person's home and place identity in a secured enclave, gated, guarded, and locked."[30] The upshot of this qualitative work is that at least some sorts of suburban environments contribute to and reinforce social attitudes generally consistent with a conservative political outlook.

A growing body of empirical research has lent support in recent years to such claims. Important work by Juliet Gainsborough using National Election Study data from the late 1980s and early 1990s shows a strong connection between suburban residence and conservative social and political views, even after controlling for many other demographic factors (including, remarkably, party identification).[31] Similarly, Alan Walks has demonstrated that the link between suburbanization and conservative political outlooks also holds for Canadian metropolitan areas. Using the Canadian Election Survey, Walks found that residence in an "inner city" was a significant predictor of support for the left-wing New Democratic Party in both the 1984 and 2000 Canadian elections, controlling for other demographic factors (including religion and region). Walks also found that by 2000, inner city residence and especially outer suburban residence fairly consistently predicted more liberal and more conservative attitudes, respectively, relative to residence in an inner suburb.[32]

Whether or not spatial arrangements shape the development of persons likely to be sympathetic to egalitarian aims should be of substantial importance to Rawlsian liberals. In the SCCBS, detailed questions about particular social issues (the kind of evidence Gainsborough draws on) are largely absent; however, individuals were asked to describe their political ideology. Specifically, respondents were asked, "Thinking politically and socially, how would you describe your own general outlook—as being very conservative, moderately conservative, middle-of-the-road, moderately liberal or very liberal?"[33]

Obviously, translating a concept such as "social solidarity" into the traditional left-right political spectrum is a messy business: a suburban resident might care deeply about the plight of the inner-city poor yet favor free-market policy responses and hence call herself a "conservative"; a self-reported "liberal" may care little about economic inequality but instead be motivated by social issues (e.g., civil liberties or abortion rights) or environmental issues; and so forth. Nonetheless, it is reasonable to assert that self-identified liberals are, on the whole, far more likely to be sympathetic to the aims of Rawlsian distributive justice than are self-identified conservatives.[34]

TABLE 5.6. Political Ideology and Spatial Context

Likelihood of describing one's political views as "moderately liberal" or "very liberal."

Central City Residents	36.7%
Suburban Residents	25.2%
Rural Town Residents	26.7%
Rural Nontown Residents	19.0%
High-Density Tract Residents (>8,000 persons/mile)	43.8%
Low-Density Tract Residents (<2,000 persons/mile)	22.2%
Residents of Older Neighborhoods (built prior to 1950)	39.3%
Residents of Newer Neighborhoods (built 1980 or later)	22.8%
Solo Commuting by Car in Tract <65%	44.7%
Solo Commuting by Car in Tract >85%	21.9%

Sources: SCCBS; 2000 U.S. Census.

Table 5.6 shows that all four sprawl-related factors appear to be substantially correlated with political ideology. How much of this correlation is actually due to contextual factors, and which of those factors is driving these observed differences? Multivariate analysis indicates that two sprawl-related variables are strongly linked with political orientation: residence in an older neighborhood, which predicts increased liberalism; and residence in an automobile-intensive tract, which predicts greater conservatism.[35] These findings are robust if we include an additional control for proportion of African Americans in one's census tract (a positive predictor of more-liberal views). Notably, these findings are also robust to local partisan environment: greater neighborhood age and reduced reliance on cars remain strongly associated with greater liberalism, even after controlling for the proportion in each respondent's county who voted for either Al Gore or Ralph Nader in 2000 in addition to individuals' religious affiliation and membership and union affiliation.[36] This set of findings suggests that the relationship between suburbanization and conservative political orientation identified by Gainsborough may actually reflect a more specific relationship between community characteristics commonly associated with sprawl and conservatism.

The cumulative relationship between sprawl-related characteristics and political ideology is substantial. The standard model (controlling for union membership, church membership, and religious affiliation but not partisan context) predicts that an individual living in an older neighborhood in which just 65 percent of workers drive alone to work will have a 31.5 percent (30.0%, 33.0%) likelihood of identifying himself as liberal.[37] A demographically

TABLE 5.7. Effects of Sprawl-Related Variables on Political Ideology

Based on a two-tiered version of the political ideology version in which respondents are coded as either "liberal" (persons indicating they hold "moderately liberal" or "very liberal" views) or "not liberal" (persons indicating they hold "middle-of-the-road" or conservative views). Both models control for union membership, religious affiliation, and church membership; the right-hand model also controls for partisan makeup of respondent's county, and includes fixed effect controls for each community sub-sample. In fixed effects model, standard errors are corrected for clustering at the census-tract level.

	Liberal Views	
	Standard Model	Fixed Effects Model
% Driving Solo in Tract	−1.004 (.160)***	−.533 (.171)**
Younger Neighborhood	−.0081 (.0015)***	−.0068 (.0013)***
% African Americans in Tract	.432 (.070)***	.423 (.095)***
Educational Level in Tract	1.06 (.156)***	.887 (.120)***

Sources: SCCBS; 2000 U.S. Census; www.uselectionsatlas.org. n = 27,883; * indicates p < .05; ** indicates p < .01; *** indicates p < .001. See appendix II for full regression table.

identical person living in a car-dependent, recently built neighborhood is predicted to have a 22.8 percent (21.9%, 23.7%) likelihood of identifying herself as a liberal. That this difference might have a profound effect on the balance of local politics is illustrated by noting that conservatives are predicted to only moderately outnumber liberals in the prototypical urban setting (37.2% to 31.5%) whereas, in the prototypical suburban setting, conservatives are predicted to outnumber liberals by roughly two to one (45.7% to 22.8%).

Notably, sprawl-related variables also help predict voting patterns at the county level. An analysis of county-by-county returns in the 2000 and 2004 presidential elections shows that both the proportion of workers driving alone in the county and the median housing age within the county have a strong effect on how counties voted, net of other demographic factors (and controlling for both density and the proportion of in-town commuters in the county). Within metropolitan areas, counties that were more recently built and had a greater proportion of solo automobile commuters were markedly more likely to vote Republican than Democrat.[38]

However, it is important here to note that the relationship between living in a sprawling location and holding conservative political views is much weaker among African Americans, Asian Americans, and Hispanics than among whites, and is much stronger among college graduates. If we demarcate the sample by race and educational status, we find that the fact of residence in a newer, more car-dependent neighborhood has much stronger implications for one's political views among white college graduates than among other groups, although even among the sub-sample of nonwhites with no college there remains a statistically significant relationship between tract spatial characteristics and ideology. As table 5.8 shows, the effect of sprawl upon political views is not a race- and class-neutral process. These findings should perhaps not, on reflection, be surprising, especially given the kinds of stories told by scholars such as Bickford and Low, who emphasize the desire of suburbanites to control space and minimize exposure to outsiders and the unfamiliar, a desire that is often bound up with white racial privilege. Intuitively, it makes sense that in the contemporary United States the effect on your worldview of what you see every day in your neighborhood should be larger among racially and socially privileged groups compared to groups (especially African Americans) that are racially marked, regardless of where they live. Such privileged groups also generally have greater capacity to move to a neighborhood of their choosing.

––––––

Sprawl-related variables clearly have an important connection with individuals' political views. As just noted, self-selection looms large as a possible explanation: it may be that liberals happen to like dense, transit-oriented neighborhoods and thus move there, or that conservatives hate them and stay away. Note, however, that the models reported above already control for the proportion of African Americans living in the census tract. For white college graduates, in particular, local spatial characteristics are strongly connected to ideology, even after controlling for willingness to live near significant numbers of African Americans.

TABLE 5.8. Effects of Sprawl-Related Variables on Political Ideology, by Race and Education Level

Based on logistic regression models in which respondents are coded as either "liberals" or "not liberals." Models contain controls for religious membership and affiliation and union membership.

	Predictors of Liberal Political Views		
	(1)	(2)	(3)
% Driving Solo in Tract	−1.326 (.306)***	−.908 (.259)***	−.827 (.177)***
Younger Neighborhood	−.0114 (.0028)***	−.0077 (.0017)***	−.0029 (.0020)
% African Americans in Tract	.797 (.236)***	.276 (.121)*	.349 (.103)***
Educational Level in Tract	1.433 (.263)***	.926 (.212)***	.324 (.197)
	n = 7,561	*n* = 14,583	*n* = 5,739

Sources: SCCBS; 2000 U.S. Census. Group (1): white college graduates; Group (2): white less than college and nonwhite college graduates; Group (3): nonwhite, less than college.

Indeed, as Gainsborough has suggested, it is equally plausible to suppose that living in a particular kind of neighborhood has an effect on how one comes to view one's own self-interest. Living in a low-density, car-dependent area in which the routines of daily life are more private cause individuals to have a different perception of the rest of the community and of the role of public goods in sustaining community life than individuals living in denser neighborhoods in which public transit is important. For instance, even purely self-interested residents of cities have good reasons, on quality-of-life grounds, to support policies that reduce urban homelessness, whereas residents of suburban enclaves have little or no direct interest in the well-being of poor urban residents.[39] Alternatively, we might think that insofar as people living in low-density areas believe their neighborhoods are objectively desirable places, they become more likely to adopt essentially conservative attitudes (i.e., "I like the community I live in and want to keep it the way it is.") Finally, we might extend a line of reasoning suggested by scholars such as Margaret Kohn and Susan Bickford by arguing that the quality of the public space we inhabit systematically informs the way we conceptualize ourselves and the world around us; these conceptions of the self and the world in turn inform our political orientations. In particular, urbanist built environments with shared space, pedestrian activity, and public transit may tend to reveal aspects of social reality (including the reality of human suffering and of people different from ourselves) that suburban car-oriented environments tend to conceal or render invisible.

Consider also the fact that residents do not have equal ability to select the neighborhoods they live in; indeed, 38 percent of respondents in the national sample of the 2006 Social Capital Community Survey said they wished to live in a different neighborhood.[40] That finding is a reminder that not everyone can reasonably be described as living where they do as matter of choice. The relationship between sprawl and conservatism remains visible even if we focus our attention on those respondents in the sample who are least likely to have chosen their current neighborhoods; namely, those with fewer economic resources (less than $30,000 in income), those who are relatively dissatisfied with their existing neighborhood (rating their local quality of life as just "fair" or "poor"), and those (excluding students) who plan to leave the neighborhood within five years.[41] Among each of these groups, a strong, statistically significant link between sprawl-related variables and ideological identification remains, although the link is not as strong as among residents with greater resources, who are happier with their neighborhood, and who plan to stay.[42] These results indicate that self-selection is indeed an important mechanism but that it cannot explain all of the observed relationship between spatial location and ideology.[43]

Yet even this evidence consistent with a self-selection story is open to multiple interpretations; after all, it may be that suburbia is producing more-conservative people, who, in turn, find suburbs more to their liking. Moreover, as Gainsborough stresses, theories of self-selection must explain *why* liberals or conservatives are systematically attracted to particular places—an explanation that inevitably must refer to specific qualities of actual places. Gainsborough thus cites Robert Huckfeldt's observation that even the self-selection hypothesis is "a rather complex contextual argument." He writes, "People choose to live in neighborhoods...because they are attracted to them or repelled by other residential alternatives. Both the attraction and the repulsion are, at least in part, contextually based."[44]

This discussion has demonstrated that there is, at the least, a substantial *affinity* between several key sprawl-related neighborhood characteristics and political conservatism, and strong evidence that this affinity is likely not simply a result of individual self-selection. Moreover, the literature presents us with two strong reasons that spatial context may affect political identity: Gainsborough's argument that spatial context shapes perception of political self-interest (an argument bolstered by the historical accounts of the new suburban historians), and Kohn and Bickford's suggestion that spatial context shapes one's perceptions of the social world itself. Moreover, even if we think that some *adults* self-select into neighborhoods that correspond to their political preferences, we might also hypothesize that local context has a politically significant effect on the *socialization* of children and teenagers: how likely is it, the concerned Rawlsian might ask, that a child growing up in a privileged suburb lacking public spaces in which one might encounter those different from oneself will come to an understanding of him or herself as inherently engaged in a system of social cooperation with unseen, less privileged others who are worthy of his or her equal moral respect?

Conclusion: Why Egalitarians Must Challenge Existing Preferences

The evidence presented in this chapter suggests that so far as weak civic virtue and social trust are concerned, sprawl presents, at most, a modest difficulty for the operation of liberal political regimes, but that sprawl is a serious obstacle to Rawlsian liberal egalitarianism. Not only is the U.S. pattern of suburbanization implicated in the creation of a regime in which opportunities are not fairly distributed (see chapter 4), key elements of sprawl are linked to the formation of a body politic that is incapable of implementing the sorts of social and economic reforms that could correct those inequalities.

This, then, is where the rubber meets the road for Rawlsian liberals: Which part of the "liberal egalitarian" formula must give way in the case of a sharp conflict between the two values—the "liberal" aspect or the "egalitarian" aspect? For, as we have stressed, the liberal will be, at least at first glance, deeply reluctant to use public action to fundamentally intrude into the adopted way of life of a given people, particularly with respect to their private lifestyles. Liberals do not want the state snooping around individuals' bedrooms, censoring religious practices, or prohibiting nose rings; nor, we suspect, would liberals happily allow the state to force people to give up their SUVs, to live within ten minutes of their job, or to ride public transit to work three days a week. But what if the lifestyle and pattern of settlement in question, while not being inconsistent (or at least not grossly inconsistent) with a liberal polity per se, makes the attainment of an egalitarian society all but impossible, both by distributing opportunities unequally and by weakening the political will and capacity to correct such inequalities?

The crucial issue is whether liberals can or would be willing to criticize suburbanite preferences and to endorse policies designed to induce different settlement patterns in our metropolitan areas. What if achieving an egalitarian polity required, as one prerequisite, substantial alterations to the way of life regarded as most desirable by most citizens, alterations that might be experienced (and in turn resisted) as a substantial encroachment on the freedom to pursue one's goals and life project as one sees fit? Would liberal egalitarians be willing to use state power to promote one sort of socio-spatial pattern rather than another in order to facilitate the formation and stability of a political order capable of realizing justice as fairness?

For liberal perfectionists the answer is presumably yes, provided there are good substantive reasons for pursuing such policies. For libertarians and other liberal adherents of "negative liberty" (liberty as noninterference) the answer is, presumably, no, as a matter of respect for individuals' preferences and choices.[45]

For Rawlsian liberal egalitarians, the answer is slightly more complex.[46] Liberal egalitarianism does not accept just any conception of the good as reasonable; those conceptions of the good that are inconsistent with the demands of justice should not be honored. Likewise, preferences that are antisocial (e.g., racist) or selfish (i.e., demanding to have more than one's fair share) can be set aside. It is thus open to the Rawlsian to judge that current preferences for suburbia, especially insofar as they are motivated by exclusionary privatism, are the sort of conception of the good that should be ruled out by justice. Indeed, it would be implausible to suggest that socio-spatial arrangements are simply beyond the proper scope of justice. Once we consider the public nature of the built environment and the public process by which it is constructed, in addition to the potentially profound effect that socio-spatial patterns can have on the basic conditions under which citizens live and the distribution of life opportunities, there is scant justification for conceptualizing the spatial organization of society as a wholly private matter. No one has the right to use geography to flee from the responsibility to contribute to a just and well-ordered society and to secure a greater share of (public and private) goods than a just society would afford. Moreover, policies aimed at preventing this outcome, even though they challenge existing preferences, are acceptable so long as they do not upset the structure of basic liberties Rawls is fundamentally concerned with.

This Rawlsian answer is appealing, and, from a rigorous egalitarian point of view, correct. But it is not a lightly reached conclusion; it is one thing to say that liberalism can dismiss blatantly antisocial preferences such as racism, and another to suggest that the predominant set of residential preferences of large parts of the population is unjust and can be legitimately overridden by public policy.

This is particularly true given two critical features of these residential preferences: First, they are indeed closely tied to individual conceptions of the good life. Second, these preferences are, in many cases, reasonably well motivated, rational, and (in the eyes of suburban residents) reasonable. Suburban residents do not generally see themselves as beneficiaries of a system of injustice, nor do they regard their own choices as morally illegitimate.

Here the liberal egalitarian might reply that the goal should be to reform the basic structure such that individual choices about what sort of community to live in do not produce results conflicting with the demands of justice. But such reform clearly would require challenging and seeking to shift or constrain strongly held existing preferences. Following this course places liberals in the uncomfortable position of having to cast judgment not simply on institutional structures but on individual choices (including perhaps their own) and of having to make the case that the public policy ought to shape the metropolis in ways that enhance prospects for egalitarian solidarity, even when this conflicts with individual preferences.[47] To cast the question in a different and perhaps more precise way, egalitarians must be willing to criticize those cultural norms that validate as moral and normal a person's seeking to live in a privileged neighborhood divorced from social problems.

In principle, liberal egalitarianism has no problem overriding current preferences—or challenging the reigning social ethos—when they conflict with the requirements of justice.[48] In practice, efforts to challenge sprawl on egalitarian grounds will be decried by many suburbanites as an assault on their liberty of choice and, indeed, as an unwarranted intrusion on their freedom to live as they choose. Liberals have two possible responses to such arguments: they might drop egalitarian aspirations and side with the libertarian defense of sprawl, or they might insist that the liberty to claim and defend a privileged place in an unjust socio-spatial order is not the sort of liberty protected by the first principle of Rawlsian justice. Indeed, policy steps aimed at constraining sprawl likely need not require that the basic political and civic liberties with which Rawls is centrally concerned be restricted.[49]

Note, however, that the justice-based case against sprawl (in a Rawlsian mode) does not require a critical judgment about the worthiness of suburban life as such. To make a judgment that living in a dense, pedestrian-friendly neighborhood is inherently better than living in an auto-dependent cul-de-sac, even if no implications for justice are involved, would violate the general commitment to liberal neutrality. Consequently, the liberal's first instinct would be to minimize the negative distributive effect of sprawl without fundamentally challenging suburbia or the suburban way of life.

The most-modest strategies along these lines, endorsed by Anthony Downs and implemented on an experimental basis during the 1990s by the Clinton administration, involve providing subsidies to poor, urban residents to permit them to move to the suburbs, while also finding other ways to "open the suburbs" to the poor.[50] A second, more ambitious approach involves bringing rich suburbs and economically stressed central cities under a common political roof through the formation of regional governments or tax-base-sharing schemes, thereby reducing local inequalities in fiscal capacity among neighboring communities, including funding for public education. A third strategy consists of reconfiguring government subsidies to encourage the economic development of poor neighborhoods within metropolitan areas; that is, paying off the "losers" that sprawl creates not with subsidies to poor individuals but with subsidies to poor communities.

All three strategies have been much discussed in policy circles in recent years, and in each case there are encouraging success stories (in addition to exceptionally formidable political obstacles). Such strategies may yet have an important role to play in redressing some of the problems of the U.S. metropolis. But none of these strategies, fundamentally, aims to contest sprawl per se or to pass judgment on the suburban way of life. Rather, they posit the (very Rawlsian) idea that suburban and urban communities alike are engaged in a common project of building a just society, and then ask more-affluent suburban communities to pay their fair share to make this enterprise successful.

Practically speaking, however, pursuing such a political project will always be a decidedly uphill struggle, given that most affluent suburban communities and affluent individual citizens lack precisely what Rawls's theory requires: a commitment to a common project of justice and a willingness to both bear social burdens and to shape one's life's aims to support that project. Moreover, the evidence considered in this chapter indicates that sprawl itself may be a substantial obstacle to the formation of the political and moral sensibility necessary to correct the inequalities generated by sprawl.

As a result, the keep-sprawl-and-redistribute-the-costs strategy is in the position of calling for reforms that both the overall political–economic structure and the specific socio-spatial structure of the United States make all but impossible. Sprawl, in short, weakens the political will required to correct its own negative impact on the ideal of equal opportunity and appears to contribute to the formation of the very kinds of citizens that Rawls decried in *A Theory of Justice,* citizens who see government and public life principally as a tool for their private advantage, and/or as a mechanism for maintaining and extending the socioeconomic status quo. If this is correct, much more radical steps aimed not just at reducing inequalities between richer and poorer areas but at challenging the "right" of more-affluent citizens to spatially segregate themselves will be required to realize Rawlsian principles of justice.[51]

———

There is a further difficulty as well: non-egalitarian liberals and others may wonder just what sort of "liberty" Rawls is committed to if the suburban preferences of the majority of Americans can be overridden, set aside, or challenged in the name of a controversial theory of justice. Liberty in ordinary popular discourse is generally taken to be freedom to do what one wants, with minimal interference or constraints. While Rawls is committed to the idea of people choosing and pursuing their own ends, his is not a theory of liberty as noninterference in the libertarian sense. But using policy to reshape preferences and choices nonetheless requires a strong justification, one that, for Rawls, must be rooted in an account of the demands of justice and not in some sectarian conception of the good life. Application of Rawlsian principles necessarily involve definitive moral judgments regarding which conceptions of the good (and which preference structures) are consistent with a just society and which are not. In practice, this means that to critique sprawl and the preferences that generate it, Rawls must appeal to a conception of distributive justice that is itself a distinctly minority view in contemporary U.S. political culture.

That observation is indicative of a more general difficulty in applying Rawlsian thought to actually existing liberal polities. Rawls wants to work out a theory of justice that reflects the self-understanding and considered moral convictions of contemporary liberal societies. To this end, he uses a thought experiment to argue that providing equal basic liberties and equal opportunity and minimizing inequalities would be the guiding principles chosen by rational agents in an original position. But the actual behavior of the U.S. public reflects only weak interest in such egalitarianism; in fact, some conservative critics have charged that Rawls's well-honed arguments for liberal egalitarian arrangements amount to relatively minor disputes with "certain philosophy professors on friendly terms with Rawls," and have little to do with the self-understanding of the U.S. people.[52] (Perhaps this tension would be less evident had Rawls been writing as, for instance, a Swedish scholar.)

Commentators more sympathetic to Rawls's aims have reached similar conclusions. The patent contradiction between the form of egalitarianism Rawls endorses and the actual views on distributive justice held by the U.S. people is especially problematic, given that his political liberalism purports to be a systematic working out of ideals that we are already committed to, that is, ideas already present within liberal democratic communities.[53] As Simone Chambers points out, while notions of equal opportunity indeed hold a strong intuitive resonance within the political culture of the United States, so too do more conservative notions of distributive justice emphasizing personal responsibility and legitimating inequalities attributable to effort, ability, or market luck.[54] As Chambers observes, the difference principle commits Rawls to a politically radical position vis-à-vis the status quo in the United States (hence his interest in replacing capitalism with "property-owning democracy"); yet the tone of Rawls's writings evinces no such radical sensibilities and gives only rare indication that the existing practice of liberal democracy in the United States is deeply flawed.[55]

In short, taking citizens as they are, politics in liberal regimes are not guaranteed to produce "just" outcomes of the type Rawls has in mind, and even a rough approximation of justice is all but impossible in liberal states where citizens are unwilling to support the steps required to realize strong, substantive equal opportunity.[56]

Rawls himself clearly did not see the tension between liberalism and egalitarianism in so problematic a light. Indeed, in the "ideal theory" society he describes (in which individuals were in fact motivated not only by private ends but by the desire to participate in a common enterprise involving securing justice for each and all), that tension would likely largely disappear. But this is not the society in which we live or in which suburbanization has become the dominant socio-spatial pattern. Indeed, if a fundamental impulse driving the long history of U.S. suburbanization, and now sprawl, is the desire of the well-to-do to separate themselves from the less well off, then the U.S. socio-spatial landscape can be seen as an *expression* of a society in which individual aspiration is prioritized over participation in a common enterprise and, in this sense, as the antithesis of Rawlsian egalitarian liberalism.

Yet the ideal of the suburban way of life has come to be embraced by many Americans, and many see enjoyment of the accoutrements of suburban existence as instrumental to pursuing their life plans. It should be abundantly clear that egalitarian arguments against sprawl, taken alone, are highly unlikely to gain sufficient political traction in the United States to compel serious change.[57]

Recognition of this point need not lead to despair, however. It is open to liberal egalitarians to turn to complementary arguments for challenging sprawl that are motivated not simply by considerations of justice as fairness, but by concerns with citizenship, self-governance, and the good life. Civic republican critics of liberalism have argued, in various ways, that Rawls's ambition of seamlessly marrying egalitarian community to liberal individualism is flawed, as both a philosophical and a practical enterprise. In the following chapter, we turn more explicitly to civic republican ideas and ask both how this tradition of thought might approach the problem of sprawl and whether this tradition might provide a more satisfactory framework for addressing the tension between the prerogatives of individuals and the claims of justice evident in the sprawl debate.

SIX | Sprawl, Civic Virtue, and the Political Economy of Citizenship

WOULD A SOCIETY PREDICATED upon the idea of active and widespread participation in civic affairs choose to organize its metropolitan areas after the fashion of contemporary sprawl? Can a society that in fact has chosen (by various actions and inactions) to develop in a sprawling manner generate sufficient civic engagement to realize any form of civic life richer than what Benjamin Barber has disparagingly termed "thin democracy"?

In this and the next chapter, we examine whether sprawl is a substantial barrier to the exercise of the demanding conception of civic virtue in which citizens must be actively engaged in the work of self-governance and assume shared responsibility for maintaining the good of the regime, associated with civic republicanism. Suburban sprawl itself has already attracted the attention of a number of civic republican thinkers, who have tended to depict sprawl as emblematic of both the manner in which private goods are systematically preferred to public purposes in U.S. life, and of a way of life (both communal and individual) of dubious moral worth. Civic republican critics of sprawl do not simply think that it would be aesthetically more desirable for middle-class families to congregate in walkable, relatively dense neighborhoods rather than go to the mall or Wal-Mart; they are concerned in a deeper way about the underlying assumption that the primary purpose of the built environment is to facilitate increased consumption and private convenience, rather than to express public aims. By calling critical attention to how sprawl may affect the practice of democratic citizenship and the broader way of life that sprawl tends to promote, civic republicanism offers resources for a more thorough interrogation of the dominant socio-spatial patterns found in U.S. metropolitan communities.

The Relationship between Liberalism and Republicanism

The recent revival of interest in republican political philosophy has sparked a fruitful outpouring of debate regarding whether republicanism and liberal egalitarianism should be seen as competing or complementary public philosophies. Initial statements of civic republican themes by theorists such as Michael Sandel framed civic republicanism explicitly as an alternative to Rawlsian liberal egalitarianism, emphasizing the contrast between republican willingness to publicly debate (and act on) controversial conceptions of the good and the commitment to liberal neutrality advanced (to varying degrees) by Rawls, Dworkin, Bruce Ackerman, and numerous other liberals.[1] In particular, a republican political regime will not be shy in advancing policies and promoting institutional structures aimed at encouraging active citizenship. But Sandel's civic republicanism similarly would not retreat from making debates about the good life a central part of political discourse, or from using policy to advance substantive conceptions of the good. To take one of Sandel's frequent examples (one of direct relevance to the sprawl debate), civic republicans contest the idea that maximizing economic growth and continually increasing individual consumption should be the organizing framework for our political economy.[2] But it is hard to see how the current political economic system could ever be substantially altered from its present priorities without robust debate about the nature of the good life and the ends an economic system should serve.

Many liberal critics of Sandel believe he overstates the contrast between republicanism and liberalism and instead emphasize the compatibility between them.[3] Most prominent in this camp is Rawls himself: in *Political Liberalism* (the sequel to *A Theory of Justice*) he argues that what we have termed "neo-Roman" civic republicanism—the promotion of political participation and other virtues needed to sustain a liberal state—is consistent with political liberalism, since such promotion of civic virtue is motivated by the ends of the liberal state rather than by a particular conception of the good life. Stronger civic republicanism in the Aristotelian mode—termed "civic humanism" by Rawls—is ruled out, however, insofar as it is motivated by the "comprehensive" view that political participation is an intrinsic and necessary part of the well-lived life.[4]

If we follow Rawls in this assessment, then liberalism and at least some forms of republicanism need not be seen in such sharp contrast, at least at the philosophical level. Even according to this view, however, political liberalism might benefit from giving attention to and uplifting distinctively republican themes. Stuart White makes the argument this way: Rawlsian political liberalism allows for but does not mandate an explicit concern with republican themes regarding the benefits of active civic participation. As Will Kymlicka remarks, in the liberal view "there will be times and places where minimal citizenship is all that we can or should require."[5] But if empirical investigation shows that engaged citizenship is sociologically necessary to win stable support for liberal political regimes, then civic republican policymaking is perfectly justified. White, invoking Tocqueville, argues that the sociological argument for engaging citizens actively is so compelling that Rawlsian political liberals should drop their conditional support for republican ideals.[6] Rather they should conclude, as Andres de Francisco elegantly puts it, that "a free republic, such as the one sought by Rawls, requires active citizens, not citizens who have withdrawn to contemplative *idiocia* and abandoned themselves to the protection and patronage of a despotically benevolent prince."[7]

Related to this, Kymlicka, taking the view that there is no compelling philosophical quarrel between republicanism and liberalism, suggests that there may be a political benefit in forwarding both republican and egalitarian arguments on public policy issues: some who may be unconvinced by purely liberal egalitarian arguments for the worth of some policy proposal might be moved by arguments cast in a republican mode, and vice versa. "From a liberal egalitarian point of view, one of the likely beneficial side-effects of promoting justice is to enrich the quality of political participation; from a civic republican point of view, one of the likely beneficial side effects of promoting the quality of political participation is to achieve greater social justice," writes Kymlicka. "In the overwhelming majority of cases, these arguments are complementary, and there is no reason to insist that only one be made."[8]

Other theorists, however, are not so certain that republicanism can simply be assimilated into the framework of political liberalism. While Rawlsian liberalism is not strictly neutral toward the good, whatever conceptions of the good life citizens adopt are acceptable so long as they are consistent with the overall scheme of justice. Civic republicanism, in contrast, supports positive measures aimed at encouraging citizens to place concern with public matters (including the realization of justice) at the heart of their plans of life and, indeed, regards this as an urgent imperative, given the many cultural and political–economic forces within modern capitalist societies that push citizens to conceive of the good life in purely individualistic terms. Moreover,

there is a substantive distinction between the minimal civic virtues celebrated by some liberals, such as trust, tolerance, civility, and basic political
awareness, and the more demanding conception of active, participatory citizenship associated with civic republicanism. Apart from his rather low-key
endorsement of classical republicanism, there is little to suggest in Rawls's
work that the good citizen *today* must be actively involved in holding power
accountable, monitoring the activities of the state, or calling attention to the
injustices and imperfections of the regime. In short, Rawls did not elaborate
in any detail a conception of citizenship appropriate for citizens in substantially flawed, non-ideal regimes.[9]

Philosophically, Richard Dagger argues that the Rawls of *Political Liberalism* wants to have his cake and eat it too: he wants to claim for liberalism
the motivational benefits associated with a republican account of civic virtue
without sacrificing the commitment to neutrality of aim. But this attempt
cannot succeed, in Dagger's view, because any account of civic virtue strong
enough to motivate citizens to change their actual behavior will necessarily
be a challenge to citizens' existing ideas about the good life. (Sandel has made
a similar argument.)[10] Dagger thus argues at length that republicanism and
liberalism are compatible, *if* liberalism drops its commitment to neutrality
of aim as an ideal for policymaking.[11]

That position has been further developed by John Maynor, who argues
that it is possible to specify a "modern republicanism" that is conceptually
distinct from liberalism yet consistent with liberalism's aims of promoting
autonomy and choice among ends. Building on Pettit's account of liberty as
non-domination, Maynor argues that republican liberty is distinct from liberalism in two key ways. First, not only the law but also demands on citizens
to exercise civic virtue are seen by republicans not as necessary constraints
that have instrumental value in producing individual liberty but as *constitutive* of liberty as non-domination. Second, republicanism aims not just to rule
out forms of the good inconsistent with social justice but to promote the
good of liberty as non-domination in all spheres of life. This in turn requires
an effort to shape not only individual's behavior but their *ends;* specifically,
citizens should be encouraged to avoid conceptions of the good that involve
the capacity to dominate (arbitrarily interfere with) other people. This will
help produce a set of social relations based on reciprocity and will contribute
both to social justice and to citizens' own good by allowing them to live more
secure lives, free from the threat of domination. "A modern republican state,"
writes Maynor, "will seek to interact with and inform individuals' conception
of the good so that they not only develop an ability to cast their ends in a
non-dominating manner, but also have the opportunity to enrich their lives

and attain certain goods that can make their lives better."[12] Promoting this ideal of non-domination in all spheres of life stands at odds with both traditional versions of liberal neutrality and the subtler version found in political liberalism. But, Maynor argues, "modern republicanism" does not involve the promotion of any unitary conception of the good life or entail the view that political participation is the highest good; in this sense, it is compatible with autonomy. Indeed, a society based on non-dominating reciprocity should strengthen individuals' ability to pursue (non-dominating) conceptions of the good and to revise those choices.

Maynor's arguments are compelling, and I share the presumption that a commitment to civic republicanism is not inconsistent with a commitment to basic liberal norms regarding respect for individual rights, or with recognition of personal autonomy as a vital political good (so long as, following Francisco, autonomy is understood as involving the rational desires of a well-ordered person, not whatever desires a person happens to have).[13] Further, I share Sandel's view that fostering robust debates about the good life and the ends public policy should promote—including the question of just how far the claims of personal autonomy should extend—would enrich our politics in important ways. Yet even if one simply accepts Stuart White's parsing of the argument—that a good Rawlsian who is well informed by the facts of political sociology in democratic society should endorse some form of republicanism—that is sufficient to motivate an inquiry into how public policy in general, and suburban sprawl in particular, might be assessed from a civic republican perspective. With respect to the substantive concerns of this chapter—the relationship between sprawl and civic engagement—we can expect there to be very substantial overlap between the views of neo-Aristotelian and what might be termed "pessimistic" neo-Roman republicans: both sorts of republicans, for slightly different reasons, think that current levels of civic mobilization in the United States are dangerously low.[14]

———

There is, in addition, a further republican critique of Rawlsian liberalism that focuses not on the question of whether republican and liberal ideals can fit together, but on whether ideal theory is the right starting place at all for thinking about politics. Stephen Elkin questions the very premise of Rawls's project: that the best way to come to judgments about practical politics and actually existing political regimes (i.e., questions of "non-ideal theory") is to develop an account of the ideal just regime, then judge existing regimes in light of that ideal. This mode of political theorizing, he charges, is too far abstracted from actual politics and the dynamics of power to make useful inferences about how existing regimes can be practically improved. In Elkin's view, political theory and political science are better served by studying the mechanics and underlying institutional theory of existing regimes, then asking how they might be made to work better in light of our shared aims. Numerous other critics of Rawls have similarly argued for the primacy of *politics*—particularly democratic politics—over abstract philosophy in assessing political regimes.[15] Engagement with the actual problems of democracy must mean, first and foremost, engagement with democracy's empirical realities. Liberal egalitarians in the Rawlsian tradition now taking up problems related to "non-ideal theory" have begun to recognize this truth, a truth that has long been central to republican thinking about politics.[16]

Rather than aiming to "depict how a political order should look among people who are already committed to a particular common sense of justice," republicans begin with the starting point that disagreement about justice is endemic and that politics is fundamentally characterized by class conflict and struggles for power. Elkin thus describes the following key "circumstances of politics": the condition of modern politics is one "in which there is a large aggregation of people who (1) have conflicting purposes that engender more or less serious conflict; (2) are given to attempts to use political power to further their own purposes and those of people with whom they identify; (3) are inclined to use political power to subordinate others; and (4) are sometimes given to words and actions that suggest they value limiting the use of political power by law and harnessing it to public purposes." Recognition of these facts, and of the unpleasant possibilities of human political nature, leads one to the view that the proper starting point for securing a political regime is preventing the worst regime, not ideal theory.[17]

Put another way, ideal theory in the Rawlsian mode is a misleading guide to engagement with concrete political problems insofar as it implies (a) that deep disagreements about justice are not an enduring part of our ordinary political life, and (b) that it is possible for citizens to neatly separate out their views about justice and public matters from their more comprehensive ethical commitments; insofar as it obscures the facts (c) that in liberal capitalist societies, political actors are commonly motivated to a high degree by self-interest of various kinds, and (d) that challenging the most powerful interests, holding government accountable, and realizing a measure of justice requires a high degree of civic mobilization; and insofar as it (e) turns our attention away from engagement with the empirical realities of democracy and the practical requirements of maintaining a stable, tolerably workable constitutional regime over time.

Seen in this vein, detailed debate about whether the ideal regime of Rawlsian theory requires sustained civic participation is interesting only as a philosophical exercise, not as a concrete political question. In the real world of concrete politics, dominant economic and political forces exercise power with only minimal constraint in the absence of sustained civic scrutiny, resistance, and opposition. According to this view, to be indifferent to the level and intensity of civic engagement in the polity is to consent to the status quo of power politics. Opposition to that status quo, in turn, is not to be conceptualized as application of a "neutral" conception of justice established outside of politics, to which any reasonable person would agree, but as a deeply partisan act that expresses the viewpoints and interests of a struggling minority (or majority, as the case may be) while at the same time appealing to values (including conceptions of justice) capable of winning assent from democratic publics. This view of politics and political engagement, in turn, permits a self-critical awareness of the contingencies of one's commitments and the partiality of one's own views not so easily attained if one equates one's political values with philosophical truth. While republicanism is perfectly consistent with a robust egalitarianism and a vigorous pursuit of social justice, here it offers a more realistic account of politics with respect to both the motive of its actors (desires for justice are always mixed in with concrete interests) and the ends to which it can aspire (ongoing conflict and struggle is unavoidable, ideal regimes unattainable).

From the standpoint of the present study, the most important contrast between civic republicanism and liberal egalitarianism in the Rawlsian mode is in the characteristic questions each tradition asks. For republicans, the most relevant political questions are not which theory of justice hypothetical persons in an original position might agree to, how such universal principles of justice might be made legitimate in the context of moral pluralism, or how to minimize the degree to which state action biases citizens toward one conception of the good or another. Rather, the central questions are how a public discourse that is shockingly devoid of serious debate about either the demands of justice or the sort of life to which we should be aspiring as a society can be reinvigorated, how the power of dominant economic groups might be restrained or re-channeled, how public action can be marshaled toward worthwhile ends, and how an ethos of privatization or indifference to public affairs can be challenged.

In particular, there is urgent need for serious discussion of the ends that public action should serve. This is particularly vital with respect to land use and the overall pattern of metropolitan development, which, as we have seen, are inextricably connected to public action. In Rawlsian terms, neutrality of effect is impossible with respect to land use, transportation, and related policies; that is why neutrality of aim must also be rejected, at least with respect to these issues. Failure to interrogate the ends that public action serves with respect to the built environment serves not neutrality but a replication of existing patterns and a reinforcement of market trends (trends that themselves have often been shaped by prior public action). Put another way, civic republicanism insists, with Aristotle, that, in an important sense, members of a political community live together, and we must live together one way or another. How the built environment is organized shapes the way of life our communities will promote, and hence it is in the purview of legitimate public action to debate what sort of life we wish the built environment to promote. To do that, in turn, we must be willing to critically assess and debate what might be reasonably termed the "American way of life"; namely, a way of life organized primarily around the pursuit of economic gain and private material comfort.[18]

That, in a nutshell, is the civic republican agenda concerning sprawl. The degree to which liberal egalitarians might share in that agenda is not a question one needs to answer definitively, other than to observe that at least some liberals will find themselves strongly sympathetic to pursuing these questions. Hence, the force of the argument that follows does not rest on a determinate view of the compatibility or lack thereof between liberalism and republicanism. Rather, it rests on the observation that the civic republican tradition highlights crucial questions that the liberal egalitarian framework, taken alone, generally has not foregrounded.

Contemporary Civic Republicanism: Crucial Themes

Contemporary civic republicanism, in either neo-Roman or neo-Aristotelian form, is thus more than just a restatement of classic themes in the history of political thought. Writers such as Ronald Beiner, Benjamin Barber, and Michael Sandel are also engaged, and self-consciously so, in situated cultural criticism. As social critics, civic republican thinkers have variously criticized the tone and content of political discourse in the United States, calling it vapid and lacking moral gravity; what is seen as the highly privatized nature of U.S. life, in which individual pursuit of self-gain is celebrated and in which various forms of "community" are thought to be in decline; the related consumerist habits of the U.S. populace; a popular culture that is largely empty of moral content; and the seeming absence of principled moral deliberation in public life.[19]

"Corruption," a favored term of Machiavelli, has always been a common theme of republican thought, and this theme echoes through many recent writings from a republican vantage point. Contemporary civic republicans charge both the practice of U.S. politics and the dominant habits of the U.S. populace with failing to foster a robust civic culture, a culture in which public goods would be widely seen as the highest ends to which our efforts should aspire and in which moral heroism (whether in the form of inspired, publicly recognized leadership, persistent political activism, or quieter lives of steadfast moral commitment) would have a prominent place. Moreover, whereas in the past, claims of corruption might have been simply unproven hypotheses, contemporary civic republicans, if they wish, can also cite powerful, well-established evidence in support of the general thesis of civic decline in the United States, drawing on the work of Putnam and a host of social scientists.[20]

Civic republican thinking about contemporary politics thus seeks to resuscitate a number of characteristic Aristotelian propositions about politics and its purposes while rebutting the common critique that the Aristotelian account of citizens coming together to deliberate about shared ends and advance a common vision of the good life is simply irrelevant to the practice of mass democracy in pluralist societies. Contemporary civic republican thinking thus makes seven substantive claims of direct relevance to the ongoing debate about suburban sprawl:[21]

1. Freedom should be understood as consisting in shared self-governance and the resistance of all forms of domination (internal and external); given this understanding, active participation in politics and active self-governance should be recognized as an essential good. Some contemporary republicans regard such participation as an intrinsic part of the good life, others as a good instrumental to warding off domination and preserving self-governance.[22]

2. The state ought not (and in practice cannot) remain wholly neutral with respect to differing ways of life. Moreover, politics should involve substantive debates about the good life itself, even when consensus on such issues is impossible.

3. More particularly, public policy should aim to honor, respect, and promote particular virtues essential to the maintenance of democratic self-governance, including awareness of our interdependence as citizens, self-restraint, a capacity for deliberative engagement with others, and the ability to think critically about the political and social institutions under which we live.

4. There are identifiable, shared common goods not reducible to disaggregated private interests to which policy should be attentive. Policy should aim not simply to maximize individual welfare but

also to protect, maintain, and expand such common goods. Political institutions themselves should be organized to promote deliberation about how best to advance the public interest.

5. Related to this, goods and social practices that are not properly viewed as commodities should be guarded from the effects of the market.

6. Relatively robust egalitarian norms comparable to Rawls's notion of justice as fairness can be grounded on a different basis; namely, the practical requirements of equal citizenship and equal participation in the work of self-governance.[23]

7. The scope of self-governance should consist not simply in oversight and participation in the activities of the state but should be extended to the political economy itself: meaningful self-governance requires that the dominant forces shaping everyday life, including most especially the economy, should be subject to effective democratic shaping and steering; that is, the economy should be embedded within society, not the other way around.

This chapter elaborates upon each of these civic republican claims and shows how they are relevant to the suburban-sprawl debate. The final section of this chapter provides a sustained analysis of how civic republicans might apply these claims to critically evaluate existing forms of residential communities in the United States, drawing on a typology of neighborhood form developed by the urban planner Sidney Brower. Simply put, civic republicanism's concern with fostering active, conscientious citizens who possess a critical consciousness, in addition to its willingness to directly challenge the existing preference structures of citizens in order to promote more civic-minded habits of thought and action, provides strong normative grounds for suspicion of both suburban sprawl itself and the motives that help generate sprawling socio-spatial environments, particularly the characteristically American desire to live in a comfortable place removed from social problems and other ills.

Freedom as Self-Governance: The Centrality of Participation in Self-Rule

The most fundamental claim of contemporary civic republican thought is that freedom should be centrally understood as the ability to influence, through participation in collective action, the social forces that shape the life of both individuals and communities: self-governance, in short, is coextensive with freedom. Societies in which citizens are subject to domination by outside forces (such as imperial rule), in which state power is not accountable to citizens, in which private influence dominates state power, or in which private relationships of domination leave many citizens dependent on other private actors all fail to meet this criterion of realizing freedom through self-governance. Civic republican thought is thus concerned with two aspects of freedom: the freedom of the regime itself and the freedom and independence of individuals from domination. Shared participation in the work of self-governance is viewed as a means to preserve both aspects of freedom; some civic republican thinkers, harkening back to Aristotle, also view participation as an intrinsic good and an integral part of the good life.

Aristotle defined human beings as "political animals," by which he meant quite literally that a capacity for shared reasoning about common ends is the characteristic feature of the human species.

> Nature, as we say, does nothing without some purpose; and she has endowed man alone among the animals with the power of speech. Speech is something different from voice, which is possessed by other animals also and used by them to express pain or pleasure; for their nature does indeed enable them not only to feel pleasure and pain but to communicate these feelings to each other. Speech, on the other hand, serves to indicate what is useful and what is harmful, and so also what is just and what is unjust. For the real difference between man and other animals is that humans alone have perception of good and evil, just and unjust, etc. It is the sharing of a common view in *these* matters that makes a household and state.[24]

Aristotle's statement reveals (at least) two core assumptions about human nature: first, that human beings are inherently social and are defined by social relationships (as exists in the household and state); and second, that human beings are not simply (as Jeremy Bentham supposed) pain and pleasure machines, but rather have a distinct set of qualities that need to be exercised if individual persons are to flourish. A fully developed human being exercises the unique capacity for speech to reason with other people about how best to fulfill some common end. The common end of the state, for Aristotle, is the fostering of the "good life," which is in turn understood as the sort of life in which distinctive human virtues are nourished and exercised.[25]

With respect to politics, Aristotle holds that participation in the common enterprise of self-governance is an intrinsic part of the good life. Without such participation, important human capabilities would go undeveloped, leading to an incomplete formation and flourishing of human virtue. This justification for political participation is very different from accounts that describe participation as instrumental to the defense of citizens' interests, or as instrumental to the perpetuation of the state. It is also distinct from (though not inconsistent with) the quintessential Tocquevillian claim that participation in politics broadens the horizons of those who participate and forces them to take a broader view of the common good by learning to accommodate other people's interests. Theoretically, an individual's interests could be defended or represented by others; or a state may be perfectly stable without depending upon significant public participation; or an individual may have a broad view of the common good without chancing to participate in politics (either by philosophical temperament, or as a result of a particular religious or moral upbringing, or as the result of abstract reasoning). Even in such cases, Aristotle would suggest, the broad-minded individual who does not participate in politics will fail to develop her distinctively human capacities to the fullest.

Among twentieth-century political thinkers, Hannah Arendt provides the most sustained arguments on behalf of understanding political engagement and active sharing in self-governance as a unique, intrinsic human good. In her 1958 work, *The Human Condition,* Arendt boldly argued for the superiority of public life to purely private existence:

> To live an entirely private life means above all to be deprived of things essential to a truly human life: To be deprived of the reality that comes from being seen and heard by others, to be deprived of an "objective" relationship with them that comes from being related to and separated from them through the intermediary of an objective world of things, to be deprived of achieving something more permanent than life itself....Being seen and being heard by others derive their significance from the fact that everybody sees and hears from a different position. This is the meaning of public life compared to which the richest and most satisfying family life can only offer the prolongation or multiplication of one's own position with its attending aspects and perspectives.[26]

Aristotelian and Arendtian arguments for the importance of political participation are relevant insofar as they help show why political arrangements in which direct participation in self-governance is minimal or is reduced to a consent (plebiscite) role are deeply problematic.[27] In Barber's terminology, "thin democracy" implies, *in practice,* government by a managerial class with effective input into the political process, participation increasingly limited to a class of political professionals. Such a democracy loses its character as a project in which citizens come together with the intention of re-visioning and remaking the world.[28] In limited democracy, the major questions facing the future of the society—such as the structure and evolution of the economy, the development of technology, changes in the structure of everyday life—are essentially beyond popular control. Voters choose between competing policy agendas on election day then largely return to the sidelines as elected officials implement policy in a climate in which the influence of organized interest groups looms large in defining and framing issues.[29] Unorganized voters are present only in the form of an amorphous "public opinion," as described in polling data, which is itself open to manipulation by elected officials. In this climate, many citizens never experience seeing themselves as agents capable of shaping a shared social world, or enjoy the internal goods associated with such agency; indeed "politics" itself often becomes degraded as an activity, more akin to marketing and fundraising than shared deliberation concerning and shared deliberation on behalf of a common future. As Sandel puts it, citizens, in this thin view of democracy, become objects of "treatment," not subjects and authors of their own destiny.[30]

Another strand of thought, echoing both Tocqueville and Arendt in addition to J. S. Mill and John Dewey, points to the importance of meaningful participation in *local* politics; according to this view, whereas the average citizen has little hope of substantially influencing the course of the national government, the more human scale of local government makes participation in local political activity more plausible and more potent.[31] Such participation is essential if citizens are to have any hope of holding leaders accountable. As Elkin argues, "If citizens of a republican regime are to judge the inclinations and capacities of their lawmakers, an essential feature of local government is that it afford them the experience of deliberating and struggling over the content of the public interest. They must themselves... have some experience of trying to answer the question, 'What is the public interest here in this case?'"[32]

Each of these strands of republican thought tends to the general conclusion that *more* participation in the political process is, on balance, a good and desirable thing for the formation of democratic citizens and is a precondition for the creation of democratic publics capable of engaging in forms of self-governance more substantive than plebiscitary democracy. Civic republicans can plausibly offer four general rationales for why high levels of political participation by individual citizens are desirable: first, widespread political participation is thought to lead to a more alert, aware, and competent public; second, through participation, it is hypothesized, citizens may come to have a broader view of their own interests; third, the process of participation may help citizens develop and hone a capacity for critical judgments about the public interest; and fourth, participation in politics—that is, the work of taking responsibility for one's community—should be considered an integral part of a well-lived human life.[33] Such an assessment differs in kind from the concerns of those who believe the primary purpose of political participation is to adequately represent the interests of citizens.[34] If the aims of participation are adequate representation, then more participation in the aggregate may not always be a good thing; analysts must also consider the socioeconomic composition of who is participating. An increase in participation only by upper-income citizens, or only by citizens of a particular race, for instance, is likely to exacerbate existing inequalities in how well particular interests are represented in the political process.

Republicanism can, of course, be taken in an aristocratic direction, in which the more enlightened citizens take the greatest share in "ruling," while the masses participate only minimally. Contemporary civic republicans and strong democrats do not intend to take this step. (For her part, Arendt envisioned a natural aristocracy of persons with a particular devotion to the political life, but explicitly said that this could not be a cultural, economic, social, or educational elite.)[35] First, civic republicans do not need to argue that defense of "interests" should have *no* role in contemporary politics, only that distributive politics should not constitute or be considered to constitute the sole purpose of political life. Aspiring to a form of democratic politics that transcends naked self-interest and aims at a broader common good does not mean imagining a world in which citizens have no legitimate interests at all to defend. Second, contemporary civic republicans think it important that as many citizens as possible gain the broadening of perspective and increased competence that is thought to be associated with political participation. Third, civic republicans might suggest that participation by individuals is (in general) an important counterweight to the influence of money and financial clout in contemporary politics. Fourth, civic republicans can contend that increased participation may also lead to a greater diversity of voices in the public sphere and a more rigorous assessment of social practices (particularly those of an exclusionary nature) that now go unchallenged.

At the same time, it needs to be stressed that civic republicans' concern with fostering participation is *not only* about increasing the raw numbers of people involved in some way with public life; it is equally or perhaps more so, as Arendt and Barber stress in different ways, concerned with *institutional* structures that permit meaningful participation in self-governance. This study does not attempt to examine the relationship, if any, between patterns of suburbanization and the existence of highly participatory local-level structures that correspond to the "spaces of freedom" invoked by Arendt (although this is a natural topic for future research).[36] Yet it can be reasonably suggested that spatial organization is itself part of the institutional infrastructure operative at local levels, which does or does not foster participation, and that civic republicans should welcome empirical evidence on which spatial practices seem most conducive to public life, even in the absence of truly participatory local-level political institutions. Detailed evidence on just this question is presented in chapter 7.

Debating the Good Life

A second constitutive element of contemporary civic republican thinking is the view that democratic societies should engage in substantive debates about what the best way of life is and that concrete policymaking should be informed by such debate. Whereas neutralist liberals believe that the state should leave debates about the best way of life to the private realm and allow individuals to pursue their own conception of the good in the way they see fit, civic republicans hold that spirited public debate about the moral worth of particular social practices and ways of life is desirable (and unavoidable).[37] For civic republicans, public deliberation about social practices must involve inquiry into the purposes and internal goods of a given practice, in addition to substantive moral arguments about the relative worthiness of those purposes and goods. For instance, a civic republican might envision public debate about the worthiness of gay marriages as revolving around a discussion of the goods such marriages are said to promote (such as, according to some, modeling a nonhierarchical form of binding adult partnership that offers a morally superior alternative to traditional patriarchal marriages), rather than a debate about whether individuals have an intrinsic "right" to marry whomever they please and have such marriages be recognized.[38] Moreover, civic republicans propose a method, derived from Aristotle, for making such inquiries: asking what the purpose of a given practice is, inquiring into what ends it seeks to promote and what internal goods it tends to foster, and then weighing the moral worth of these goods (both intrinsic and extrinsic) against other considerations. In some cases, competing goods can be effectively balanced or reconciled with one another; in other cases, there may be irreconcilable conflicts between competing values requiring difficult social choices—social choices that civic republicans contend will be made best when they are informed by robust inquiries into the nature of the goods at stake and rigorous scrutiny of the ends they promote.

It is important to recognize that civic republicans who question the appropriateness of settling controversial moral questions such as abortion or gay marriage by appealing to state neutrality may often agree with the practical conclusions drawn by a state-neutrality approach in particular cases. But civic republicans raise three kinds of concerns. The first is that by bracketing debate regarding contested issues, certain goods pertaining to the contested practices themselves may become obscured (e.g., the sense in which egalitarian same-sex marriages might be seen as a positive model for all marriages and partnerships). Second, emptying politics of moral debate has a negative effect on not only the tenor of politics but the citizenry as a whole, to the degree that moral passions are not simply tamed but extinguished altogether. Third, a populace unable to engage morally contested issues might also become unable to resist or object to socially dubious practices in the future: thinkers like Sandel have the commodification of existing social practices foremost in mind. The neutral state, Sandel's writings suggest, leaves the public unable to effectively challenge the ever-expanding reach of the market and market-oriented thinking; objections to the contemporary political economy within a strict liberal framework generally only pertain to distributive consequences, not to the consequences of economic structure on civic life (or upon other valued human goods).[39]

Civic republicans want to revive the notion that politics, at its heart, involves making collective judgments about how we might best live together. Within this framework, civic republicans might in the end endorse state neutrality with respect to a large number of matters pertaining to how individuals live. Yet civic republicans would characteristically insist that public institutions and public policy ought to be concerned with fostering both active citizens and fully flourishing human beings. Such human beings must be capable of exercising the autonomous judgment that liberalism itself requires, must be able to appreciate a diverse range of goods, must possess the basic capabilities with which to pursue a well-lived life, and must *actually pursue* morally meaningful lives.[40]

Civic republicanism thus highlights the importance in democratic politics of morally informed public deliberation and judgments about contested social practices. In addition, civic republicans can also plausibly argue that, as a practical matter, state neutrality is often simply impossible, not just in the trivial sense that the law itself necessarily presupposes that a law-abiding and -respecting society is a good to be advanced, but in the more substantive sense that in modern societies, state policies in certain areas inevitably have a strong substantive effect on how individuals live their lives. Land use planning is an excellent case in point; to take an obvious example, Americans could not possibly have developed a lifestyle heavily dependent upon private automobile ownership in the absence of state action to build roads (indeed, lots and lots of roads). The question with regard to land use is not *if* public policies will favor one particular version of the good life rather than another, but which *kind* of community and social life public policy should aim to enhance as it shapes and reshapes the landscape and the built environment.

What Then Should the State Promote? Republican Virtues

If state "neutrality" is neither desirable nor possible with respect to many important public questions, what is the substance of the way of life and habits of thought and action that civic republicans would seek to promote in public policymaking? In chapter 5 we briefly discussed those "liberal virtues" that many contemporary writers in the liberal tradition regard as vital to the maintenance of liberal regimes. We can now enumerate a list of "republican virtues" that civic republicans would regard as essential to the realization of public freedom, whose promotion should be a paramount consideration in public policymaking (including policymaking regarding the built environment). Iseult Honohan usefully groups republican virtue into three central themes:

1. Awareness, described as becoming cognizant of "the interdependencies and common economic, social, and environmental concerns of the polity." Honohan notes, "[Citizens] recognize how they are related to other citizens in being dependent on practices supported by them, and affecting them by their actions.... Citizens pay *attention* to political issues, and contribute to policy decisions directly or indirectly."

2. Self-restraint in "pursuing personal interests in wealth, power, or status: this corresponds to the classical idea of accepting duties and putting the common good before the individual." Citizens exhibiting this virtue approach public life seeking not maximal personal gain from policy decisions but the good of the state as a whole; the citizen is to "[take] responsibility as a citizen for what happens in the common world rather than [focus] on personal integrity alone." Related to this, Maynor stresses that republican citizens must develop the capacity to "track the interests" of other citizens and to

form conceptions of the good life not contingent upon dominating others.

3. Deliberative engagement, which consists in being willing to enter into dialogue with people who hold other perspectives: "Citizens listen to other points of view, and are prepared to explain their own position and revise it in deliberation." Under this heading Honohan also specifies the related theme of vigilance "with respect to abuses of power, public or private." Finally, the virtue of active, deliberative engagement also requires "active solidarity with other citizens—sometimes against government and institutions—rather than passive obedience to laws."[41]

To this list of civic virtues we might also add the development of a *critical consciousness* among citizens; that is, a capacity to critically evaluate institutions, power relationships, economic structures, and other central phenomena of social life from a morally principled framework. Rather than regard such institutions as permanent givens unamenable to conscious human intervention, they should be viewed as humanly created artifices that citizens have the capacity to influence, reform, or even overthrow. Such a capacity for critical scrutiny can be contrasted to unreflective patriotism, unreflective materialist individualism, and other socio-ideological attitudes that promote a passive orientation toward the social world.

We thus have four interrelated but conceptually distinct civic virtues: awareness of the facts of interdependence, self-restraint, deliberative engagement, and critical civic consciousness. Connecting these virtues is the presumption that citizens must be willing and able to take responsibility for the shared civic and social condition of their society, and must come to see their own good as intertwined with the good of the polity as a whole. Which if any of these virtues is potentially at stake in the suburban sprawl debate?

Civic republicans can plausibly portray sprawl as both the *result* of habits of thought and action that prioritize individual well-being and desires above the common good, and a cause, or a perpetuating factor, of such an orientation. A civic republican perspective might critique sprawl not simply on the grounds that individuals, in pursuing their private goals and seeking to satisfy their preferences, unwittingly produce social bads or under-produce social goods, leading to "sprawl," such that intervention in the market to help secure such public goods is desirable. Civic republicans also wish to critically assess the *motives*—the content of the preferences—underlying citizens' engagement in the land and housing markets, particularly the motives of suburban residents.

Take the example of affluent white homeowners who choose to live in a prosperous, fairly homogeneous suburb. We can identify two likely motives for this decision that civic republicans might regard as problematic. First are those moves to suburbia that are fundamentally motivated by a desire to escape responsibility for urban social problems, to escape being taxed to fund city services benefiting the worst off urban residents, and to separate one's self from the poor and/or concentrations of racial minorities. The second sort of motive is more innocent in content: a person simply prefers quiet suburbs to urban bustle and is essentially oblivious to the larger-order social and civic consequences of suburbanization. The first sort of motive can be critiqued by civic republicans as straightforwardly elevating private aims over a concern for the whole; the second sort of motive can be criticized for lacking awareness of the interdependencies and interrelationships among different communities within a metropolitan area, or perhaps for lacking a critical civic consciousness.

Notably, however, there is also a third sort of motive that civic republicans might have more difficulty critiquing: that of the anguished suburbanite who is reluctant to abandon the city and sincerely deplores the consequences of socioeconomic segregation, but feels obliged to move his or her family and children to the safest area with the best possible school, even if this is in a distant suburb. Only a very strong version of civic republicanism would insist that such a person has a positive obligation to absolutely prioritize civic goods over individual or private ones, especially in situations (such as this commonplace one) in which the civic benefit of a given action may be slight or diffuse whereas the private cost of the same action is powerful and far-reaching. Indeed, minimizing the circumstances in which this sort of very sharp conflict between civic and individual goods occurs should be a prime goal of policymaking from a civic republican point of view (though such conflicts cannot be eliminated completely).

Civic republicans can also contest sprawl insofar as it encourages a way of life that undermines the civic virtues described above. Separation from the city and the construction of suburbs as normal, and central city areas as the "other," undermines awareness of both social interdependence and the recognition of other citizens as equals. Further, self-serving exclusionary zoning in the suburbs exhibits a lack of self-restraint. To the extent that sprawl is correlated with segregation, it may decrease citizens' ability to enter into deliberative engagement with persons different than themselves. To the extent that homogeneous suburbs have by their very demographic makeup "solved" core political problems (by, in effect, externalizing them), they may encourage depoliticization and weaken the virtue of vigilant attentiveness to public matters. To the extent that suburbs are constructed to facilitate a way of life oriented around private consumption, they may act against the development of a critical civic consciousness among citizens.

Is There a Public Good? Are There Common Goods?

Civic republicans frequently evoke the notion of a public good that is more than simply the sum of all individuals' private interests. In one sense, the meaning of this public good is straightforward: republicans often simply mean the good of the regime itself. By "regime," republicans might mean simply "nation," or they might mean a particular kind of regime that is seen as having intrinsic moral worth, such as "democracy." In any case, because institutional regimes outlive (or ought to outlive, if they are desirable) individuals, activities that support these regimes can be seen as a higher kind of good than activities that benefit individuals in purely private ways. Civic republicans thus ask citizens to see themselves as stewards of the regime, with responsibility not only to themselves but to future generations to maintain and improve the regime (or simply the nation). Embedded in this concept of stewardship is a deeper philosophical point: civic republicans want to challenge the dichotomy between private interests, or the private self, and that of the "public." Why would one care whether one's country, or one's town, or one's local church, continues to flourish after we no longer are part of that community? Because one may have a sense of oneself as inherently connected to the good of this larger community and may recognize that our own selves are *constituted* by membership in particular communities.[42]

Civic republicans, then, need not conceptualize "society" as a determinate force having a life of its own and capable of human-like agency to derive a workable concept of the "public good," or, as Iseult Honohan properly clarifies, "public *goods*." Nor need the public good be conceptualized as some shared pre-political values, a unitary good (such as maximum utility) that can be unproblematically identified and implemented, or communitarian attachment. Rather, as Honohan specifies, "the model of common good central to republican politics is that of intersubjective recognition in the joint practice of self-government by citizens who share certain concerns deriving from their common vulnerability."[43] Importantly, these goods are shared, tangible matters of common concern, and they are established *through* politics. Communitarian consensus regarding values is not required to sustain a conception of common goods; as Honohan puts it, "A republic does not necessarily start from clearly agreed purposes but from sharing a common world and common fate." What are examples of such common goods? Freedom itself, or non-domination, is one such good; others cited by Honohan include public health, public education and "the existence of public spaces in which citizens can act and deliberate on the shape of their society and social practices."[44]

Underwriting a concept of shared goods is a view of the self that assumes that selves are constituted in relationship to particular communities and obligations. To be sure, Rawlsian liberalism, too, explicitly requires that citizens see themselves as participating in a larger-order scheme of cooperation. *Why* ought citizens possess this desire to participate in a just regime? On this point, Ronald Dworkin has supplied the compelling argument that private individuals derive a great good from living in a just regime; namely, they are free to pursue their private lives with a clear conscience.[45] For civic republicans, however, the very separation between private lives and the public good is problematic: To the question, Why care about the society in which I live? the proper answer is not simply, Because when society goes well, I am likely to obtain more private benefits. Instead, it is that I cannot even conceive of my own good without reference to the good of the community to which I belong. As Rousseau observed,

> Even if I could procure for myself well-being of an exclusive sort and a few dubious pleasures by sacrificing everything else solely for my own sake, I still would not be able to assure myself of peace and lasting happiness except in a well-ordered society.... The individuals to whom I owe my life, who gave me what I needed, who cultivated my soul, who communicated their talents to me, may no longer exist, yet the laws that protected my childhood live on. The good habits that I was fortunate enough to receive, the assistance that I found ready to meet my every need, the civil liberty that I enjoyed, the goods that I acquired, the pleasures that I savored—I owe all of these things to the universal order that directs public concern for the benefit of all, that anticipated my needs before I was born and will command respect for my ashes after I am gone.[46]

To be sure, a civic republican conception of the public good is not required to specify more-generic types of "public goods" of the kind identified by economists, goods such as clean air or public safety. All individual citizens have a stake in such goods, but no citizen can obtain them individually. In the suburban sprawl debate, these sorts of goods most commonly come to mind when discussing the "public good."[47]

What civic republicanism might add to the conventional understanding of the public goods at stake in debates about sprawl is an insistence that urban design ought to be compatible with the fostering of citizens who possess a deep sense that their own good is linked to that of the communities to which they belong. Even if civic republicans believe they have a philosophically superior conception of the self as inherently connected to particular communities and attachments, it is not sociologically guaranteed that citizens will actually think of themselves this way. Indeed, it is all too possible that individuals might come to think of themselves as separate in the most thorough sense from all obligations and commitments—completely unencumbered—or equally troubling, that they will possess only narrow "encumbrances" and identify only with a very particularistic reference group and not the community as a whole. Plausibly, spatial arrangements might be one important mechanism by which citizens come to view themselves as strongly, weakly, or not at all connected to the larger public; whether and how sociospatial arrangements and sprawl in particular might affect the formation of civic identity and civic virtue is thus a central question for civic republicans evaluating the goodness of sprawl.[48]

Misplaced Commodification

Civic republicans worry that commodification of distinctive human goods has gone too far in contemporary U.S. society; the relevant question here is the degree to which land and housing ought to be viewed as commodities to be bought and sold on the market.[49] As noted above, civic republicans insist that the proper method for investigating this question is to ask what the *purpose* of the built environment is and then discern whether this purpose would be undercut or enhanced by commodification.

The case of land use patterns and suburban sprawl is complex. On the one hand, the most obvious purpose of the built environment is to house people in an orderly way and provide an acceptable material environment in which they may carry out daily activities. While commodification of housing units might work tolerably well in performing this basic function, in no advanced society is housing purely commodified: interventions into the market are made to assist poor people, to regulate the construction and maintenance of buildings, and so on. On the other hand, the built environment also has the function of constituting communities and establishing the broader neighborhood environment that structures residents' daily lives. As a resident, I am affected by the size and amenities my own house provides, but I am also affected by how the streets leading to my house are organized, how neighboring houses are laid out, the level of street activity in the immediate environment, whether there is public space present, and so forth. Residents do not solely inhabit their own homes; they have an interest in (at least) their immediate surroundings as well. More specifically, the local built environment helps constitute the daily life of a given people and may demarcate particularistic identities and communities; as well, larger-order social-spatial patterns reflect and express social relationships within the community. Put another way, collective identity is at stake in the way local environments are built.

If these points are accepted, then the reasonable fear arises that unrestrained commodification of land use and housing-development decisions might undermine important goods. For instance, the market may fail to recognize or value specific neighborhood goods widely considered important by residents; for example, a housing developer may not know (or may know and not care) that a small commercial building torn down to construct high-profit condominiums has particular significance to the identity of a particular neighborhood or a particular community within that neighborhood. Or market processes may lead to a process of gentrification, whereby long-term residents and/or poor people are forced out of the neighborhood altogether. Most importantly, when neighborhoods become wholly commodified, the scope for democratic mastery over the specific goods and specific character of neighborhood life is constrained. Neighborhood character and conditions become (on the upper end of the socioeconomic spectrum) commodities sold to the highest bidders or (on the lower end of the socioeconomic spectrum) conditions thrust upon residents by forces beyond their control. Ought not the character of the places we live in and the specific goods they provide instead be a matter of shared deliberation?

According to civic republicans, yes. As a result, civic republicans will be likely to treat residential environments as the sort of good that should be only partly commodified. (For slightly different reasons, many utilitarians and most egalitarian liberals would surely agree.) To be sure, contemporary civic republicans do not want the state to assign housing arrangements to citizens, preferring to leave scope for citizens to choose where to live, how much money to spend on housing, and how to decorate their homes. Equally important, the civic republican need not—and ought not—forward the implausible and morally dubious claim that local communities ought to be wholly autonomous agents. Yet civic republicans will likely insist upon a substantive role for public deliberation at multiple scales of government, regarding, first, what *kinds* of neighborhood choices are offered to citizens, and second, the specific goods supplied by particular neighborhoods. Civic republicanism sees a public role in deliberating whether policy ought to favor, say, central city areas or, instead, suburban bedroom communities in a macro-level sense; but it will also see a public role within specific communities (be they high-density urban clusters or classic bedroom communities) for deliberation among citizens as to what exactly that neighborhood is going to look like. Much attention in the literature and in popular discussion has been placed on this second type of micro-level public deliberation about the built environment, particularly with respect to New Urbanist developments; but macro-level, higher-order deliberation about what sorts of communities larger-scale public policies should foster is probably of greater substantive importance.[50]

Egalitarianism and the Requirements of Equal Citizenship

Just as we asked what sort of individual virtues civic republicans seek to promote, we also must ask which sort of political regime best matches the civic republican conception of freedom as shared self-governance. Answering this question requires a deeper articulation of the ends that civic republicanism wishes to realize. Participation in politics is seen as a good to be promoted for its own sake because only through participation in self-governance can we preserve our freedom and (in some accounts) realize our human nature most fully. From this initial premise, we can draw more substantive conclusions about the regime that civic republicans ought to promote; a regime that fully allows for active self-governance must be democratic in character and free from domination by both outside forces and internal private power. A regime built on democratic participation, in turn, requires a relatively strong form of social equality to ensure that all are able to actively share in self-governance and that no citizens are dominated by others. Probably, in practice, this requires a level of social equality akin to the egalitarian program sketched by Rawls.[51]

As Honohan remarks, "Citizens need a material basis, not just 'social capital' or civic virtue to be able to act as active and independent citizens. Extremes of economic inequality present a serious obstacle to the possibilities for political equality and freedom." Fundamental concepts of non-domination may provide a rationale for limiting inequality, at the least; but stronger notions of freedom as active participation provide a still stronger argument for robust norms of equality. When such equality is absent, Honohan notes, "participatory politics may favor the economically powerful, amplifying the existing inequalities of civil society."[52]

Thus, the logic of a specifically civic republican argument for a relatively egalitarian state unfolds; from the premise that participation in self-governance is an essential component of freedom flows the requirement of democracy and in turn of meaningful social equality.[53] Yet each point in this chain of argument requires further stipulation. First, it is assumed that all human beings, as opposed to a select elite, are inherently capable of actively participating in civic affairs and self-governance. Empirically, even if we believed that many actual human beings in formally democratic societies are not well prepared for or capable of such participation, this should be attributed to what Mill termed "wretched social arrangements" rather than, as Plato and Aristotle implied, natural distinctions of rank among human beings.[54] Second, it is assumed that plebiscite democracy is inadequate as a form of active self-governance and that periodic assent to managerial government followed by long periods of public inactivity does not foster the specifically human excellences of shared public deliberation to which civic republicanism aspires. Rather, citizens need to be involved in civic affairs as part of their daily lives (though such involvement need not always be explicitly political). Third, it is assumed that vast inequalities of skill, resources, time, and other civic capacities are inimical to the operation of "strong democracy." Work on the relationship between socioeconomic status and political participation undertaken by Sidney Verba et al. strongly indicates that better educated and more affluent citizens are far more likely to be engaged in the political process in the United States.[55] Consequently, socioeconomic inequalities must be substantially curbed if citizens are to have anything approaching equal capacity to participate effectively in political life.

Sprawl and the Political Economy of Citizenship

The final central claim of contemporary civic republican thought concerns the proper scope of democratic politics: civic republicans argue that the public should have the capacity to exercise "mastery" over the predominant social forces shaping everyday life, including the political economy itself. Civic republican concern with sprawl is thus linked to a larger concern with the effect of contemporary corporate capitalism upon the civic fabric of the United States. Civic republican thinkers have claimed that there is something wrong when shared public spaces are neglected or ignored while privatized or commercialized space expands, and that there is something wrong when locally owned enterprises are put out of business by big-box chains such as Wal-Mart. The "something" that is wrong is a loss of public capacity to steer the economy toward ends that sustain the polity itself and that foster a praiseworthy way of life. In the Wal-Mart case, a town's economic future may become wholly dependent on the actions of an out-of-town corporate conglomerate, as opposed to being held in the hands of local merchants with strong ties to one another and to the local community.[56] It might also be argued that local retail keeps more financial capital re-circulating locally and may be more favorable to the creation of local social capital than enterprises like Wal-Mart; or that a strong and independent citizenry is better fostered by maximizing the numbers of people running their own enterprises rather than the number working as Wal-Mart employees.

Civic republicans thus have a qualitative objection to enterprises such as Wal-Mart and want the state to actively favor smaller enterprises and retard the growth of mega-retail operations. Moreover, civic republicans have reason to suspect that *sprawl* may be centrally linked to the growth of such enterprises (whether as cause or effect). Wal-Mart's strategy of locating just outside the municipal borders of small and medium-sized towns, away from existing downtowns, is well documented; the new stores direct traffic of persons and vehicles away from existing community centers.[57]

Consequently, civic republicans tend to look favorably upon efforts by local communities to shape their immediate economic environment in support of civic ends. But if it is acceptable for localities to use zoning and other regulations to slow down or keep out the growth of conglomerate retail, why should it not also be acceptable for localities to pursue exclusionary zoning to make it difficult for the poor to enter a given community? This is the hard question that the liberal inclined toward a neutralist state will ask of civic republicans with respect to sprawl; as seen in chapter 4, exclusionary zoning is widely recognized as a major factor contributing to spatial segregation and metropolitan inequalities. Advocating that government act to advance substantive notions of the good life opens the door to potentially dangerous policies, liberals might argue: there might appear to be a number of good "civic" reasons for wanting to keep the poor out of one's community (e.g., the poor, needing to stretch their dollars, might be more likely to want a community-destroying Wal-Mart to come to town).

Civic republicans have two potent replies to this objection. The first is that the worth of a given intervention by the locality into the local political economy needs to be judged on its merits by examining the ends toward which the intervention is directed. While local voters might describe both exclusionary zoning and anti-big-box zoning in terms of "preserving local character," the substance of the local character being preserved is, in the one case, class privilege; in the other case, it is the economic basis for a civic community. Civic republicans of a progressive bent might argue that these are substantially different cases, from a moral point of view. Moreover, civic republicans could push further and hypothesize that a democratic public in the habit of connecting public deliberation to substantive notions of the good (especially the good of a robust citizenry) would easily be able to make this distinction.

This hypothesis connects to the second reply of civic republicans to liberal questions on the exclusionary zoning issue: civic republicans can reasonably observe that liberal political culture itself, described by civic republicans as involving an emptying out of moral deliberation from politics, has hardly impeded the spread of exclusionary zoning policies at the local level. Indeed, civic republicans might further argue that the narrowing of politics to concern merely with the size and distribution of the economic pie has encouraged citizens to view politics and the state apparatus primarily as mechanisms for protecting or advancing economic self-interest. Citizens conditioned to think of politics this way would find it perfectly natural to resist encroachments on their property values as strongly as possible, leading to exclusionary zoning. It is the absence of serious moral deliberation from political life rather than its presence that allows exclusionary zoning to go unchallenged, the civic republican might continue. Reinvigorating political debate to include more substantive debates about the nature of community life might create a climate in which exclusionary zoning policies would be more frequently challenged.

Consideration of the exclusionary zoning issue illustrates how issues of scale and citizenship necessarily come to the fore when one considers what an applied civic republicanism might look like in the contemporary United States. Civic republicans want citizens to have experience with exercising self-governance and a concern with the good of advancing a morally desirable, shared way of life. It is vitally important, however, that these citizens do not take their immediate geographic community as the sole or even primary reference point in pursuing these goals, but rather that they identify with the good of the larger-order political community. In the context of an economically and spatially segregated United States, pure localism is a straightforward recipe for hardening social and economic inequalities, with devastating effects on the health of national civic life.[58] This is not what contemporary civic republicans, at least those of a progressive bent, have in mind.

But such civic republicans can persuasively argue that if the larger-order political community is accepted as the relevant frame of reference for public policymaking, and if citizens somehow come to have a sense of the good of the whole, then in practical terms it would become quite easy to provide normative justifications for ending or relaxing exclusionary zoning—*and,* simultaneously, for slowing down the growth of Wal-Mart and similar mega-chains. J. Eric Oliver has shown how economic segregation at the municipal level leads to weakened engagement in local politics, as rich communities are able to "solve" political problems of how rich and poor are to coexist, the "solution" being simply to segregate themselves into rich localities where all substantive political problems have been solved.[59] This observation might underwrite a powerful civic case for reducing exclusionary zoning. On the other hand, the efforts of local communities to stop Wal-Mart from coming to town are unlikely to generate negative effects on residents of neighboring towns (and, indeed, may have a positive effect since superstores would drain business from those communities as well) or to undermine the overall civic life of a given metropolitan region.

A coherent civic republicanism, then, cannot be equated with or reduced to localism, but neither can it a priori rule out local communities as potential actors in taking concrete steps to shape their local political economy—or local spatial design—for the sake of some concrete good. Whether any specific proposed action ought to win approval depends on the nature of the end being advanced, in addition to its likely effects on not only the locality but on the larger-order community of which each locality is a part. Necessarily, then, if civic republican regimes are to be successful, the public must learn to exercise collective judgment and become skilled in the art of practical wisdom and of discerning good proposals from bad, with respect to both intent and likely effect. This, in turn, likely requires the further development of institutional mechanisms designed to facilitate such public deliberation.[60]

Yet, as this discussion has already noted, there is reason to suspect that something more may be required; namely, a sense of the overall normative principles that ought to inform this exercise of practical wisdom. Within contemporary democratic regimes, these principles—even when invoked by civic republicans—are likely to be thoroughly democratic and liberal in character. As we have seen, contemporary civic republicanism starts from the premise that self-governance (or "non-domination," in Pettit's formulation) is the heart of freedom; from that initial premise it is possible to derive robust principles regarding equal respect for persons and their life prospects, and strong commitment to democratic norms of inclusionary decision making. But the precise meaning of such general principles, and, even more so, the particular claims that arise from them, is and must be a matter for democratic debate. Put another way, policymaking should not be seen as a matter of mechanically applying to politics moral principles established outside of the political realm; rather, it is within politics itself that regimes establish the meaning and practical application of claimed principles. Instead of assuming universal consent to a given standard (strong natural rights to property, utility maximization, the principles of justice that would be chosen in the original position) as the precondition for politics, civic republicans argue that it is through politics itself—both public debate and the public action that follows—that citizens forge a (always tentative and shifting) practical understanding of the moral and political principles shaping their common life.[61]

Applying Civic Republicanism to the Built Environment

We are now in position to more thoroughly elicit the implications of civic republican thought for the assessment of suburban sprawl. The first point to make is that "utilitarian" concerns with sprawl—that sprawl might be too expensive, that it might be aesthetically unpleasant—can be fully acknowledged as a legitimate object of concern and public debate by civic republicans. Debate about concrete material concerns (costs and benefits) and about the stock of common goods in a given community must be at the very heart of a robust civic republican politics.[62] Likewise, concern with the distributive implications of sprawl, as well as the potential effect of sprawl on possibilities for meaningful social solidarity of the kind needed to sustain a just society, is also consistent with civic republicanism—or at least those versions of civic republicanism that derive relatively robust egalitarian norms from the demands of equal citizenship and active participation in self-governance. Finally, civic republicans are capable of speaking to the actual and potential environmental harms associated with sprawl, and of doing so in ways that may be more consonant with environmentalists' understandings of the worth of ecological goods (see chapter 8 for elaboration). Civic republicans are thus fully capable of speaking to the diversity of practical concerns raised by sprawl in an adequate and even compelling manner.

Yet civic republicans also bring at least two distinctive concerns to the ongoing public debate about sprawl. The first is the suggestion that the public should be concerned with the qualitative dimensions of our urban and suburban communities, particularly those dimensions that affect, and indeed help constitute, citizens' common life; the second is the suggestion that the public (through the state) may legitimately aim to foster certain kinds of urban arrangements rather than others for the sake of promoting particular habits, especially those habits of participation and related civic virtues that are essential to sustaining an ideal of freedom as self-governance.

This normative framework can be contrasted with approaches that see built communities simply as products of individual choices in the marketplace and that would permit overriding or revising such choices only in rare circumstances. As we saw in chapter 5, liberal egalitarians have good reason to challenge both socio-spatial patterns that prove inimical to the realization of social solidarity and the cultural preferences associated with such patterns. The egalitarian civic republican can offer another reason to challenge such patterns and preferences, which is that the ways of life produced or constituted by such choices may not be morally praiseworthy and may in fact be inimical not only to larger-order social solidarity but also to the local practice of civic virtue.

WHAT ARE TOWNS, CITIES, AND NEIGHBORHOODS FOR?
SOCIO-SPATIAL ARRANGEMENTS AS A SOCIAL PRACTICE

One further observation is in order before we consider how civic republicans might interrogate the goodness of specific residential environments: civic republicans understand the spatial organization of communities as a "social practice," rather than simply as the aggregate of many individual, unrelated decisions. Civic republicans can make this case on two grounds. First, the organization of space is intimately intertwined with the social relations of any coherent political community. Centuries ago Native American tribes in present-day Alabama, for instance, molded the earth into a series of large mounds rising up to sixty feet; elite groups occupied the largest and most central mound.[63] In modern cities, public buildings and public space both constitute and signify the presence and power of the state. The spatial design of communities and cities has, historically, reflected the interests and prerogatives of (relatively) privileged groups in fairly obvious ways (hence the term "socio-spatial organization" used in chapter 4). This is also demonstrably the case in the United States with respect to the creation of suburbs, where an entire infrastructure of public funding and subsidies has helped create and sustain the process of suburbanization.

Secondly, civic republicans can argue that socio-spatial arrangements embody the aspirations of a given society and the way of life its members will lead and that spatial arrangements have profound effects on both the sorts of lives individuals lead and also the cultural norms that predominate in society as a whole. "Sprawl," for instance, is often thought to promote the following social practices, which are constitutive of the mainstream U.S. way of life: households are grouped into private homes accessible only by private transportation; most publicly accessible space is oriented toward commercial ends, with the aim of facilitating efficient consumption; the places created have relatively low densities and assure minimal intrusions on privacy; and the home, the workplace, and the market are functionally and spatially separated. This sort of socio-spatial environment, in turn, is generally thought to discourage the sorts of vitality that thinkers such as Iris M. Young often associate with urban space (see chapter 1), and the formation of "third places," identified by the urban sociologist Ray Oldenburg as vital to the formation of civic and political life.[64] To return to a formulation developed in chapter 5, this sort of environment, especially when combined with spatial segregation by class and race, might have the effect of concealing or obscuring, rather than making visible, troubling aspects of social reality. Civic republicans thus worry about whether sprawl discourages both the habits of citizenship and the critical civic consciousness that a robust practice of shared self-governance requires.

THE VARIETY OF BUILT ENVIRONMENTS: A TYPOLOGY

Understanding the built environment as a social practice, an artifact of conscious human decisions, allows analysts to examine the degree to which socio-spatial arrangements succeed or fail in realizing normatively important substantive goods.

It may be, of course, that certain kinds of socio-spatial arrangements are advantageous for some purposes, but not for others. Sidney Brower thus usefully identifies thirty-three distinct qualities of residential living that might plausibly be seen as desirable, then creates a four-pronged typology of desirable neighborhood types.[65] Type 1 are central urban locations, described by Brower as "a part of the city that is lively and busy, with lots to see and do...[which] has a mix of many different people and uses and...attracts visitors from other parts of the city and beyond." Type 2 locations are areas that have "the feeling of a small town, with its own institutions and meeting places. People who live here know one another and are able to recognize those who do not live here." Type 3 locations, "residential partnerships," are exclusively oriented toward domestic life. "Residents go to other parts of the city for work, shopping, and entertainment." Type 4 locations, "retreats," are areas "where one feels removed from other people and their activities. People who live here tend to be independent and go their separate ways."[66]

Each of these distinct locations has a typical clientele and distinctive requirements for being successful. Urban areas tend to attract young singles and couples without children; small-town environments attract settled families and people who "like to live in a cohesive neighborhood where they know everyone"; residential areas attract higher-income families who "do not like the city"; and retreat environments attract individualists and people who are "antisocial, lonely, and out of the mainstream." Survey findings cited by Brower indicate that the "small-town" setting is the most preferred environment, favored by some 48 percent of his sample; 27 percent favor urban locations, and 22 percent residential partnerships. Only 3 percent favor retreat settings.[67]

Brower does not attempt to pass judgment on the worthiness of each of these settings or on the content of individuals' preferences. Instead, he argues that each kind of place will be most successful when it meets its own distinctive requirements. Good central cities need the following characteristics: ample public spaces and pedestrian environments; nonwork-related facilities within easy access; housing units designed to relieve noise concerns and provide a sense of privacy and intimacy; impressive public buildings and landmarks; varied activities, especially those geared at meeting residents' desires (e.g., for luxury and entertainment); effective public transportation; a comprehensible design layout that is welcoming to visitors and newcomers; housing that can accommodate a variety of social classes; and effective policing and surveillance to offset the sense of chaos and diversity that define cities yet also weaken social barriers to crime. As Brower summarizes, "A good Center is active and lively, has a full range of facilities, offers a wide range of choice, serves visitors and newcomers, has a diversity of people and places, is constantly changing and evolving, provides special protection against incivilities, and represents a wide range of needs, tastes and values."[68]

Small-town neighborhoods, according to Brower, should be "visually distinct," "bounded," and "small enough so that each resident knows many others by face or name and reputation." "Typically," Brower adds, "it has a concentration of stores, institutions, and public places (perhaps 'Main Street,' 'The Avenue,' or 'The Center'), which serves as the focus of common identity." The focus in small-town environments is on stability, with high rates of homeownership and the development of "local social networks"; consequently, it takes time for newcomers to be accepted and settle in. Overall, Brower writes, "a good small-town neighborhood has a clear center and defined boundaries, a full complement of local facilities and institutions, a stable residential population and a network of friendships. It favors residents over outsiders, is protected from change, and represents a range of needs, tastes, and values."[69] Brower cautions that while many people say they want small-town neighborhoods, numerous social trends are undermining the viability of small towns, such as the proliferation of chain stores at the expense of local operations, cosmopolitan consumer preferences that may not be satisfied by shopping only locally, and the increasing capacity of citizens to develop social ties and forms of community outside the geographic neighborhood.

Brower suggests that the "residential partnership" form of neighborhood appears likely to grow in importance, as small-town settings have a difficult time sustaining themselves. Residential partnerships are essentially bedroom communities, and are based on the principle of exclusion; as Brower puts it, such a neighborhood "is attractive to those who want an environment that provides minimal distractions outside the home, that reflects their own needs, tastes, and values, and over which they can exercise a great deal of control." He notes, "It is attractive to people who are fearful of conditions of the larger society, to those for whom home rather than community is the center of domestic life, and those who grew up in the suburbs and think of themselves as 'not city people.'" For such a neighborhood to be successful on its terms, it needs to be tranquil and homogeneous and to provide amenities to residents only. Notably, Brower observes, "the Residential Partnership is the most common type of neighborhood being built in the United States."[70]

The fourth type of neighborhood, the retreat, merits less attention in this discussion. These neighborhoods are oriented entirely around individual living units and are intended to maximize individuality and privacy. Such a neighborhood, Brower writes, will be "private and secluded" and "[will represent] the individual householder's needs, tastes, and values"; it will also be "not easily accessible to strangers."[71]

Brower argues that instead of attempting to promote a single ideal type of neighborhood, planners and builders should recognize that people have diverse needs and desires with respect to the kind of place they want to inhabit. Brower does not question or problematize these preferences (although he does acknowledge criticisms of each type of neighborhood). To be sure, Brower's typology still leaves plenty of room for a critique of "sprawl," insofar as sprawling places might fall outside these categories and fail to provide any desirable goods at all.[72] But Brower deliberately refrains from asking whether one sort of place might be better than another, and, in particular, whether one kind of neighborhood might be more conducive to the formation of active citizens than another.

BEYOND THE NEUTRAL STATE: THE PROBLEM WITH RESIDENTIAL PARTNERSHIPS

In this sense, Brower's approach corresponds with the emphasis of neutralist liberalism on withholding judgment on the worth of different ways of life. As we have already seen, criticism of the liberal "neutral state" has been at the heart of contemporary civic republican criticisms of both liberal theory and contemporary democratic practice in the United States. For both principled and practical reasons, civic republicanism will insist that what sorts of built communities we ought to foster should not be theorized as simply a matter of individual preferences working themselves out in the market but instead as a matter of shared deliberation, deliberation that itself is explicitly connected to basic moral values and ideals—particularly, the ideal of the engaged democratic citizen. Civic republicans, then, are unlikely to share—at least not as an a priori assumption—Brower's implicit notion that the various kinds of built environments in contemporary U.S. society are to be regarded as equally valid and praiseworthy. The civic republican can thus respond to claims such as Brower's with three observations.

First, to reiterate, even if we ultimately conclude that there is no unitary "best" sort of socio-spatial environment, or ideal form of the neighborhood, inquiry into the kinds of goods various neighborhoods facilitate is, in itself, essential.

Second, civic republicans may insist that well-functioning democracies have certain relatively firm *requirements* for civic engagement and participation and may insist that all neighborhoods are subject to critique according to whether or not a given neighborhood promotes active citizenship. (Indeed, civic republicans may point out that the quality of facilitating robust civic and political participation is notably absent from Brower's discussion of desirable residential traits.)

Third, even as civic republicans insist that all neighborhoods need to be conducive to a least some baseline standard of active participation, they can concede that there are legitimate grounds for variation among neighborhoods along many other dimensions, and that active citizens can reasonably differ among one another regarding which sort of neighborhood they would choose to inhabit (or how they would like to see their existing neighborhood evolve). Grounds for such diversity of opinions may include the individual's life-cycle stage, personal conception of the well-lived life (rural solitude vs. urban vibrancy), biographical factors, or simply "preferences" in the classical sense (i.e., individual tastes not amenable to intersubjective analysis and discussion). In short, it is possible, if not probable, that civic republicans will conclude that a variety of neighborhood forms could potentially both permit reasonably active citizenship and also promote a way of life that could be regarded as morally worthy or at least morally acceptable.

With these qualifications and clarifications in place, how then might civic republicans critique the set of preferences that Brower (quite plausibly) associates with "residential partnerships"? These preferences include, to recount, a desire to control one's personal space with a minimum of outside influence and the desire to escape the "conditions in the larger society." Residential partnerships thus embody an ideal of negative liberty—freedom from intrusion by others. Civic republicans may not look too harshly upon that desire, but it is the further desire to live one's life without being impinged by the circumstances of larger society that is more likely to be regarded as objectionable. Such a set of preferences reflects both an attitude of *withdrawal* from the larger social order as opposed to seeking to balance one's own legitimate self-interest in connection with the interests of others and the maintenance of shared common goods; it declares the lexical priority of egoistic goods over common concerns. To return to a distinction made by Rawls, such a set of preferences reflects a conception of society itself as an arrangement for maximizing private interests and utilities rather than as a system of social cooperation.

Yet some further parsing is needed to isolate the exact nature of the civic republican objection to privatistic preferences. Can anyone who, like Wendell Berry, prefers to live on a quiet farm in the country be considered an escapist privatist? And what of the fact that modern societies and, specifically, modern urban agglomerations, do evidently produce stress, irritation, and even alienation in substantial numbers of people, such that the desire for a private, secure space, the proverbial "haven in a heartless world," appears as natural to a significant portion of people in the contemporary United States?

The Wendell Berry question can be resolved straightforwardly. Living in a rural community does not intrinsically imply withdrawing from community life; it simply means that one is living in a qualitatively different sort of community than a metropolitan area.[73] This is different in kind from living within a metropolitan area and claiming access to the benefits of living in a metropolitan community, while simultaneously seeking to shield oneself from the negative aspects of such a community. This argument is coherent, however, only to the extent that we conceive of suburbs and cities as inherently interdependent, such that, in moving to a suburb (say, Falls Church, Virginia), one is in fact not entering an entirely new center of social cooperation distinct from Washington, D.C. Simply put, well-off suburbs such as those that ring Washington, D.C., or any number of central city areas could not exist were it not for the presence of a metropolitan agglomeration that acts as a center and stimulant of economic activity. Although one may feel oneself to be in an entirely different community when one leaves the streets of Washington and walks (or more likely, drives) around the streets of Falls Church, this immediate sense experience belies a larger-order inherent relationship between relatively tranquil Falls Church and bustling Washington.

Indeed, a central goal of critics of U.S.-style suburbanization is to reveal the apparent separateness of suburban communities from central city areas as essentially illusory.

But is it not the case that society (especially urban society) itself is stressful and sometimes dangerous? Is there anything wrong with the prevalent desire to escape the unpleasant aspects of society, a desire, Fishman reminds us, that dates back at least to the dawn of the industrial era in Anglo American society? Civic republicans can acknowledge and to some extent accommodate the reality of this desire; Hannah Arendt, for instance, explicitly urged the formation and preservation of private spaces, arguing that such spaces are needed as a relief from activity in the public sphere.[74] But civic republicans might, following the lead of Richard Sennett, cogently argue that the desire to live in a purified social environment reflects a fundamental immaturity, an unwillingness to accept "risk, uncertainty, incompleteness," to expose oneself to vulnerability and suffering, and, in short, to accept the reality of the human condition.[75]

Additionally, civic republicans might argue that the desire for private space and respite from the outside world should not give moral sanction to some to avoid unpleasant aspects of modern life that others cannot. Such avoidance is a sort of free-riding, a prioritizing of individual comfort over the shared goods of the civic regime. It also reflects and reinforces the erroneous perception that the conditions of the larger society are simply a given confronting individuals, rather than a product of social processes for which the citizenry has collective responsibility. Indeed, to the extent that the polity objectively is, or feels itself to be, unable to shape broad social processes, it logically follows that individuals will want to escape something they have no hope of controlling or altering.

This is the deeper import of contemporary civic republicans' insistence on exerting democratic influence over the political economy. Without a shared sense that social conditions, the conditions of modern life, can somehow be shaped by public activity, there is no reason for individuals to regard the conditions of modern life—including the specific condition of our urban environments—as anything other than a given, an unchangeable backdrop, more similar to a mountain or an ocean than to a discernible product of human activity. If it is the case that "unpleasant" aspects of modern society (crime, congestion, distrust, etc.) cannot be changed, modified, or ameliorated, then the only remaining question is how these "bads" will be distributed, and it is perfectly natural that persons conditioned to prioritize private over common ends will seek to minimize their share of these bads. The absence of a shared "sense of mastery" over the forces that govern modern life is itself an impulse to privatization and, in turn, to the rise of the suburban residential partnership. In a regime in which such a sense of mastery existed, perhaps individuals' preferences for the privatism offered by residential partnerships would subside; parallel to the observations made in chapters 2 and 3, concerning the contingency of observed suburban preferences upon the conditions of urban environments, civic republicans can hypothesize that existing preferences for privatism may be inauthentic distortions. But civic republicans would also argue that even if such preferences were *not* in any sense distorted (being not a case of Elster's adaptive preferences), then they would still be morally suspect. To wish to enjoy the fruits of the regime (security, tranquility, etc.) while avoiding its costs reflects a lack of commitment to the good of the whole. A regime might, in favorable circumstances, survive indefinitely if such an attitude predominated, but would be unlikely to realize the republican vision of a society based on widespread, meaningful participation in the work of self-governance.

———

To summarize, then, civic republican suspicion of sprawl is based on the following logic: The practice of freedom as shared self-governance requires that citizens actively take responsibility in public life for matters of common concern; it requires that citizens possess particular virtues that motivate them not only to action but to a certain kind of public action that is concerned with the good of the whole and that recognizes social interdependencies; it requires that citizens be relatively equal in their capacities to shape political life; and it requires that citizens actually possess the collective capacity to shape and steer the dominant forces and institutions of modern life. In order to forward this conception of freedom, civic republicans are willing to criticize not only existing institutions and social practices, but also existing preferences and cultural norms, to the extent that they undercut freedom as self-governance. But the history of suburbia in the United States reveals sprawl to be a response precisely to Americans' desires for individual private space in which they might escape larger social problems, not an attempt to build communities that would foster active citizenship. In seeking to come to terms with the de-politicization and lack of civic engagement characteristic of modern American, suburban sprawl appears, at least at first glance, to be part of the problem.

Not surprisingly, then, the tenor of civic republican–inspired social commentary concerning suburban sprawl to date has been critical in tone; thus, Sandel has described campaigns against Wal-Mart as indicative of the substance of an active political economy of citizenship, Dagger has charged that the libertarian "cafeteria or shopping-mall conception of the metropolis…undermines both community and citizenship," Barber has critiqued the rise of the shopping mall and decline of noncommercial public spaces, and Pettit has warned that the shape of metropolitan public space "bodes extremely ill for public life, for it ensures that the view which people have of others in their society, in particular the view that they have of those who do not belong to their own class and coterie, becomes hostage to fantasy."[76] In general, the image of spread-out, low-density communities in which the built environment is dominated by the needs of the automobile and in which there is little noncommercial shared space lacks intuitive appeal for many civic republicans; the strong suspicion is that this sort of built environment shares a natural affinity with Americans' general commitment to prioritizing achievement of private ends (being able to shop conveniently) over engagement in the public forum (being able to actively deliberate with others on matters of common concern).

Nonetheless, it remains an empirical question whether sprawl, or aspects thereof, deserves the opprobrium that civic republican thinkers (and urban design professionals and anti-sprawl activists who cite republican-sounding themes in critiquing sprawl) commonly deliver.[77] Chapter 7 considers just this question, but before moving on to that investigation, it needs to be stated that while civic republicans may suspect that there is a *tendency* for sprawl to undermine civic virtues as described above, this should not imply a return to environmental determinism (the view that geography is destiny). For civic republicans to make a very strong claim that it is *impossible* for sprawling environments to nurture concerned, active citizens who have the good of the whole in mind would not only likely be an empirical overreach, but would also imply an unwarranted conclusion that there is *no* possibility of meaningful civic and political engagement emerging in suburban environments in the future. What is in question in the analysis to follow is the more limited claim that local spatial attributes may affect the *likelihood* of Americans actively engaging in politics in predictable ways, given the present state of political mobilization and engagement in the society as a whole—ways that civic republicans need to be aware of both when evaluating sprawl and when envisioning how to reinvigorate U.S. democracy.

SEVEN

You Can't March on a Strip Mall

Sprawl and Political Disengagement

A N ACTIVE, POLITICALLY ENGAGED citizenry is both a precondition and a product of a regime based upon the practice of shared self-governance. Civic republicans (and others) thus want to know whether sprawl hinders or helps the practice of active citizenship. Put simply, what sorts of spatial characteristics are most conducive to active participation in civic life? By active participation, we mean not simply being interested in politics in the abstract, but actually participating, beyond merely voting, in some sort of common enterprise involving the public good.

This is, at bottom, an empirical question, and one the Social Capital Community Benchmark Survey (SCCBS) is well suited to explore. This chapter examines the effect of sprawl-related variables on basic awareness of and interest in politics, in addition to the following specific measures of active civic engagement: participation in local reform organizations, attendance at political meetings and rallies, participation in protest-type activities, membership in political organizations, petition signing, attendance at public meetings, and, finally, an overall index measure of political participation. Together, these measures span a wide spectrum of civic activity, ranging from quite widespread, relatively low-cost activities, such as petition signing, to much rarer, time-intensive activities, such as participating in a protest.

This chapter demonstrates that there is, minimally, a strong affinity between residence in an older, less car-dependent central city neighborhood and the propensity to be engaged in nonelectoral political activity, controlling for a range of factors (including individuals' political ideology). The strength of this relationship, moreover, compares favorably to three long-established predictors of political participation that are related to the sprawl debate: homeownership, length of residency in the same community, and city size. Indeed, using simulation analysis we find that the cumulative effect of sprawl-related variables on depressing civic participation substantially outweighs the positive benefits of higher homeownership and smaller city size associated with suburbs. After establishing this relationship, we go on to consider the more difficult question of whether this observed correlation represents a *causal* relationship, in which more sprawl leads to lower participation—while also pointing out that from a specifically civic republican point of view, simply establishing an affinity between spatial characteristics and a lack of civic engagement is sufficient to inform robust normative judgments concerning sprawl.

The empirical findings of this chapter, juxtaposed with the findings of chapter 6 indicating that low-density areas are associated with increased social trust, show that sprawl-related variables have divergent effects on Americans' social habits and attitudes; specifically, more sprawl is associated with lower political engagement but higher levels of local social cohesion. The final section of this chapter revisits civic republican theory in some depth to assess how civic republicans might negotiate this apparent tension between vibrant political engagement and social cohesion.

The Rediscovery of Place in Recent Political Science

The general relationship between local contexts and political engagement and/or social capital has received increasing attention from political scientists in recent years. Pioneering work by J. Eric Oliver on the relationship between local context and specifically local political participation, using the 1990 Citizen Participation Survey and 1990 U.S. Census data, found that both smaller city size and high levels of local economic diversity were strong predictors of increased individual participation. Oliver found relatively little evidence of a direct relationship between broad land use patterns and participation, although he hypothesized that neighborhood design might account for an observed positive relationship between older city age and increased political participation in the Sunbelt.[1]

Adding to this picture, Lance Freeman's study of the effect of local spatial context on neighborhood ties in three U.S. cities found that residence in a census block group with a relatively low percentage of workers driving alone to work is a significant positive predictor of both the existence and number of neighborhood social ties, after controlling for a range of individual characteristics in addition to local population density and the local poverty rate.[2] Reaffirming Sidney Verba and Norman Nie's earlier finding of a link between "boundedness" and increased political participation, Stan Humphries's multilevel analysis of political participation drawing on 1996 National Election Study data found that the percentage of out-of-town commuters in a locality has a negative effect on political participation.[3] Analysis of the SCCBS by Dan Hopkins shows that (controlling for local population density) the presence of big-box retailers in one's zip code is a negative predictor of rates of nonelectoral political participation, especially the more confrontational political activities, such as protests.[4] Finally, the political scientist Kevin Leyden has demonstrated a link between residence in a walkable neighborhood and increased political participation in a study of 258 residents of cities and suburbs in Ireland.[5] In short, recent literature provides tantalizing suggestions that at least some contextual variables affect individual-level social capital and political participation in important ways.

Does Physical Form Really Influence Individual Behavior? The New Urban Sociology

The urban sociologist Lyn Lofland points out that, for decades, social scientists tended to view "geographic determinism" as a badge of shame.[6] Yet the notion that physical structures, though they are first and foremost human creations, might influence the behavior and consciousness of those who live in their shadow is, as Lofland notes, "a commonplace among geographers and environmental psychologists," and, we might add, among contemporary New Urbanists. Nonetheless, in testing the notion that spatial form might have predictable effects on individual behavior, it is important to clarify that it is theoretically possible to affirm such a hypothesis without concluding that "geography is destiny" in any straightforward determinist way; rather, the claim is, again echoing Lofland, that physical form can help *structure* the nature of interactions that occur in the "public realm," so as to make some forms of interactions more likely and others less likely.[7] The claim is not that it is impossible that there would ever be a large protest march through the parking lots of a mega-retail site on the suburban fringe, or that it is inevitable that there will be such marches in the downtown areas of the fringe's associated center city, but that if we had to predict where the next march would occur we would bet on the central city environment (and we would bet, too, that a disproportionate number of the marchers would be central city residents).

Several urban theorists have gone beyond general claims that sprawl impacts "community" to hypothesize a specific link between spatial design and political participation. Lofland, for instance, argues, "In the place of a 'lively street life' we have millions of adult Americans who have as an option a round of life consisting of (1) leaving their autoresidences [homes whose principal outward feature is the garage]—which are located in megmono-neighborhoods [single-use neighborhoods] of similarly priced and designed detached houses, (2) driving through autostreets to the antiparks [corporate "parks"] or megastructures where they work, (3) stopping at the counterlo-cale shopping mall after work, and then (4) returning via autostreets to the autoresidences they call home. This is an option for a life of privatism."[8]

Margaret Kohn's recent work on the privatization of public space also identifies the character of shared space as essential in facilitating political activity. "Public sidewalks and streets are practically the only remaining sites for unscripted political activity," writes Kohn. She adds, "Access to public space is important because public forums are used to communicate ideas to allies and adversaries through techniques such as street speaking, demonstrations, picketing, leafletting, and petitioning. The face-to-face politics that takes place in public places requires no resources except perseverance and energy."[9]

David Brain's recent work examining the sociological assumptions of the New Urbanism points in a similar theoretical direction. Employing an important distinction between "community" and "civility," Brain argues that while suburban places may facilitate certain types of community interactions (among similar persons) as effectively as urban places, they are unlikely to facilitate civility, which involves interaction and cohabitation with strangers. Such civility is the "quintessential normative dimension" of urbanism, and, unlike "community" itself, is inherently place-based. "What has broken down is not our relations with those with whom we share intimate relations," Brain writes, "but our relations with everyone else, with strangers: in both the actual spaces between our various engagements in the private realm and in the metaphorical public space of politics." Brain goes on to suggest that "the erosion of meaningful public space by suburban development patterns (with their emphasis on the parochial communities at the expense of what comes between) is part of what has become a kind of trained incapacity for public life."[10]

Related to this, the social theorist Fran Tonkiss has provided a useful discussion of urban space as both a "point of struggle" and a *resource for* mobilization" for social movements. First, theorists of urban social movements have long noted that it is in urban space that power and power relationships become visible and concrete; as Tonkiss notes, "the architecture of authority gives physical form to official sites and concentrations of power, whether we think of this instrumentally in terms of social elites or structurally in terms of the sheer weight of institutions." It is thus natural that the spaces where government and corporate power are most visible also act as the spaces where resistance (in the form of social movements) becomes most visible. Second, "urban spaces provide a stage for wider political conflicts," not just in the specific sense of providing usable space where protest activity may be manifested but in the broader sense of serving as the terrain in which social inequalities of various kinds can be challenged. Specifically, control of the city and of public space itself often becomes the focal point for political conflict and oppositional movements.[11]

To be sure, not all political activity and political communication occurs in public spaces. But these scholars suggest that public spaces and places are critical mechanisms both for making political life visible and for drawing citizens into political engagement (even if much of such engagement is subsequently pursued in private spaces). Kohn and Brain, in particular, go beyond general claims made by New Urbanist writers positing a negative relationship between sprawl and community life to make what is at once a more specific and a more modest claim, which is that whatever its relationship with informal social life and social capital more broadly, prominent features of sprawl tend to inhibit specifically *political* activity. In contrast, pedestrian-friendly spaces with vibrant face-to-face street life and opportunities to reach a broader public can act as incubators of enhanced, visible political engagement: public political communication is easier and likely to be more effective in such locations. Further, cities themselves may often generate enhanced political engagement, for the reasons identified by Tonkiss. This chapter confines itself to testing these claims. Inferences concerning the relationship between sprawl and political activity should *not* be extended to form broader generalizations about sprawl and nonpolitical forms of social life.

Plausible as the hypothesis of negative correlation between sprawl and political participation may be, however, it runs counter to a long-held view among some urban scholars that the metropolitan fragmentation associated with sprawl, by creating smaller localities, should actually *increase* opportunities for meaningful political participation. Indeed, *The Costs of Sprawl—2000* report discussed in chapter 2 counted increased civic participation as a *benefit* of sprawl precisely because it groups citizens into smaller places, where participation might be seen as more efficacious.[12]

This discrepancy highlights, once again, the importance of being very specific about both what we mean by sprawl and the importance of recognizing that various dimensions of sprawl may have contradictory effects on civic behavior. With those considerations in mind, we now more specifically examine how the core sprawl-related variables used in this study affect various forms of political participation.

The Effect of Sprawl on Basic Political Consciousness

We begin by considering the relationship between sprawl and three measures of what might be termed "basic political consciousness": ability to name one's U.S. senators, propensity to read newspapers, and stated interest in politics.

TABLE 7.1.   Basic Political Consciousness by Place of Residence

	Can Name Both Senators	Days/Week Read Paper	"Very Interested" in Politics
Central City Residents	27.2%	3.51	34.0%
Suburban Residents	24.2%	3.58	31.8%
Rural Town Residents	24.5%	3.76	30.5%
Rural Nontown Residents	24.4%	3.37	29.5%
Density >8,000 persons/mile	27.6%	3.25	33.1%
Density <2,000 persons/mile	24.0%	3.59	31.1%
Neighborhood Built prior to 1950	28.4%	3.54	33.6%
Neighborhood Built 1980 or Later	24.9%	3.47	32.5%
Drive Alone in Tract <65%	26.4%	3.18	33.8%
Drive Alone in Tract >85%	24.1%	3.78	34.1%
Tract Average Commute <18 Min.	32.2%	3.89	32.4%
Tract Average Commute >30 Min.	20.5%	3.17	32.1%

Sources: SCCBS; 2000 U.S. Census.

Respondents to the SCCBS were asked whether they could name their state's two U.S. senators; their responses were ranked on a five-level scale, ranging from being able to name both (about 25 percent of the sample) to being unable to name either (roughly 50 percent of the sample). They were also asked how many days a week they read a newspaper, and how interested they are in politics.

Table 7.1 shows that as a descriptive matter, there is no consistent relationship between sprawl-related variables and these three measures of basic political awareness. While it is striking that ability to name both one's senators is higher in traditional urban environments, newspaper reading is higher in lower-density settings. Interestingly, abstract interest in politics appears to vary very little across spatial settings.

Regression analysis reveals a stronger set of relationships (see table 7.2). The proportion of people in the census tract driving alone and neighborhood age are jointly significant predictors of interest in politics, with interest being higher in less sprawling areas, among the 79 percent of respondents who are white and/or a college graduate. Among this sub-sample, a resident

TABLE 7.2.   Effect of Sprawl-Related Variables on Political Awareness

Ability to name senators scored on 1–3 scale, with 3 being able to name both senators correctly (D.C. residents excluded); newspaper reading scored as three-category scale (non-readers, those who read 1–6 days a week, and everyday readers); interest in politics scored on 1–4 scale from lesser to greater interest. Ordered logistic regression employed in each case.

	Ability to Name Senators	Newspaper Reading	Interest in Politics
Central City Residence	.189 (.072)**	.105 (.034)**	—
% Driving Solo in Tract	−1.555 (.422)***	—	−.523 (.157)***
Younger Neighborhood	—	—	−.0020 (.0011)
Commuting Time in Tract	−.030 (.011)**	−.017 (.004)***	—
Educational Level in Tract	.949 (.262)***	.471(.142)***	.992 (.104)***
Homeownership	.374 (.041)***	.141 (.036)***	.064 (.042)
	n = 28,532	n = 28,640	n = 22,628 (whites and/or college graduates only)

*Sources: SCCBS; 2000 U.S. Census. *** indicates $p < .05$; ** indicates $p < .01$; *** indicates $p < .001$. See appendix II for full regression table.*

TABLE 7.3. Cumulative Effect of Sprawl on Basic Political Knowledge and Newspaper Reading

Predicted likelihood of being able to name both U.S. senators (95% confidence interval).

Central City Resident Living in a Low-Automobile Dependency Tract	25.6% (22.2%, 29.2%)
Suburban Resident Living in a High-Automobile Dependency Tract	17.3% (15.0%, 19.7%)
Owner	22.8% (20.1%, 25.6%)
Renter	16.9% (14.6%, 19.3%)
Living in Census Tract with 18-Min. Commute	23.7% (19.8%, 28.0%)
Living in Census Tract with 30-Min. Commute	17.7% (15.5%, 20.1%)

Likelihood of reading newspaper 7 days a week.

Central City Resident	34.8% (33.3%, 36.3%)
Suburban or Rural Town Resident	32.4% (31.0%, 33.8%)
Owner	34.0% (32.7%, 35.2%)
Renter	30.9% (29.4%, 32.4%).
Worker with 18-Min. Commute Living in Census Tract with 18-Min. Commute	34.2% (32.7%, 35.6%)
Worker with 30-Min. Commute Living in Census Tract with 30-Min. Commute	29.3% (27.7%, 31.0%)

Sources: SCCBS; 2000 U.S. Census.

living in a tract built in 1980 in which 85 percent of workers drive alone to work is predicted to have a 31.4 percent (30.3%, 32.4%) likelihood of saying they are very interested in politics, compared to 35.0 percent (33.5%, 36.5%) for a demographically identical resident of a tract built in 1950, where just 65 percent drive alone.[13]

Urban residence is a significant predictor of greater ability to name one's senators and of more frequent newspaper readership. Living in a highly automobile-dependent census tract is associated with reduced basic political knowledge; living in a newer neighborhood is also associated with less newspaper reading, though this relationship falls just short of statistical significance. Notably, long commuting times are a sharp predictor of both reduced political knowledge and newspaper reading.

In cumulative terms, the effect of sprawl on political knowledge is substantial; as table 7.3 shows, an individual living in a less car-dependent central city tract is more than 40 percent more likely to be able to name both senators than a demographically identical person living in a car-dependent suburb.[14] Homeownership and commuting times also have large substantive effects on such political knowledge. As table 7.3 also reports, the cumulative effect of central city residence on newspaper reading is similar to the effect of homeownership but smaller than the effect of commuting times.

In short, sprawl-related variables have a modest effect on interest in politics but a marked effect on two measures of political awareness: basic knowledge about politics, and the habit of newspaper reading. In the case of political knowledge, the cumulative effect of sprawl-related variables is larger than that of homeownership. Long commuting times are also significant predictors of reduced newspaper reading and political knowledge.

Sprawl and Low-Intensity Political Participation

We now consider the possible effect of sprawl on three forms of lower-intensity, relatively common forms of political participation: voting, signing petitions, and attending public meetings.

SCCBS respondents were asked whether they had voted in the most recent (1996) presidential election. The declining voting rate in this country between the 1960s and 2000 has (until recently) been Exhibit A for those criticizing the quality of U.S. democracy.[15] Do spatial factors have a tangible relationship with citizens' likelihood of participating in the democratic process in at least this minimal way?

Table 7.4 indicates that (among eligible voters) self-reported voting rates differ only slightly across spatial contexts. Petition signing, however, is slightly less common in lower-density, car-dependent locales.[16] Both voting and petition signing are less common in areas where commutes are long. Finally, public meeting attendance is somewhat higher in lower-density suburban and rural areas than in central cities.

Multivariate analysis shows, however, that after controlling for individual and other contextual factors as well as region, living in a traditional urban area is not a significant predictor of increased voting, although it is a substantial predictor of petition signing.[17] Interestingly, commuting time does *not* depress either type of activity. Likewise, the effect of sprawl on meeting attendance is mixed; small city size and light population density are predictors of increased attendance, but so is living in an older, less car-dependent neighborhood. On balance, residents of non-sprawling areas are predicted to be about as likely as residents of sprawling areas to have attended a public meeting in the past year.[18] Sprawl does, however, appear to have a quite

TABLE 7.4. Lower-Intensity Political Participation by Place of Residence

	Reported Voting in National Election*	Signed Petition in Previous Year	Went to Pub. Mtg.
Central City Residents	83.4%	41.8%	42.2%
Suburban Residents	82.6%	38.6%	44.5%
Rural Town Residents	83.8%	43.2%	46.2%
Rural Nontown Residents	81.1%	36.0%	47.4%
Density >8,000 persons/ mile	81.4%	44.0%	41.3%
Density <2,000 persons/ mile	81.6%	37.5%	46.1%
Neighborhood Built prior to 1950	82.5%	43.5%	45.4%
Neighborhood Built 1980 or Later	82.5%	38.1%	47.0%
Solo Commuting by Car in Tract <65%	81.7%	43.0%	41.8%
Solo Commuting by Car in Tract >85%	84.3%	39.1%	45.2%
Tracts Commute <18 Min.	84.1%	42.2%	44.9%
Tract Commute >30 Min.	81.6%	39.0%	46.1%

*Sources: SCCBS; 2000 U.S. Census. *Citizens twenty-two years old and older living in their current community at least five years only.*

TABLE 7.5. Effect of Sprawl-Related Variables on Low-Intensity Political Participation

	Petition Signing	Public Meetings
Central City Residence	.104 (.038)**	—
Tract Density (ln)	—	-.077 (.012)***
% Driving Solo in Tract	-.504 (.192)**	-.723 (.119)***
Younger Neighborhood	-.0039 (.0012)**	-.0043 (.0011)***
City Size (ln)	—	-.066 (.018)***
Educ. Level in Tract	.556 (.143)***	.447 (.118)***
Homeownership	.192 (.032)***	.341 (.030)***
	$n = 28,517$	$n = 28,643$

*Sources: SCCBS; 2000 U.S. Census. * indicates $p < .05$; ** indicates $p < .01$; *** indicates $p < .001$. Logistic regression. See appendix II for full regression tables for petition signing and public meetings.*

TABLE 7.6. Cumulative Effect of Sprawl on Petition Signing

Predicted rate of participation (95% confidence interval).

	Signed Petition in Past Year
Resident Living in an Urbanist Tract*	42.3% (40.5%, 44.1%)
Resident Living in Prototypical Suburbanist Tract**	34.7% (32.8%, 36.7%)
Owner	39.6% (38.2%, 41.0%)
Renter	35.1% (33.2%, 37.1%)

*Sources: SCCBS; 2000 U.S. Census. *Central city resident, neighborhood built in 1950, 65% of residents drive alone to work. **Suburban or rural resident, neighborhood built in 1980, 85% of residents drive alone to work.*

substantial effect on rates of petition signing, exceeding the effect of homeownership status.

Sprawl and High-Intensity Political Participation

We now consider four forms of more demanding, higher-intensity political activity: membership in a political organization, membership in a group involved in local reform, attendance at a political rally, and participation in a march, demonstration, or boycott. Each of these activities is markedly less common than petition signing and public meeting attendance. Participation in each activity also generally means committing oneself to a particular viewpoint on a given issue or signaling support for political or social change of some type in a way that simply showing up at a school board meeting does not necessarily imply. As Wendy Cho and Thomas Rudolph have shown, the SCCBS reveals that among urban residents political participation of this kind is clustered geographically in ways that are not reducible to individual demographic factors, individual engagement in social networks, or aggregate-level demographic factors.[19] Whether one participates in politics is shaped to a significant degree by the political activity of one's neighbors.

The analysis presented here asks, "Where is there more intense political participation?" The most straightforward answer is that it occurs in central cities, relatively dense census tracts, places not exclusively dependent on the automobile, and older neighborhoods. This general pattern is evident for all four explicitly political activities examined here (see table 7.7). This descriptive pattern is especially striking when we consider that, insofar as they tend

	Pol. Grp.	Ref. Grp.	Rally	March
Central City Residents	11.6%	24.4%	20.7%	10.9%
Suburban Residents	8.8%	19.0%	16.7%	6.3%
Rural Town Residents	9.1%	18.9%	19.3%	7.9%
Rural Nontown Residents	8.6%	16.1%	16.7%	4.7%
Density >8,000 persons/mile	12.8%	25.5%	21.9%	13.3%
Density <2,000 persons/mile	8.8%	17.9%	17.0%	5.7%
Neighborhood Built prior to 1950	12.3%	25.0%	22.6%	12.3%
Neighborhood Built 1980 or Later	9.0%	19.5%	17.3%	6.0%
Solo Commuting by Car in Tract <65%	12.7%	25.3%	23.2%	14.5%
Solo Commuting by Car in Tract >85%	9.3%	19.8%	17.2%	5.9%
Tracts with Average Commute <18 Min.	11.1%	22.1%	19.3%	7.5%
Tracts with Average Commute >30 Min.	9.6%	19.8%	18.7%	8.5%

Sources: SCCBS; 2000 U.S. Census.

to be more likely to own homes and to have higher incomes, we would expect suburbanites, on the basis of their individual characteristics, to be *more* likely to be engaged in politics.[20]

Multivariate analysis (see table 7.8) shows that three of the four sprawl-related variables—central city residence, automobile dependence, and neighborhood age—are consistent, independently significant predictors of high-intensity political participation. In each case, higher sprawl is associated with less participation: suburban residence, residence in a more car-oriented place, and residence in a more recently built neighborhood are each statistically significant predictors of four types of activism.

On the other hand, small city size and in some cases low neighborhood density are shown to be positively related to each of these forms of higher-intensity participation. In substantive terms, however, this countervailing effect is overwhelmed by the cumulative effect of the sprawl-related variables. Table 7.9 shows that a resident of an older, denser, less car-dependent neighborhood in a central city (population 450,000) is estimated to be far

TABLE 7.8. Impact of Sprawl-Related Variables on Higher-Intensity Political Participation

	Belong to Political Group	Belong to Reform Organization
Central City Residence	.224 (.059)***	.200 (.065)**
Tract Density (ln)	−.040 (.014)**	−.021 (.012)
% Driving Solo in Tract	−1.012 (.223)***	−.624 (.180)***
Younger Neighborhood	−.0065 (.0014)***	−.0061 (.0013)***
City Size (ln)	−.094 (.034)**	−.045 (.032)
Educational Level in Tract	.601 (.134)***	.833 (.126)***
Homeownership	.203 (.062)***	.117 (.039)**
Years Lived in Community	.0057 (.0018)**	.0024 (.0012)*
	n = 28,648	n = 28,228

	Attendance at Rally	Attendance at Protest
Central City Residence	.156 (.066)*	.274 (.068)***
Tract Density (ln)	−.052 (.015)***	—
% Driving Solo in Tract	−1.162 (.187)***	−1.433 (.298)***
Neighborhood Age	−.0068 (.0014)***	−.0090 (.0020)***
City Size (ln)	−.093 (.028)***	−.089 (.033)**
Educational Level in Tract	.709 (.136)***	.654 (.186)***
Homeownership	.210 (.045)***	.115 (.053)*
Years Lived in Community	.0044 (.0014)**	.0020 (.0016)
	n = 28,663	n = 28,656

*Sources: SCCBS; 2000 U.S. Census. * indicates p < .05; ** indicates p < .01; *** indicates p < .001. Logistic regression. See appendix II for full regression table.*

more likely to participate in these four types of high-intensity activism than is a demographically identical resident in a more car-dependent, recently built neighborhood in a lower-density suburban area (population less than 100,000). Notably, as table 7.9 also shows, this cumulative effect of sprawl is markedly larger than the estimated effect of homeownership, which is also a consistent predictor of increased political participation.[21]

Sprawl and Overall Activism

Regression analysis thus confirms what the descriptive data suggest: residence in a non-sprawling area is a very substantial predictor of increased involvement in higher-intensity forms of political participation. If we collate the four

Predicted likelihood of political participation (95% confidence interval).

	Political Org.	Reform Group
Urbanist Central City Tract*	9.2% (8.5%, 10.0%)	21.4% (20.2%, 22.6%)
Sprawling Suburban Tract**	6.5% (6.0%, 6.9%)	15.4% (14.6%, 16.1%)
Owner	8.4% (8.0%, 8.8%)	18.6% (17.9%, 19.3%)
Renter	6.9% (6.3%, 7.6%)	16.8% (15.9%, 17.8%)

	Political Rally	Protest

Central City Resident
  Living in an Older
  Low-Automobile
  Dependency Tract*
	18.2% (17.1%, 19.4%)	8.7% (8.0%, 9.5%)

Suburban Resident
  Living in a Newer
  High-Automobile
  Dependency Tract**
	13.8% (12.8%, 14.7%)	4.6% (4.2, 4.9%)

Owner	17.3% (16.5%, 18.1%)	6.5% (6.1%, 7.0%)
Renter	14.5% (13.3%, 15.7%)	5.9% (5.3%, 6.4%)

*Defined as a census tract in a central city with population of 450,000 with 65% solo auto commuting, median housing unit built in 1950, and density of 8,000 persons/square mile. **Defined as a census tract outside a central city, with population under 100,000 with 85% solo auto commuting, median housing unit built in 1980 and density of 1,000 persons/square mile. (Density dropped from protest and reform models; city size dropped from reform model.)

measures of higher-intensity political participation into a single-index measure of political activism, central city residence, residence in an older neighborhood, and residence in less car-dependent areas are all strong, independent predictors of increased activism, with a substantive effect that far outweighs the counter-vailing positive effect of living in a smaller municipality. A resident of a central city (population 450,000) living in a census tract built in 1950 in which only 65 percent of workers drive alone to work and with a population density of 8,000 persons per square mile is predicted to have a 36.1 percent (34.7%, 37.5%) likelihood of participating in at least one form of high-intensity activism. In contrast, a demographically identical suburban resident living in a census tract built in 1980 in which 85 percent of workers drive alone to work and the population density is 1,000 persons per square mile is predicted to have just a 28.5 percent (27.4%, 29.6%) likelihood of participating in at least one type of activism.[22] Notably (see table 7.10), this relationship remains robust

Based on an indexed measure of high-intensity participation, calculated as reform group membership + political group membership + political rally participation + march/protest participation

	Basic Model	Basic Model + Fixed Effects
Central City Residence	.186 (.053)***	.092 (.046)*
Tract Density (ln)	−.029 (.013)*	−.019 (.011)
Driving Solo in Tract	−1.022 (.168)***	−.735 (.152)***
Younger Neighborhood	−.0068 (.0011)***	−.0056 (.0012)***
City Size (ln)	−.078 (.025)**	−.036 (.024)
Educational Level in Tract	.818 (.107)***	.748 (.133)***
% African Americans in Tract	.249 (.100)*	.308 (.084)***
Homeownership	.175 (.036)***	.167 (.034)***
	n = 28,156	n = 28,156

*Sources: SCCBS, U.S. Census. * indicates p < .05; ** indicates p < .01; *** indicates p < .001. Left-hand table utilizes the basic regression model employed in this chapter; right-hand table adds fixed-effect controls for community sub-sample; see appendix II for full regression table. Standard errors corrected for clustering at county level in right-hand tables. Ordered logistic regression.*

even if we add fixed-effect controls for a respondent's community sample. This is significant because it helps rule out the possibility that the observed findings are being driven by other unmeasured metropolitan-level factors, such as differences in local political institutions.

The relationship also remains robust when we add additional individual and community- level controls. These additional controls include individuals' interest in politics, the frequency with which they read newspapers, how much time they spend watching television, their political ideology, their local quality-of-life evaluations, whether they are union members, and their local partisan context (at the county level), as measured by vote totals in the 2000 presidential election. Even with these additional controls in place, central city residence, neighborhood age, and automobile dependence are all independent predictors of overall activism, with statistical significance past the p < .001 level. Indeed, even if we add metropolitan-level fixed effects and these additional individual controls simultaneously, central city residence, neighborhood age, and automobile dependence remain jointly significant predictors of activism significant past the p < .001 level.[23]

One final wrinkle should be noted. As was the case with political ideology, sprawl's impact on political activism is markedly higher among college graduates than among other groups. If we divide the sample into college graduates (n=9,560) and non–college graduates (n=18,596) and employ a simplified model in which proportion driving alone in the tract is the only sprawl-related variable, we find that the effect of driving alone on overall activism is stronger (both in terms of significance and substantive effect) among college graduates than among other groups. This is worth noting both for its own sake and because, as a group, college graduates in the SCCBS participate in more than twice as many forms of political activism as non–college graduates. Spatial attributes appear to affect participation most strongly among just those respondents who, on the basis of their individual characteristics, are more likely to be engaged in activism.

Where Sprawl Matters Most

Sprawl-related variables are a consistent predictor of reduced participation in higher-intensity forms of political involvement. The other consistent and resilient contextual predictor of increased participation is the proportion of college graduates in one's census tract. Building on our observation that sprawl has the largest effect on participation among college graduates, an interesting question becomes whether the effect of spatial variables on political involvement matters more in some demographic settings than in others. Table 7.11 illustrates how political participation varies by spatial setting in each of four distinct demographic settings: high-education, high-income tracts (where both education and income levels are above the median); high-education, low-income tracts; low-education, high-income tracts; and low-education, low-income tracts.

Table 7.11 suggests that while the relationship between increased sprawl and reduced participation is evident across demographic settings, the connection is much stronger in neighborhoods with more college graduates. This result is confirmed by regression analysis. If we divide the SCCBS sample into higher-education and lower-education sub-samples (based on whether a tract has greater or lesser than the median proportion of college graduates), regression analysis shows that the effect of sprawl on participation is more powerful in tracts with higher education levels, particularly if we focus on propensity to be engaged in multiple forms of participation.[24] In substantive terms, among respondents living in higher-education tracts, residents in less sprawling central city tracts are estimated to have a 18.2 percent (16.8%, 19.7%) likelihood of engaging in at least *two* forms of higher-intensity political involvement, compared to 12.7 percent (11.8%, 13.7%) for a resident of

TABLE 7.11. Relationship between Automobile Dependence and Higher-Intensity Political Participation, by Demographic Setting

Average number of types of higher-intensity participation (political-rally attendance, protest, belonging to a local reform group, belonging to a political organization) respondents participated in, measured on 0–4 scale.

	Low-Income Tracts	High-Income Tracts
Low-Education Tracts		
% Driving Alone <.7	0.535 (n = 3,968)	0.514 (n = 333)
% Driving Alone >.85	0.455 (n = 941)	0.425 (n = 1,185)
High-Education Tracts		
% Driving Alone <.7	0.883 (n = 1,396)	1.006 (n = 1,555)
% Driving Alone >.85	0.520 (n = 502)	.566 (n = 3,806)

Sources: SCCBS; 2000 U.S. Census. Low- and high-education tracts are categorized by whether tract has greater or less than the sample median (22.73%) college graduates among adults in tract; low- and high-income tracts categorized by whether tract has greater or less than sample median income ($42,209) among households in tract.

a sprawling suburban tract. Among respondents living in lower-education tracts, residents of prototypical non-sprawling center city tracts are estimated to have a 10.6 percent (9.4%, 11.9%) likelihood of participation in at least two forms of political involvement, compared to 8.1 percent (7.4%, 8.9%) for a resident of sprawling suburban tract.[25]

The effect of sprawl on political participation is thus larger in both proportional and absolute terms in better-educated tracts. What this means, in effect, is that less automobile-dependent, less sprawling places appear to more powerfully elicit engaged political participation in relatively favorable demographic settings. By the same token, urban settings cannot (on their own) transform neighborhoods with relatively low levels of education into hotbeds of participation, though the effect of space on participation within such neighborhoods is important and substantial.

Supply-Side Mechanisms

The hypothesis of scholars such as Lofland, Kohn, and Brain is that the specific qualities of urban space, particularly the presence of public, pedestrian-scaled spaces shared by strangers, facilitates civic consciousness (awareness of a world beyond our own personal networks) and political engagement. We might further predict that car-oriented suburban places may be particularly inhospitable for those political activities that occur in space—that is, in particular places—such as political rallies and marches. Evidence presented so far in this chapter is consistent with those hypotheses.

A complementary hypothesis explaining the observed link between urban space and higher political participation focuses on the supply side: it may be the case that political organizers and political organizations focus their attention in traditional urban areas, thereby creating more opportunities for political participation. This may happen for one of three reasons: because activists and organizations believe that it is easier to reach and recruit members and participants in urban settings, because urban locations are geographically closer to the targets of activism (e.g., city and state governments, media outlets), or simply for historical or symbolic reasons. Indeed, a review of the institutional affiliates of three of the largest community organizing networks in the United States—the Industrial Areas Foundation, Direct Action and Research Training Center (DART), and the Gamaliel Foundation network—shows that multi-issue, often congregation-based community organizing networks are overwhelmingly based in central cities (and in some cases, inner suburban counties).[26]

Evidence from organizational data collected by the Department of Commerce's County Business Patterns (CBP) survey supports the idea that activist organizations are more likely to be located in traditional urban settings than in sprawling environments, a finding that is interesting in its own right and that helps corroborate the individual-level evidence presented in the SCCBS.[27] I examined the relationship between county-level sprawl variables and 2005 county-level data on "social advocacy organizations" from the CBP survey of all businesses.[28] Such organizations are markedly more prevalent in more urban counties than in newer, more car-dependent counties. Among metropolitan counties (excluding Washington, D.C.), both the proportion of persons driving alone to work and older housing stock are significant predictors (jointly significant past the $p < .001$ level) of higher proportion of social-advocacy organizations per capita, controlling for county-level income, education levels, racial demographics, region of the country, and whether or not the county hosts a state capital (itself a large positive predictor of the prevalence of such organizations).[29]

Regression analysis indicates, however, that the disproportionate concentration of advocacy groups in urban areas cannot entirely explain the link between urban spaces and activism. In regressions in which we control for *both* sprawl-related variables and the proportion of advocacy organizations in one's

TABLE 7.12. Prevalence of Social Advocacy Organizations among Metropolitan Counties, 2005

Metro Counties	Social Advocacy Organizations/100,000 Residents
<78% Drive Alone to Work (n = 221)	6.81
>83% Drive Alone to Work (n = 220)	3.04
Median Home Built before 1966 (n = 206)	5.66
Median Home Built after 1979 (n = 193)	3.23

Sources: 2005 County Business Patterns Data; 2000 U.S. Census. Washington, D.C., excluded.

county, both factors remain independently significant positive predictors of individual-level political participation among metropolitan-area residents. The number of advocacy organizations per capita in one's county is a positive predictor of individual-level nonelectoral activism at the p < .01 significance level, but neighborhood age, tract-level automobile dependence, and central city residence all remain significant predictors of activism when included in the same model (though their cumulative effect is somewhat weaker, as we would expect). The greater availability of opportunities to engage politically provided by the higher proportion of formal advocacy organizations in urban areas partly explains higher rates of urban nonelectoral engagement but is not in itself the sole mechanism driving the observed findings.

Overall, the evidence in this chapter suggests that the effect of urban spatial settings is strongest on forms of political engagement that generally occur in public spaces (petition signing), require engagement with other people (belonging to a local reform group or a political organization), or have both characteristics (participation in rallies and protests). Reported effects are much weaker with respect to voting, and we might expect the effects of local spatial characteristics to be smaller (or nonexistent) on more individualistic forms of participation such as contacting public officials donating money to a candidate online, actions that do not require associating with others or using public space in any way. (Those specific measures are not included in the SCCBS, but recall Glaeser and Gottlieb's finding in the DDB Needham data that central city residence did not increase one's likelihood of contacting public officials.) What the SCCBS data show is not a relationship between neighborhood spatial characteristics and all conceivable forms of political participation (let alone all forms of civic participation) but a strong and consistent relationship between urban spatial characteristics and more demanding, conflict-oriented forms of political engagement.

Do Activists Self-Select into Non-Sprawling Places?

We now consider the question of whether the relationship between spatial characteristics and activism might simply be a function of individual self-selection. Oliver asserts that preferences for higher (or lower) political engagement are not a plausible reason for people to move (an assertion that can be corroborated by studies of mobility and the reasons people give for moving).[30] Yet it is possible that such a concern might motivate a person to choose to move to a particular place, once they have decided to make a move for a different, primary reason. Freeman, however, provides a useful response to this possibility: if politically motivated people move to areas that they already know will facilitate higher social and political participation, then it must be the case that such areas do in fact have qualities that facilitate such participation.[31]

As Gainsborough has noted, recent cross-sectional analyses demonstrating a link between suburban residence and political attitudes and behavior overcome the most straightforward version of the self-selection hypothesis, precisely by controlling for a range of individual-level characteristics that might be thought to predict political orientation. As Gainsborough asks, "If preexisting attitudes cause self-selection into suburbs, where do these preexisting attitudes come from, given that the most obvious source—socioeconomic characteristics—has already been accounted for?"[32] A self-selection objection to the present study must hypothesize that residents of auto-dominated suburbs must have some unobserved characteristic—one not captured by race, income, education, or other demographic factors—that predisposes them not to participate in politics.

In the present case, the fact that the link between sprawl and reduced participation remains intact even after controlling for interest in politics, political ideology, and media-consumption habits suggests that more is going on than a simple process of activists and non-activists sorting themselves into more- or less-politicized communities according to their preferences. Nor can differences in quality-of-life assessments explain differences in activism rates across the metropolitan area; that is, activism is not higher in non-sprawling places simply because people there are less satisfied with their communities.

Still another way to get at this question is to ask, as we did in chapter 5, with respect to political ideology, whether we can observe the relationship between sprawl-related variables even among respondents in the sample least likely to have selected into their current neighborhoods; to recall, in a 2006 national survey, some 38 percent of respondents said they would leave their current neighborhoods if they could.[33] Among respondents in the working sample with household incomes of less than $30,000, the proportion of workers in one's tract commuting alone by car is a significant predictor of reduced political activism at the $p < .01$ level (see table 7.13).[34] The proportion of solo commuters in the tract has a similarly significant effect ($p < .01$) on activism among nonstudents who plan to leave their community in the next five years. Finally, automobile dependence is also a significant negative predictor of political participation among persons who are most dissatisfied with their local community; that is, those rating local quality of life only "fair" or "poor." As was the case with political ideology, the correspondence between spatial context and activism is indeed higher among persons who are best situated to live in a neighborhood of their choice (higher income), who have

TABLE 7.13. The Effect of Spatial Attributes on Higher-Intensity Political Participation by Income, Community Satisfaction, and Quality-of-Life Ratings

	Income <$30,000	Income >$75,000
Central City Residence	.160 (.134)	.405 (.084)***
% Driving Alone	−1.078 (.397)**	−1.078 (.211)***
City Size (ln)	−.066 (.052)	−.145 (.040)***
Educational Level in Tract	.704 (.211)***	.723 (.198)***
	$n = 7,641$	$n = 5,595$
	Quality of Life "Poor" or "Fair"	Quality of Life "Excellent"
Central City Residence	.292 (.124)*	.197 (.074)**
% Driving Alone	−.971 (.370)**	−1.374 (.234)***
City Size (ln)	−.100 (.054)	−.082 (.043)
Educational Level in Tract	1.020 (.270)***	.913 (.199)***
	$n = 3,861$	$n = 11,279$
	Plan to Leave (nonstudents)	Plan to Stay (nonstudents)
Central City Residence	.279 (.088)**	.173 (.061)**
% Driving Alone	−.882 (.284)**	−1.491 (.236)***
City Size (ln)	−.133 (.050)**	−.076 (.026)**
Educational Level in Tract	.601 (.209)**	.904 (.158)***
	$n = 5,667$	$n = 20,230$

Sources: SCCBS; 2000 U.S. Census. Census tract density and neighborhood age omitted from these analyses. Otherwise based on same regression model used in this chapter, including full controls for region.

the strongest commitment to their current neighborhood, and who are in fact relatively pleased with their local community, indicating that self-selection must be part of the explanation. But the self-selection hypothesis, again, does not help us account for the persistence of a significant and consistent spatial effect among persons who are not happy with their current environment and/ or lack the resources to move elsewhere.

Obviously, as in the case of individual political ideology discussed in chapter 5, an absolutely airtight response to all claims of self-selection is not possible in the absence of longitudinal data permitting us to track how participation varies within individuals' lives over time as they come to inhabit different spatial contexts. Yet there is good reason to think that self-selection likely plays only a partial role in the observed relationship between urbanism and higher political participation. Relatively few individuals who are not professional politicians are so motivated by political engagement as to organize their entire life, including where they live, to facilitate such participation, and even if such individuals flock to places like Berkeley, where politics is assumed to always be in the air, it seems implausible to claim that there is nothing particular about Berkeley that facilitates political participation.

If we conceive of individuals as having varying predispositions to participate in politics, which local contexts may or may not activate, there is a strong theoretical basis for believing that spatial context—whether one frequents an area characterized by public space and many pedestrians, or instead lives strictly a "doorstep to parking lot" existence—may affect the degree to which one is drawn into public life. At a minimum, even if the findings here cannot establish beyond doubt a *causal* connection between spatial context and political participation in the way a well-designed experiment might, the findings are certainly strong enough to suggest that there is a substantial *affinity* between certain kinds of spatial contexts and increased political participation.

Indeed, from a specifically *civic republican* point of view, it matters relatively little whether sprawl is understood as a *cause* of privatistic attitudes and behavior among Americans, an *expression* of such attitudes, or both. Precisely because civic republicans do not hold a reverential attitude toward preexisting individual preferences, they are capable of judging that a particular way of life that individuals—or a class of individuals—pursue is both detrimental to the good of the civic whole and (yet more controversially) a deficient way for human beings to live. Even if sprawl were conceived of *only* as an expression of individuals' privatistic preferences, such that the findings reported above could be wholly explained by supposing that persons with no interest in civic engagement self-select themselves into newer, car-dominated neighborhoods on the suburban fringe, civic republicans would still maintain a negative assessment of sprawl and could coherently argue that the phenomenon of citizens moving to locales where they can avoid political activism and political activists is unhealthy. To be sure, civic republicans would also have an analytic interest in knowing whether changes in spatial arrangements would likely induce changes in individual behavior, but civic republicans' normative judgment about whether sprawling neighborhoods are desirable does not rest on which is the cause and which the effect where privatistic preferences and sprawling spatial contexts are concerned.

REVERSE CAUSALITY?

Related to the self-selection question is a second methodological issue, which has been less considered in the literature to date: the possibility of reverse causality, especially over the long haul, between political participation and the existence of the kinds of urban spaces considered the antithesis of sprawl. That is, it may be that while sprawl weakens political engagement, political engagement in turn can weaken sprawl, and hence a correlation between less sprawl and more participation may reflect causal arrows in both directions. This is especially important to note, given that many commentators involved in the New Urbanist and smart-growth movements cite increased civic participation as a precondition for creating more livable spaces in the future.

Looking prospectively, then, the likelihood of mutual causality is certain to increase as a relevant methodological issue, precisely to the extent that New Urbanism and smart growth succeed as social movements. Looking retrospectively, however, it is far from clear that those places that have the least sprawl now have less sprawl because they are better mobilized now or were so in the past. First, exogenous geographic factors account, sometimes decisively, for many (if not most) of the nation's relatively non-sprawling metropolitan areas; cities that are geographically hemmed in by water or mountains, such as Boston and San Francisco, are far less likely to be sprawling places. Second, the proportion of instances in which the design of urban spaces has been significantly affected by popular mobilization in the past, though much celebrated, has historically been small compared to the total quantity of land use–related policy decisions in the United States. To be sure, in large cities, growing resistance in the 1960s and 1970s to the crude slum clearance and urban redevelopment policies of the postwar era impacted subsequent patterns of urban public investment and likely contributed to the preservation of some older urban neighborhoods.[35] But there is little reason to believe that such activism had a major impact on metropolitan-wide growth patterns or the continued proliferation of sprawling areas. Put another way, urban protests may account for long-term shifts in redevelopment strategies within central cities, and may even in some cases affect the long-term character of particular urban neighborhoods, but they do not account for the fundamental contrast between older, denser, less car-oriented places and newer, low-density, automobile-dependent places. Thus a high degree of public mobilization and engagement concerning planning proposals in downtown Richmond, Virginia, might influence the city's development plans and the future of particular neighborhoods but will have only minimal and very indirect impact on the degree of sprawl present in the suburban counties circling the city.

Twenty years from now we might see prior levels of civic participation as a primary factor in shaping the degree to which "sprawl" is present or absent in a given community. But, with the possible exception of Oregon, where current land use patterns reflect explicitly anti-sprawl policies adopted in the 1970s, policies that were directly shaped by a popular movement,[36] it seems reasonable to conclude that existing levels of sprawl in local neighborhoods are generally not a function of the extent of the degree of political participation in those same communities. Even if doubt remains on this point, it is again crucial to recognize that civic republican concern with the observed affinity between sprawl and lower participation does not hinge on a claim that the causal arrow between spatial characteristics and participation runs only in one direction.

Discussion

The most straightforward conclusion to draw from the preceding empirical investigation is that just as civic republicanism places more demanding expectations upon citizens to actively participate in self-governance and upon social and economic arrangements to facilitate such participation than do most varieties of liberal thought, so, too, does civic republicanism invite a substantially stronger critique of sprawl's effect on civic life. Whereas sprawl-related spatial features in general have only a modest effect on abstract interest in politics and lower-intensity forms of political participation (voting and attending public meetings), these features do appear to affect citizens' basic political awareness and their likelihood of engaging in higher-intensity civic participation to a quite significant degree.

Interestingly, the strength of this effect appears to increase to the degree that the activity examined reflects "conflictual" rather than "consensual" modes of political engagement. As recent work by David E. Campbell has stressed, civic participation might be a result of two distinct motivations: a civic motivation, which he associates with "consensual" local political cultures in which there are strong norms favoring civic participation, and an interest-based motivation, which is said to be associated with "conflictual" local political cultures.[37] As demonstrated above, components of sprawl have effects on all types of political behavior, but the specific negative impact of highly automobile-intensive areas is weakest for voting and public meeting attendance—forms of participation that tend to be less conflictual and confrontational in content. On the other hand, the overall effect of sprawl is strongest upon protest activity, the most conflictual mode of political engagement examined here.

Conversely, recall our finding in chapter 3 that sprawl was not significantly linked to differences in, for instance, volunteering (what Campbell terms "civic" behavior) or to more generic forms of community (such as overall group membership). That finding matches Campbell's conclusions (derived in part from his own analysis of the SCCBS, using community samples as the unit of analysis) that social context affects various kinds of activities differently. (Campbell thus finds that specifically political activity is higher in ideologically diverse communities but that volunteering and social trust are higher in ideologically homogeneous settings.)[38] It is also consistent with David Brain's argument (discussed above) that while urban settings may do no better than suburbs in producing "communities," distinctively urban spaces produce contexts that both facilitate awareness of difference and facilitate political engagement.[39] What the evidence provided in this book has shown is not that sprawl is bad for all forms of "community," but that it seems to undermine specifically political forms of civic participation, at least those requiring face-to-face contact of some kind.[40]

Conflictual or Consensual Communities:
What Do Civic Republicans Want?

The evidence presented above naturally raises broad questions about just what sort of communities civic republicans should seek to promote: Classical republican rhetoric and language often appeals implicitly to an image of the Roman republic, or perhaps a Greek city–state, or a New England town meeting, in which citizen–lawmakers each seeking a common good meet to deliberate policy matters. Such an image seems to correspond to a unitary, consensual model of politics. Likewise, civic republican thought typically expresses admiration for civically motivated political participation, as opposed to participation rooted fundamentally in self-interest. Civic republicanism's normative thrust is to admire the citizen who attends a public hearing out of heartfelt concern for the good of the city more than the citizen who attends the same hearing in order to file a complaint about how a proposed development in one's neighborhood would be bothersome and unwelcome.

Yet social conflict of various kinds, particularly in the local community, may act as a tremendous stimulus to political participation, which in turn might be conceptualized as a first step in the formation of citizens capable of considering a good larger than their own. The man who actually goes to a public hearing for selfish reasons may from time to time be forced to take account of considerations that expand his position. More broadly, interest groups pursuing particular agendas in a conflictual political arena may be forced to develop alliances with other groups in order to accomplish political goals and, in this way, may have their horizons gradually broadened to encompass some sense of the good of the whole.

In chapter 6, we sketched an outline of the connection between civic republican commitments and egalitarian distributive justice. For the sake of this discussion, let us assume that this line of reasoning connecting civic republicanism to substantive egalitarianism is sound, or at least plausibly defensible. How then might egalitarian civic republicans approach the question of whether the present-day U.S. polity ought to encourage "consensual" political cultures at the local level, or instead encourage "conflictual" local political cultures, as defined above?

Three considerations on this question should be noted. First, we may take it as a given that the present-day United States exhibits levels of inequality unlikely to be defensible from a difference-principle point of view (or any other plausible egalitarian principle), and that part of this inequality is embodied in spatial segregation (see chapter 4 for this discussion). In this situation, an egalitarian civic republican cannot endorse the present socioeconomic status quo and would see changes in the direction of more-egalitarian policies as highly desirable. This in turn implies substantial political conflict; in particular, it may involve finding ways to prevent affluent Americans from simply *escaping* local political conflicts via economic segregation.[41]

Second, John Maynor, drawing on themes from Machiavelli, has made the case that civic republicans ought not to view conflictual politics as inherently bad or deplorable. Given the pervasiveness of class conflict, conflicts over the meaning of justice, and the presence of social diversity, a robust political culture in which contrasting, conflicting perspectives are voiced may be a sign of civic health—if such conflict occurs within the context of a well-ordered constitutional system. What is important is not that conflict be minimized but that no one group be permitted to dominate others; instead, such conflict must be mediated by deliberative conversations and, ultimately, the legislative process. This in turn means that the contending parties must have a capacity to seek the common good and to revise their own demands in light of the reasonable demands of others, a capacity that is necessarily the product of well-formed institutions and of civic virtue. To endorse the legitimacy of conflictual politics, then, is not to say that broader civic motivations have no important role to play in contemporary politics; indeed, such motivations are essential.[42]

Third, civic republicans take the observation and judgment that many (perhaps most) Americans are substantially depoliticized as a starting point for practical reflection. Average turnout in the 2000, 2004, and 2008 presidential elections amounted to 54 percent of the voting-age population, and in state and local elections the voter turnout rate is still lower apart from voting. The proportion of the population that participates in any single form of the political activities described in this chapter is a minority.[43] Indeed, some 65.6 percent of the SCCBS sample participated in *none* of the higher-intensity forms of political activity noted here. Evidence assembled by U.S. political scientists over decades further indicates that a large number of Americans do not hold systematic or internally coherent views about politics, and surveys (including the SCCBS, in which just 25 percent of respondents could name both their U.S. senators) frequently reveal embarrassingly low levels of basic political knowledge. Moreover, Putnam's research shows that rates of political mobilization have declined since the early 1970s.[44]

Within *this* context, it might be reasonably proposed that civic republican beggars ought not to be choosers, or at least not overly persnickety choosers, when it comes to evaluating modes of political participation and motivations for such activity. Any form of nonelectoral political engagement might stimulate greater political awareness and, possibly, greater awareness of the good of the polity as a whole. In short, from a civic republican point of view, *any* entry point into public engagement, even one concerned primarily with preservation or enhancement of self-interest, is a possible stepping stone in the formation of publicly minded citizens who are both in the habit of public engagement and motivated by civic as opposed to purely self-interested concerns. It is not necessary for civic republicans to show that participation always or even usually has this effect, only that it *might* in some cases have this effect; and, that, generally speaking, citizens who do participate in politics out of interest-based motivations do not become *worse* citizens for having participated.

To be sure, situations can be identified in which self-interested participation might indeed have a perverse effect; for instance, a successful effort to employ exclusionary zoning at the local level might teach wrongheaded lessons about the purposes of politics, from a civic republican perspective. This possibility must be acknowledged. Moreover, numerous specific *organizations* that are engaged in politics might be structured according to narrow, self-interested concerns. In well-functioning pluralist polities, ordinarily such self-interested political actors must form coalitions with other organizations—that is, take at least a slightly broader view—in order to achieve or partially achieve their own ends, and in this manner the contrast between self-interested and civic motivations may break down. But many suburban communities in the United States are not pluralist polities in the least, and it is particularly likely to be true at the local level, in socially homogeneous communities, that a politics of fairly narrow self-interest may in fact be quite successful and become a self-perpetuating habit.

This observation points again to the need to detach civic republicanism from localism, but it is at most a caveat, not an objection, to the general proposition that civic republicans ought to regard individuals' increasing participation (of any kind) in politics as a positive step. For, as we have observed, individual-level participation for the sake of self-interest is ordinarily *not* necessary in truly homogeneous communities, unless or until some concrete issue becomes contested. Once a claim is contested, however, even purely self-interested participants in politics must at least become cognizant of their political opponents, and this itself is a first (though, sadly, often no more than first) step in the formation of citizens guided by a truly civic consciousness. In short, civic republicans need not and ought not lose the distinction between more and less admirable modes of political participation, but they might simultaneously conclude that, especially in the context of a very depoliticized citizenry, even bad politics is more likely to produce admirable citizens than no politics at all.

The fourth observation pertinent at this point is that civic and self-interested motivations for political engagement can substantially overlap in many particular cases. If a trade union seeks to block the shutdown of a local steel plant and preserve an Ohio town's primary employer via some political or regulatory intervention, should such behavior be characterized as self-interested or civic in character? Clearly, both sorts of motivations are present in such a case; and since a special emphasis of many contemporary civic republicans is expanded democratic governance of the political economy (recall Sandel's "political economy of citizenship"), this case is hardly an anomaly but very much what civic republicans, and especially egalitarian civic republicans, conceive as a model of desirable political engagement. Broadly speaking, policies to reduce inequalities, as a practical matter, will always require support from both self-interested and civically motivated parties.[45]

Indeed, civic republicans can plausibly go further, arguing that it is legitimate and just for groups experiencing injustice to advance their own interests in the political arena, and to do so not just because they care about the abstract good of the whole polity but because they want to improve their own life situations. No civic republican would criticize civil rights–era activism on the grounds that many African Americans engaged in the movement were concerned with advancing their own interests; yet civic republicans might properly insist that it was the character of advancing oppressed groups' interests *and* simultaneously claiming to redeem the project of U.S. democracy that gave the civil rights movement its special moral force (and perhaps, too, its practical success). Likewise, civic republicans can claim that any serious movement to correct economic inequalities in the United States must appeal not only to the self-interest of who are getting the short end of the stick, but also to broader civic concerns.[46]

This last point leads us directly to a summary statement of the attitude egalitarian civic republicans are likely to take toward "conflictual" political motivations involving contests between persons or groups with contrasting interests. Namely, such a form of politics is *necessary* in order to correct existing injustices and *may* help stimulate the formation of expanded civic consciousness among at least some participants. But such a politics needs *also* to be connected, as frequently as possible, to explicit discussion of the good of the whole—that is, to broader civic motivations—and, moreover, that it must do so in an honest and compelling way.[47] (It is not hard to find examples of base self-interest dressing itself up in civic airs.)

Having made what one hopes is a productive detour to flesh out civic republican theory, we are now in better position to understand how contemporary civic republicans might approach the question of whether we should prefer "conflictual" to "consensual" communities. A long and venerable tradition of communitarian and utopian thinking and practice regarding spatial design, dating back to Fourierist experiments, Shaker communities, and other nineteenth-century initiatives, has emphasized the promise of communities designed to promote a particular way of life, with special emphasis on themes of social cohesion, such as "harmony" and "cooperation."[48] A well-planned community oriented towards cooperative living can serve as a model for exhibiting seamless social cooperation in a context of social equality and relative trust, all in proper relationship with the natural environment. Such communities are not only good in themselves, it is thought, but also act as a positive example for the rest of society. This conception of the harmonious local community parallels common (or latent) civic republican conceptions of the state as governed fundamentally by shared public deliberation.

As historians of suburbia such as Dolores Hayden note, however, there has always been a tension between the hopeful, utopian aspirations of planned new suburban communities and a tendency toward social exclusion. (Some nineteenth-century efforts at building a community oriented toward wholesome living centered around shared public space, such as Llewellyn Park, New Jersey, evolved into privatized enclaves for the rich during the twentieth century.)[49] The danger, from an egalitarian civic republican standpoint, is that attempts to build model communities become just another effort to secede from society and its social conflicts. (Precisely this sort of criticism has been leveled in recent years at prominent New Urbanist–inspired communities such as Celebration, Florida.)[50]

Within the context of a society marked by sharp inequalities and serious conflicts of interest, achieving a measure of harmony, trust, and calm repose in particular communities without simultaneously addressing the sources of such conflict in the larger society becomes a morally dubious enterprise. Rather than looking to foster placid and harmonious communities marked by social trust as a near-to-midterm social ideal, civic republicans might more properly look to communities whose structure encourages active participation in collectively dealing with shared problems, including problems arising from conflicting material interests.

This might mean strengthening cities...but it also (in theory) might mean strengthening those suburbs which are themselves more diverse, incorporate the elements of civic conflict, and possess public space and other spatial attributes that facilitate the expression of such conflict. The key criterion is that local boundaries should not be used as an instrument whereby a privileged segment of society can separate itself from core social problems; placing all residents of metropolitan areas under one civic roof opens the door to a re-politicization of metropolitan life (and also, inevitably, increases in local political conflicts). Yet from a civic republican point of view, even if conflictual politics is endorsed as an appropriate motivation for civic engagement within the context of unjust societies, such motivations need to be supplemented with broader civic concern for the good of the whole. And in the case that metropolitan areas were reformed such that rich and poor shared a common political roof, if citizens' political engagement were motivated solely by self-interest, we would expect to see local civic life consist of pure power politics—and also, far more often than not, for the affluent to success-fully defend their privileges. At most, we might think that the proposed new political structure would force the well-off to make some concessions they currently avoid, but unless concern for the regime as a whole, or for a broader common good, is an active motive in political life, more-promising political outcomes will be achieved only irregularly.[51]

Conclusion

It is worth briefly restating why the issue of whether civic republicans should prioritize enhanced political engagement over higher levels of trust—and even subjective quality-of-life satisfaction—looms so large with respect to the sprawl debate. Existing evidence suggests that within the social con-text of the contemporary United States, it is not possible to identify a form of spatial organization or a neighborhood type capable of maximizing local social cohesion, community satisfaction, and extensive political participation all at once. Spatial policies aimed at boosting political participation would appear to require strengthening central cities in addition to encouraging the development of places less oriented to the automobile. Each of those tasks, however, necessarily involves increasing local densities within U.S. metro-politan areas—which in turn appears to lead to both reduced social trust and reduced satisfaction with one's community (given the existing preferences of Americans).

The full force of this dilemma is explored further in chapter 9, where we take up two distinct questions: First, whether it is possible, as a practi-cal matter, to specify a nontrivial consensus regarding policy reform options upon which utilitarians, liberal egalitarians, and civic republicans might agree; and second, to what extent a civic republican approach justifies a more aggressive policy approach to sprawl than can be sustained by the resources of liberalism and utilitarians alone. At the heart of this last issue is whether satisfaction of existing preferences and freedom of choice to live as one wants ought to be the highest priorities for the polity, or whether we should, with Aristotle, conceive of individuals as belonging in some sense to the polity as a whole, and hence regard the encouragement of civic duty and active par-ticipation in political life as a critical and at times decisive consideration in public policymaking.

First, however, we must reengage one additional substantive issue with major significance for both the debate about sprawl and for the general question of the proper relation between existing preferences and practices and public policy: the connection between sprawl and environmental concerns, particularly the threat and reality of long-term climate change.

| EIGHT | Sprawl, the Environment, and Climate Change |

IN THE PREVIOUS FOUR chapters, we examined evidence suggesting that continuing the dominant pattern of metropolitan development in the United States—automobile-oriented development on the fringe of existing metropolitan areas—is a recipe for perpetuating entrenched social inequalities and weakening active political participation. Yet even if sprawl had no implications whatsoever for social justice or civic health and were thought to be quite efficient in cost–benefit terms, it would still constitute a morally problematic form of development if it contradicted the requirements of long-term ecological sustainability.

There is now an enormous literature detailing the environmental consequences of sprawl, including loss of agricultural land, species loss, wetlands destruction, runoff water pollution, and auto-generated air pollution.[1] These costs need to be taken into account in evaluating local land use decisions. As noted in chapter 2, the traditional cost–benefit matrix associated with utilitarian policy analysis is of limited usefulness in this regard, precisely insofar as utilitarians insist on placing a price on goods that environmentalists (and others) regard as priceless. As the philosophers Elizabeth Anderson and Mark Sagoff have each shown, people commonly (and properly) value some ecological goods—such as the good of a local ecosystem, a plot of open land, an old-growth forest—as *ends in themselves,* not for the pleasure or economic gain they provide human beings.[2] For instance, opponents of oil drilling in the Arctic National Wildlife Refuge commonly invoke this argument by claiming that there is a value to the existence of pristine ecosystems more or less untouched by human activities.[3] According to this view, destroying or significantly altering such an environment could not be justified by any increase in national wealth that might result from exploitation of the underlying natural resources.

Local policy trade-offs between damage to local ecosystems and new development should therefore not turn on the results of purportedly scientific cost–benefit analyses that use dubious methods to assign quantitative value to environmental goods.[4] Rather, judgments on trade-offs must be based, inevitably, on more qualitative judgments about the importance of a particular ecological good to the integrity of the local environment, judgments that are inherently local in nature and highly dependent on specific local conditions. It is impossible, for instance, to state with any certainty that it is never acceptable to develop new housing or commercial space on a previously undeveloped piece of land, *or* to assume that such development is *always* acceptable. The answer will depend on local conditions and ultimately on the shared judgment of local democratic publics.

What kinds of ecological concerns should democratic publics take into consideration in making practical judgments about appropriate land use? At least four kinds of environmentalist arguments against the conversion of land and ecosystems into development can be usefully specified. The first (and least compelling) argument is that such development threatens existing owners of private property who feel entitled to continue to derive aesthetic enjoyment from the scenic vistas afforded by undeveloped farmland and rolling, road-free hills. In many practical battles against sprawl, such as the failed proposal to build a Disney-themed American history park in Northern Virginia during the early 1990s, private landowners threatened in this way have played a prominent role in fending off proposals for sprawl-type development.[5] While reasonable consideration of the interests of property owners affected by new development should be afforded by policymakers, such interests should not be cast as trumps on what policy can and cannot do. Policymakers thus should carefully assess the claims of property holders threatened by new development, giving the least weight to claims (such as those of owners of beachfront property in California who seek to limit public access to beaches) that are exclusionary in intent.[6]

A second argument rests not on private property rights but on the view that development policies must respect ecosystems in general, and that human beings should not increase the quantity of damaged ecosystems. Consider, for instance, a no-net-loss wetland policy that has been advocated by many environmentalists and is now a standard aim of federal policy. Because wetlands are of particular importance to the maintenance of biological diversity, environmentalists believe human development should show special regard for these areas and should ensure that wetlands are not depleted over time. Such a policy does not mean that any *particular* wetland is entitled to preservation from development for all time, however. Developers of a new suburban community might pledge, for instance, to create new wetland acres elsewhere in the region in order to win public permission to drain, bulldoze, and develop acres critical to the creation of a new shopping complex or a development of condominiums. Such a policy acknowledges that wetlands have special worth not reducible to economic terms, and, in this sense, modifies strict cost–benefit analysis-based policies. Even so, however, a no-net-loss policy would be consistent with very substantial destruction of many specific ecosystems and even with banishing natural areas from much urban development—so long as it could be assured that the destroyed acres could be "replaced" elsewhere.

A third argument against unchecked development goes further to argue for the intrinsic worth of *particular* ecosystems—ecosystems whose loss would be irreplaceable. To take an extreme example, most people would agree that it would be at least questionable to allow developers to build a strip mall at the base of the Grand Canyon and would be horribly wrong to allow developers to take actions that would fundamentally alter the character of the site itself. The sense that developing the Grand Canyon is horribly wrong rests on a valuation of the canyon as a unique geologic formation. For instance, showing respect for the canyon as a product of the natural world is a way to acknowledge that human beings are only in a very partial sense the creators of their own circumstances. The sense of awe the canyon evokes is an important good insofar as it inspires or compels human beings to reflect on their own situatedness on a planet not of their own shaping.

Most ecosystems are not the Grand Canyon, however. Can the logic of a Grand Canyon–type argument be applied by citizens who wish to block the construction of a new shopping mall that would intrude upon a local creek system? Would there be grievous and irreplaceable harm comparable to the harm that would attend the obliteration of the Grand Canyon if a local creek system were sacrificed or significantly compromised in order to accommodate new development? An affirmative answer to that question is implausible, and not simply because the Grand Canyon is much larger in scale than a local creek. The organization of our built communities already implicates everyday Americans in the notion that particular ecosystems can be modified or destroyed in order to accommodate human activities. Why should we care about the destruction of another creek system when so many similar ecosystems have already been altered in order to build our cities and towns? And in the American case, why exactly should we be so concerned about saving a particular piece of land in an urban region when, in point of fact, the vast majority of land in the country remains undeveloped?[7] Residents of New Jersey who want open space can always move to South Dakota if they wish to inhabit ecosystems largely untouched by urban development.

This last observation points in the direction of a fourth, more far-reaching argument for not treating all ecological goods as commodities that can be monetarily valued and hence entered into cost–benefit equations. This argument for valuing particular places and ecosystems does not depend on claims of ecological uniqueness, or upon implausible claims that no human activity can ever defensibly displace an existing ecosystem. Rather, it argues that *each* existing region should maintain a sense of balance between developed and undeveloped areas. Particular ecosystems can be defended from development for the sake of maintaining an appropriate balance and also because such an ecosystem may define the region. The case for maintaining balance in inhabited areas can be made in two ways: first, it might be claimed that human beings feel healthier and happier when they are not entirely divorced from the natural world.[8] Such a claim locates the moral value of a balance between nature and human activities in its effects on human well-being. A second, non-instrumental argument for balance might claim that complete separation from and lack of access to nature is not only unpleasant but also distorts our recognition that human activities are ultimately embedded within the natural world. This impoverished view in turn damages our ability to properly value the environment.

If this last argument is accepted, it follows that cost–benefit analyses that posit a trade-off between environmental goods and economic goods will not be able to account properly for the sense of balance between the natural world and the human environment that may be at stake in a given land use decision. Such an analysis may fail to grasp how citizens might accept or welcome disrupting a pristine ecosystem to build a shopping center but oppose or regret a development twenty years on that turns the last significant chunk of undeveloped forest land in the area into the county's ninth shopping district. In short, the application of cost–benefit analyses must always be contextual; while it seems excessive to claim that ecological goods can *never* be assigned a price and never traded off against other goods, a still more grievous error would be to assume that ecological goods must *always* be assigned a price and treated as a commodity. This is obviously true with respect to some truly unique landmarks and natural features (e.g., the Grand Canyon), but it is also likely to be true in many much more routine and localized analyses, where cutting down a forest or endangering a local watershed might negatively affect an ecosystem's integrity or a place's identity.

Given these considerations, it is not feasible to construct a simple formula for guiding localities on how to judiciously trade off environmental goods against potential economic benefit. It is possible, however, for environmentalists to insist upon an *ethic* of minimizing damage to the local ecosystem. At a minimum, such an ethic would insist that new development projects refrain from unnecessarily or gratuitously affecting ecological features; that among development projects promising roughly equivalent economic benefit, the proposal with the least ecological impact be selected; and that, when necessary, the public be willing to incur monetary costs to minimize the ecological damage associated with any new development.[9]

A large body of research has in fact connected suburban sprawl and its characteristic components with substantial environmental destruction, destruction that has local, regional, and potentially global implications. At the local level, large parking lots and increases in paved areas have been linked with increased water pollution, resulting from runoff water; when runoff water collects on man-made surfaces, it passes into local water sources at high speeds and quantities compared to water collected by natural habitats. Erosion and damage to water tables also can result from runoff water pollution.[10] At the regional level, sprawl has been linked to over-consumption of top-quality farmland in addition to wetland destruction (in turn leading to a threat to biodiversity as the natural habitats available to support species shrink). Estimates by the Center for Urban Policy Research suggest that pursuing a policy of uncontrolled urban growth would lead to the development of 4 million additional acres of land in the United States between 2000 and 2025, including 1.5 million acres of environmentally sensitive land, compared to a policy of controlled growth.[11] Car-centered transportation systems have been linked to more than $20 billion in annual health-related costs attributable to congestion and to local air pollution.[12] (Although local air-pollution trends in the United States show decreasing pollution, cars remain a primary source of remaining pollution.)[13]

Defenders of suburban sprawl often argue that such costs are acceptable given that sprawl is thought to promote broader benefits, given that there remains an enormous supply of undeveloped land in the United States, and given that advancing technology may continue to reduce some of the ecological costs associated with sprawl. Such arguments are much less compelling, however, if we shift the focus of our analysis from large-scale aggregate statistics to preserving the integrity of existing ecosystems. At a minimum, development that alters existing land uses needs to be rigorously scrutinized, and local publics can justifiably reject development that has substantial undesirable effects on ecosystems and upon the balance of ecological settings to which metropolitan-area residents have access. Importantly, however, such decisions need to be implemented primarily at the regional level; as is widely recognized, resolutions by individual localities to limit development may have the perverse effect of pushing development farther outside the metropolitan core, leading to greater, rather than fewer, ecological costs. Consequently, policies aimed at curtailing the ecological costs of new development need to be implemented at the regional level to be effective.[14]

As Peter Cannavó has eloquently argued, moving from a mode of urban development that treats places as disposable commodities to one that treats them as landscapes to be cherished requires striking an appropriate balance between the activities of "founding" (creating new places) and "preservation" (maintaining that which is essentially meaningful in existing places.)[15] Cannavó describes sprawl as a cheapened corruption of the original ("founding") ideal of suburban communities as well-designed refuges from urban density that would afford residents access to open air, trees, and nature. "Under the impetus of private developers, retailers, and local governments seeking tax revenue and job creation, the founding project no longer aims at something enduring and thus the preservationist element is entirely lost. This is founding in its narrowest, most crude, debased form. The existing landscape is swept away and something new is put there without any real attention to its ultimate viability—it is consumed and allowed to degrade."[16] Ecologically motivated critics of sprawl have no hope of arresting this trend unless they can succeed in forwarding non-commodified conceptions of both urban and undeveloped places. Yet critics of sprawl, Cannavó argues, go awry when they are based on either rigid architectural determinism or a fundamentalist form of preservationism that refuses to allow places to evolve over time in idiosyncratic ways—two faults he finds evident in some New Urbanist rhetoric and practice. What local publics need in order to steer development toward the formation and sustenance of meaningful human place and respect for ecological limits is not a dogmatic emphasis on either founding or preservation as ends in themselves, but an understanding of the proper role of each and the achievement of a balance between them.[17] Achieving this balance, in turn, would require the development at the local level of a robust, politically aware ecological consciousness of the kind so sorely lacking in most U.S. communities.

_____

The problem of sprawl-related localized ecological damage, while serious, pales in significance when compared to the potential harm associated with long-term climate change. The rest of this chapter thus focuses on the role car-centered urban environments play in contributing to global warming, and how taking account of that role should affect our overall evaluation of sprawl.

Emissions of the greenhouse gas carbon dioxide from motor vehicles have been identified by climate scientists as a primary source of human-generated climate change. Vehicle-based carbon emissions are far higher in the United States than in any other nation, partly because of the enormous (and growing) number of vehicle miles traveled per year and partly because the United States lags behind other nations in effective fuel efficiency.[18]

If we accept the overwhelming scientific consensus that urgent action is needed to reduce carbon emissions in the United States in order to minimize the future effects of climate change, then the question becomes whether the United States can continue to develop in a sprawling, automobile-intensive fashion into the indefinite future. It is estimated that the United States needs (acting in concert with other countries) to achieve a reduction of greenhouse-gas emission of 60 to 80 percent, relative to 1990 levels by the year 2050 if the climate is to be stabilized with the increase in average global temperature limited to just two degrees Celsius. In practical terms, this means that greenhouse emissions in the United States need to fall by 2 percent a year every year between 2010 and 2050. Yet current suburban development patterns generally assume (a) that there is universal or near-universal car usage among the adult population and (b) that there is no intrinsic problem with development that has the effect of increasing the total vehicle miles traveled, apart from limits the preferences of consumers themselves may set. Indeed, carbon emissions in the United States actually rose at an annual rate of 0.9 percent between 1990 and 2007, before declining slightly in 2008 as a consequence of the economic downturn and higher gas prices.[19]

From a theoretical point of view, there is a close parallel between the challenge of climate change and our discussion of civic engagement in chapter 7. In both cases, advancing an important good fundamental in the one case to the health and vitality of a democratic political order and in the other case to the health of the planet itself requires directly challenging the existing preferences that help produce sprawl. Put another way, confronting the full seriousness of climate change requires a fundamental reconsideration of central aspects of the American way of life.

———

There is widespread agreement among scholars and policy analysts that tackling climate change must include, as an important component, attention to the built environment. A 2008 research brief published by the economists Edward Glaeser and Matthew Kahn calculated per household carbon dioxide emissions for sixty-six large metropolitan areas, finding that suburbs generally emitted substantially more than central cities within the same metropolitan statistical area (MSA), although there was substantial variation across MSAs both in level of emissions and in the discrepancy between central city and suburban areas. Glaeser and Kahn noted that their results "suggest that low-density development, particularly in the South, is associated with far more carbon dioxide emissions than higher density construction."[20] Another 2008 study by researchers at the Brookings Institution quantifying the carbon footprint of America's hundred largest MSAs found that higher-density MSAs with greater use of rail transit generally have smaller-than-average carbon footprints; the study notes that "reducing carbon emissions further from compact development will require a major change in the way U.S. urban systems have been evolving during the past half-century."[21] The bivariate correlation between the 2005 carbon footprint estimates produced by the Brookings researchers and the proportion of workers in each metropolitan area who drove alone to work in 2005 is a robust $r = .55$.[22]

International comparisons with other wealthy nations also help reveal the strong linkage between U.S. automobile dependence and climate emissions. In 2005, per capita carbon dioxide emissions in the United States were nearly twice as high as those in Germany (19.6 v. 9.9 tons), and emissions per dollar of GDP were more than twice as high in the United States as in Germany.[23] Different transportation patterns are a major factor in this discrepancy. A Brookings Institution study published in 2009 reported that the average American in 2001 traveled more than twice as many miles by car (9,200) as the average German (4,400 in 2002) and that Americans took two-thirds of all trips of less than one mile by car, compared to 27 percent in Germany. The average German took six times as many public transportation trips as the average American, and took nearly one-third of all trips by bicycle or foot, compared to 10 percent in the United States.[24]

These large-scale differences reflect the different price structures for travel by car in the United States and Germany. The Brookings researchers report that the per-mile cost of operating a Honda Accord in 2006 was $0.72 in the United States, compared to $1.09 in Germany; that sales taxes on cars are 19 percent in Germany compared to 6 percent in most U.S. states; that obtaining a driver's license costs more than $2,000 in Germany, compared to roughly $100 in the United States; and, most significantly, that gas taxes in Germany total $3.60 a gallon, compared to $0.42 in the United States. In addition, traffic layouts in German cities are designed to slow traffic (making alternative transportation modes more appealing, and also reducing traffic fatalities), and parking is scarcer and more expensive in German cities.[25]

Although it may seem obvious that places in which residents drive more also emit larger quantities of carbon, the idea that dealing with climate change requires reversing sprawl has been challenged by some commentators, such as Robert Bruegmann. While acknowledging that global warming may someday require dramatic action, including possibly moving away from car-centered forms of urban development, Bruegmann argues that it would be premature to move in that direction at this point. Why? Because doing so likely will not "solve" the problem of global warming, and because if the goal is to help human lives right now, taking direct action to solve urgent public health problems in the developing world would be a better investment of resources.[26] The latter point is on its own terms correct, but it is irrelevant to the question of whether curbing automobile use would also be a good thing: perhaps we need to take dramatic public action on both counts.

The former point completely ignores the broader geopolitical dimensions of climate change: it is certainly true that no single action or package of actions taken by the United States can "solve" the problem of long-term climate change, but if the United States, as the world's leading generator of greenhouse gases, does not take whatever steps it can to cut back its emissions, there is little hope of persuading other important players such as India and China to take similar steps.[27]

An alternate approach is to put all one's hopes in the possibility of dramatically increasing fuel efficiency in the near future. If the United States' fleet of motor vehicles suddenly was twice as fuel-efficient as it currently is, vehicle-related emissions should fall by half, a major step toward meeting long-term goals of reduced overall emissions.

But banking on this possibility is quite unrealistic and imprudent. First, improvements in fuel efficiency that simply reduce the cost of driving would likely stimulate an increase in vehicle miles traveled, leading to limited or zero net reductions in greenhouse-gas emissions. Second, even if laws introducing dramatically tighter fuel-efficiency standards were passed immediately or if alternatively fueled vehicles, such as plug-in hybrid electric vehicles, became dramatically more cost competitive, it would take a considerable number of years before the fleet as a whole became dramatically more fuel efficient. Third, moving toward more-efficient vehicles would likely require a permanent consumer shift from larger and larger SUV-type vehicles toward smaller cars. SUV sales have fallen since 2004, but large vehicles remain a staple of the typical suburban lifestyle and are perceived by middle-class families accustomed to spending a significant portion of their lives on the road transporting children as a virtual necessity, for reasons of both convenience and safety. Even if the decline in SUV sales proves permanent, the continued presence of large numbers of SUVs on the roads will slow movement toward improved fuel efficiency.

Fourth, any effort to dramatically increase fuel efficiency will likely invite severe opposition from the automotive industry and other parties with a vested interest in the status quo. Of course, this is true (at the moment) of almost all serious efforts to constrain carbon emissions in the United States. But the political difficulty in achieving substantial policy change in any particular area makes it all the more crucial not to put all one's policy eggs in a single basket. Rather than assuming it will be possible to achieve the best possible reform in a particular aspect of climate change policy, it would be more prudent (both politically and substantively) to take steps aimed *both* at limiting total vehicle miles driven *and* at increasing fuel efficiency.

Bruegmann and other skeptics of dramatic action aimed at stemming climate change characteristically point to the possible waste associated with investments in expensive policy shifts that may prove ineffective (or even unnecessary) in the future. This common argument fails on three grounds. First, given the significant possibility that people and property will suffer catastrophic displacement and destruction from climate change by the end of this century, taking steps now to mitigate the possibility of future catastrophe is prudent policy.[28] In addition, given that decisions made today about development patterns will have consequences for decades or longer, taking precautionary action now provides future decision-makers with better options and more flexibility to address climate change as greater certainty about the magnitude of the problem emerges with time. As with a nuclear holocaust, the very possibility of catastrophic climate change causing irreversible damage should be sufficient to stimulate policy action aimed at reducing the probability of such an event. That such action may later turn out to have been unnecessary is not a sufficient reason to refrain from the action, just as a student who closely studies a question that may or may not be on a final exam should not be regarded as wasting her time.[29]

Second, corrective steps aimed at limiting future climate change may have other policy benefits besides limiting carbon emissions. Indeed, wise policy aimed at adjusting to the threat of climate change would do well to focus first on those policy steps that might have broader benefits. Limiting oil consumption surely fits that category, given both the geopolitical and economic consequences of long-term U.S. dependence on foreign oil and the fact that oil is a nonrenewable resource.

Third, this sort of response often implies that efforts to adjust America's spatial arrangements in light of the risks of climate change will in the first instance require extremely expensive efforts to remove Americans from existing suburbs and push as many as possible back into cities. But such a policy, even if it were desirable, would be wildly implausible in political terms. A realistic spatial policy aimed at limiting future climate change would have as its primary focus not undoing the *existing* built environment, but ensuring that *future* metropolitan development promotes ecological efficiency to the furthest degree possible and that future population growth is channeled into more ecologically sound locales. (This may often involve higher-density development in locations now identifiable as "sprawl.")[30]

Consider the numbers: In 1975 passenger cars (excluding SUVs) accounted for just over 1 trillion vehicle miles traveled per year in the United States. By 2005, that figure had risen to just under 1.7 trillion miles traveled per year. Total highway usage rose even faster over the same period: from 1.33 trillion total miles in 1975 to nearly 3 trillion total miles in 2005.[31] If total highway usage increases at the same pace over the next thirty years, then by 2035 some 6.8 trillion total miles a year will be traveled on U.S. highways.

To be sure, while automobiles are a significant source of greenhouse gas emissions, a larger share of carbon dioxide emissions (67% in the United States) can be attributed to households, and to commercial and industrial operations.[32] But this observation only strengthens the case for taking policy steps to curb vehicle emissions, for two reasons: First, it is critical to tackle the challenge of reducing emissions at as many pressure points as possible; second, the larger task facing the United States as it comes to terms with climate change is how to build a *culture* of ecological sustainability. Such a culture necessarily must adopt an ethos of conservation, limiting unnecessary and wasteful energy use. Such steps must extend not only to curbing wasteful transportation practices but also to reexamining broader patterns of household energy use—including the long-term trend in the United States toward much larger house sizes, which is itself facilitated by sprawl.[33]

———

Probably the most thorough assessment to date of the linkage between the built environment and greenhouse-gas emissions has been published by the research team of Reid Ewing, Keith Bartholomew, Steve Winkleman, Jerry Walters, and Don Chen. Ewing et al. stress the need for drastic, simultaneous progress in three key areas: improving fuel efficiency, reducing the carbon content of fuel, and stabilizing total vehicle miles traveled. Focusing on fuel efficiency and carbon content alone may be politically more straightforward, but gains in those areas will simply be canceled out if vehicle miles traveled continue to increase at anything like the rate seen in recent decades. To stabilize vehicle miles traveled, we must confront the issue of how our communities are designed and the geographic expanse of our metropolitan areas.

Based on existing evidence and simulation analysis, Ewing et al. suggest that building more-compact metropolitan areas in combination with other policies could reduce vehicle miles traveled by nearly 40 percent by 2030, relative to the expected trend.[34] Consequently, they recommend a comprehensive effort to "get *all politics and practices, funding and spending, incentives, and rules and regulations pointing in the same direction*, toward smart growth and away from sprawl."[35]

The imperative of finding ways to limit total miles traveled is clear enough from an ecological point of view. But how could such a goal be accomplished? Here we might distinguish between two goals: the first, getting Americans to use cars less; the second, laying out future development in a fashion that permits residents to perform their everyday tasks without driving much.

Spatial design is clearly relevant to both goals. First, higher-density neighborhoods facilitate the development of functional and relatively efficient mass transit systems, which (when efficiently used) consume much less energy per passenger than private-vehicle travel does. Second, mixed-use development offers residents the possibility of taking care of most daily needs in the immediate or nearby neighborhood, without using a car. Third, traditional cities with smaller land parcels and narrower streets facilitate pedestrian activity, as opposed to superblocks flanked by four-lane thoroughfares, which mandate motor-vehicle travel.[36] Finally, shifting away from pod-style development, in which compartmentalized neighborhoods are connected by a single access road to arterials, and toward a more traditional grid arrangement with multiple routes from one point to another, would foster more non-car local travel.

Facilitating alternatives to the car will require changes in both cities and suburbs. Riding a bicycle can be hazardous in many U.S. cities, and many urban places are hostile to pedestrian traffic. But generally speaking, higher-density, mixed-use development offers a greater possibility for minimizing automobile travel than does scattered low-density development. The economist Matthew Kahn has usefully demonstrated the link between more-compact, transit-oriented metropolitan areas and reduced personal gasoline consumption. Drawing on the 2001 National Household Travel Survey, Kahn uses regression analysis to estimate that a household earning $45,000 a year and living in New York City is predicted to consume less than 784 gallons of gasoline a year, compared to more than 1,400 for an identical household in Houston.[37] A similar study by the economist Antonio Bento found that households in Atlanta drive 25 percent more than do demographically identical households in Boston.[38]

There has been a marked long-term trend in the United States since 1960 toward less public transportation use and greater reliance on the car. Whereas just 64 percent of workers drove or carpooled to work in 1960, nearly 88 percent did so in 2000.[39] This shift from public transit creates a self-reinforcing political dynamic in which those who abandon public transit for the automobile become less willing to pay taxes to support public transportation, further weakening public transit's prospects. Kahn usefully documents this point in the case of California, showing that among residents living within twenty miles of a metropolitan center, support for a 1994 gas-tax referendum (Proposition 185) was highest among residents living near the urban center.[40]

Even more worrisome, the low-density layout of so many U.S. metropolitan areas, combined with the ever-larger shift of jobs to suburbs, makes the construction of mass-transit rail a difficult proposition in many areas. Such systems typically have a hub-and-spoke design, being organized around a central city, and are less efficient for transporting persons from one suburb to another. They also require substantial densities in order to generate enough riders and income to offset operating costs. (Some localities might be willing to run such systems at a loss indefinitely, or the federal government might agree to cover such losses, but betting on this possibility would not be wise.)

Consequently, in many metropolitan areas, increasing the use of public transit is likely to first involve buses. But bus transit is commonly perceived as—and often, objectively, is—the least attractive form of public transit because travel is relatively slow and wait times long. Riding the bus in a U.S. city also often involves traveling with poor, minority residents, a prospect some affluent whites find unappealing. However, it might be possible to improve the efficiency and attractiveness of bus transportation, such as by creating bus-only lanes (where possible) to facilitate faster travel or by waiving fares. Such changes might make a difference on the margins and could help change perceptions of bus travel. But persuading large numbers of households now affluent enough to use cars to use buses instead will likely prove very difficult (unless or until the cost of driving rises substantially).

A somewhat more promising possibility is the further growth of telecommuting. Again, however, the proportion of telecommuters is small, and telecommuters living in car-oriented areas will still be required to drive a substantial amount to meet their other daily needs. Moreover, the recent increase in telecommuting has been at least partially offset by the sharp growth since 1990 of "extreme commuting"; between 1990 and 2005, the proportion of workers commuting at least ninety minutes roundtrip nearly doubled.[41]

Given these considerations, many analysts have long been skeptical about the possibility of inducing significant behavior changes in places already dominated by cars.[42] Sharply rising gasoline prices in the first half of 2008 sparked some reconsideration of that proposition, as total vehicle miles driven declined compared to 2007, and large urban-transit systems saw increases in ridership of 5 to 15 percent, including in many highly car-dependent areas, pushing some systems to the brink of capacity.[43] These declines in driving in turn helped ease congestion in some metropolitan areas, such as New York.[44] Automakers reported sharp declines in sales of larger vehicles, such as SUVs, and articles began appearing in leisure sections of newspapers about how to have an enjoyable "stay-cation." The implications of those trends are twofold: First, if—even in the absence of sustained policy intervention—gasoline prices were to reach and remain at $4 per gallon or higher over the long term, then it is reasonable to believe that public demand for mass transit would increase and that vehicle miles traveled by car would begin to stabilize. Second, if policy were to go further and make a concerted effort to increase the consumer's cost of driving (via gasoline taxes) to the point at which drivers paid the full marginal social cost of each mile driven, that would likely have quite a dramatic effect on both individual behavior and public attitudes toward transit.[45]

Enthusiasm for the higher gas prices of 2008 was limited primarily to environmental activists, with most citizens (and the major political parties) viewing the relatively higher prices (still low by international standards) as a problem to be corrected. Consequently, while the recent developments are salutary in indicating that behavioral change is possible, even given the existing metropolitan landscape, a serious strategy for substantially reducing automobile dependence over the next twenty-five to fifty years should not rely on price-induced behavior modifications alone. Any workable strategy would additionally need to focus on ensuring (a) that new developments be oriented around transit and create possibilities for allowing residents to accomplish most of their daily business on foot or by bicycle, and (b) that new population growth in metropolitan areas be funneled into less car-oriented places. Both goals, in turn, would require a concerted effort to stabilize the economic basis of existing urban centers.[46]

Achieving those goals is clearly an enormous challenge, but the possibilities for meaningful change should not be dismissed. Arthur Nelson estimates that by 2025, one-half of our metropolitan buildings will have been built in the twenty-first century.[47] This rebuilding process provides ample opportunity to begin moving away from an automobile-oriented paradigm. Ewing et al. estimate that if the United States could achieve a 20 to 40 percent reduction in travel requirements for *new* developments and redevelopments in the coming generations, that could lead to a "7 to 10 percent reduction in total transportation CO_2 emissions by 2050 relative to continuing sprawl." Higher-density development would also increase the value of land, creating strong incentives for people to live in smaller residences and thus reducing household energy consumption.[48] While more compact development alone will not be enough to markedly reduce greenhouse-gas emissions, if coupled with drastic improvements in fuel efficiency and in the carbon content of fuel—and "complementary strategies" such as congestion pricing—significant reductions could be achieved. Other scholars have called for massive public investments in alternative modes of transportation, particularly inter-city rail.[49] But for any of this to happen, there would have to be a strong political will to implement policy measures capable of steering development this way, a will that the U.S. public has yet to display concerning climate change.

———

Given the difficulty of reversing a decades-long trend, it is understandable that policymakers might wish to avoid confronting the inherent conflict between automobile-centered ways of life and ecological requirements for as long as possible. Cars have a long, honored history in the U.S. imagination and the national mythology; to recall, the sociologist Orlando Patterson's investigations into what Americans mean by freedom found that a substantial portion of men, especially young working-class men, virtually equated freedom with mobility by car. The automobile industry and adjunct operations also remain a potent political force in U.S. politics. It is the rare locality where directly critiquing the automobile and our collective use of it will win a politician many friends or much admiration.[50]

And yet, the green concerned with tackling climate change may insist, someone has to do it. Indeed, a central theme in the environmental movement of the past forty years has been the importance of altering daily habits at the individual and community levels, and building new habits based on being mindful of one's ecological footprint and minimizing unnecessary consumption and waste. On this point, the green can make common cause with civic republicans, who also are willing to challenge the preferences and mindset of the majority when they conflict with the common good.

Indeed, I contend that it is possible to speak coherently of a *green civic republicanism*. As Philip Pettit points out, while republicans generally cannot embrace the non-anthropocentric stance of some strands of environmentalism, they can appreciate the real threat that severe ecological problems pose to the security and good of the community.[51] Likewise, implicit in the environmentalist attitude toward contemporary industrial society is a stance of non-neutrality toward our existing preferences and lifestyles. Environmentalists want people to change the way they live and think, and indeed to change more profoundly than even the most ambitious contemporary civic republican is generally willing to imagine.[52]

This proposed link between civic republicanism and a green political orientation is not simply a marriage of convenience. At least six points of connection between the civic republican tradition and prominent strands of green political theorizing can be identified. First, green political theorists share republican skepticism (indeed, often hostility) toward attempts to treat ecological goods as commensurate, monetized values whose worth can be plugged into the equation of a cost–benefit analysis.[53] Second, green political theorists reject aggregative conceptions of democracy as simply tallying people's preferences, and instead favor more-deliberative conceptions.[54] Third, green political theorists generally reject any implication that the state should be value-neutral; indeed, green political theorists seek to politicize and subject to critical scrutiny a whole range of practices regarding consumption, travel patterns, and the like, which are now regarded in liberal democracies as matters of private choice.[55] (This need not, however, commit green theorists to a totalizing version of eco-fundamentalism.) Fourth, green political theorists also stress the fundamental importance of much stronger, more effective civic engagement and political participation as a prerequisite for advancing ecological sustainability.[56] Fifth, as pointed out by Peter Cannavó, both republicans and greens share a skepticism toward the market and, in particular, toward the ideals of economic growth as a good in itself and maximal consumption as the marker of the good life.[57] Sixth, it is simply a fact that many contemporary critics of sprawl are concerned with both promoting democratic civic engagement and ecological sustainability. Some, such as Randolph Hester, have gone further and argued explicitly that the two concerns are intrinsically linked: "Together—and only when integrated— ecology and democracy provide the foundation for making informed choices and better cities and for discovering more fulfilling lives."[58]

The ideal green republican citizen is one who takes into account both the civic requirements of maintaining a political system based on self-governance and the ecological requirements of maintaining a sustainable planet in shaping both her public identity and her private ends. Neither sustainability nor civic engagement can be reduced to periodic votes for the "right policies"; rather, both must become everyday habits of thought and action. That ideal poses a serious challenge to dominant conceptions of the good life in the United States that identify the well-lived life with high and rising material consumption. Sprawl, as we have seen, is substantially the byproduct of such an orientation, and both greens and civic republicans are correct to think that that orientation must be challenged directly (and without regret) if substantial alterations to sprawl are to be achieved.[59]

———

Climate change represents the most urgent rationale considered in this book for dramatically altering the structure of our built environment. Interestingly, however, politically serious support for such changes will almost certainly not emerge from the usual actors now engaged in debates about suburban sprawl, but from a much wider group of people whose primary concern is reducing greenhouse gases as quickly as possible. Supporters of ardent action might be willing to advocate far more radical and dramatic change than is usually heard in contemporary debates about sprawl.[60]

Indeed, as public understanding of the climate crisis grows, so, too, will political pressure and the boldness of challenges to the status quo. In fall 2008, California enacted a landmark bill intended to curb both sprawl and greenhouse-gas emissions, and there is good reason to think that coalitions based on shared concerns about traffic, rising fuel costs, and climate change might make substantial political progress in other states and regions over the next decade.[61] As understanding of the necessity for change emerges, the tension between how Americans now live and the need to reduce our ecological footprint may subside to some degree, as individuals become less insistent about holding on to the status quo. But that tension is most unlikely to disappear. Indeed, the politics of climate change will probably involve activists voicing a good deal of judgmental public rhetoric about the U.S. way of life, the costs of gas-guzzling SUVs, the moral obliviousness of continuing to buy more and bigger cars. Such rhetoric, in turn, will invite responses—and, no doubt, a fair amount of social tension and resentment. For some, the emerging politics of confrontation over what addressing climate change actually means for our built environment and life in the United States is a troubling phenomenon. For green civic republicans, however, such conflict is a welcome sign and nothing short of the price of meaningful change.

NINE | Reforming Sprawl, and Beyond

N ORMATIVE JUDGMENTS ABOUT SUBURBAN sprawl cannot be divorced from normative judgments about the current condition of U.S. society and the American way of life. It is not surprising that conservative and libertarian-minded defenders of the status quo should also tend to take a favorable view of suburban sprawl and tend to emphasize the real benefits it brings to many people. By the same token, in the United States egalitarians distressed by manifest inequalities and the rightward turn in political life over the past generation, civic republicans alarmed by the decline and devaluation of engaged political activism in contemporary society, and green activists disturbed by the profligate, climate-threatening nature of the mainstream way of life all have good reason to be suspicious of suburban sprawl, a constituent of that way of life. The evidence reviewed in this book lends strong support to each of those suspicions.

The aims of this concluding chapter are, first, to briefly review the key findings of this inquiry; second, to briefly sketch a positive vision of a metropolis compatible with the normative concerns discussed in this book (efficiency, fairness, citizenship, and sustainability); and third, to draw out some of the general policy implications that follow both from those normative concerns and from our empirical examination of sprawl and its consequences for civic life. Dozens of specific tactics to slow, combat, or reverse sprawl have been forwarded in the academic and popular literature, and reviewing the pros and cons of each of these approaches would be impractical. It is possible, however, to comment on the merits of several broad policy strategies in light of what we have learned and argued. Consequently, I distinguish six broad types of anti-sprawl strategies and assess how well they cohere with utilitarianism, liberal egalitarianism, and green civic republicanism.

I then go on to argue for a two-pronged approach to policy reform. Based on what we have learned, it *is* possible to spell out a terrain of policy reform that merits the support of a wide set of philosophical views. Harsh critics of sprawl's negative effects and those who are less persuaded of sprawl's evils or of the need to alter U.S. living habits might at least agree on the rationality of taking steps to roll back current policies that promote and even mandate continued sprawling development.

Pursuing this first prong of policy reform would, in itself, represent a formidable political challenge and would be sure to invite resistance from many quarters. But addressing the worst consequences of sprawl—in particular, its exclusionary elements, the way it shrinks usable public space, and its ecological consequences—will likely require a more aggressive approach, involving policy strategies that deliberately favor urban and older suburban neighborhoods over sprawling fringe development, that seek to steer Americans into more-compact forms of development, and that seek to create a new political architecture for metropolitan government. This more aggressive set of strategies challenges market outcomes, the "American dream," and Americans' existing preferences in a more fundamental fashion; consequently, it will prove more controversial. Here, or so I argue, the civic republican framework—fused with green elements—provides the most compelling normative justification for pursuing aggressive socio-spatial policies aimed at reshaping the nature of the U.S. metropolis.

Utilitarianism, Liberal Egalitarianism, and Green Civic Republicanism: The Argument Revisited

As we have seen, it is difficult to mount a compelling case either for or against sprawl on utilitarian criteria alone. Residents of sprawling communities are happier with their locality than are residents of dense environments, and while sprawl may be more expensive than compact development, the cost difference is not necessarily an overwhelming consideration, particularly if residents are willing to pay more to move into more-expensive developments. Nonetheless, in the absence of experimental evidence, there is no way of gauging the degree to which the common preference for suburban life is conditional upon the substandard state of central cities in the United States. Moreover, Jonathan Levine has introduced compelling evidence that, in at least some metropolitan areas, there may be a latent unsatisfied demand for alternatives to sprawl that, due to zoning regulations mandating low-density development, the market is not presently satisfying.[1] Both of these points suggest utilitarian rationales for promoting greater diversity of neighborhood choices, both within and across metropolitan areas—particularly if these goals can be pursued without direct interference in people's efforts to satisfy their own preferences.

Similarly, liberal egalitarians have grounds for favoring some consequences of sprawl but rejecting others. On the positive side, there is an internal connection between the idea of widespread homeownership and the liberal ideal of independence and creating private spaces independent of the state. Likewise, levels of social trust—a highly valued liberal virtue—appear to be higher in sprawling locations. Lastly, liberals characteristically emphasize respect for individual choices about how to live one's life, including choices about what kind of community to live in.

But sprawl is a threat to the egalitarian project. The history of suburbanization in the United States has been driven by exclusionary impulses, impulses inseparable from the American dream itself; the desire to live in a safe neighborhood that is divorced from crime and social problems and has good public amenities motivates the exclusionary impulse. Suburbanization, then, has had the effect of locking in and reinforcing racial and economic inequalities and of weakening (if not eliminating) the possibility of meaningful redress of social and economic inequalities within metropolitan regions. What is decisive about this dynamic is less the particular spatial configurations of suburbs than the process of suburbanization itself.

Several specific attributes of sprawl *are*, however, strongly associated with more conservative political attitudes. If we accept Gainsborough's highly plausible suggestion that (apart from any other contextual or environmental effects that may be in play) where you live will affect how you identify your political self-interest, then we can see suburbanization and sprawl as a kind of inequality machine: Households of means move to the suburbs to escape problems associated with the central cities, then they construct barriers to exclude poor and working-class families from joining them; they escape fiscal responsibility for coping with urban social problems, and become more likely to support the political status quo and to resist efforts to alter the structure of opportunity in the United States in the direction of greater fairness and equality.

Green civic republicanism—especially in its egalitarian form—provides the strongest rationale for demanding reform of U.S. socio-spatial structures. The process of sprawl can be linked to the decline in usable public space, to the rise of powerful big-box chains (at the expense of independent business), and to the weakness of municipal governments vis-à-vis highly mobile businesses. As we have seen, it also can be linked to lower rates of political engagement and activism. Last, but certainly not least, sprawl is complicit in both the generation of greenhouse gases and, more generally, in a way of life oriented around profligate consumption, not ecological mindfulness.

A Just, Efficient, Civically Engaged, and Ecologically Sustainable Metropolis

This book has particularly emphasized distinctions among utilitarianism, liberal egalitarianism, and civic republicanism. Yet, as noted in the introduction, the distinctive values of each political philosophy—efficient satisfaction of rational preferences, respect for people's choices, maintaining a just structure of equal opportunity, upholding a solidaristic political culture, active civic engagement, and ecological sustainability—are, in many cases, not in zero-sum conflict with one another. Civic republicans, in particular, do not care *only* about having an engaged citizenry; they also care about material prosperity, maintaining sufficient social equality so that no citizen can be dominated by any other, building trust and solidarity among citizens, and sustaining the ecological basis for stable human communities. In practice, there will often be trade-offs at the margins among these various goods. But, in principle, a green civic republican's first impulse is to try to maximize *each* of these goods, to the fullest extent possible.

Before considering specific policy strategies, then, it will be helpful to briefly sketch the basic features of a "good" twenty-first-century metropolis, from the point of view of green civic republicanism. A healthy metropolitan area should provide for a variety of residential settings, to accommodate a variety of neighborhood preferences, and each sort of neighborhood should have as high a quality of life as possible. In particular, no type of neighborhood or particular section of the metropolitan area should be markedly more unpleasant, unsafe, or unsanitary than the rest of the region. Nor should there be dramatic differences in the quality of public goods available to each neighborhood. In particular, the quality of opportunity available to young people to develop their capacities should not be significantly affected by one's area of residence in the metropolis. Municipalities within the region should not have the capacity to economically, socially, and politically segregate themselves from the larger region to defend or extend a privileged position in the provision of public goods.

All neighborhood types within the metropolis should provide a rich quality and quantity of public, noncommercial space, to encourage public contestation and a culture of political engagement and activism. Special care should be given to preserving those neighborhoods that already have a vibrant street-life culture facilitating face-to-face interactions. Often, this will require paying attention to the economic base of such neighborhoods (e.g., traditional Main Streets) and taking steps to ensure that older commercial areas are not discarded in favor of car-oriented big-box development. In spatial environments lacking effective public space or walkable street connections, creating such spaces should be a priority.

A good metropolitan area should provide a variety of transportation options. The goal should be to enable all members of the metropolitan area—including those who do not own or cannot drive cars—to effectively get around at as little ecological cost as possible. The social and ecological costs of driving should be accounted for in siting new developments, and any new development should be connected to—if not primarily oriented around—transit nodes. The proportion of neighborhoods in which individuals are required to drive to meet the basic demands of everyday life should be as small as is feasible.

While absolute size of the metropolis is in itself not necessarily a decisive evaluative criterion, fringe development that tends to undercut the goals laid out above is to be discouraged and certainly not subsidized. Further, metropolitan areas should attempt to limit the incidence of very long personal commutes, particularly long commutes by solo drivers. Whether achieving this last set of goals requires a growth boundary or another "hard limit" on sprawl will likely vary from region to region. Metropolitan development should also show respect for other ecological goods, including ecosystem and watershed integrity and the preservation of open space. Finally, metropolitan areas should take steps to offset the possible negative effects of policy reforms, especially those reforms that (at least debatably) may negatively affect low- and middle-income residents. Community land trusts, limited-equity cooperatives, and other structural means of permitting poorer and working-class households to remain in their neighborhoods in the wake of gentrification should be encouraged, assisted, and even capitalized.

From Here to There: A Two-Tiered Approach to Reform

Above we have sketched a vision of a just and healthy metropolis that should be attractive to people from a wide range of political viewpoints. This vision represents a formidable challenge to the status quo, however. In particular, it challenges Americans' widespread preference (examined or not, fully rational or not) for living in low-density, privileged neighborhoods divorced from serious social problems. This vision thus presents a challenge for policymakers, who are obliged to take account of their constituents' existing preferences. How might it be possible to bring about meaningful policy reform, given the opposition some, perhaps even many, residents are likely to have to this agenda?

When goods are in tension with one another, a reasonable policy approach—echoing the Pareto principle in economics—is to first seek strategies that could maximize some goods without undercutting other goods (such as the satisfaction of existing preferences) or undercutting them only minimally. To the extent that it is possible to bolster some goods without causing significant harm to other valued goods, this approach to reform can be conceived simply as making public policy more efficient.

At a certain stage, however, the potential of such non-confrontational reforms to effect change may be exhausted. At that point, it will become necessary to consider policy strategies that do place higher priority on some goods than on others, and in which value conflict is indeed inevitable. Proposed reforms along those lines will inevitably prove more controversial.

The following section consequently lays out six broad strategies for reforming the United States' socio-spatial structures. The first two of these strategies are "Pareto optimizing" with respect to valued goods. In principle, they could be endorsed by utilitarians, liberal egalitarians, and civic republicans alike. Further, because they do not fundamentally challenge existing preference structures, they do not require trading one value against another in zero-sum fashion.

The remaining strategies for reform are more far-reaching in nature, more controversial, and more likely to inspire opposition from at least some utilitarians and liberals (in addition to libertarians). These policy strategies explicitly challenge Americans' existing residential preferences, particularly the reigning, exclusionary vision of the "American dream."

STAGE 1 REFORM: UNDOING EXCLUSIONARY ZONING
AND SUBSIDIES

Sprawl is not simply the product of market forces but also the result of extensive state and federal subsidies (see chapter 1) and a longstanding patchwork of local zoning regulations aimed at excluding higher-density suburban development in addition to less affluent potential residents.[2] All three normative perspectives examined here would be highly sympathetic to a reform agenda whose goal was to roll back such exclusionary zoning.

Utilitarians might support such an agenda on the grounds that a more diverse set of local spatial arrangements would both increase the likelihood of individuals getting to choose a neighborhood that matched their preferences and would allow both residents and policymakers to make better-informed comparisons between sprawling and non-sprawling places. Liberal egalitarians might support ending exclusionary zoning as a matter of fairness toward individuals and populations typically excluded from suburban neighborhoods. Finally, green civic republicans might endorse such reform measures on substantive grounds: rolling back such zoning measures is an essential precondition of any movement toward developing twenty-first-century spatial forms that are more inclusive, more hospitable to rich civic and political life, and more consistent with the demands of ecological sustainability.

All three perspectives might likewise favor ending federal policies that now disproportionately favor suburbs and big-box style retailers, on similar grounds. These policies include home loans that disproportionately finance construction in suburbs, the home-mortgage subsidy (available to urban homeowners, but disproportionately claimed by suburbanites), in addition to various subsidies for driving, parking, and highway construction. Of particular importance is the failure to make drivers pay the full marginal social cost of driving.

We might call this agenda "stage 1 sprawl reform": this agenda does not directly challenge the market itself; rather, its goal is to minimize the degree to which government policy pushes the market in a sprawling direction. Nonetheless, this agenda would represent a massive challenge to the status quo and attract the determined opposition of many existing suburbanites. The existing forms of exclusionary zoning, for instance, did not develop by accident; at some point, local communities thought it in their shared interest to adopt those policies. It would be entirely too optimistic to suggest that all of those same local communities would now be prepared to alter long-standing zoning regulations just because they happen to violate free-market principles and basic norms of fairness.

Indeed, rolling back local zoning regulations will, in most cases, require state-level legislative action, action that will be opposed by some localities in the name of maintaining local control. It is rather difficult to imagine that appeals to free-market norms alone will suffice to overturn exclusionary zoning. Put another way, asking localities to take measures making higher-density suburbs possible is unlikely to be successful if it is not coupled with a substantive account of why higher-density suburbs might be desirable. Here, appeal to norms of inclusivity and fairness, and to civic and ecological aims, would be most appropriate in building a multilayered argument for, at the very least, *permitting* denser, less sprawling forms of development in suburbs.

STAGE 2 REFORM: IMPROVING URBAN QUALITY OF LIFE AND EDUCATION

"Stage 2" of a sprawl reform agenda also might command at least partial support from all three normative perspectives. The substance of this agenda would consist in making central cities dramatically more livable places and in taking concrete steps to improve the quality of public goods, especially public education, available to urban residents. In theory, this could be done without seeking to reshape the political structure of the metropolis itself; federal-level taxation could be used to finance efforts to bolster schools, encourage community development, and improve public safety, building on many past policy precedents. Internal reform efforts aimed at minimizing corruption and waste and at better capitalizing on cities' existing assets and capabilities would also be a crucial ingredient of this approach.

There are severe limits to this strategy, however, both political and practical. The political limit is that party leaders have little appetite for large increases in federally funded public assistance to central cities. The practical limit consists in the fact that even somewhat improved central cities might not be significantly more attractive to mobile, middle-class households than suburban alternatives if a marked disparity between suburban and urban public goods remained. It is possible that both of these dynamics might change, however, if market shifts in coming years led relatively affluent households to increasingly demand urban living, as some analysts predict they will, or if continued increases in the cost of driving makes living nearer the center significantly more attractive to households.[3]

STAGE 3 REFORM: REDRESSING LOCAL INEQUALITIES

"Stage 3" reform would involve steps not just to strengthen the condition of central cities but to break down the walls between suburban and urban locations at the local level. Two major strategies for redressing such inequalities are commonly noted: first, urban annexation of suburban municipalities, and second, the formation of regional-governance structures. The annexation strategy, however, is inherently limited; there are legal (to say nothing of political) obstacles to annexation in many states, and it is not plausible to think that central cities will be able to annex all or even most of their surrounding suburbs.[4]

This leaves some form of regional government as the most plausible possibility. But any proposal for regional government is sure to invite serious political opposition as well (in the name of maintaining local control and of allowing suburban residents to escape responsibility for urban problems). Implementing regional reform involves directly challenging the suburban prerogative to be left alone. Whereas stage 2–type reform imposes only very diffuse costs on suburban residents (in the form of at least some redistributive taxation), stage 3 reform involves challenging the nature of suburban governance and hence suburban life itself. Consequently, it is likely to attract opposition not simply from self-interested suburbanites but also from those utilitarians and liberals who believe that infringing on existing forms of suburban governance might be tantamount to restraining suburbanites' liberty to live in a community of their own choosing.

Egalitarians counter this claim by insisting that that there is no inherent right to insulate oneself in a particular municipality, apart from the community as a whole. Here again, though, political prudence suggests that regional governments be framed not simply as vehicles for redistribution—essential as that may be—but as institutions capable of bringing broader benefits, including to suburban residents themselves.

Some scholars skeptical of regionalist approaches have raised a different kind of concern, which is that regional governance structures, rather than enhancing the position of central cities, might weaken cities' ability to aggressively pursue progressive policies, and thus might effectively lock existing inequalities into place. This concern points to the importance of carefully thinking about how to organize regional structures that are politically plausible and that facilitate progressive rather than regressive outcomes.

By far the most sophisticated work on what such a regional-governance structure might look like has been undertaken by the legal scholar Gerald Frug. Frug rejects conventional "two-tiered" models of regional governance in which localities retain control over purely local issues while ceding power on regional issues to regional bodies, on the grounds that this would create an unstable, zero-sum conflict between localism and regionalism. He instead argues that a properly designed regional framework might give localities *more* control over some decisions over which they now have little influence (such as transportation planning and revenue generation), while also requiring them to take account of the effect of local policies on neighboring localities. To this end, Frug proposes a regional legislative body based roughly on the European Union (EU) model of regional governance. This body would have the power to forge regional approaches to metropolitan policy problems, not via a top-down regional planning directive but as a result of a process of consultation and negotiation among representatives of all localities in the region, with each locality being given seats or votes in proportion to their share of the region's population.[5]

Frug argues that a regional legislature of this kind should be able to develop and enforce region-wide policies on taxes, zoning, land use, housing, economic development, transportation, and other crucial issues; when appropriate, policy implementation might be left to individual localities. In some cases, moreover, the regional body should permit localities to craft localized policies on these issues, so long as they take the concerns of other localities into account. Such a regional structure would derive legitimacy from the fact that (unlike existing regional institutions, such as metropolitan planning organizations) all localities in the region would be represented democratically. Further, localities would have far more input into a variety of policy areas now controlled by state governments; Frug envisions state governments relinquishing decision-making power regarding transportation, for instance, to regional bodies.

Frug suggests that regional legislatures could eventually help address longstanding inequalities between central cities and poorer older suburbs, on the one hand, and more affluent suburbs, on the other. At the most basic level, the regional structure would require localities to cooperate with one another and to at least recognize one another's problems, as opposed to acting in a wholly self-regarding manner that is oblivious to the needs of other localities in the region. Frug argues that recognizing such commonality of interest might lead localities to implement policies to improve the worst-off neighborhoods and cities. Here Frug argues that rather than relying on a shared-tax-base paradigm, regions could (following EU practice) establish "structural funds" aimed at financing initiatives and projects in poorer areas. Such funds might be raised through regional sales taxes, for example. Residents of poorer metropolitan neighborhoods would shape specific proposals to improve their neighborhoods; those proposals would then be considered by the legislature as a whole, which in Frug's view would have the positive benefit of forcing wealthier communities to consider the concrete problems of poor communities rather than simply allowing a formula to mechanically distribute tax revenues. Indeed, a crucial aim of Frug's proposed framework is not simply to establish revenue sharing but also to compel individual localities to recognize their interdependence; compared to the status quo, the regional-legislature proposal at least creates the possibility of meaningful social solidarity between better-off suburban communities and poorer cities and suburbs.[6]

STAGE 4 REFORM: GOVERNMENT-STEERED
DEVELOPMENT IN OLDER AREAS

"Stage 4" of a reform agenda does, at last, involve challenging the market itself, and/or using state power to steer development toward specific areas. Levine is again persuasive in suggesting that while "smart growth"–type regulations have the capacity to allow localities to accommodate higher-density development, they do not have the capacity to create such developments where there is no underlying demand for them.[7] Put another way, if no one wants higher-density developments, no one is going to build them either, whatever inducements zoning or other state policies may provide.

This does not mean, however, that the state needs to remain neutral or refrain from intervening in the market in ways that might encourage more compact, walking and transit-oriented development. First, as in Maryland, it can steer its own monies and the construction of new public facilities and infrastructure toward more compact development, efforts that help facilitate the development of higher-density places. Second, it can provide incentives to developers doing in-fill work, cleaning up brownfields, participating in transit-oriented development, and supplying other alternatives to low-density development on the suburban edge. Third, the state might attempt to shape the preferences of individuals directly, whether by bully-pulpit marketing of the virtues of more-compact communities, provision of incentives to individuals who minimize automobile use, or other methods.

Clearly, these policy approaches involve steering the market, and therefore only green civic republicans are likely to embrace such "stage 4" reform in unalloyed fashion. Civic republicans can point out, however, that public policy is already involved in steering or shaping the market in countless (sometimes contradictory) ways, from support for home ownership and small businesses to procurement practices to decisions about where to locate government facilities. Government involvement in market activity is ubiquitous; civic republicans argue that it's better to recognize that fact and openly debate what ends such involvement should be directed toward, rather than cling to an unattainable ideal of neutrality that, in practice, allows government interventions to be steered more by private influence than public purpose. Just as government activity has played a key role in the construction of American suburbia, so might it also play a key role in redirecting new growth toward existing central cities and suburbs.

STAGE 5 REFORM: SETTING HARD LIMITS
ON SUBURBAN EXPANSION

Next, we consider policies that go beyond simply leveling away pro-sprawl public biases or using incentives to attempt to steer the behavior of individuals, firms, and localities. Stage 5 sprawl reform involves the setting of hard limits on suburban expansion. This might happen in two principal, not mutually exclusive ways.

First, following the famous example of Portland, Oregon, reformers may impose a flexible urban-growth boundary in metropolitan areas. This hard limit slows sprawl on the perimeter of the metropolis in the most direct way possible, and redirects new development and residential growth back toward the central city and existing suburbs.[8]

Second, state and local governments may simply refuse to finance any additional rounds of automobile-oriented development and instead insist that new development within the metropolis be transit-oriented. In its most dramatic form, this strategy might even involve planned "new towns" (harkening back to Howard's Garden City model). The basic idea is for new development in a given metropolitan area to take the form of a coherent locality organized around transit nodes or other central geographic points, rather than evolving in a scattered, free-form manner. The reasoning here is that to the extent that further development in suburbia is necessary, it should result in coherently planned new communities that have, even from their inception, strong transit links to the rest of the metropolis.[9]

Whereas "stage 4" reform simply involves "indicative" planning—government action intended to encourage certain kinds of market developments—"stage 5" reform involves more-explicit public planning. States and localities choosing to implement such planning are making a deliberate choice to ensure that future development does not bring unconstrained sprawl, precisely by setting the rules of the market to preclude such a possibility. The *legitimacy* of such a course of action is widely accepted by all political viewpoints that reject strong property rights libertarianism (see the introduction); but many utilitarians and some liberals believe that public policy best maximizes costs and benefits when it avoids dictating market outcomes. Civic republicans can respond by pointing out the ways in which public policy already restricts certain kinds of transactions on both moral grounds (hiring child labor) and in order to promote other public ends that unconstrained market processes are unlikely to produce; more fundamentally, they question the very idea that there is such a thing as a pure "market outcome" detached from the specific rules and regulations in which markets operate. In a fundamental sense, public planning aimed at shaping the contours of the metropolitan region as a whole reflects the sense that regional landscapes are a shared matter of common concern, not simply an aggregation of privately held properties. Consequently, civic republicans are likely to be generally sympathetic to proposals for direct public planning at the state and local levels to curb sprawl; however, any particular proposal needs to be judged on its merits, and if enacted, its consequences.

STAGE 6 REFORM: DIRECT INTERVENTION INTO INDIVIDUAL CHOICES

Finally, we come to the most controversial and most difficult-to-justify set of policy strategies, those that attempt to affect individual behavior directly, not simply through giving positive incentives aimed at steering persons one way rather than another, but by employing more-punitive or even coercive techniques to ensure the desired behavior.

Perhaps the mildest and most palatable policy along these lines would be imposing dramatic increases on the cost of driving, through gasoline taxes, vehicle-registration fees, more frequent toll collection, and so forth. Note, however, that *punitive* tax increases that principally aim to stop the behavior itself can be distinguished from tax increases that aim simply to force drivers to pay for a greater share of the costs of maintaining the automobile infrastructure or to offset the externalities (including greenhouse-gas emissions) associated with driving. Tax increases—even very sharp tax increases—undertaken for those purposes can easily be justified by liberals and utilitarians alike. But taxes that go beyond this, and that implicitly condemn automobile driving itself, invite much greater suspicion from these traditions. Indeed, J. S. Mill explicitly denied the permissibility of levying taxes of this kind.[10]

Another type of punitive, coercive policy would involve large-scale intervention in the private housing market, with the aim of effectively *forcing* people to live in central cities or older suburbs. What might such intervention look like? In theory, governments might impose draconian taxes on outer suburban households, might impose a financial penalty on urban households seeking to move to the suburbs, or might construct other direct barriers to residential choice. In the most extreme scenario, exurban residents might be literally forced out of their homes and resettled in urban apartments.

Essentially no one in the suburban sprawl debate favors this last set of policies, or thinks they could be justified in the absence of emergency conditions requiring a rapid relocation of U.S. households. (Moreover, emergencies associated with immediate threats to national security or severe weather events that require rapid relocation are more likely to involve rapid decentralization of people out of, not back into, central cities.) Yet libertarian defenders of sprawl often suggest that the real intent of planners and others who favor some form of sprawl reform actually intend this level of intrusion into individual choices—or imply that there is an equivalency between direct coercion of individuals and milder reform strategies.[11]

From a civic republican point of view, there is a key distinction to be made between state action that *encourages* and *rewards* praiseworthy behavior or actions, and state action that punishes individuals for actions that do not cause direct harm to others or themselves. From a civic republican point of view, honoring an excellent citizen, or providing an incentive to someone who acts to bolster the health of the community is permissible; punishing or coercing someone who is merely an indifferent citizen is not. In terms of the sprawl debate, policies and incentives aimed at encouraging future growth and residential move toward older parts of the metropolis are justified, as would be policies aimed at getting suburban residents to pay for the full social costs of activities such as driving; imposing a large, punitive head tax specifically targeted at suburban residents for no other reason than that they live in the suburbs would not be so justified. Obviously, this position is at odds with a strict neutrality view that insists the state must remain completely neutral and indifferent toward the individual decisions and attitudes of its members. But neither does it mandate *forcing* people to alter the way they live their lives, so long as they are not harming or externalizing costs onto others.[12]

In practical terms, the harm principle itself, with the corollary notion that persons should pay for the full social costs of their actions, might justify taxes likely to be experienced as "coercive" by people unaccustomed to having to take into account the social costs of their own behavior. This is particularly likely with respect to environmental goods. But policies that go beyond this and attempt to not just encourage but to coerce individuals into exhibiting a particular set of attitudes or behaviors cannot ordinarily be justified by any of the normative perspectives considered here. This sixth set of policy reforms then is of interest insofar as it helps illustrate the proper *limits* of acceptable policy strategies aimed at reforming sprawl and building a better metropolis.

Beyond Anti-Sprawl

This book has been organized principally around the question of whether sprawl is a good or bad thing, or, more specifically, in what sense it is praiseworthy and in what sense it is blameworthy. It has also repeatedly stressed that one's overall assessment of the advantages and disadvantages of sprawl will inevitably be intimately linked with one's broader views of politics and its purposes.

"Sprawl" is and will probably continue to be a useful shorthand for describing the dominant urban pattern in the metropolitan United States. Indeed (as shrewd observers have noted), the word itself functions brilliantly in political terms: the very use of the word implies that there is something wrong with the pattern of metropolitan growth in the United States.[13]

But both the complex findings of this book and the internal logic of the various normative perspectives we have considered suggest that it may be time to move beyond "stopping sprawl" as the guiding metaphor for reforming our metropolitan areas. Four considerations underlie this judgment. The first is the inherent ambiguity of the term itself, and how it lends itself to the problematic assumption that each aspect of sprawl has the same sorts of consequences for goods that we care about. Second, a focus on sprawl often invites a too-exclusive focus on the spatial form of metropolitan communities. Such form is not unimportant, and we have demonstrated some ways in which it appears to influence individual attitudes and behavior. But from the standpoint of justice, especially, what is decisive is not the form itself but the underlying social purposes for which the forms are employed. In short, the "socio" part of the term "socio-spatial structure" too often evaporates from both friendly and critical commentaries on sprawl.

Third, from the standpoint of the various normative perspectives considered here, the primary purpose of policy reform cannot be to stop "sprawl" for its own sake. We may choose to stop or slow sprawl, but we would do so in order to secure the substantive ends we care about. From a utilitarian perspective, the principal end of socio-spatial policy is to maximize well-being, or alternatively, to satisfy preferences as efficiently as possible, relative to other alternatives. Liberal egalitarians seek to create a metropolis in which opportunity and life chances are not significantly correlated with where one lives within the metropolis; in short, a socio-spatial structure that tends to mitigate rather than exacerbate background inequalities, and a socio-spatial structure that facilitates rather than inhibits meaningful social solidarity based on the idea that we are all in this together. Civic republicans, without denying the importance of these themes, place special stress on whether socio-spatial arrangements tend to encourage or discourage a robust public life, facilitate public contestation of political decisions, and contribute to the formation of engaged citizens. Lastly, green thinkers and activists emphasize the importance of minimizing our collective ecological footprint, particularly with respect to greenhouse-gas generation.

To be "against sprawl" does not necessarily mean to favor taking policy steps to better secure all or even most of these valued goods. Consequently, reform efforts might gain greater analytical and political clarity by framing their goals in positive rather than negative terms: the long-term goal should not be to stop "sprawl" but to build a just, efficient, civically engaged, and ecologically sustainable polity. Hence the potential importance of sketches of the just metropolis such as those laid out above.[14]

The need to develop a positive account of the just metropolis becomes particularly urgent when we consider a fourth, crucial point: it is possible that long-term trends toward ever-higher levels of suburbanization and fringe development may begin to reverse themselves in the coming generation. An increasing number of important urban planning voices, such as Robert Fishman and Arthur C. Nelson, now think it quite likely that the demand for alternatives to low-density development will increase significantly in the coming decades; Fishman goes so far as to speak of a possible "Fifth Migration" of affluent households back into central cities and older suburbs.[15] If such a trend comes to fruition, it would obviously lend support to and help facilitate some of the metropolitan reform strategies outlined above, and, in particular, create welcome possibilities for substantially improving quality of life and public goods in long-neglected older places (central cities and suburbs alike). It might also contribute substantially to the goal of reducing the metropolitan United States' dependence on automobiles and reducing greenhouse-gas emissions. The current (2008–9) economic crisis already has slowed or stalled new suburban development in many parts of the United States, and the abandoned shopping mall is becoming an increasingly common feature of the U.S. landscape.[16]

But such trends, even if they truly amounted to the end of sprawl, would not in itself create a just or civically engaged metropolis; it's quite possible that spatial inequality and the degradation of shared public space might simply take on a new, somewhat more compact form. Put another way, while any substantial trend of urban resettlement would create significant new possibilities for lasting metropolitan reform, sustained political action on behalf of socio-spatial justice will be required to take advantage of those positive possibilities and to mitigate any negative byproducts (i.e., displacement of poorer residents) that might accompany a migration of the relatively affluent back to central city and inner suburban neighborhoods.

Conclusion: Policy Experimentation and the Limits of New Urbanism

This chapter has argued that a green civic republican perspective speaks more fully to the motives and concerns of critics of the contemporary U.S. metropolis than either utilitarianism or liberal egalitarianism, taken alone.

It has also shown how green civic republicanism underwrites a more aggressive policy orientation toward the reform of our socio-spatial structures, both with respect to its diagnosis of the existing metropolis and with respect to the range of reform strategies it is willing to endorse.

This is not to say that liberals and utilitarians have no reason to be concerned about sprawl. Indeed, liberals and especially utilitarians might agree that there is a good case for policy diversity and experimentation with various types of spatial development. So, too, will civic republicans who—quite properly—have only limited faith in findings generated by cross-sectional quantitative studies regarding the apparent relationships between socio-spatial characteristics and individual behavior of the kind presented in this study. Might substantial metropolitan-level changes in socio-spatial arrangements create circumstances conducive to increased political participation? Might they lead to the creation and maintenance of economically diverse neighborhoods? Might they alter Americans' attitudes toward cities and their general preference for suburban life? Might they even enhance possibilities for meaningful solidarity between well-off and less well-off Americans? Active policy innovation aimed at limiting sprawl and strengthening center cities while reducing overall dependence on the automobile would serve as a natural experiment, with the potential to provide rich evidence with which to address those questions—evidence that could well alter how liberals, utilitarians, and civic republicans alike assess sprawl in the future.

From a green civic republican perspective, however, two cautionary notes to this call for policy innovation need to be added. First, serious, comprehensive reform strategies involving entire metropolitan regions that address both the spatial and the social dimensions of sprawl need to be distinguished from piecemeal, ad hoc reforms that may carry a "smart growth" or "New Urbanist" banner but have (even in intent) only very limited or specific effects. Second, building on the theme of the previous section, insofar as the long-term goal of civic republicans is to encourage ways of life that balance both public and private concerns and include active participation in self-governance as a central component, the inherent limitations of focusing simply on sprawl as a lever of change must be recognized.

Those limitations do not consist simply in the fact that the predicted effect on, say, protest activity, of shifting from "sprawl" to denser, transit-friendly areas is finite—and certainly not large enough to constitute an overwhelming shift in the civic habits of Americans. (Even in those places most conducive to active participation, a majority of citizens sit largely on the sidelines of civic life.) The more serious limitation is that the built environment (and Americans' current preferences regarding how to live) is but one aspect of a larger way of life associated with the U.S. version of consumer capitalism. If many Americans now highly value the convenience and sense of liberty that cars (and a nearby Wal-Mart) provide, this is not unrelated to the stress, time pressure, and economic insecurity many Americans experience in everyday life. If many Americans have come to primarily emphasize the private sphere as a source of personal happiness, this is not unrelated to the lack of satisfaction many feel in the experience of work, or to a perceived lack of opportunities to engage in meaningful political engagement. If many Americans now prefer the comforts of a sterile subdivision to the stresses of a bustling city, that is not unrelated to the reality of urban crime and poverty, and, in turn, broader socioeconomic patterns of income and poverty.

Put another way, insofar as green civic republicanism aims at a holistic critique of the U.S. way of life, it cannot train its sights solely on one sphere of life while ignoring others. Nor can it place undue hopes on the possibility that changes in one such sphere (such as the built environment) will lead to profound alterations in the way Americans balance private and public commitments in the absence of changes in other spheres as well.

Equally important, civic republicans must provide substantive reasons why the U.S. way of life should be altered, beyond expanding civic participation for its own sake; otherwise, the civic republican is stuck in a chicken-and-egg problem where civic renewal is required to produce the institutional changes that would in turn make more robust civic engagement a permanent feature of U.S. life. Citizens are most likely to be engaged in politics when substantive, material questions affecting their lives are in play. Civic republicans understand this—and it would be a grievous mistake to suppose that civic republicans care *only* about the formation of better citizens, and not also about concrete material goods and harms.

In the case of sprawl, civic republicans can point to the socio-spatial injustices associated with sprawl, the ecological and aesthetic costs of more cars on the roads and more land consumed by development, the negative social (and spiritual) consequences of a spatial environment oriented around consumerism, and questions about the cost of sprawl-type growth (especially when such costs are subsidized by the public rather than borne by private actors)—in addition to arguments that less sprawl would help enhance political engagement. Moreover, the civic republican can comfortably talk about these issues without being confined to the straightjacket of an ideal of state "neutrality," and without being bashful about naming and critiquing sprawl as a shared way of life. Unlike the utilitarian, the civic republican can speak to the concrete harms of sprawl not in terms of inherently ambiguous comprehensive cost–benefit analyses but by arguing that the private and public harms associated with sprawl are inimical to engaged citizenship and cannot be adequately compensated by sprawl's promised benefits.

Critically, there is also reason to believe that an anti-sprawl reform coalition *without* a strong civic republican sensibility would be short-lived and limited in scope; if participants in the coalition see their goals as simply advancing their own interests and maximizing their personal welfare, it would be difficult, if not impossible, to maintain a coalition on behalf of new socio-spatial policies that necessarily impose costs on certain groups or that challenge the existing preferences of a substantial portion of the population.[17] Civic republicans demand that citizens learn to think in terms of the good of the whole and learn to contextualize legitimate material claims within the claims and needs of other parts of the community. The presence, or emergence, of this particularly lofty republican virtue is probably a prerequisite for the formation of lasting political coalitions aimed at redressing sprawl and shaping a more just metropolis (as opposed to short-term political alliances based solely on the accident of converging interests).[18]

To be sure, civic republicans cannot avoid making arguments for the politically engaged life and hope simply to smuggle in civic republican benefits through the backdoor of policies adopted for other reasons. The dominant cultural ideals of life in the United States stand largely athwart the civic republican ideal of the engaged citizen possessing both a keen critical consciousness and a deep moral responsibility, unable to conceive of his or her good apart from that of the larger political community. Civic republicans can offer one of three responses to this reality: they may abandon democratic principles entirely and call for state actions that simply ignore citizens' existing preferences, they may take advantage of the notorious imperfections of democratic social-choice procedures and devise sophisticated political strategies aimed at getting citizens to adopt policies at odds with their own preferences, or they may use argument and reason to challenge dominant cultural ideals and make the case for the politically engaged life—arguments that might draw on both the neo-Roman emphasis on active citizenship as a requirement for preserving liberty and self-rule, and the neo-Aristotelian claim that through political engagement we may come to "know a good in common that we cannot know alone."[19]

Indeed, sprawl is an issue with special interest for civic republicans precisely because it is multilayered and offers the possibility of forming coalitions involving actors motivated by both concrete, material concerns and by more-abstract normative principles. In pointing to the ways that public policies and private actions that for decades escaped serious public scrutiny helped create the reality of sprawl in the metropolitan United States, civic republicans have an opportunity to enter the sprawl debate with more than an abstract argument for the goodness of the civically engaged life. They can also cite sprawl as a case study in the tangible costs of civic disengagement, and an example of the inherent risk that democratic publics run in turning over our shared landscapes to the care of either impersonal market forces or unaccountable public decision making.

Equally important, as a new era unfolds in U.S. politics, one seemingly more attuned to the importance of sustained civic and political activism and more open to constructive public action on behalf of public ends than in the recent past, civic republicans have a rare opportunity to raise fundamental questions about how and why we organize the socio-spatial patterns of our metropolitan areas as we do and to reconsider what ends those development patterns promote. For perhaps the first time in decades, there is growing and widespread understanding that the way Americans have lived is ecologically, economically, and civically unsustainable, as well as fundamentally unjust. Sprawl is a constituent of that way of life, and it is inconceivable that a serious reassessment of that way of life could ignore the manifold consequences of our high dependence on the automobile or the geographically structured inequalities that mark our metropolitan areas. Civic republicans and their allies can contribute to this reassessment not just by critiquing the status quo but by taking up the work—at once visionary and practical—of carefully thinking through how to reshape our metropolitan areas in ways that befit our civic aspirations as a free people, respond to the demands of social justice, and meet the urgent ecological demands of a warming planet.

Summary of Dependent and Independent Variables Used in Data Analysis

DATA SOURCES

Social Capital Community Benchmark Survey (2000), carried out by the Saguaro Seminar, Kennedy School of Government, Harvard University in conjunction with community partners. Restricted-use, geo-coded version provided courtesy of the Saguaro Seminar. Public data set and geo-codes available from the Roper Center for Public Opinion Research (www.ropercenter.uconn.edu).

2000 United States Census, Summary Files 1 and 3. Most indicators are from Summary File 3, except for the Herfindahl Index and proportion of African Americans and Hispanics in census tract, which are based on Summary File 1.

County Business Patterns Data (2005), U.S. Department of Commerce.

City and County Data Book 2000, U.S. Census Bureau.

Additional Data Sources Cited

Social Capital Community Survey (2006), carried out by the Saguaro Seminar, Kennedy School of Government, Harvard University in conjunction with community partners. Public data set available from the Roper Center for Public Opinion Research (www.ropercenter.uconn.edu).

2005 American Community Survey, conducted by the U.S. Census Bureau.

The Metro Poll (1999), Richmond, Virginia, carried out for the Virginia Center for Urban Development, Virginia Commonwealth University.

County sprawl index developed by Reid Ewing, National Center for the Study of Smart Growth, University of Maryland, provided courtesy of Reid Ewing.

Almanac of American Politics 2000 and 2002, published by National Journal Press; used for information on senators and Senate candidates in the 2000 election.

uselectionatlas.org, source for county voting data in the 2000 presidential election.

2000 Uniform Crime Report, U.S. Department of Justice.

DEPENDENT VARIABLES

Note: All binary outcomes (yes or no) coded as 1 = yes, 0 = no.

Utility-Related Variables

Description of "how happy you are" ("happiness"), (categorical variables on 0–3 scale, with 3 indicating greater happiness). Sample mean: 2.32.

Self-reported overall health ("health") (categorical variable on 0–4 scale, with 4 indicating greater health). Sample mean: 2.70.

Rating of "your community as a place to live" ("quality of life") (categorical variable on 0–3 scale, with 3 indicating higher quality of life). Sample mean: 2.24.

Social Capital–Related Variables

Total informal socializing: number of times in previous year respondents did any of the following: attended a club meeting, played cards with friends, attended an artistic event, attended a parade or community event, played a team sport, hung out with friends in a public place (count variable with range between 0 and 360). Sample mean: 54.0.

Total group memberships, excluding religious congregations, political organizations, and labor unions (count variable with range between 0 and 16). Sample mean: 2.95.

Trust-Related Variables

Overall "social trust": summary measure of overall trust based on responses to questions about general interpersonal trust, trust of neighbors, trust of coworkers, trust of fellow congregants, trust of employees in local stores, and trust of police (categorical variable on 1–3 scale, indicating low, medium, or high trust). Sample mean: 2.04.

How much one can "trust people in your neighborhood" ("trust neighbors") (categorical variable on 0–3 scale, with 3 indicating more trust). Sample mean: 2.26.

Tolerance-Related Variables

Whether one has an African American friend (yes or no): 64.2% yes

Whether one has an Asian friend (yes or no): 37.8% yes

Whether one has a Hispanic friend (yes or no): 48.7% yes

Whether one has a gay friend (yes or no): 42.1% yes

Believe immigrants are "too demanding in their push for equal rights" (categorical variable on 1–5 scale, from strongly disagree [1] to strongly agree [5]). Sample mean: 2.58.

Believe that "a book most people disapprove of should be kept out of the public library" (categorical variable on 1–5 scale, from strongly disagree [1] to strongly agree [5]). Sample mean: 2.06.

Politics-Related Variables

Voted in previous presidential election (1996), yes or no. 74.7% yes (eligible voters only).

Ability to name both senators from one's state ("political knowledge") (1–5 scale, with 5 indicating ability to name both senators correctly). Sample mean: 2.50; 25.4% correctly named both senators.

Number of public meetings attended in past year; self-reported count; converted into a binary measure of attendance or non-attendance at least one meeting. 44.0% yes.

Self-reported political ideology ("ideology") (categorical variable coded along a 1–5 scale, with 1 being "very conservative" and 5 "very liberal"). Sample mean: 2.84; 29.1% described themselves as "moderately" or "very" liberal. Respondents who volunteered "something else" were excluded from the analysis.

Days/week read a newspaper (0–7 scale). Sample mean: 3.53; 34.4% read 7 days a week.

Nonelectoral Political Participation

Signed a petition in previous year ("petition"), yes or no. 39.7% yes.

Participated in protest, demonstration, march, or boycott in previous year ("march"), yes or no. 8.0% yes.

Belonged to any group that took local action for reform in previous year ("reform"), yes or no. 20.8% yes.

Attended a political meeting or rally in previous year ("rally"), yes or no. 18.4% yes.

Participated in a political group ("political group"), yes or no. 9.9%.

Index of intensive nonelectoral political participation, based on participation in a protest, attendance at a political rally, membership in a political organization, and membership in an organization involved in local reform. (0–4 scale, with 0 indicating no participation and 3 indicating participation in each type of activity). Sample mean: 0.57; 35.4% participated in at least one such activity.

INDEPENDENT VARIABLES

Independent Variables Included in Core SCCBS Data

Respondent's citizenship status (yes, no, or missing): 94.5% yes.

Language survey conducted in (English or Spanish): 96.4% English.

Respondent's age (mean substituted for missing cases; missing age dummy included in regressions when significant). Sample mean age: 44.8.

Respondent's race (dummy variables for African American, Hispanic or Latino, Asian American, Native American, "other race," and missing race are employed; 0 on all six dummy variables=white). Sample: 71.6% (non-Hispanic) white, 12.3% (non-Hispanic) African American, 8.4% Hispanic or Latino, 2.4% Asian American, 2.3% other race, 1.2% Native American or Alaskan, 1.8% race missing.

Respondent's gender (0=male, 1=female): 59.0% female.

Respondent's household income (separated into the following categories, with dummy variables for each: under $30,000 (27.1%), over $75,000 (19.6%), $30,000–75,000 or over $30,000 unspecified (43.6%), income data missing (9.8%).

Years respondent has lived in community (imputed from a categorical measure of years lived in the community). Sample mean: 16.6 years.

Respondent's education level, separated into the following categories: high school diploma or less (33.1%); some college, technical training, or two-year degree (32.2%); bachelor degree or higher (33.8%); education level missing (0.9%).

Whether respondent is homeowner, yes or no. 69.2% yes.

Whether respondent is currently married, yes or no. 51.1% yes.

Number of children 17 or under living in household with respondent. Sample mean: 0.76.

Occupational status: employed (66.6%), unemployed or laid off (4.3%), disabled (3.4%), student (3.4%), retired (15.9%), homemaker (6.4%).

Daily commute time of respondent in minutes (coded as zero for non-workers): 24.0 (employed respondents only).

Residence within metropolitan area (central city, suburban, rural town, rural nontown residence): 39.9% central city, 46.2% suburban, 11.2% rural nontown, 2.7% rural town.

Independent Variables Derived from Summary File 3 of the 2000 U.S. Census and Matched to SCCBS Data

Population density within respondent's census tract (operationalized as natural log of raw density). Sample mean: 5,064 persons/square mile.

Median age of housing unit within respondent's census tract ("neighborhood age"). Sample mean: 1965.

Percentage within respondent's census tract driving alone to work ("solo driving"). Sample mean: 74.9%.

Size of respondent's city in 2000 (coded as 1 for cities under 100,000 population; 2 for cities with population between 100,000 and 199,999, etc.; operationalized in natural log form). Sample mean: 3.28.

Average commuting time in respondent's census tract. Sample mean: 23.4 minutes.

Median household income (1999) in respondent's census tract ("median neighborhood income"). Sample mean: $46,352.

Proportion of households in respondent's census tract earning greater than $75,000 ("proportion rich in tract"). Sample mean: 23.2%.

Proportion of households in respondent's census tract earning less than $25,000 ("proportion poor in tract"). Sample mean: 27.8%.

Herfindahl Index of Racial Dissimilarity; 0–1 scale, in which higher values indicate greater racial homogeneity ("neighborhood racial homogeneity"). Sample mean: .716. Derived from Census Summary File 1.

Proportion of single-race individuals in census tract who are African American: 13.5%. Derived from Census Summary File 1.

Proportion of single-race individuals in census tract who are Hispanic: 8.8%. Derived from Census Summary File 1.

Mean education level in census tract, measured as percentage of adults over 25 in tract with bachelor's degree or higher ("neighborhood education level"). Sample mean: .277.

Residential stability in census tract, measured as proportion of persons aged 5 or above in tract living in same housing unit as 5 years previously: ("neighborhood stability"). Sample mean: 53.0%.

Proportion of workers in census tract living and working in the same place (town or city), i.e. not commuting to a different community. Used to help distinguish rural town from rural nontown areas and test as an alternative to the dichotomous central-city status meaure. Sample mean: 53.0%.

Proportion of persons in census tract living in an urbanized area. Used to help distinguish rural town from rural nontown areas. Sample mean: 35.5%.

County partisan context measured as proportion of presidential vote in county in 2000 for Al Gore and for Ralph Nader, derived from uselectionsatlas.org. Operationalized as two separate variables. Sample mean: 49.5% for Gore and 3.0% for Nader.

Residence in South, Northeast, Midwest, West Census regions. 29.2% South, 30.3% Midwest, 25.6% West, 15.0% Northeast.

ADDITIONAL TECHNICAL NOTES

Construction of City-Size and Urban Variables

The urban and city-size variables employed in this study were constructed using information about residents' place of residence. Respondents were designated urban residents if they lived in one of more than four hundred cities designated by the U.S. Census as of 1999 as a center of a metropolitan statistical area (MSA) or primary metropolitan statistical area (PMSA), excluding those cities with population less than 25,000. Up to three cities per area were so designated. Respondents were designated as rural residents if they lived outside an MSA. Note that I do not employ the variable "METSTAT" included in the public release of the SCCBS for this purpose; METSTAT's designation of central city status for respondents does not consistently correspond to central city political boundaries.

City-size values were assigned based on whether a respondent lived in a place with a population less than 100,000 (assigned a value of 1), between 100,000 and 200,000 (assigned a value of 2), and so forth. While this measure does not capture differences between very small and moderately sized places, it does capture the fundamental difference between smaller and much larger urban communities.

Urban designation was assigned based on whether a respondent's census place and county codes indicated residence in a census-designated center city. Because the SCCBS contains incomplete data with respect to resident's' place codes, I imputed whether a not a resident lived in a central city, and the city size, for 7,740 cases in the sample, based on the respondents' census block group. Respondents for whom the geographic center ("internal point") of their block group lay within the boundaries of a central city (as determined by use of Google Earth) were coded as central city residents. This process designated some 39.9 percent of the sample as central city residents, compared to 51.4 percent so designated by METSTAT.

The certainty of some measurement error in the construction of the central city and city-size variables resulting from the fact that a significant portion of the census tract and block group codes in the SCCBS are imputed from zip codes should be acknowledged. (Any inaccuracies or discrepancies in the SCCBS's own place codes are another potential source of measurement error.) The use of the constructed urban variable as opposed to METSTAT does not alter the overall effect of sprawl on outcomes of interest, though (because the constructed central city variable is more "urban" than the MET-STAT central city variable), it does slightly alter the relative importance of central city residence relative to the tract-level sprawl variables in predicting outcomes such as political participation. Readers should be aware that these estimates of the relative importance of central city residence vis-à-vis other spatial variables necessarily carry a degree of imprecision.

For discussion of the effect of measurement error resulting from the SCCBS's imputation of census tract location, see chapter 1, note 67.

Missing Data

Roughly 98 percent of cases in the original SCCBS data (29,140 of 29,733) contained geo-codes at the census tract level. For 29,136 cases, I was able to append complete census tract demographic and spatial information (the remaining cases were located in tracts lacking complete demographic data).

Additionally, data was missing for one or more variables at the individual level in roughly 10 percent of the SCCBS cases. Some 2,847 cases in the final working sample with missing income data were coded as "missing income," with the missing-income dummy variable entered into the equations alongside the other income-level dummy variables. Similar procedures were performed for 531 cases with missing race data, 268 cases with missing education level, 255 cases with missing commuting time (among employed persons not telecommuting), and 176 cases with missing citizenship status. Handling missing data in this way allows us to make use of the information available in these cases; any distortion in the estimates of the contextual-level variables that results from this process should be slight. In the case of the age variable, a process of mean substitution for 592 cases in which age was missing was used; a dummy variable for "age missing" was tested for in each analysis and included as a control in a small number of instances in which it proved statistically significant.

Cases in which data about an individual's community tenure, home-ownership status, employment status, marital status, or number of children in the home were missing were deleted list-wise from the reported regressions.

Alternative specifications of these models in which *all* cases with missing data are deleted list-wise do not generate results significantly different from those reported here.

Comparison of Logit Results with Results Obtained by Alternative Models

As a check, in addition to the results reported here, based primarily on logit and ordered logit analyses with standard errors corrected for clustering at the community sample level, I also performed the core analyses using a number of other modeling techniques, including probit models, OLS, and models employing fixed-effect controls for each community sample.

Results generated from these alternative procedures do not differ appreciably with respect to the relationship between the sprawl-related measures and the dependent variables in question. In "no-pool" fixed-effect models that include a control for each community sample (while correcting standard errors for clustering at the county level) the cumulative effects of sprawl on reported outcomes remained statistically significant in each case, though (as we would expect) generally the reported impacts are weakened, since such models, in effect, rule out variance between communities.

The core results also hold up if we shift the scale of analysis to the zip code or county level. Results at the zip code level are generally as strong or stronger than those reported here; results at the county level are generally somewhat weaker than those obtained at the tract level but nonetheless remain statistically significant. The robustness of the findings at multiple geographic scales alleviates potential concern that the core reported findings are simply an artifact of how the census tracts themselves are defined.

APPENDIX 2 | Regression Tables

This appendix reports results for each regression analysis noted in the text that yielded positive findings. All contextual variables (except as noted) are measured at the census-tract level. All models report robust standard errors corrected for clustering at the community sample level, unless otherwise noted. Commuting times at both the individual and tract level are denominated in minutes. Throughout the tables, *** signifies $p < .001$; ** signifies $p < .01$; * signifies $p < .05$. Reported pseudo R-squares in the tables refer to McFadden's R-squared statistic for models analyzing categorical data.

TABLE A. Individual and Neighborhood Determinants of Individual Happiness

Based on a four-category measure of self-reported personal happiness, with higher values indicating greater happiness.

	Coefficient (SE)
U.S. Citizen	.301 (.074)***
Spanish-Speaking	−.309 (.103)**
Age	−.0024 (.0010)*
Homeowner	.165 (.039)***
Years Lived in Community	.0030 (.0009)***
Married	.534 (.029)***
Children in Home	−.038 (.014)**
Female	.205 (.031)***
African American	−.094 (.045)*
Asian American	−.488 (.089)***
Hispanic	−.170 (.063)**

	Coefficient (SE)
Native American	−.058 (.113)
Other Race	−.076 (.071)
Income <$30,000	−328 (.041)***
Income >$75,000	.249 (.032)***
High School or Less	−.158 (.027)***
Bachelor Degree or Higher	.153 (.033)***
Unemployed	−.432 (.074)***
Disabled	−.540 (.078)***
Student	.025 (.067)
Homemaker	.094 (.045)*
Retired	.118 (.050)*
% College Education in Tract	.523 (.112)***
Proportion Poor in Tract	−.141 (.128)
Proportion Rich in Tract	−.420 (.161)**
Racial Homogeneity in Tract	.288 (.065)***
Year Median Housing Unit Built	.0041 (.0009)***
Commuting Time (Employed)	−.0024 (.0005)***
Commuting Time in Tract	−.0043 (.0020)*
Rural Town Resident	.174 (.067)**
Rural Nontown Resident	.145 (.041)***
Midwest	−.066 (.034)*
West	.040 (.024)

n = 28,554. Pseudo R-square: .047. Ordered logistic regression. Additional controls not reported: Dummy variables for missing citizenship, education, commuting time, race, and income status. Omitted dummy variables (reference categories) for race, income, employment status, education, and region are white, $30,000–75,000 income bracket, employed, some college or associate's degree, and Northeast or South, respectively.

TABLE B.   Spatial Determinants of Individual Health

Based on a five-category measure of self-reported personal health, with higher values indicating better health.

	Coefficient (SE)
U.S. Citizen	.153 (.058)**
Spanish-Speaking	−.354 (.061)***
Age	−.018 (.0011)***
Homeowner	.255 (.026)***
Years Lived in Community	−.0006 (.0009)
Married	.196 (.029)***
Children in Home	−.004 (.012)

(continued)

	Coefficient (SE)
Female	.019 (.024)
African American	−.152 (.034)***
Asian American	−.441 (.068)***
Hispanic	−.100 (.037)**
Native American	−.197 (.125)
Other Race	−.243 (.069)***
Income <$30,000	−.351 (.034)***
Income >$75,000	.265 (.035)***
High School or Less	−.184 (.029)***
Bachelor Degree or Higher	.406 (.029)***
Unemployed	−.560 (.056)***
Disabled	−2.41 (.087)***
Student	.010 (.077)
Homemaker	−.190 (.054)***
Retired	−.383 (.048)**
One Adult Household	.145 (.036)***
Three-Adult Household	−.132 (.037)***
Four or More Adults in Household	−.165 (.047)***
% College Education in Tract	.736 (.081)***
Median Income in Tract (Thousands)	−.0007 (.0009)
Population Density (ln) in Tract	−.023 (.006)***
Commuting Time (Employed)	−.0023 (.0005)***
South	−.091 (.026)***

n = 28,634. Pseudo R-square: .064. Ordered logistic regression. Additional controls not reported: Dummy variables for missing citizenship, education, race, commuting time, income, and household size status. Omitted dummy variables (reference categories) for race, income, employment status, education, household size, and region are white, $30,000–75,000 income bracket, employed, some college or associate's degree, two-adult household, and Northeast, Midwest or West, respectively.

TABLE C. Spatial and Individual Determinants of Community Quality of Life

Based on a four-category measure of subjective evaluations of community quality of life, with higher values indicating greater satisfaction.

	Coefficient (SE)
U.S. Citizen	.136 (.062)*
Spanish-Speaking	−.182 (.071)**
Age	.013 (.001)***

Homeowner	.442 (.038)***
Years Lived in Community	.0024 (.0009)**
Married	.189 (.030)***
Children in Home	−.021 (.014)
Female	.106 (.030)***
African American	−.236 (.064)***
Asian American	−.082 (.091)
Hispanic	−.013 (.052)
Native American	−.307 (.095)***
Other Race	−.199 (.087)**
Income <$30,000	−.244 (.031)***
Income >$75,000	.183 (.043)***
High School or Less	−.146 (.032)***
Bachelor Degree or Higher	.154 (039)***
Unemployed	−.252 (.049)***
Disabled	−.106 (.082)
Student	−.096 (.085)
Homemaker	−.036 (.050)
Retired	−.041 (.038)
% College Education in Tract	1.95 (.195)***
Proportion Poor in Tract	−.898 (.186)***
Proportion Rich in Tract	−.865 (.199)***
Residential Stability in Tract	.658 (.207)***
Racial Homogeneity in Tract	.419 (.114)***
% African American in Tract	−.602 (.114)***
% Hispanic in Tract	−.562 (.187)**
Central City Residency	−.146 (.044)***
Population Density (ln)	−.037 (.012)**
Year Median Housing Unit Built	.0065 (.0018)***
Rural Town Resident	.267 (.143)

$n = 28,618$. *Pseudo R-square: .087. Ordered logistic regression. Additional controls not reported: Dummy variables for missing citizenship, education, race, income status. Omitted dummy variables (reference categories) for race, income, employment status, education, and spatial location are white, $30,000–75,000 income bracket, employed, some college or associate's degree, and suburban or rural non-town residence, respectively. Regional controls omitted from this model.*

TABLE D. Individual and Spatial Determinants of Informal Socializing

Based on total number of times one attended a club meeting, played cards with friends, attended an artistic event, attended a parade or community event, played a team sport, or hung out with friends in a public place in past year.

	Coefficient (SE)
U.S. Citizen	11.30 (2.09)***
Spanish-Speaking	−8.49 (1.60)***
Age	−.943 (.030)***
Homeowner	−2.31 (.704)**
Years Lived in Community	.169 (.020)***
Married	−11.02 (.819)***
Female	−.658 (.718)
African American	−5.72 (1.19)***
Asian American	−16.12 (1.24)***
Hispanic	−5.51 (1.43)***
Native American	2.11 (3.82)
Other Race	−.244 (1.565)
Income <$30,000	−6.291 (.810)***
Income >$75,000	6.023 (.859)***
High School or Less	−8.89 (.818)***
Bachelor Degree or Higher	1.420 (1.047)
Unemployed	−3.675 (1.608)*
Disabled	−8.544 (1.32)***
Student	11.42 (2.43)***
Homemaker	1.32 (1.17)
Retired	10.55 (.960)***
One-Adult Household	−2.56 (.900)**
Three-Adult Household	3.40 (1.07)**
Four or More Adults in Household	5.71 (1.47)***
Commuting Time (Employed)	−.064 (.010)***
Commuting Time in Tract	−.223 (.072)**
% College Education in Tract	11.54 (3.55)**
Median Income in Tract (Thousands)	−.111 (.034)**
Racial Homogeneity in Tract	5.17 (2.17)*
Central City Resident	−1.44 (.786)
Rural Town Resident	1.56 (.953)

Midwest	3.70 (.879)***
West	3.14 (1.18)*

n = 28,536. R-square: .119. OLS regression. Additional controls not reported: Dummy variables for missing citizenship, education, commuting time, race, income, household size, and age status. Omitted dummy variables (reference categories) for race, income, employment status, education, household size, spatial location, and region are white, $30,000–75,000 income bracket, employed, some college or associate's degree, two-adult household, suburban or rural (nontown) residence, and Northeast or South, respectively. Note: control for children in household, which is not a significant predictor of socializing net of other factors, dropped from reported model to conserve parameters.

TABLE E.   Individual and Spatial Determinants of Group Involvement

Based on total number of groups one formally belongs to (excluding religious congregations, labor organization, and political organization), sorted into seven categories: member of no groups, one group, two groups, three groups, four groups, five groups, and six or more groups.

	Coefficient (SE)
U.S. Citizen	.508 (.067)***
Spanish-Speaking	−.321 (.059)***
Age	.012 (.0013)***
Homeowner	.242 (.035)***
Years Lived in Community	.0043 (.0008)***
Married	−.001 (.025)
Children in Home	.154 (.012)***
Female	−.018 (.022)
African American	.299 (.049)***
Asian American	−.298 (.081)***
Hispanic	−.029 (.047)
Native American	.418 (.093)***
Other Race	.253 (.079)***
Income <$30,000	−.359 (.024)***
Income >$75,000	.299 (.034)***
High School or Less	−.735 (.034)***
Bachelor Degree or Higher	.555 (.024)***
Unemployed	−.281 (.045)***
Disabled	−.124 (.066)
Student	.275 (.067)***

(continued)

	Coefficient (SE)
Homemaker	−.189 (.041)***
Retired	−.110 (.050)*
Commuting Time (Employed)	−.0016 (.0004)***
% College Education in Tract	.713 (.096)***
Median Income in Tract (Thousands)	−.0021 (.0013)
% African Americans in Tract	.357 (.065)***
Population Density (ln) in Tract	−.030 (.007)***
Rural Town Resident	.204 (.079)**
Northeast	−.104 (.030)***

n = 28,617. Pseudo R-square: .048. Ordered logistic regression Additional controls not reported: Dummy variable for missing citizenship, commuting time, race, and income status. Omitted dummy variables (reference categories) for race, income, employment status, education, and region are white, $30,000–75,000 bracket, employed, some college or associate's degree or education missing, and South, Midwest, and West, respectively.

TABLE F.   Individual and Spatial Determinants of Overall Social Trust

Overall index of social trust; respondents are coded as having "high," "medium," or "low" overall trust based on their responses to all trust-related questions.

	Coefficient (SE)
Spanish-Speaking	−.679 (.118)***
Age	.023 (.0012)***
Homeowner	.208 (.032)***
Years Lived in Community	.0022 (.0009)*
Married	.237 (.029)***
Children in Home	−.027 (.013)*
Female	.128 (.025)***
African American	−1.23 (.044)***
Asian American	−.575 (.102)***
Hispanic	−.840 (.065)***
Native American	−.634 (.116)***
Other Race	−.655 (.085)***
Income <$30,000	−.165 (.029)***
Income >$75,000	.082 (.033)*
High School or Less	−.314 (.030)***
Bachelor Degree or Higher	.451 (.030)***

Unemployed	−.477 (.064)***
Disabled	−.477 (.072)***
Student	−.000 (.070)
Homemaker	−.048 (.056)
Retired	−.201 (.054)***
% College Education in Tract	.996 (.134)***
Proportion Poor in Tract	−.559 (.202)**
Proportion Rich in Tract	−.584 (.253)*
Racial Homogeneity in Tract	.231 (.087)**
% African American in Tract	−.196 (.082)*
Central City Residency	−.085 (.033)**
Population Density (ln)	−.068 (.018)***
Commuting Time in Tract	−.015 (.004)***
Individual Commuting Time (Employed)	−.0021 (.0005)***
Rural Nontown Resident	.140 (.078)
Rural Town Resident	.160 (.097)
South	−.250 (.049)***
Northeast	−.076 (.053)

$n = 28,565$. *Pseudo R-square: .118. Ordered logistic regression. Additional controls not reported: Dummy variables for missing education, race, commuting time, and income status. Omitted dummy variables (reference categories) for race, income, employment status, education, spatial location, and region are white, $30,000–75,000 income bracket, employed, some college or associate's degree, suburb, and Midwest or West, respectively.*

TABLE G. Spatial and Individual Determinants of Trust of Neighbors

Four-tiered measure of trust of neighbors, coded from 1 ("not at all") to 4 ("a lot").

	Coefficient (SE)
Spanish-Speaking	−.418 (.069)***
Age	.023 (.0012)***
Homeowner	.592 (.030)***
Years Lived in Community	.0053 (.0010)***
Married	.229 (.030)***
Children in Home	−.028 (.011)*
Female	.148 (.023)***

(continued)

	Coefficient (SE)
African American	-.779 (.049)***
Asian American	-.467 (.089)***
Hispanic	-.673 (.049)***
Native American	-.619 (.121)***
Other Race	-.536 (.074)***
Income <$30,000	-.272 (.034)***
Income >$75,000	.165 (.040)***
High School or Less	-.294 (.034)***
Bachelor Degree or Higher	.312 (034)***
Unemployed	-.178 (.048)***
Disabled	-.306 (.075)***
Student	.167 (.056)**
Homemaker	.040 (.062)
Retired	-.080 (.047)
% College Education in Tract	1.365 (.154)***
Proportion Poor in Tract	-.497 (.186)**
Proportion Rich in Tract	-.568 (.246)*
Residential Stability in Tract	.614 (.163)***
Racial Homogeneity in Tract	.368 (.081)***
% African American in Tract	-.223 (.094)*
Central City Residency	-.143 (.027)***
Population Density (ln)	-.085 (.014)***
Proportion in Tract Driving Alone	.404 (.169)*
Commuting Time in Tract	-.010 (.004)**
Rural Resident (all)	.121 (.065)
South	-.071 (.046)
West	.077 (.055)

n = 27,930. *Pseudo R-square: .129. Ordered logistic regression. Additional controls not reported: Dummy variables for missing education, race, and income status. Omitted dummy variables (reference categories) for race, income, employment status, education, spatial location, and region are white, $30,000–75,000 income bracket, employed, some college or associate's degree, suburb, and Midwest or Northeast, respectively.*

Respondents' agreement with idea that controversial books should be censored, based on five-category measure from 1 (strong disagreement) to 5 (strong agreement).

	Coefficient (SE)
U.S. Citizen	−.537 (.074)***
Spanish-Speaking	.279 (.079)***
Age	.019 (.001)***
Homeowner	.018 (.036)
Years Lived in Community	.0037 (.0009)***
Married	.244 (.027)***
Children in Home	.084 (.010)***
Female	−.004 (.022)
African American	.413 (.043)***
Asian American	1.066 (.087)***
Hispanic	.477 (.056)***
Native American	.168 (.146)
Other Race	.066 (.093)
Income <$30,000	.291 (.030)***
Income >$75,000	−.296 (.033)***
High School or Less	.463 (.024)***
Bachelor Degree or Higher	−.372 (.037)***
Unemployed	.159 (.051)**
Disabled	.217 (.072)**
Student	.081 (.078)
Homemaker	.294 (.050)***
Retired	.157 (.041)***
Commuting Time (Employed)	.0015 (.0006)*
% College Education in Tract	−.892 (.152)***
Median Income in Tract (thousands)	.0018 (.0012)
% Residential Stability in Tract	.446 (.124)***
Year Median Housing Unit Built in Tract	.0057 (.0011)***
South	.307 (.071)***
Midwest	.211 (.040)***

n = 28,063. Pseudo R-square: .063. Ordered logistic regression. Additional controls not reported: Dummy variables for missing citizenship, education, commuting time, race, income, and age status. Omitted dummy variables (reference categories) for race, income, employment status, education, and region are white, $30,000–75,000 income bracket, employed, some college or associate's degree, and West or Northeast, respectively.

TABLE I. Individual and Spatial Determinants of Opposition to Immigrant Rights

Respondents' agreement with the statement that immigrants are "getting too demanding in their push for equal rights" based on five-category measure from 1 (strong disagreement) to 5 (strong agreement). As in table H.

	Coefficient (SE)
U.S. Citizen	−.195(.102)
Spanish-Speaking	.158 (.179)
Age	.0087 (.0011)***
Homeowner	.026 (.040)
Years Lived in Community	.0065 (.0011)***
Married	−.002 (.027)
Children in Home	.004 (.013)
Female	−.229 (.025)***
African American	−.267 (.074)***
Asian American	.395 (.108)***
Hispanic	.072 (.127)
Native American	.244 (.204)
Other Race	−.222 (.1??)
Income <$30,000	.176 (.029)***
Income >$75,000	−.088 (.024)***
High School or Less	.414 (.035)***
Bachelor Degree or Higher	−.637 (.033)***
Unemployed	.097 (.068)
Disabled	.163 (.092)
Student	−.223 (.093)*
Homemaker	.070 (.041)
Retired	.096 (.044)*
% College Education in Tract	−1.258 (.144)***
Median Income in Tract (thousands)	.0016 (.0012)
% Hispanic in Tract	.488 (.181)**
Year Median Housing Unit Built in Tract	.0054 (.0012)***
% Driving Alone in Tract	.980 (.225)***
South	.269 (.065)***
Midwest	.118 (.056)*
West	.089 (.072)

n = 21,536. Pseudo R-square: .053. Analysis limited to whites and/or college graduates only. Ordered logistic regression. Additional controls not reported: Dummy variables for missing citizenship, education, race, and income status. Omitted dummy variables (reference categories) for race, income, employment status, education, and region are white, $30,000–75,000 income bracket, employed, some college or associate's degree, and Northeast, respectively.

Spatial Determinants of Political Ideology

Respondents' likelihood of saying they are "moderately" or "very" liberal.

	Coefficient (SE)
Spanish-Speaking	−.344 (.090)***
Age	−.001 (.0010)
Homeowner	−.103 (.032)***
Years Lived in Community	−.0033 (.0010)***
Married	−.237 (.029)***
Children in Home	−.067 (.016)***
Female	.375 (.030)***
African American	.239 (.062)***
Asian American	−.363 (.103)***
Hispanic	.284 (.069)***
Native American	−.018 (.155)
Other Race	.161 (.099)
Income <$30,000	−.053 (.045)
Income >$75,000	.095 (.028)***
High School or Less	−.214 (.043)***
Bachelor Degree or Higher	.410 (.037)***
Disabled	.256 (.082)**
Student	.148 (.077)
Homemaker	−.230 (.061)***
Retired	−.141 (.046)**
Unemployed	.097 (.060)
Member of Religious Congregation	−.339 (.033)***
Catholic	−.628 (.052)***
Protestant or Other Christian Denom.	−.760 (.045)***
Jewish or Other Religion	.287 (.064)**
Labor Union Member	.353 (.044)***
% College Education in Tract	1.058 (.156)***
Median Income in Tract (thousands)	−.0020 (.0014)
% African American in Tract	.432 (.070)***
Year Median Housing Unit Built	−.0081 (.0015)***
Proportion Driving Alone to Work	−1.004 (.160)***
West	.172 (.048)***

n = 27,883. Pseudo R-square: .100. Logistic regression. Additional controls not reported: Dummy variables for missing education, race, income, and religious congregation-member status. Omitted dummy variables (reference categories) for race, income, employment status, education, religion, and region are white, $30,000–75,000 income bracket, employed, some college or associate's degree, atheist or religion missing, and South, Midwest or Northeast, respectively.

TABLE K. Individual and Spatial Determinants of Newspaper Reading

Likelihood of reporting reading the newspaper, sorted into three groups: nonreaders, those who read 1–6 days a week, and daily readers.

	Coefficient (SE)
U.S. Citizen	.354 (.084)***
Spanish-Speaking	−.806 (.115)***
Age	.026 (.0016)***
Homeowner	.141 (.036)***
Years Lived in Community	.012 (.0009)***
Married	.077 (.031)*
Children in Home	−.012 (.012)
Female	−.219 (.023)***
African American	.080 (.042)*
Asian American	.219 (.097)*
Hispanic	−.132 (.058)*
Native American	.092 (.101)
Other Race	.049 (.066)
Income <$30,000	−.246 (.025)***
Income >$75,000	.188 (.031)***
High School or Less	−.185 (.031)***
Bachelor Degree or Higher	.224 (.026)***
Unemployed	−.133 (.063)*
Disabled	−.440 (.077)***
Student	.018 (.056)
Homemaker	−.158 (.048)***
Retired	.430 (.049)***
Commuting Time in Tract	−.017 (.004)***
Commuting Time (employed)	−.0015 (.0006)**
Live in One-Adult Household	−.271 (.033)***
% College Education in Tract	.471 (.142)***
Median Income in Tract (thousands)	−.0005 (.0016)
Central City Residency	.105 (.034)**
Rural Nontown Resident	−.132 (.053)*
Northeast	.198 (.043)***

n = 28,640. Pseudo R-square: .080. Ordered logistic regression. Additional controls not reported: Dummy variables for missing citizenship, education, race, commuting time, and income status. Omitted dummy variables (reference categories) for race, income, employment status, education, spatial location, household size, and region are white, $30,000–75,000 income bracket, employed, some college or associate's degree, suburb or rural town resident, two or more adults in household or household size missing, and Midwest, West, or South, respectively.

TABLE L. Individual and Spatial Determinants of Interest in Politics

Based on 1–4 scale of interest in politics, from not interested (1) to very interested (4)

	Coefficient (SE)
U.S. Citizen	.580 (.110)***
Spanish-Speaking	−.059 (.128)
Age	.028 (.0014)***
Homeowner	.064 (.042)
Years Lived in Community	.0012 (.0009)
Married	.132 (.028)***
Children in Home	−.016 (.015)
Female	−.275 (.028)***
African American	.191 (.083)*
Asian American	−.533 (.147)***
Hispanic	−.088(.089)
Native American	.598 (.193)**
Other Race	.335 (.142)*
Income <$30,000	−.281 (.041)***
Income >$75,000	.166 (.033)***
High School or Less	−.679 (.032)***
Bachelor Degree or Higher	.370 (.034)***
Unemployed	−.064 (.075)
Disabled	−.004 (.102)
Student	.402 (.083)***
Homemaker	.021 (.057)
Retired	.129 (.049)**
% College Education in Tract	.992 (.104)***
% Poor in Tract	−.392 (.218)
% Rich in Tract	−.564 (.184)***
% African American in Tract	.271 (.113)*
% Hispanic in Tract	.428 (.149)**
Proportion in Tract Driving Alone	−.523 (.157)***
Year Median House in Tract Built	−.0020 (.0011)
South	.081 (.047)
West	.083 (.052)

n = 22,628. Pseudo R-square: .059. Whites and/or college graduates only. Ordered logistic regression. Additional controls not reported: Dummy variables for missing citizenship, education, race, age, and income status. Omitted dummy variables (reference categories) for race, income, employment status, education, and region are white, $30,000–75,000 bracket, employed, some college or associate's degree, and Midwest or Northeast, respectively.

TABLE M.   Individual and Spatial Determinants of Political Knowledge

Based on ability to name the U.S. senators from one's state, grouped into three categories: know neither, know one, or know both; persons getting one or two name "close" counted as knowing one.

	Coefficient (SE)
U.S. Citizen	.902 (.118)***
Spanish-Speaking	.157 (.081)
Age	.0228 (.0014)***
Homeowner	.374 (.041)***
Years Lived in Community	.0077 (.0013)***
Married	.197 (.034)***
Children in Home	−.020 (.016)
Female	−.525 (.025)***
African American	−.692 (.065)***
Asian American	−.176 (.092)
Hispanic	−.645 (.072)***
Native American	−.543 (.104)***
Other Race	−.063 (.092)
Income <$30,000	−.272 (.043)***
Income >$75,000	.098 (.041)*
High School or Less	−.567 (.042)***
Bachelor Degree or Higher	.573 (.035)***
Unemployed	−.091 (.075)
Disabled	−.124 (.082)
Student	−.021 (.073)
Homemaker	−.060 (.054)
Retired	−.149 (.050)**
% College Education in Tract	.949 (.262)***
% Poor in Tract	−.577 (.307)
% Rich in Tract	−.604 (.342)
Residential Stability in Tract	1.142 (.361)**
Commuting Time in Tract	−.030 (.011)**
Central City Residency	.189(.072)**
Proportion in Tract Driving Alone	−1.555 (.422)***

	Coefficient (SE)
Incumbent Running for Senate in State	.437 (.155)**
Open Seat Senate Race in State	−.514 (.138)***
Years Senators in State Have Served	.020 (.005)***
West Census Region	.355 (.157)*

n = 28,532. Pseudo R-square: .125. Ordered logistic regression. Additional controls not reported: Dummy variables for missing citizenship, and income status. Omitted dummy variables (reference categories) for race, income, employment status, education, and region are white or race missing, $30,000–75,000 income bracket, employed, some college or associate's degree or education missing, and Midwest, South, or Northeast, respectively. Incumbent, open seat, and senatorial service variables based on 2000 elections. Washington, D.C., residents excluded.

TABLE N. Individual and Spatial Determinants of Petition Signing

Respondents' likelihood of saying they signed a petition in the previous 12 months.

	Coefficient (SE)
U.S. Citizen	1.143 (.092)***
Spanish-Speaking	−.496 (.123)***
Age	−.000 (.001)
Homeowner	.192 (.032)***
Years Lived in Community	.0020 (.0009)*
Married	.064 (.028)*
Children in Home	.041 (.013)**
Female	.122 (.028)***
African American	−.239 (.063)***
Asian American	−.811 (.106)***
Hispanic	−.400 (.059)***
Native American	−.097 (.134)
Other Race	.171 (.089)
Income <$30,000	−.265 (.032)***
Income >$75,000	.054 (.031)
High School or Less	−.574 (.037)***
Bachelor Degree or Higher	.237 (.034)***
Unemployed	−.144 (.071)*
Disabled	−.209 (.088)*
Student	.089 (.082)
Homemaker	−.113 (.055)*
Retired	−.386 (.049)***

(*continued*)

	Coefficient (SE)
% College Education in Tract	.556 (.143)***
Median Income in Tract (thousands)	−.0022 (.0016)
Racial Homogeneity in Tract	.256 (.129)*
Proportion in Tract Driving Alone	−.504 (.192)**
Year Median House in Tract Built	−.0039 (.0012)**
Central City Resident	.104 (.038)**
South	−.401 (.096)***
Midwest	−.166 (.084)*
West	.373 (.096)***

n = 28,517. *Pseudo R-square: .079. Logistic regression. Additional controls not reported: Dummy variables for missing citizenship, education, race, and income status. Omitted dummy variables (reference categories) for race, income, employment status, education, and region are white, $30,000–75,000 bracket, employed, some college or associate's degree, and Northeast, respectively.*

TABLE O.   Individual and Spatial Determinants of Attendance at a Public Meeting

Likelihood of having attended at least one public meeting in the previous 12 months.

	Coefficient (SE)
U.S. Citizen	.358 (.087)***
Spanish-Speaking	−.261 (.120)*
Age	−.0035 (.0013)**
Homeowner	.341 (.030)***
Years Lived in Community	.0057 (.0010)***
Married	.198 (.033)***
Children in Home	.364 (.018)***
Female	.091 (.025)***
African American	.372 (.046)***
Asian American	−.377 (.065)***
Hispanic	.053 (.114)
Native American	.155 (.115)
Other Race	.154 (.106)
Income <$30,000	−.249 (.035)***
Income >$75,000	.206 (.047)***
High School or Less	−.580 (.034)***
Bachelor Degree or Higher	.380 (.035)***
Unemployed	−.294 (.078)***
Disabled	−.301 (.082)***

	Coefficient (SE)
Student	.149 (.086)
Homemaker	−.196 (.049)***
Retired	−.405 (.060)***
Commuting Time (employed)	−.0014 (.0007)*
% College Education in Tract	.447 (.118)***
Median Income in Tract (thousands)	−.0012 (.0012)
Population Density in Tract (ln)	−.077 (.012)***
Proportion in Tract Driving Alone	−.723 (.119)***
Year Median House in Tract Built	−.0043 (.0011)***
City Size (ln)	−.066 (.018)***

n = 28,643. Pseudo R-square: .089. Logistic regression. Additional controls not reported: Dummy variables for missing education, race, commuting time, citizenship status, and income status. Omitted dummy variables (reference categories) for race, income, employment status, education, and region are white, $30,000–75,000 bracket, employed, and some college or associate's degree, respectively.

TABLE P. Individual and Spatial Determinants of Local Reform-Group Membership

Respondents' likelihood of saying they belonged to an organization involved in local reform in the previous 12 months.

	Coefficient (SE)
U.S. Citizen	.788 (.119)***
Spanish-Speaking	−.265 (.163)
Age	.0051 (.0017)**
Homeowner	.117 (.039)**
Years Lived in Community	.0024 (.0012)*
Married	−.022 (.035)
Children in Home	.029 (.012)*
Female	−.060 (.030)*
African American	.068 (.059)
Asian American	−.478 (.114)***
Hispanic	−.070 (.085)
Native American	.030 (.179)
Other Race	.274 (.117)*
Income <$30,000	−.276 (.048)***
Income >$75,000	.149 (.043)***
High School or Less	−.718 (.053)***
Bachelor Degree or Higher	.637 (.039)***

(continued)

	Coefficient (SE)
Unemployed	−.282 (.100)**
Disabled	.048 (.105)
Student	.294 (.078)***
Homemaker	−.170 (.077)*
Retired	−.344 (.060)***
% College Education in Tract	.833 (.126)***
Median Income in Tract (thousands)	−.0016 (.0012)
Racial Homogeneity in Tract	−.252 (.100)*
Population Density in Tract (ln)	−.021 (.012)
Proportion in Tract Driving Alone	−.624 (.180)***
Year Median House in Tract Built	−.0061 (.0013)***
Central City Resident	.200 (.065)**
City Size (ln)	−.045 (.032)
West	.180 (.046)***

n = 28,228. Pseudo R-square: .087. Logistic regression. Additional controls not reported: Dummy variables for missing citizenship, education, race, and income status. Omitted dummy variables (reference categories) for race, income, employment status, education, and region, are white, $30,000–75,000 bracket, employed, some college or associate's degree, and Midwest, South, or Northeast, respectively.

TABLE Q. Individual and Spatial Determinants of Political-Rally Participation

Respondents' likelihood of saying they attended a political meeting or rally in previous 12 months.

	Coefficient (SE)
U.S. Citizen	.795 (.126)***
Spanish-Speaking	−.159 (.129)
Age	.0049 (.0016)**
Homeowner	.210 (.045)***
Years Lived in Community	.0044 (.0014)**
Married	−.014 (.036)
Children in Home	.024 (.017)
Female	−.214 (.031)***
African American	.259 (.072)***
Asian American	−.212 (.098)***
Hispanic	.246 (.072)***
Native American	.488 (.142)***
Other Race	.331 (.121)**
Income <$30,000	−.289 (.038)***

	Coefficient (SE)
Income >$75,000	.230 (.055)***
High School or Less	-.682 (.047)***
Bachelor Degree or Higher	.350 (.043)***
Unemployed	-.073 (.086)
Disabled	.022 (.089)
Student	.387 (.083)***
Homemaker	-.274 (.080)***
Retired	-.121 (.061)*
% College Education in Tract	.709 (.136)***
Median Income in Tract (thousands)	-.0021 (.0015)
% African American in Tract	.309 (.100)**
Population Density in Tract (ln)	-.052 (.015)***
Proportion in Tract Driving Alone	-1.162 (.187)***
Year Median House in Tract Built	-.0068 (.0014)***
Central City Resident	.156 (.066)*
City Size (ln)	-.093 (.028)***
Rural Town Resident	.176 (.091)
Midwest	-.077 (.056)

n = 28,663. *Pseudo R-square: .061. Logistic regression. Additional controls not reported: Dummy variables for missing citizenship, education, age, race, and income status. Omitted dummy variables (reference categories) for race, income, employment status, education, and region are white, $30,000– 75,000 bracket, employed, some college or associate's degree, and West, South, or Northeast, respectively.*

TABLE R. Individual and Spatial Determinants of Political Group Participation

Respondents' likelihood of saying they belonged to a political organization in the previous 12 months.

	Coefficient (SE)
U.S. Citizen	.558 (.128)***
Spanish-Speaking	-.414 (.151)**
Age	.011 (.002)***
Homeowner	.203 (.062)***
Years Lived in Community	.0057 (.0018)**
Married	.134 (.052)**
Children in Home	-.022 (.025)
Female	-.301 (.044)***
African American	.056 (.093)
Asian American	-.390 (.143)**
Hispanic	.204 (.084)*
Native American	.355 (.204)
Other Race	.201 (.141)

(continued)

	Coefficient (SE)
Income <$30,000	−.351 (.070)***
Income >$75,000	.235 (.054)***
High School or Less	−.765 (.064)***
Bachelor Degree or Higher	.529 (.052)***
Unemployed	−.280 (.130)*
Disabled	.110 (.103)
Student	.305 (.117)**
Homemaker	−.346 (.117)**
Retired	−.276 (.082)***
% College Education in Tract	.601 (.134)***
Median Income in Tract (thousands)	−.0021 (.0014)
Population Density in Tract (ln)	−.040 (.014)**
Proportion in Tract Driving Alone	−1.012 (.223)***
Year Median House in Tract Built	−.0065 (.0014)***
Central City Resident	.224 (.059)***
City Size (ln)	−.094 (.034)**
South	.085 (.069)
Midwest	.115 (.061)
West	.243 (.067)***

n = 28,648. *Pseudo R-square: .074. Logistic regression. Additional controls not reported: Dummy variables for missing citizenship, education, race, age, and income status. Omitted dummy variables (reference categories) for race, income, employment status, education, spatial location, and region are white, $30,000–75,000 bracket, employed, some college or associate's degree, suburb or rural area, and Northeast, respectively.*

TABLE S.   Individual and Spatial Determinants of Protest Activity

Respondents' likelihood of saying participated in a march, protest, or boycott in the previous 12 months.

	Coefficient (SE)
U.S. Citizen	.528 (.119)***
Spanish-Speaking	−.050 (.152)
Age	−.017 (.002)***
Homeowner	.115 (.053)*
Years Lived in Community	.0020 (.0016)
Married	−.129 (.052)*
Children in Home	.046 (.017)**
Female	−.035 (.060)
African American	.185 (.082)*
Asian American	−.363 (.185)*

Hispanic	.140 (.097)
Native American	.292 (.176)
Other Race	.659 (.128)***
Income <$30,000	−.088 (.070)
Income >$75,000	.019 (.064)
High School or Less	−.462 (.063)***
Bachelor Degree or Higher	.301 (.064)***
Unemployed	.043 (.110)
Disabled	−.103 (.131)
Student	.312 (.107)**
Homemaker	−.312 (.117)**
Retired	−.659 (.155)***
% College Education in Tract	.654 (.186)***
Median Income in Tract (thousands)	−.0003 (.0020)
Proportion in Tract Driving Alone	−1.433 (.298)***
Year Median House in Tract Built	−.0090 (.0020)***
Central City Resident	.274 (.068)***
City Size (ln)	−.089 (.033)**
Midwest	.108 (.072)
West	.349 (.092)***

n = 28,656. Pseudo R-square: .074. Logistic regression. Additional controls not reported: Dummy variables for missing citizenship, education, race, age, and income status. Omitted dummy variables (reference categories) for race, income, employment status, education, spatial location, and region are white, $30,000–75,000 bracket, employed, some college or associate's degree, suburb or rural area, and South or Northeast, respectively.

TABLE T.   Individual and Spatial Determinants of Overall Activism: Basic Model

Likelihood of participating in the following activities: membership in a local reform organization, membership in a political organization, attendance at a rally, and participation in a protest. Based on a simple index tallying participation in each type of activity, scaled from 0–4.

	Excluding Sample Fixed Effects Coefficient (SE)	Including Sample Fixed Effects Coefficient (SE)
U.S. Citizen	.733 (.088)***	.715 (.090)***
Spanish-Speaking	−.233 (.108)*	−.248 (.118)*
Age	.0033 (.0014)*	.0035 (.0014)*

(continued)

	Excluding Sample Fixed Effects Coefficient (SE)	Including Sample Fixed Effects Coefficient (SE)
Homeowner	.175 (.036)***	.167 (.034)***
Years Lived in Community	.0037 (.0009)***	.0038 (.0010)***
Married	−.052 (.033)	−.051 (.031)
Children in Home	.030 (.011)**	.031 (.013)*
Female	−.168 (.023)***	−.167 (.026)***
African American	.102 (.059)	.108 (.059)
Asian American	−.381 (.115)***	−.341 (.108)**
Hispanic	.098 (.067)	.145 (.068)*
Native American	.272 (.144)	.283 (.132)*
Other Race	.342 (.115)**	.342 (.099)***
Income <$30,000	−.299 (.039)***	−.292 (.041)***
Income >$75,000	.210 (.040)***	.222 (.037)***
High School or Less	−.684 (.040)***	−.686 (.041)***
Bachelor Degree or Higher	.519 (.036)***	.519 (.032)***
Unemployed	−.127 (.067)	−.127 (.065)*
Disabled	.029 (.074)	.010 (.072)
Student	.413 (.077)***	.421 (.076)***
Homemaker	−.219 (.063)***	−.218 (.061)***
Retired	−.239 (.051)***	−.241 (.051)***
% College Education in Tract	.818 (.107)***	.748 (.133)***
Median Income in Tract (thousands)	−.0020 (.0012)	−.0011 (.0012)
% African American in Tract	.249 (.100)*	.308 (.084)***
Population Density in Tract (ln)	−.029 (.013)*	−.019 (.011)
Proportion in Tract Driving Alone	−1.022 (.168)***	−.735 (.152)***
Year Median House in Tract Built	−.0068 (.0011)***	−.0056 (.0012)***
Central City Resident	.186 (.053)***	.092 (.046)*
City Size (ln)	−.078 (.025)***	−.036 (.024)
Rural Town Resident	.075 (.054)	.039 (.077)
West	.155 (.060)**	.164 (.089)
Pseudo R-square:	.056	.058

n = 28,156. Ordered logistic regression. Additional controls not reported: Dummy variable for missing education, race, citizenship and income status. Omitted dummy variables (reference categories) for race, income, employment status, education, spatial location, and region are white, $30,000–75,000 income bracket, employed, some college or associate's degree, suburb or rural nontown area, and South, Midwest, or Northeast, respectively. Sample-level fixed effects in right-hand model also not reported. Standard errors corrected for clustering at county level in right-hand model.

Introduction

1. According to the Texas Transportation Institute, annual hours of delay per automobile traveler increased from 14 hours in 1982 to 36 hours in 2007 in the nation's urban areas. See 2009 *Urban Mobility Report*, Exhibit 1.

2. In February 2009, Barack Obama stated that "the days we're just building sprawl forever, those days are over" and that "everybody recognizes that that's not a smart way to design communities" ("Remarks by the President," February 10, 2009, Fort Myers, Florida, available at www.whitehouse.gov). While these (and similar) statements are notable, at the time of publication it is premature to evaluate the urban and transportation policies of the Obama administration and their possible effectiveness in altering long-term growth patterns.

3. For an excellent discussion of recent trends, including the period since 2000, see Knox, *Metroburbia USA*, esp. chs. 3 and 8.

4. Thus, see Bruegmann, *Sprawl*; Bogart, *Don't Call It Sprawl*; and, in a decidedly less academic vein, Brooks, *On Paradise Drive*. Many of these themes are also taken up in Martinson, *American Dreamscape*. While Martinson calls for better and more attractive design of suburban communities, the thrust of his book is a strong defense of suburbs and suburban living as meeting U.S. "Yeoman" aspirations: "Anyone can have their own plot of land, and everybody is reasonably free from being told how to live their lives" (*American Dreamscape*, 242).

5. Calthorpe and Fulton, *Regional City*. This general point is a key theme of two of the keenest critical observers of the New Urbanism, Emily Talen and David Brain. Talen stresses that "there is a recurrent normative content" underlying the project of urbanism in the United States, old and new; ideas about planning are inextricably linked to ideas about "what the best possible human settlement in America should be" (Talen, *New Urbanism and American Planning*, 3). Likewise, Brain observes that "in the context of the urban landscape, every design and planning decision is a value proposition, and a proposition that has to do with social and political relationships" (Brain, "From Good

Neighborhoods to Sustainable Cities," 233). For another critical overview of the New Urbanism, see Grant, *Planning the Good Community*.

6. Flint, *This Land*, 5.

7. For a comprehensive list of desirable qualities associated with neighborhoods, see Brower, *Good Neighborhoods*. See ch. 7 for a discussion of Brower's work.

8. See, for example, Baxandall and Ewen, *Picture Windows*, 251–60.

9. See, e.g., Gutmann and Thompson, *Democracy and Disagreement*; Richardson, *Democratic Autonomy*; Goodin, *Reflective Democracy*.

10. Cohen, "Deliberation and Democratic Legitimacy."

11. See, e.g., Rawls, *Political Liberalism*.

12. Bruegmann, *Sprawl*, 135–36.

13. See Knox, *Metroburbia USA*, 66–88, for a discussion of the modern development industry and its role in producing new suburban neighborhoods; see also Levine, *Zoned Out*, for evidence on how developers' project choices are shaped by local zoning rules not simply consumer demand. Other critical accounts of sprawl, however, have stressed the political influence of developers and homebuilders' associations on local planning bodies and state government, which in turn facilitates government approval of and support for new low-density suburban development. See, e.g., the numerous examples of developer influence on local and state government provided in Hirschhorn, *Sprawl Kills*, ch. 1.

14. See Wiewel and Persky, eds., *Suburban Sprawl*.

15. For a recent scholarly examination of the effect of metropolitan-level policies aimed at addressing sprawl, see Nelson, Dawkins, and Sanchez, *Social Impacts of Urban Containment*.

16. On the concept of "policy learning," see Hall, "Policy Paradigms, Social Learning and the State."

17. For a balanced but critical assessment of Maryland's Smart Growth Initiative under Governor Parris Glendening by one of the principal state officials involved in the effort, see Frece, "Twenty Lessons from Maryland's Smart Growth Initiative." See also Lewis, Knaap, and Sohn, "Managing Growth with Priority Fund Areas."

18. Williamson, Imbroscio, and Alperovitz, *Making a Place for Community*, 92–94.

19. See Altshuler, "Ideo-logics of Urban Land Use Politics."

20. See Putnam, "E Pluribus Unum," for further description and discussion of the Social Capital Community Benchmark Survey.

21. Altshuler, "Ideo-logics of Urban Land Use Politics."

22. See Cohen, "Choice-Based Libertarianism."

23. As Jonathan Wolff has stressed (drawing on related work by G.A. Cohen), it is unclear why the relevant baseline for judging whether an appropriation has made someone worse off should be the case in which no appropriation at all takes place, as opposed to the case in which appropriation proceeds under alternative rules that do not wholly exclude some persons. See Wolff, *Robert Nozick*, 112–15. For a more recent comprehensive critique of Nozick and related libertarian thinkers, see Attas, *Liberty, Property and Markets*; see also Waldron, *Right to Private Property*, 253–83, and Singer, *Entitlement*, 171–74.

24. Nozick, *Anarchy, State and Utopia*.

25. Locke, *Second Treatise of Government*, Paragraph 25; Locke, *First Treatise of Government*, Paragraph 42.

26. Waldron, *Right to Private Property*, ch. 6.

27. The meaning and coherence of this "proviso" is hotly debated. Often it has been interpreted as meaning that others in the state of nature must have the same opportunity to acquire desirable land as the first acquirers, as a straightforward reading of Locke's phrasing here might indicate. Both Nozick and Waldron have critiqued that interpretation as incoherent. Waldron argues that the proviso is best understood as a restatement of the general right to subsistence (i.e., private-property rights cannot be used to exclude others from the ability to support themselves), which need not entail a positive right to acquire property. See Waldron, *Right to Private Property*, 209–18.

28. As Waldron notes, Locke ignores the possibility that such cultivation might have taken place under more collective systems of ownership. See Waldron, *Right to Private Property*, 171.

29. Locke, *Second Treatise of Government*, Paragraph 139. As Thomas Horne neatly puts it, "For Locke, property led to constitutionalism, not to libertarianism or a radical redistribution." Horne, *Property Rights and Poverty*, 63. See also Waldron, *Right to Private Property*, 232–41.

30. See Epstein, *Takings*, 7–18. Epstein recognizes the limitations Locke places on acquisition of private property but treats this as an aberration resulting from Locke's theological commitment to the idea that God gave the world to humanity in common; "if we correct his account of the original position to remove all traces of original ownership in common," Epstein writes, "then the soundness of his position is true."

31. Rousseau makes this point in different ways in both the *Discourse on the Origins of Inequality* (Part Two) and the *Social Contract* (Book I, ch. 9).

32. This acknowledging community need not be the government; it is possible for "informal" land-tenure regimes assigning de facto property rights to households and individuals to arise in the absence of formal government ratification. But the legitimacy of such arrangements nonetheless rests on the consent of the concerned communities, not the mere assertion of a property claim.

33. For a fuller explication of this conception of rights, drawing on the work of J. S. Mill, see Zivi, "Cultivating Character."

34. Waldron, *Right to Private Property*, 190.

35. Related to this, Amartya Sen observes that Nozick also allows for the possibility that his ideal libertarian framework of justice might be legitimately overridden if it produced "catastrophic moral horror" (Nozick, *Anarchy, State, and Utopia*, 30). As Sen remarks, "If catastrophic moral horrors are adequate for abandoning the reliance on the allegedly right institutions altogether, could it be the case that bad social consequences that are not absolutely catastrophic but still quite nasty might be adequate grounds for second-guessing the priority of [libertarian] institutions in less drastic ways?" Sen, *The Idea of Justice*, 85.

36. Anderson, "How Not to Complain About Taxes (II): Against Natural Property Rights." Nozick's view is that the end-state distribution of a given resource is to be judged as just on the basis of the process by which the distribution arose; whether the resulting pattern of holdings is highly unequal or not is irrelevant to judging its justice. Nozick believes that his proviso preventing deliberate acquisition of a monopoly of an essential good does not open the door to allowing property rights to be "overridden" by other concerns, since the limitation is internal to the theory of property itself. Indeed, Nozick

even suggests that a person owning a water hole who had the foresight to take steps to keep his hole from drying up when other water hole owners did not would have a moral right to wield a (local) monopoly on water; similarly, a medical researcher discovering a new life-saving drug is entitled to control how that drug is distributed (Nozick, *Anarchy, State and Utopia*, 180–81). But this view fails to account for the moral intuition concerning *why* it is wrong for someone to keep all the water in the desert for himself. Intuitively, it seems the wrongness of such a monopoly consists in the likelihood that people will needlessly die or suffer for want of a scarce resource controlled by someone who withholds it not for the sake of his or her own survival, but in order to command a profit or to force others to obey his or her will in exchange for access. A monopoly of this kind is, simply put, a recipe for a regime of domination. If *this* is what is morally wrong about a desert water monopoly, then the manner in which such a monopoly came about (i.e., whether or not it violated Nozick's proviso) is morally irrelevant.

37. As Waldron further stresses, a theory of natural property rights creates moral obligations that are likely to conflict with other, more fundamental moral obligations a person may have (such as the obligation to try to provide for his or her family without resort to theft, deceit, etc.). See Waldron, *Right to Private Property*, 266–71.

38. This last point applies with greater force to Nozick's conception of property rights than to Locke, who does insist that the general right to subsistence trumps property claims in the case of a conflict.

39. Thus, Martha Nussbaum (in a particularly interesting example) includes the right to own property as one of the ten essential capabilities that just social policies aimed at promoting human development should respect and cultivate; see Nussbaum, *Women and Human Development*. For a succinct and persuasive conventionalist account of property rights that places positive value on the connection between property and autonomy, see Brettschneider, *Democratic Rights*, 114–37. Brettschneider argues that rights to private property can be justified if they are coupled with (and trumped by) a more general right to welfare.

40. Anderson, "How Not to Complain About Taxes (II)."

41. See Singer, *Entitlement*.

42. Murphy and Nagel, *Myth of Ownership*.

43. These two sentences, of course, cannot begin to do justice to the complexity and importance of the historical, constitutional, and legal issues in play here. For a particularly instructive discussion, see Nedelsky, *Private Property and the Limits of American Constitutionalism*.

44. However, various Supreme Court rulings in the past two decades have had the effect of raising the standard public land use regulations must meet. For an overview from a scholar sympathetic to the property rights movement, see Ely, *Guardian of Every Other Right*, 160–65.

45. See Singer, *Entitlement*, and Singer, *Introduction to Property*. See also, e.g., Waldron, *Right to Private Property*, and Radin, *Reinterpreting Property*, esp. "Problems for the Theory of Absolute Property Rights" (ch. 3), a critique of Epstein's influential libertarian treatise, *Takings*.

46. For recent discussions of this movement, see Hannah Jacobs, "Searching for Balance in the Aftermath of the 2006 Takings Initiatives," and the critical response by Harvey M. Jacobs, "New Actions or New Arguments over Regulatory Takings." See also Flint, *This Land*, 127–48.

47. Cohen, "Choice-Based Libertarianism."

48. Friedman: "What the market does is to reduce greatly the range of issues that must be decided through political means, and thereby to minimize the extent to which government need participate directly in the game. The characteristic feature of action through political channels is that it tends to require or enforce substantial conformity. The great advantage of the market, on the other hand, is that it permits wide diversity" (*Capitalism and Freedom*, 15).

49. The phrase is that repeatedly invoked by Bruegmann in *Sprawl*; see, especially, 109–12.

50. Levine, *Zoned Out*.

51. Polanyi, *Great Transformation*, 72–73.

52. Beatley, *Ethical Land Use*, 261.

53. For an eloquent statement of this theme, see Singer, *Edges of the Field*.

54. See Beatley, *Ethical Land Use*, for further elaboration of each of these responsibilities. See also Freyfogle, *Land We Share*.

Chapter 1

1. Fulton, Pendall, Nguyen, and Harrison, "Who Sprawls Most?"

2. See Bruegmann, *Sprawl*, 58–70, for estimates of changing urban densities between 1950 and 1990 using the census definition of urbanized areas (1,000 persons/square mile). For an alternative approach that seeks to include lower-density areas that are functionally connected to urban centers, see Wolman, Galster, Hanson, Ratcliffe, Furdell, and Sarzynski, "Fundamental Challenge in Measuring Sprawl." For yet another approach to the question (excluding tracts in which density is less than 200 persons/square mile), see Lopez and Hynes, "Sprawl in the 1990s."

3. Glaeser and Kahn, "Sprawl and Urban Growth"; Burchfield, Overman, Puga, and Turner, "Causes of Sprawl."

4. Galster, Hanson, Wolman, Coleman, and Freihage, "Wrestling Sprawl to the Ground." Quoted material here taken from the shorter version of the article that appeared in *Housing Facts and Findings* (Winter 2000).

5. Duany, Plater-Zyberk, and Speck, *Suburban Nation*, 7.

6. See Barber, "Malled, Mauled and Overhauled"; and Jacobs, *Mall*.

7. Gillham, *Limitless City*, 146.

8. For discussion along these lines, see Hayden, *Building Suburbia*, 172–79.

9. See, e.g., Mitchell, *Big-Box Swindle*.

10. Kunstler, *Geography of Nowhere*.

11. Hayden, with Wark, *Field Guide to Sprawl*, 13.

12. For a theoretically rich discussion of the qualitative characteristics of suburban places, see Kolb, *Sprawling Places*. Kolb emphasizes the importance of "place complexity."

13. Mumford, *Culture of Cities*, 538.

14. Peter Cannavó: "Sprawl presents a disorienting, illegible experience of placelessness.... To call sprawl placeless is not to say there are no locations. Rather, sprawl offers relatively little in the way of meaningful, distinctive places with which one can identify, that communities can call home, that visitors will appreciate; i.e., places with which people can truly engage" (*Working Landscape*, 111–12).

15. Thus, for instance, this discussion sets aside discussion of exogenous geographic factors such as climate and presence of physical barriers to outward development (i.e.,

mountains, water), though these are relevant factors in explaining variation in the degree of sprawl between different metropolitan areas; see Burchfield et al, "Causes of Sprawl."

16. Hobbs and Stoops, *Demographic Trends in the 20th Century*. See Figures 1.1, 1.14, 5.3.

17. 2008 National Population Projections, United States Census, released August 14, 2008.

18. Blair, *Local Economic Development*; O'Flaherty, *City Economics*, ch. 6.

19. A point well emphasized by Bruegmann, *Sprawl*, 21–32.

20. See Howard, *Garden Cities of To-Morrow*.

21. For an argument that developers have no inherent interest in low-density development, see Bruegmann, *Sprawl*, 100–101. For accounts of the political influence wielded by developers and real estate interests on public policy, especially during the critical period of the 1930s, see Hayden, *Building Suburbia*, and Hornstein, *A Nation of Realtors*.

22. For an insightful discussion of the role contemporary developers play in shaping new developments in suburbia, see Knox, *Metroburbia USA*, esp. ch. 4.

23. See, e.g., Marshall, *How Cities Work*, and Gutfreund, *Twentieth-century Sprawl*.

24. Glaeser and Kahn, "Sprawl and Urban Growth," 2497.

25. Gordon and Richardson, "Are Compact Cities a Desirable Planning Goal?"; and Lang, "Office Sprawl."

26. Glaeser and Kahn, "Sprawl and Urban Growth."

27. Sugrue, *Origins of the Urban Crisis*.

28. See, e.g., Downs, "How Is Suburban Sprawl Related to Urban Decline?" This argument is conceptually distinct from the converse argument: that suburban growth directly causes urban decline. For a critique of that argument, see Beauregard, "Federal Policy and Postwar Urban Decline."

29. For discussion of these points, see Lewis, *Shaping Suburbia*; Frug, *City Making*; Cannavó, *Working Landscape*.

30. See, e.g., Cannavó, *Working Landscape*, 230–58.

31. Gutfreund, *Twentieth-century Sprawl*.

32. Gutfreund, *Twentieth-century Sprawl*.

33. See, e.g., Caro, *Power Broker*; Lassiter, *Silent Majority*.

34. Nivola, *Laws of the Landscape*, 13.

35. Gutfreund, *Twentieth-century Sprawl*, 58–59.

36. Dreier, Mollenkopf, and Swanstrom, *Place Matters*, 109.

37. Jackson, *Crabgrass Frontier*, see 211, table 11–2.

38. Lewyn, "Five Myths about Sprawl."

39. For a detailed discussion of this point, see Cohen, *Consumer's Republic*, ch. 5. See also Beauregard, *When America Became Suburban*, ch. 6.

40. Bruegmann, *Sprawl*, 103–4.

41. Lewyn, "Five Myths about Sprawl."

42. Dietz, "Local Use of the Mortgage Interest and Real Estate Tax Deduction." For a related analysis of the impact of federal housing subsidies on sprawl in the Chicago metropolitan area, see Persky and Kurban, "Do Federal Spending and Tax Policies Build Cities or Promote Sprawl?"

43. Pendall, Puentes, and Martin, "From Traditional to Reformed."

44. Levine, *Zoned Out*.

45. Beauregard, "Federal Policy and Postwar Urban Decline," 146.

46. Bruegmann thus suggests that federal policies encouraging suburbanization simply tracked preexisting consumer preferences for suburban residence. See *Sprawl*, 224.

47. Frank, *Falling Behind*.

48. Alexander, "U.S. Homebuilding Industry."

49. Patterson, "American View of Freedom."

50. Texas Transportation Institute, *2009 Annual Mobility Report*.

51. Harvey, *Social Justice and the City*, 270–271. For a more recent discussion of sprawl drawing on a similar analytical framework see Gonzalez, *Urban Sprawl, Global Warming, and the Empire of Capital*.

52. Hackworth, *Neoliberal City*, 96.

53. A good example of recent scholarship showing how each of these processes predominated at different points in time is Self, *American Babylon*. Self shows how the creation of white industrial suburbs based on the ideal of homeownership in the 1940s and 1950s created and locked into place spatial inequalities in the Oakland area. This process in effect redistributed "social problems, especially poverty, to the central city, and public resources, namely the tax base, to suburban communities" (175). That redistribution subsequently both made Oakland a less attractive residential location for working and middle-class whites and increased suburban resistance to policies intended to redress spatial inequalities, such as fair housing legislation.

54. Perhaps the most prominent critic of the idea of "architectural determinism" is Herbert Gans; see, e.g., his *People and Plans*.

55. The following discussion is informed by the more detailed accounts of urban space and urban life provided by (among other sources) Tonkiss, *Space, the City and Social Theory*; Tickamyer, "Space Matters!"; Demerath and Levinger, "Social Qualities of Being on Foot"; Cannavó, *Working Landscape* (esp. ch. 1); Talen, *New Urbanism and American Planning*; and Brain, "Social Theory of the New Urbanism." Tonkiss's volume provides a thorough, critical review of twentieth-century urban social theory, with informative discussions of the work of prominent scholars such as Georg Simmel, Robert Park, Ernest Burgess, Louis Wirth, Richard Sennett, Manuel Castells, and many others. Talen's volume provides a valuable intellectual history of urban planning in the United States and the way such planners (and their critics) have thought about urban space.

56. For more detailed analysis of the nature of pedestrian space and the sorts of interactions and experiences characteristic of pedestrian activity, see Demerath and Levinger, "Social Qualities of Being on Foot."

57. See Staeheli and Mitchell, "USA's Destiny?" for an interesting case study of the speech control policies of a Syracuse-area mall.

58. Levine, *Zoned Out*.

59. Young, *Justice and the Politics of Difference*, 238–241.

60. In a similar vein, Emily Talen argues that the "urbanist" tradition in the United States is based on the "recurrent principles" of "diversity, equity, community, connectivity, and the importance of civic and public space"; anti-urbanism, in contrast, consists of "separation, segregation, planning by monolithic elements like express highways, and the neglect of equity, place, and the public realm." See Talen, *New Urbanism and American Planning*, 3. David Kolb provides an analogous, more succinct way of making this distinction: some places exhibit "complexity" of uses and meanings, while others are "simple" and hence in his view less interesting. Kolb, *Sprawling Places*.

61. Indeed, each of the four principal empirical findings of this book: the positive relationship between sprawl and trust, quality of life, and political conservatism, and the negative relationship between sprawl and political participation, are evident in models considering *only* the national sub-samples of the SCCBS (roughly 3,000 cases). Specifically, in models controlling for age, gender, race, education level, income, homeownership status, years lived in the community, median income in the census tract, educational attainment in the census tract, marital status, language spoken, and region of the country, and correcting standard errors for clustering at the county level, older neighborhood age (median year housing unit built in tract) is a highly significant predictor (p < .001) of greater likelihood of being a liberal (see ch. 5) and greater political activism (p <.01), as measured by an index of four types of nonelectoral political activity—participation in protests and rallies and membership in political organizations or groups involved in local reform (see ch. 7). Likewise, the natural log of census tract density is a highly significant negative predictor (p <.001) of both trust of neighbors and overall social trust, as well as community quality-of-life evaluations, when controlling for the same factors noted above as well as tract-level racial homogeneity (see chs. 3 and 5). The same patterns are evident whether or not we include the sample weights in the regressions.

Further confirmation of these basic patterns is provided by analysis of the 2006 Social Capital Community Survey, also conducted by the Saguaro Seminar at Harvard University. This survey of 12,100 persons asked many of the same questions as the SCCBS in a much smaller, nonrepresentative set of communities (for instance, more than 20% of the total sample consists of a subsample from the state of Kansas). The 2006 survey, however, does contain a nationally representative sample of 2,740 persons. At the time of publication, geo-codes for this data are not publicly available; however, the publicly released data do include a designation of respondents as either "urban," "suburban," or "rural." This measure is obviously not nearly as subtle as the disaggregated measures of sprawl considered in this book but still offers a rough measure of the difference between urban and suburban places. In the national sample of this data, the general relationship between trust, quality of life, political ideology, and political activism and spatial setting mirrors what we find in the 2000 SCCBS. Among respondents marked "urban," just under 36 percent trusted their neighbors "a lot" compared to 47 percent for suburban residents; just under 33 percent rated their community quality of life as "excellent" compared to 41 percent of suburban residents; nearly 33 percent of urban residents described themselves politically as a "liberal," compared to 22 percent of suburban residents; self-described Democrats outnumbered self-described Republicans 36 percent to 23 percent among urban residents, whereas among suburban residents, self-described Republicans outnumbered Democrats 34 percent to 29 percent. Urban residents were also over one-quarter more likely in the past year to have belonged to an organization involved in local reform (24% to 19%) and nearly 50 percent more likely to have engaged in protest activity (9.6% to 6.6%); they were also modestly more likely to have attended a political rally (19.5% to 18.0%). Reported figures here are weighted by the sample weights. A t-test of the unweighted data shows that the difference in means between urban and suburban areas with respect to each of these variables is highly significant (p <.001) in all cases noted, except for protest activity, which is significant at the p < .02 level, and attendance at a rally, which approaches significance at p < .075. In short, the basic empirical patterns described in this book using the 2000 SCCBS are as a descriptive matter replicated in an entirely separate national survey conducted in 2006.

For further discussion of the 2000 SCCBS and how it approximates a national sample, see Putnam, "E Pluribus Unum."

62. In addition, many cases include identifiers of the respondent's place of residence (i.e., city, town, or census designated place); I draw on this identifier to construct a measure of central city residence and city size, as explained in the appendix. Zip code level data is missing in roughly 1.4 percent of cases for which the census tract data are available.

63. See Galster, Hanson, Wolman, Coleman, and Freihage, "Wrestling Sprawl to the Ground"; Ewing, Pendall, and Chen, "Measuring Sprawl and Its Impact"; Malpezzi and Guo, "Measuring 'Sprawl.'" In recent work, Jackie Cutsinger and George Galster argue against conceptualizing metropolitan-level sprawl as a unified phenomenon; they instead identify four distinct patterns of sprawling development. See Cutsinger and Galster, "There Is No Sprawl Syndrome."

64. The disaggregated approach has several advantages: First, it does not make the investigation excessively dependent on a formal definition of sprawl—definitions that can always be critiqued and challenged. For instance, scholars constructing an index of sprawl face dilemmas regarding not only which indicators to include and which to exclude, but also how to weight each of the various indicators. Findings contingent upon how a particular index of sprawl is constructed are likely to be met with understandable skepticism. Second, a disaggregated approach helps avoid reifying "sprawl," as if "sprawl" were an inherent characteristic of built communities and not, in fact, a label placed upon communities by scholars and commentators. Focusing attention on the more specific characteristics that are visible and measurable in communities—e.g., transportation patterns—can avoid that problem. Third, and perhaps most important, the disaggregated approach does not assume that each element of "sprawl" necessarily has the same sort of effect on the dependent variables with which we are concerned and allows us to isolate which characteristics (if any) are of greatest importance in affecting, for instance, an individual's likelihood of having signed a petition in the past twelve months. Fourth, the disaggregated approach need not assume that the various community characteristics commonly associated with sprawl are in reality always present in the same places. Neighborhoods can be sprawling along one dimension but not another.

65. Places designated as central cities include those listed by name as the center or co-center of a metropolitan statistical area or primary metropolitan statistical area by the census as of 1999 (up to three cities per area). The use of the 25,000-population threshold for central city designation excludes some quite small cities listed as metropolitan centers. This threshold was selected to correspond with the definition of a city (a census place with more than 25,000 persons) used by the census in the *County and City Data Book* 2000 (U.S. Census, 2002). One town with a significant number of cases (Auburn, Maine) is not listed as a central city under this coding procedure because it falls below the population threshold; an alternative specification according to which Auburn residents are coded as central city residents does not produce significantly different results from those reported in the text.

66. Because the SCCBS provides incomplete data on municipal residence, in some cases it was necessary to impute urban residence or non-residence based on other geographical information (i.e., the location of one's census tract block group). See appendix I for more discussion of the procedure by which this variable was constructed. While there is necessarily measurement error in this variable, I believe (and the reported findings suggest) that it is sufficiently accurate to allow us to judge in a least a general way between the relative importance of whether one lives in an urban center or not compared to the importance of more-specific neighborhood attributes in predicting outcomes of interest.

67. For 67.7 percent of the cases in the SCCBS, census tract locations are identified directly from each respondent's street address (or nearest intersection). In 31.2 percent of the sample, for which street addresses are unavailable, tracts were imputed using the geographic midpoint of the respondent's zip code. (In the remaining cases, the method by which the census tract was identified is not recorded.) Consequently, there is at least some measurement error in the identification of census tracts. The expected result of this error is to bias findings downward (e.g., the correlation between tract-level education and individuals having a bachelor's degree or higher is estimated to be $r=.345$ among respondents in exactly matched tracts compared to $r=.298$ among respondents whose tract location was imputed). If we divide the sample into those in which tracts are matched from addresses ($n=19,729$) to those that were imputed ($n=9,080$), the key findings of this book (of a positive linkage between sprawl and trust of neighbors, higher quality of life, greater conservatism, and reduced nonelectoral political participation) can be replicated in both sub-samples. In each case, however, the linkages are stronger among the exact-matched cases. The results of this procedure suggest that the practical result of this measurement error inherent in the SCCBS is to bias the overall results downward with respect to the effects of sprawl. It should also be noted that each of the core findings in this book can be replicated at higher levels of analysis (the zip code and the county level), where this issue does not arise.

68. In 2000, the exact figure was 75.7 percent. 2000 U.S. Census data, Summary File 3.

69. Freeman, "Effects of Sprawl on Neighborhood Social Ties." It should be noted here that the proportion of solo driving at the tract level is correlated with the proportion of all car commuters (i.e., solo drivers and carpoolers) at (among SCCBS respondents) $r=.92$. Use of the latter measure would not substantially alter results reported in this study, but in my judgment the solo-driver measure more tightly corresponds to the concept of sprawl. Carpooling rates are much more heterogeneous across spatial context (and in fact are somewhat higher among older neighborhood and urban respondents in the SCCBS), and correlate only weakly with density, whereas solo driving is substantially higher in suburbs and newer neighborhoods and is highly correlated with low density. Including carpoolers would, in effect, dilute the measure's effectiveness in capturing sprawl.

70. Unfortunately, the SCCBS does not include a measure of individual-level transportation mode.

71. To be sure, the proportion of solo automobile commuters is shaped by other factors besides neighborhood-level spatial features; most notably, it is shaped by neighborhood affluence (more people have and drive cars in more affluent areas), a factor controlled for in the analysis, and it is influenced by broader metropolitan-wide transportation

patterns and networks. Nonetheless, there are very significant variations in neighborhood reliance on automobiles, even within the same metropolitan areas and even after accounting for differences in neighborhood income.

72. Oliver, *Democracy in Suburbia*, ch. 5.

73. Jargowsky, "Sprawl, Concentration of Poverty, and Urban Inequality."

74. To quantify this relationship, I first devised a composite sprawl measure from the variables concerning neighborhood age and the proportion of those driving alone, defined as [median year neighborhood built -1900] + [% driving alone in tract* 100]. I then took photos of the geographic midpoint of representative tracts (oversampling non-sprawling tracts located outside central cities) from each tail (up to the 10th percentile) in the distribution of the composite measure, with no more than five cases in each tail taken from any one community sub-sample (apart from the national sample), to assure wide regional distribution of selected cases. These photos were then coded by myself and research assistants as being on a traditional urban grid, not being on a grid, or as being ambiguous or exhibiting a mixed design. The vast majority (more than 90%) of the 137 tracts taken from the "less sprawling" tail (bottom 10th percentile), were located on an urban grid or in a central business district, with a few cases exhibiting mixed design features. Of the 153 tracts taken from the "more sprawling" tail, roughly 85 percent were not part of an urban grid; some cases were ambiguous or had a mix of design features, and one tract exhibited a predominant grid pattern. Census tracts that have a low proportion of persons driving alone to work and are relatively old thus have very little chance of being a curvilinear, suburban neighborhood located on the urban fringe; conversely, census tracts that have a relatively high proportion of persons driving alone to work and that are relatively recently built have very little chance of being a traditional urban neighborhood with a high level of street accessibility. In short, while not perfect, these measures do capture meaningful differences in urban design. My thanks to Daniel J. Hopkins, Jordan Wade, Deanna Boyd, and Patrick Scanlan for help in designing and executing this test. For useful discussion of the differences between high-connectivity grid street designs and low-connectivity "hierarchical" designs and explanation of how pedestrian activity can vary dramatically among places with similar density according to neighborhood design characteristics, see Frank, Engelke, and Schmid, *Health and Community Design*.

75. The bivariate correlations between the four core sprawl measures among respondents to the SCCBS is presented below (n=29, 136). In no case is the relationship between the various variables stronger than r=.52. In short, we can be confident that these measures capture distinct yet interrelated dimensions of the spatial contexts Americans inhabit.

	(1)	(2)	(3)
Population Density (log) (1)	*	*	*
% Solo Drivers in Tract (2)	−.40	*	*
Year Neighborhood Built (3)	−.38	.49	*
Central City Residence	.52	−.45	−.37

76. It is important to note that the measures of sprawl employed here are not idiosyncratic. They track fairly closely the (2000) county-level index of sprawl constructed by Reid Ewing and used in several studies of the relationship between sprawl and health and other outcomes. The Ewing index is based on four separate sets of indicators measuring density, "land-use mix," "degree of centering," and "street accessibility," compiled from a variety of data sources. Weighting for population size, the bivariate correlation between Ewing's sprawl index (which is coded so that higher values signify less sprawl) and the proportion of workers driving in a county alone to work is $r = -.92$. The correlation between the Ewing measure and county population density (natural log) is $r = .79$, and the correlation between the Ewing and the median year a county's housing units were built is $r = -.58$. These correlations are calculated for the 950 counties (all currently designated as metropolitan, excluding Hawaii and Alaska) for which the Ewing index is currently available. Together, over 228 million people, or roughly 80 percent of the 2000 population, resided in these counties in 2000.

Analyses of this data conducted at the county level substituting the Ewing index for these disaggregated measures of sprawl yields results highly similar to the results reported here for the disaggregated, neighborhood-level measures of sprawl. In short, these measures of sprawl correspond fairly closely to other approaches in the literature, increasing confidence that the overall results here are not an artifact of how sprawl is measured.

Specifically, analysis at the county level using the same battery of individual-level controls described in note 61 and county-level control measures of income, education, and racial composition shows that low scores on the Ewing index of sprawl—that is, more sprawl—are statistically significant predictors of increased satisfaction with neighborhood quality of life (see ch. 3), and of higher trust of neighbors and greater political conservatism (see ch. 5). Conversely high scores on the Ewing index (less sprawl) are significant positive predictors of an index of four forms of nonelectoral political participation (protests, political rallies, membership in a group involved in local reform, and political-group membership) discussed in ch. 7, and of increased political knowledge. In short, the key empirical findings of this book can be largely replicated using the Ewing index, although the strength of the results produced at the county level of aggregation are, naturally, weaker than those produced at the census tract level.

See Ewing, Pendall, and Chen, "Measuring Sprawl and Its Impact"; Ewing, Schmid, Killingsworth, Zlot, and Raudenbush, "Relationship between Urban Sprawl and Physical Activity, Obesity, and Morbidity"; Ewing, Brownson, and Berrigan, "Relationship between Sprawl and Weight of United States Youth." County-level measures of sprawl were provided to the author courtesy of Reid Ewing.

77. Previous studies linking sprawl with long commuting times often assumed a straightforward relationship between suburbanization and increased commuting time (e.g. Putnam, 2000). In fact, central cities with high levels of public transit use and traffic congestion may have longer average commute times than some suburbs, and the overall difference in commuting time between cities and suburbs is modest. The effect of commuting time on a variety of outcomes remains of substantive interest but should be distinguished from the core sprawl-related measures.

78. Commuting times are reported for currently employed workers, some homemakers, some unemployed or laid-off workers, and some students. The SCCBS also reports whether respondents are telecommuters or not. I have operationalized the commuting-time

information as follows: I created a variable consisting of commuting-time information for currently employed workers *only*; values for this variable are set to zero for the unemployed (including the temporarily laid off), the disabled, the retired, students, and homemakers. In most cases, workers who primarily work at home (telecommuters and those with home-based businesses) did not report a commuting time; for those workers, effective commuting time is assumed to be zero. The resultant variable measures commuting time among currently employed workers only. In estimating the substantive impact of commuting time on outcomes of interest it is thus necessary to also control for employment status (as all models in these analyses do).

79. Oliver, *Democracy in Suburbia*.

80. As with the measure of central city residence, in some cases city size had to be imputed rather than directly measured. Due to data limitations it was impractical to construct a reliable measure distinguishing among smaller cities, but this control measure does capture the essential difference between living in a relatively small community and living in a much larger city. I also examined the possible relationship between city size and other measures beyond political participation; in almost all cases, however, city size did not have a significant relationship with other measured outcomes.

81. For a critical overview of the literature on this point, see Dietz and Haurin, "Social and Private Micro-level Consequences of Homeownership."

82. Verba, Schlozman, and Brady, *Voice and Equality*.

83. On patterns of rising and falling city population in the United States between 1980 and 2000, see Williamson, Imbroscio, and Alperovitz, *Making a Place for Community*, Introduction.

84. See, for instance, Putnam, "E Pluribus Unum."

85. For instance, conditional on respondents' educational levels, high proportions of both poor *and* rich people in the neighborhood are negatively related to trust of neighbors and local quality-of-life evaluations. Put another way, local trust and quality of life are reported as higher in neighborhoods with a high proportion of middle-income residents. See ch. 3.

86. A difficult question in conducting research on sprawl is how to treat residents in or bordering rural areas. Some analysts recommend excluding rural areas from examinations of sprawl. It should be acknowledged that the measures of sprawl used in this book are conceptualized principally with metropolitan settings in mind and that these measures correlate with one another in different ways in urban and rural settings. For instance, higher density is strongly correlated with reduced automobile dependence within metropolitan areas, but at the much lower densities in non-urbanized rural areas, density and car use are positively correlated among SCCBS respondents. (However, in urbanized clusters of rural areas—that is, small towns—the relationship between density and automobile dependence is an inverse one, as in metropolitan areas.) Lopez and Hynes, "Sprawl in the 1990s," thus argue that "rural sprawl" requires a separate analysis, and Wolman et al., in "Fundamental Challenge in Measuring Sprawl," develop an instrument for distinguishing rural from "sprawling" land based on a measure of functional connection to the central city. Those distinctions are especially important when measuring sprawl at the metropolitan level. Likewise, Oliver excludes rural cases from consideration in most analyses in his *Democracy in Suburbia*, a decision that makes sense given that his unit of analysis was municipalities within metropolitan areas. Despite these considerations, I include rural residents in the reported results for three reasons: first, excluding rural residents would limit the number of communities and range of variation in the data; second, the data itself

was collected in "community" samples that in several cases covers substantial numbers of residents in both metropolitan and rural counties; third, excluding rural residents might exacerbate concerns about self-selection driving reported findings. The overall findings reported in this book remain robust whether we include or exclude rural residents.

87. I test for regional effects in all models using the complete set of controls (i.e., South, Midwest, and West, with Northeast as the reference category), but I only include controls that are statistically significant or approach statistical significance in the reported results. In some models, for instance, residence in the South may be included as a control variable, with residence in the rest of the nation the implicit reference category. Except in one case as noted (reported voting), substantive conclusions regarding the results of tract-level sprawl-related variables are not sensitive to which specific regional controls are included.

88. Wooldridge, *Econometric Analysis of Cross-Sectional and Panel Data*; Long and Freese, *Regression Models for Categorical Data Using Stata*.

89. Tomz, Wittenberg, and King, *CLARIFY*. See also King, Tomz, and Wittenberg, "Making the Most of Statistical Analyses."

90. This approach to multilevel data, in which the researcher's interest is the effect of community-level variables on individual outcomes, is recommended both by Primo, Jacobsmeier, and Milyo, "Estimating the Impact of State Policies and Institutions with Mixed-Level Data," and Angeles, Guilkey, and Mroz, "Impact of Community Level Variables on Individual Level Outcomes." For explanations of the specific cluster estimating technique employed by Stata to compute these standard errors, see Snijders and Bosker, *Multilevel Analysis*, 250–51, and Statacorp, *Stata User's Guide Release 9*.

By correcting standard errors at the community sample level of aggregation, I allow for the possibility that individuals within the same community may not be independent of one another (even if they live in different neighborhoods). This procedure produces standard error estimates substantially more conservative than those produced by correcting standard errors for clustering at the census tract level and dramatically more conservative than estimates produced by failing to account for the clustered nature of the data (what Angeles et al. term "naïve standard errors").

Given that the community samples in the SCCBS are geographically heterogeneous, a reasonable alternative approach is to correct standard errors for clustering at the county level; this approach has the further statistical advantage of dramatically increasing the number of clusters. Clustering at the county level generally produces results quite similar to clustering at the community sample level, and in no case does clustering at the county as opposed to the community level affect the statistical significance of key variables. Similarly, models including metropolitan area residents only with standard errors corrected for clustering at the MSA (metropolitan statistical area) level also produce similar results.

In addition, I have confirmed key reported findings using more conservative, "no-pool" models which include fixed-effect controls for each community sub-sample in addition to the tract-level variables.

Chapter 2

1. For a discussion of this issue, see Marglin, *Dismal Science*.

2. Mill, *Utilitarianism*, 12–15.

3. Mill's insistence that utilitarianism can distinguish between higher and lower pleasures and better and worse ways to live—in short, his attempt to marry utilitarianism
and perfectionism—has been frequently challenged, of course, by both utilitarians and
non-utilitarians; thus, Amy Gutmann argues that Mill's claim that those who have
experienced both sorts of pleasures are equipped to judge which is superior "smuggles
in a particular conception of the good life under the guise of a universally acceptable
choice criterion of pleasure." Gutmann suggests that Millian utilitarianism cannot be
neutral with respect to a conception of the good life—a bad thing, in her view ("What's
the Use of Going to School?" 263).

4. Interestingly for the present investigation, some of the specific goods described by Mill
as crucial to happiness correspond closely to the common critique of stereotyped suburban life: U.S. social critics have for half a century painted a picture of suburbs as intellectually stultifying, isolating places that encourage (or even require) individuals to be
predominantly preoccupied with their own affairs. Put more bluntly, there is much in
the body of Mill's work to suggest that he would not regard a way of life that is fundamentally apolitical and in which watching television for four hours a day is the norm as
one utilitarians ought to admire or promote.

5. See Mill, *On Liberty*.

6. Following David Brink, I understand Mill to have an objective view of human well-
being; namely, to hold that happiness consists not in hedonism or in preference satisfaction but in the exercise of rational deliberative capacities. This understanding of
Mill allows us to comprehend how he could simultaneously suggest that some goods
and some modes of living—those that involve the exercise of these deliberative capacities—are of greater worth than others and also provide a strong defense of individual
liberty and allowing people to make their own choices. See Brink, "Mill's Deliberative
Utilitarianism."

7. Altshuler, "Ideo-logics of Urban Land Use Politics."

8. For a telling case study illustrating this point, see Susan Fainstein's discussion of the
fate of the Bronx Terminal Market in her "Planning and the Just City."

9. Campbell and Marshall, "Utilitarianism's Bad Breath?"

10. Campbell and Marshall, "Utilitarianism's Bad Breath?" 177. Note that Campbell and
Marshall carefully distinguish their favored view from forms of utilitarianism that
assume the public interest can be defined through a simple counting exercise or that
the state must take an uncritical view toward individuals' existing preferences. Campbell and Marshall's position, however, is quite consistent with broader conceptions of
utilitarianism—such as Robert Goodin's—that do allow a role for public deliberation
and do view existing preferences through a critical lens in determining the public
interest.

11. Goodin, *Utilitarianism as a Public Philosophy*, 8–12; Mill quote (cited by Goodin, 12) is
taken from his 1838 "Essay on Bentham."

12. For an overview of cost–benefit analysis on related policy-evaluation methods commonly employed by economists, see Smith, "Economic Techniques." For critical discussions of both the Pareto standard and the cost-benefit standard, see Sen, *On Ethics and
Economics*, esp. 31–51, and Marglin, *Dismal Science*, esp. 60–66 and 179–83.

13. Related to this, James Bailey's recent defense of utilitarianism acknowledges that it
may be the case that "costs of information and causation do not allow us to make global

estimates of what would lead to the best outcomes overall"; nonetheless, "utilitarianism does enable us to make piecemeal reforms in our practices whenever new information or calculative techniques become available.... Utilitarianism is thus often a doctrine of marginal rather than global analysis." Bailey, *Utilitarianism, Institutions, and Justice*, 15. For further discussion of the increasingly conservative tenor of much academic utilitarianism, see Kymlicka, *Contemporary Political Philosophy*, 45–48.

14. See Braybrooke and Lindblom, *Strategy of Decision*, 83–90. Braybrooke and Lindblom go on to argue that use of utilitarian criteria in policy analysis ultimately necessitates marginal analysis of policies and makes comparisons among larger-scale alternatives difficult if not impossible. As elaborated in ch. 3, this conclusion, if accepted, should count as a major deficiency in utilitarianism as a public philosophy.

15. U.S. urban-growth patterns are also often compared by scholars to patterns in cities in other advanced industrialized nations (especially those in Europe).

16. See Wiewel, Persky, and Sendzik, "Private Benefits and Public Costs."

17. Glaeser and Kahn make precisely this argument in "Sprawl and Urban Growth."

18. Transit Cooperative Research Program, *Costs of Sprawl—2000*, 12, table ES.12. See also Burchell et al., *Sprawl Costs*.

19. Altshuler and Gómez-Ibáñez, *Regulation for Revenue*, 74.

20. Data on Americans' subjective income needs suggest that the average American believes he or she needs at least $100,000 a year (1994 dollars) to live comfortably. Schor, *Overspent American*, 15. If one defines a comfortable life as including private home ownership in a neighborhood with good schools, ownership of one automobile per adult in the household, good childcare provision, adequate savings for children's college education, health and other forms of insurance, etc., this belief may in fact be well grounded. In societies with relatively few public goods and an underdeveloped system of social insurance, it is natural that most families will believe they need a great deal of money before they can feel completely secure: in short, the point at which the hypothesized diminishing return begins to curve steeply downward and additional money is not experienced as a very substantial good with important real-life benefits is likely very, very high in the contemporary United States.

21. Wilson, *When Work Disappears*.

22. Evidence that efforts at urban containment can in fact produce increased central city investment has been provided by Nelson, Dawkins, and Sanchez and is based on a study of 144 central cities, 21 of which implemented urban-containment policies prior to 1985. They report that "[these] programs...had an effect on the level of construction activity in central cities over the eleven-year period between 1985 and the end of 1995," adding that, "central cities located in urban regions with containment programs attracted more development per capita than central cities in regions without containment programs" (Nelson, Dawkins, and Sanchez, *Social Impacts of Urban Containment*, 109–19, quote at 118). In related research, Nelson et al. also find that over the same time period, metropolitan areas with "smart growth" policies in places had greater investments in rehabilitation of older buildings (and hence higher construction investments per new resident in the region) (103–7).

23. An excellent example of a textbook economist's approach to sprawl is Brueckner, "Suburban Sprawl."

24. O'Flaherty, *City Economics*, 49. For a detailed but accessible discussion of the externalities associated with motor vehicle use, see Litman, "Policy Implications of Full Social

Costing." See also Delucchi, "Do Motor-Vehicle Users in the United States Pay Their Way?"

25. Anderson, *Value in Ethics and Economics*. See also Sagoff, *Price, Principle and the Environment*. For related critical discussion of cost–benefit analysis and related economic techniques, see Wolff and Haubrich, "Economism and Its Limits."

26. The issue would become more complicated, of course, if it could be shown that the effect on human health of 2.2 tons of air pollution is markedly more severe than that of 2.0 tons of air pollution, to the extent that permitting the higher level of pollution would cause markedly more deaths. For an interesting critical discussion of attempts by EPA administrators during the 1980s to use utilitarian methods to adjudicate a jobs-versus-health trade-off in Tacoma, Washington, see Gutmann and Thompson, *Democracy and Disagreement*, 165–98.

27. See Sagoff, *Price, Principle and the Environment*; see also Daly and Cobb, *For the Common Good*.

28. Anderson, *Value in Ethics and Economics*, 215. Anderson objects, however, to aggregating information about costs and benefits into a single, seemingly authoritative analysis. Rather, she recommends that costs and benefits be analyzed in disaggregated form.

29. Gutmann and Thompson envision precisely this role for utilitarian analysis; see *Democracy and Disagreement*.

30. The following summary of Persky and Wiewel's work draws heavily on Williamson, Imbroscio, and Alperovitz, *Making a Place for Community*, 85–89.

31. Persky and Wiewel, *When Corporations Leave Town*.

32. Persky and Wiewel, *When Corporations Leave Town*, 72.

33. Williamson, Imbroscio, and Alperovitz, *Making a Place for Community*, 84.

34. For similar argumentation, see Bogart, *Don't Call It Sprawl*.

35. Glaeser and Kahn, "Sprawl and Urban Growth."

36. Glaeser and Kahn, "Sprawl and Urban Growth." For an interesting argument that the move to bigger houses may have only a limited effect on boosting utility, see Frank, *Falling Behind*. Frank argues that to the extent moves toward bigger houses reflect social pressures to have as big a house as possible, they add nothing to utility (and may detract from it by causing us to ignore other goods).

37. Garreau, *Edge City*, 222.

38. Garreau, *Edge City*, 234.

39. Brooks, *On Paradise Drive*.

40. Mill, *Utilitarianism*, ch. 2.

41. Goodin, *Utilitarianism as a Public Philosophy*, 137–41.

42. Ignorance or distorted perception of the existing alternatives, corresponding to Goodin's first category, may also play a role; in particular, suburban residents may have an exaggerated view of the problems of central cities. Evidence from a 1999 survey of 1,086 residents in the Richmond metropolitan area found that suburban residents were much more likely than city residents to view downtown crime as a severe problem. Forty-four percent of residents from Henrico, Chesterfield, and Hanover counties stated that crime in downtown Richmond was "very serious," compared to just 19 percent of residents in the city of Richmond; interestingly, the same general pattern held for both white and African American respondents. Author's analysis of Virginia Center for Urban Development (Virginia Commonwealth University) Metro Poll. Consistent with the findings from the SCCBS, 45 percent of suburban residents rated their neighborhood as an

"excellent" place to live, compared to 21 percent of residents of the city of Richmond. Data provided courtesy of Donelson Forsyth.

43. Bayoh, Irwin, and Haab, "Determinants of Residential Location Choice."

44. The classic account of this process is found in Horkheimer and Adorno's essay on the "culture industry" as "mass deception" in their *Dialectic of Enlightenment*.

45. On this theme, see Cohen, *Consumer's Republic*; Hayden, *Building Suburbia*; and Hornstein, *Nation of Realtors*.

46. As noted by Hayden, "What Is Suburbia?" See also Beauregard, *When American Became Suburban*.

47. On this theme, see Schor, *Born to Buy*.

48. This is not to say that the virtual reality world would be the best of all possible worlds from the standpoint of well-being; as Robert Nozick has observed by way of critiquing hedonic utilitarianism, we have good reason to prefer actual experiences to such virtual experiences as might be provided by an "experience machine." See Nozick, *Anarchy, State and Utopia*, 42–45. Utilitarians might conclude, however, that the "virtual reality helmet"-wearing society would be the best attainable one, given that real life for most people is not a continuous stream of highly desirable actual experiences.

49. Such a critique might be available, however, to a Millian utilitarian with an "objective" understanding of the sources of human happiness.

50. Anderson, *Value in Ethics and Economics*, 10–11. For a parallel argument, see Taylor, "Diversity of Goods."

51. For related discussions, see Walzer, *Spheres of Justice*, and Sandel, "What Money Can't Buy."

52. For similar argumentation, see Frug, *City Making*.

53. Gutmann and Thompson, *Democracy and Disagreement*; see also Richardson, *Democratic Autonomy*.

Chapter 3

1. Montesquieu, *Spirit of the Laws*.

2. Obviously, many other indicators that are by most accounts closely related to "utility" will also be of interest to utilitarians, such as most of the measures related to social trust taken up in ch. 5. Utilitarians value social trust, however, as an intermediate good (because it is thought to promote numerous positive outcomes), not as a good that is worthy in itself. As an intermediate good, social trust will be of only secondary interest to the utilitarian, especially when the data provides means to more directly measure the primary goods of subjective individual well-being and individual satisfaction. Health, friendship, and social interaction are intermediate goods as well, but these goods are so closely linked to individual well-being that it is reasonable to conclude that most utilitarians would regard them as primary goods. Put another way, it's much easier to imagine a fundamentally happy person who does not have a high degree of trust for everyone they interact with than it is to imagine a fundamentally happy person who is lonely and/or socially isolated, or who is plagued by health problems. Following Goodin's observations regarding implicit "preferences for preferences," it should be uncontroversial for utilitarians to attribute to human beings a desire for health and a desire for friendship or companionship, even if people on occasion themselves do not recognize these goods as primary to their own well-being. (Many, of course, do!)

3. Putnam, *Bowling Alone.*

4. See, e.g., Rodgers, "Residential Satisfaction in Relationship to Size of Place." For more detailed summary of much of this literature, see also Gonzalez, *Urban Sprawl, Global Warming and the Empire of Capital*, ch. 1.

5. Simmel, "The Metropolis and Mental Life," and Wirth, "Urbanism as a Way of Life" (quoted words from 16).

6. Oliver, "Mental Life and the Metropolis in Suburban America." Oliver did not examine the possible effect of transportation patterns or average commuting time in his analysis.

7. Throughout this book, I use the unweighted sample totals when presenting descriptive data. Differences between these figures and totals using the SCCBS sample weights are small, and in no case alter the basic spatial patterns in the distribution of various attitudes and behaviors with which we are concerned.

8. The analyses reported are based on unweighted regression analyses; that is, analyses that do not include the survey sample weights. The key elements comprising the survey weights for the SCCBS—race, age, education, gender, household size, and, in some cases geography—are already controlled or tested for in the analysis, and unweighted regressions are a more efficient tool. For each regression, however, I have also run the analyses with sample weights included. Results from weighted analyses are generally very similar to those reported here. In a few cases where the point estimates for the sprawl-related variables are substantially different between weighted and unweighted models, I test for the presence of significant interactions between the sprawl-related variables and key demographic variables such as race and education. (This procedure draws on recommendations made in Winship and Radbill, "Sampling Weights and Regression Analysis.") In instances where there are substantial, theoretically interesting differences across demographic groups concerning the impact of sprawl on outcomes of interest, I break out the sample into sub-groups and report separate regression results for each demographic sub-group (see chs. 5 and 7).

9. For reasons of space and to keep the analytical focus on sprawl, reporting on the effect of other community-context variables upon the dependent variables examined in this book will be kept to a minimum in the main text, even though in many cases these are noteworthy in themselves and worthy of further attention. For instance, the finding in table 3.2 that (controlling for a range of individual variables) living in a richer neighborhood actually depresses subjective well-being is quite interesting (and consistent with Oliver, "Mental Life and the Metropolis in Suburban America"). Further exploration of such findings is necessarily beyond the scope of the present enterprise.

10. See Tomz, Wittenberg, and King, *CLARIFY*; see also King, Tomz, and Wittenberg, "Making the Most of Statistical Analyses."

11. Obviously, the SCCBS includes fairly rough measures of some variables, such as subjective well-being. In general, within the SCCBS there is also likely the presence of a "golden glow" effect that may have caused respondents to exaggerate their degree of community attachment upon discerning that such attachments formed the core of the interview questions; Putnam estimates this effect to inflate estimates of community attachment and participation by 5–10 percent. (See Putnam, "E Pluribus Unum," n. 14). It should also be stressed that for a variety of reasons both general to survey research (measurement error) and specific to the SCCBS data, there is some inherent

uncertainty in the precision of these estimates of substantive effects; moreover, different methods of modeling this data are sure to yield at least slightly different results.

12. Dummy variables for unemployed persons, the disabled, students, retirees, and homemakers are set to zero so that we are comparing the effect of commuting times among employed persons.

13. Comparison values for the key independent variables in reported simulation analyses in this book are selected to correspond roughly to the comparison between a census tract in the 80th percentile and the 20th percentile of the metropolitan-area distribution of each variable (for SCCBS respondents). However, for presentation purposes I have elected to use relatively "round" values in each case to make the comparisons as easy to comprehend in real-world terms as possible, and the correspondence of the selected variables to the percentile distribution of each variable and to the standard deviation of each variable varies from case to case. In statistical terms, the difference between tracts in which 65 percent and 85 percent of workers drive alone is roughly 1.4 standard deviations; the difference between neighborhoods whose median house was built in 1950 in one case and 1980 in the other is roughly 1.9 standard deviations; the difference between tracts with 1,000 persons/square mile and 8,000 persons/square mile is roughly 1.1 standard deviations (of the log-transformed variable); and the difference between tracts with average commuting times of thirty minutes and eighteen minutes, respectively, is roughly 2.1 standard deviations.

14. Glaeser and Kahn, "Sprawl and Urban Growth."

15. Mill, *Utilitarianism*, 15.

16. See, for instance, Ewing, Schmid, Killingsworth, Zlot, and Raudenbush, "Relationship between Urban Sprawl and Physical Activity, Obesity, and Morbidity." Whether this relationship is simply a product of self-selection is a hotly debated topic; see Harder, "Weighing In on City Planning," 43, for a summary overview of recent studies.

17. In the full model that includes all four sprawl-related variables and tract commuting time, proportion driving alone to work has a negative relationship with health, albeit not at a statistically significant level. This conditional relationship is more than offset by the significant inverse relationship between neighborhood density and health.

18. Simulation analysis predicts that residents of a tract with a density of 8,000 persons/square mile will have a 20.7 percent (20.0%, 21.4%) likelihood of saying they are in excellent health, compared to 21.6 percent (21.1%, 22.1%) for a resident of a tract with a density of 1,000 persons/square mile.

19. For a review of research linking the built environment to walking and health, see Frank, Engelke, and Schmid, *Health and Community Design*.

20. See Nasar, *Evaluative Image of the City*, for a discussion of what sorts of places tend to be regarded by most observers as visually attractive and appealing. Drawing on empirical work about individuals' perceptions of specific places in two Tennessee cities, Nasar concludes that well-maintained places in which the presence of nature is evident, that present an open vista, that have historical significance and character, and that are perceived as organized and coherent are the best-regarded sorts of places; commercial strip malls of the sort most associated with "sprawl" tend to fail most or all of these tests: one such area in Chattanooga is described as being "disliked for parking lots, lighting, dilapidation, pollution, litter, disorder and confusion, crowding, congestion, and signs" (53, 62). On the other hand, respondents in Chattanooga

and Knoxville also disliked the city's central business districts and several inner-city neighborhoods, and spoke favorably of some residential environments with many new houses. Aesthetic considerations of this kind will be of potential significance interest to the utilitarian; such aesthetic evaluations will form a part (greater or larger, depending on individual preferences) of residents' overall evaluation of the local quality of life.

21. Controls for residence in a rural area are dropped from the analysis used to produce this estimate.

22. It should be acknowledged that there is ambiguity as to the exact scale of "community" respondents had in mind in answering this question about quality of life; persons living in a city or town likely were judging the municipality as a whole, but alternatively some respondents (particularly in larger cities) may have been judging only their immediate residential environments or some sub-set of the city. Likewise, some suburban residents may have conceptualized "community" as an area larger than their residential locality. Persons living outside a municipality presumably were referring to their surrounding area. Nonetheless, it is reasonable to assume that this measure provides a useful estimate of respondents' views of their local environments as places to live.

23. Freeman, "Effects of Sprawl on Neighborhood Ties."

24. Leyden, "Social Capital and the Built Environment."

25. Putnam, *Bowling Alone.*

26. Glaeser and Gottlieb, "Urban Resurgence and the Consumer City."

27. Brueckner and Largey, "Social Interaction and Urban Sprawl." Brueckner and Largey also employ a two-stage least squares model in which several measures of metropolitan-level density are used as instruments for tract level–density. These results show a negative relationship between the resulting instrument and neighborhood sociability and group membership.

28. Dropping other sprawl-related variables from the model, there is a slight inverse, though not statistically significant relationship between central city residence and reduced informal socializing; see appendix II for the full regression table. An alternative model in which we undertake a log transformation of the dependent variable by taking the natural log of (number of times informally socialized + 1) generates similar estimates of commuting time's substantive impact on informal socializing.

29. There is a significant negative relationship between tract density and reported number of friends, but the substantive effect is negligible.

30. This is a measure of membership in sixteen distinct kinds of organizations: fraternal groups, artistic groups, hobby clubs, ethnic organizations, Internet-based groups, religious groups (not churches), youth groups, parent–teacher groups, neighborhood groups, elderly groups, sports groups, veterans' groups, self-help groups, professional groups, charity organizations, and other unclassified groups. (Membership in political organizations is analyzed separately in ch. 7.) This measure was recoded into seven categories, with persons belong to six or more groups collapsed into a single category.

Simulation analysis shows that, controlling for other factors, residents of a tract with a density of 1,000 persons/square mile have a 50.1 percent (49.2%, 50.9%) likelihood of belong to three or more groups, compared to 48.6 percent (47.2%, 49.9%) for residents of a tract with a density of 8,000 persons/square mile.

31. Based on a simplified analysis employing proportion of workers in the neighborhood driving alone to work as the only sprawl-related variable. Using instead a measure of neighborhood age yields similar results.

32. Simulation analysis using a model in which only proportion driving alone to work is included (the other sprawl-related variables are omitted) suggests that controlling for other factors, residents of a neighborhood in which 85 percent of workers are solo commuters have a 57.3 percent (55.5%, 59.0%) likelihood of belonging to a religious congregation, compared to 54.8 percent (52.3, 56.9%) for residents of a neighborhood in which 65 percent of workers are solo commuters.

33. Glaeser and Gottlieb, in "Urban Resurgence and the Consumer City," report similar findings, although, as we shall see in ch. 7, their conclusion that sprawl has no effect on political activism is premature.

34. A worker with a forty-five-minute commute living in a tract with an average commute of thirty minutes is predicted to engaged in 49.1 (47.9, 50.2) instances of informal socializing during a year, compared to 54.3 (52.4, 56.2) for a worker with a fifteen-minute commute living in a tract with an average commute of fifteen minutes.

35. Proper policy response to the existence of such effects is indeterminate; however, to echo an ongoing debate in urban policy scholarship, we might opt to try to make the most-dense areas better places to live, we might opt to encourage dispersion of such areas or to provide assistance to families seeking to move to other areas, or we might do both. See Imbroscio, "Fighting Poverty with Mobility."

36. Increasingly, this has been exactly what has been happening, as increasing numbers of white-collar offices have relocated to suburban locations. See Lang, "Office Sprawl," as well as his *Edgeless Cities*.

37. Similar conclusions obtain if we ask the inverse question: since Americans report higher quality of life in the suburbs, why not embark on a program to empty cities out even further and move as many Americans as possible to a low-density, car-oriented suburb? Two considerations against this proposal present themselves. First, it likely is the case that such a strategy is self-defeating on its own terms. For instance, "quality of life" is likely at least partially a positional good; to say that one's neighborhood is not just "good" but "excellent" suggests that it is *better* than others, and not all neighborhoods can be "excellent" in this sense. Second, such a wave of further suburbanization would likely impose additional costs of the kind already discussed in this chapter, as well as severe environmental costs (see ch. 8).

38. Persky and Wiewel, *When Corporations Leave Town*.

39. See Frank, "Why Is Cost–Benefit Analysis So Controversial?" quote at 93. More generally, see, in the same volume, Sen, "Discipline of Cost–Benefit Analysis."

40. Richardson, "Stupidity of the Cost–Benefit Standard."

41. Burchell et al., *Sprawl Costs*.

42. Levine, *Zoned Out*.

43. Some evidence on the impact of urban-containment policies on neighborhood quality and satisfaction is provided by Nelson, Dawkins, and Sanchez, *Social Impacts of Urban Containment*, 137–46. The authors find evidence of a small but positive impact of containment policies on neighborhood satisfaction and suggest that a very long time horizon may be needed to assess the long-term effects of urban-containment programs.

44. Hahn, "On Some Difficulties of the Utilitarian Economist."

45. See Dixon, "Virtue of Density."

46. This way of stating the issue draws on Jon Elster's discussion of how utilitarians might answer the question of whether the industrial revolution was a good thing for workers; see Elster, "Sour Grapes," 231 ff.

47. Braybrooke and Lindblom, *Strategy of Decision*, 89. Braybrooke reiterates this commitment to "incrementalism" in his *Utilitarianism*; see ch. 2. Conversely, Lindblom in subsequent work undertook the sort of larger-scale comparative evaluation of institutional systems that an incrementalist approach to policy eschews; see especially his *Politics and Markets*.

48. Taylor, *Sources of the Self*, 78–79.

49. On this point, see, among others, Duany, Plater-Zyberk, and Speck, *Suburban Nation*.

50. Elster, "Sour Grapes," 234.

51. Goodin, *Political Theory and Public Policy*, ch. 2.

52. See Kahn, "Does Sprawl Reduce the Black–White Housing Consumption Gap?" As noted in the introduction, Kahn measures sprawl in terms of the percentage of jobs within a metropolitan region located outside a given radius (in this study, 10 miles) of the central business district.

53. Campbell and Marshall, "Utilitarianism's Bad Breath?"

54. This is, in fact, roughly the approach taken by the Transit Cooperative Research Program's *Costs of Sprawl—2000*, which tallies up costs and benefits associated with sprawl and concludes that the benefits are slightly outweighed by the costs, without explaining clearly how different kinds of costs were traded off against different kinds of benefits (or taking account of issues pertaining to the malleability of preferences discussed here). The honest yet fundamentally equivocal conclusion of the report's Executive Summary speaks volumes about the limitations and indeterminacy associated with utilitarian approaches to policy analysis: "Sprawl has benefits that can be measured, and these are reasonably significant. It has more costs that can be measured, and these are more significant. Sprawl has some benefits that cannot be measured empirically; these may be significant. Overall, *from what can be measured*, sprawl has more costs than benefits" (emphasis added) (Burchell et al., *Costs of Sprawl—2000*, 17).

55. Sophisticated utilitarians such as Goodin have recognized these dangers; Goodin now endorses a version of deliberative democracy in which ordinary citizens are called upon to practice "deliberative democracy within"; that is, to practice considering in their own minds differing points of view on a given context, coming to a judgment about what the public interest requires, and then voting for representatives on the basis of that judgment. See Goodin, *Reflective Democracy*. Goodin's agenda overlaps very substantially with nonutilitarian advocates of deliberative democracy and with civic republican concerns about fostering good citizens skilled in thinking about the good of the whole. Within this conception, utilitarianism as such might continue to play two broad roles—guiding policymakers and social planners in making decisions, and serving as a meta-criterion by which citizens might come to judge the public good and the skill of their representatives in advancing it. With respect to policymaking, Henry Richardson in *Democratic Autonomy* has developed a powerful argument for requiring policymakers to include a substantial measure of participatory deliberation in reaching decisions and applying rules, rather than just relying on procedures such as cost–benefit analysis or upon the best judgments of social planners about how well policy changes might affect

citizen's future satisfaction (as endorsed by Goodin in his 1982 work *Political Theory and Public Policy*).

56. One caveat is in order here. Those utilitarians who are persuaded that sprawl involves unacceptable ecological harms (see ch. 8) might come to judge sprawl to be in net terms unacceptable, primarily for that reason. For instance, it is possible that one might apply rigorous cost-benefit methods and arrive at a monetary assessment of the cost of current environmental damage, as well as an estimate of the cost associated with the risk of future damage resulting from global warming. All such estimates would necessarily involve value judgments about the monetary worth of environmental goods, as well as extremely difficult decisions about how to discount future costs and the like.

57. Bailey's interesting defense of utilitarianism recognizes this point; his strategy is to argue that given plausible assumptions about a social world that resembles our own, the rules and institutional structures that utilitarianism would recommend will produce a set of social conditions that would preclude the possibility of utilitarianism recommending absurd, intuitively wrong courses of action. These institutions turn out to be something resembling liberal democracy in a relatively egalitarian form, and they rest on Bailey's derivation (from the principle of utility) of a norm of non-exploitation (i.e., agents cannot be required to give all their resources away to maximize the utilities of others). Bailey thus suggests that *once* ideal institutions have been established, *then* policymakers can focus on marginal analysis (Bailey, *Utilitarianism, Institutions, and Justice*).

58. This does not mean that we all are, or should be, unconditional consequentialists, even with respect to public policy; see Taylor, "Diversity of Goods." Taylor nonetheless acknowledges the importance of consequentialist and utilitarian reasoning as a necessary *part* of our public life.

59. This point is especially well made by Bailey, *Utilitarianism, Institutions, and Justice*.

Chapter 4

1. Downs's analysis is presented most thoroughly in chapter 13 of Burchell et al., *Costs of Sprawl—2000*.

2. For more on this theme, and the broader relationship between social justice, geography, and urban life, see the collected works of Harvey, especially *Social Justice and the City*; and *Justice, Nature, and the Geography of Difference*; Smith, *Geography and Social Justice*; Mitchell, *Right to the City*; and Lynch, *Good City Form*, ch. 12.

3. For evocative description of such ghettoes, see Richard Sennett's discussion of the Renaissance Jewish ghetto in Venice, in his *Flesh and Stone*.

4. See Smith, *Geography and Social Justice*, ch. 8.

5. Marx, "German Ideology." For a defense of liberal concepts of justice against Marxist critiques, see Kymlicka, *Liberalism, Community and Culture*, ch. 5.

6. While Rawls's *Theory of Justice* is the canonical statement of his view, much contemporary discussion among philosophers focuses on the revised view set forth in *Justice as Fairness*.

7. Rawls, *Theory of Justice*, 29. All page references to *A Theory of Justice* are from the revised 1999 edition.

8. Dworkin, *Sovereign Virtue*.

9. For related recent discussions of how Rawlsian ideas about justice might be applied to contemporary metropolitan areas, see King, "Democratic Hopes in the Polycentric City"; Shelby, "Justice, Deviance, and the Dark Ghetto"; and Fainstein, "Planning and the Just City." The standard treatment of metropolitan inequalities in the urbanist literature is Dreier, Mollenkopf, and Swanstrom, *Place Matters*; see also Briggs, *Geography of Opportunity*; Altshuler, Morrill, Wolman, and Mitchell, *Governance and Opportunity in Metropolitan America*; and Orfield, *Metropolitics*, and *American Metropolitics*.

10. Rawls, *Theory of Justice*, 53.

11. I deliberately set aside here the complex question of immigration and freedom to travel across borders, despite its practical importance in the United States and worldwide. A major feature and limitation of Rawls's theory of social justice is that it is set within the assumed context of a discrete nation–state and hence has limited leverage for treating what Seyla Benhabib terms "the rights of others." See Benhabib's very critical discussion of Rawls on this point in *Rights of Others*. But this limitation may be intrinsic to the idea of social justice; David Miller thus argues that "social justice" is inherently a project for nation–states. See Miller, *Principles of Social Justice*.

12. See, e.g., Moe and Wilkie, *Changing Places*.

13. The following discussion is inspired by a session on justice and cities at the 2002 Annual Meetings of the American Political Science Association in Boston, organized by Loren King, at which I was a panelist. Fiss was also a panelist, and Young participated as an audience member.

14. On the idea of racial stigma and its application to the current condition of African Americans, see Loury, *Anatomy of Racial Inequality*.

15. Fiss, *Way Out*.

16. Young, *Inclusion and Democracy*, 204–10.

17. Rawls, *Theory of Justice*, 179.

18. Rawls, *Theory of Justice*, 63.

19. See Hochschild and Scovronick, *American Dream and the Public Schools*, 52–76; Anyon, *Radical Possibilities*.

20. Alexander and Salmon, "Warranting Failure." On proportion of public school revenue generated by local property taxes, see National Center for Education Statistics, *Condition of Education 2008*, appendix I, table 34–2.

21. Young, *Inclusion and Democracy*, 207.

22. See Porter, "New Strategies for Inner City Development"; see also Grogan and Proscio, *Comeback Cities*.

23. See, among others, Fishman, *Bourgeois Utopias*.

24. Tiebout, "Pure Theory of Local Expenditure."

25. Cannavó, *Working Landscape*, 110.

26. King, "Democracy and City Life," quote on 111.

27. Imbroscio, "Fighting Poverty with Mobility."

28. King, "Democracy and City Life," seems to suggest that the hegemony of suburban forms of life can be traced to unjust and problematic political decision-making processes in contemporary metropolitan areas.

29. While Rawls's discussion of political economy in *A Theory of Justice* deliberately gives "efficiency" a very subordinate role, he does appeal to the "advantages of efficiency"

in making the case for markets as allocative instruments (238–42). Efficiency is not Rawls's priority, but he certainly counts it as an advantage.

30. On the claim that healthy metropolitan regions should exhibit a variety of neighborhoods oriented toward various preferences or conceptions of the good life, see Brower, *Good Neighborhoods*.

31. Rawls describes the move from the original position to concrete application as a "four-stage" sequence involving selection of principles of justice, drafting of an appropriate constitution, consideration of specific laws by the legislature, and application of those laws by public officials. Knowledge of specific facts about the world and particular persons increases at each succeeding stage. See Rawls, *Theory of Justice*, 171–76.

32. Rawls, *Theory of Justice*, 78.

33. Gainsborough, *Fenced Off*. See also Thomas, *United States of Suburbia*.

34. Rawls's conception of community—termed by Michael Sandel a "sentimental" conception"—can, however, be usefully distinguished from the stronger, "constitutive" concept of community favored by Sandel: "Rawls' account is individualist in the sense of assuming the antecedent individuation of the subjects of co-operation, whose actual motivations may include benevolent aims as well as selfish ones. As a result, the good of community for Rawls consists not only in the direct benefits of social co-operation but also in the quality of motivations and ties of sentiment that may attend this co-operation and be enhanced in the process" (*Liberalism and the Limits of Justice*, 149).

35. Rawls, *Theory of Justice*, 457.

36. Rawls, *Theory of Justice*, 458.

37. Rawls, *Theory of Justice*, 461.

38. Rawls, *Theory of Justice*, 462.

39. Rawls, *Theory of Justice*, 463.

40. Hence, Rawls, in the penultimate paragraph of *Justice as Fairness*: "Those who grow up in a society well ordered by justice as fairness, who have a rational plan of life, and who also know, or reasonably believe, that everyone else has an effective sense of justice, have sufficient reason founded on their own good (rather than on justice) to comply with just institutions. This is not to say that they do not also have reasons of justice so to act" (202).

41. A point well demonstrated in a different context by Walzer, *Spheres of Justice*.

42. For discussion of how Social Security and other programs affecting the elderly reshaped norms and practices of citizenship, see Campbell, *How Policies Make Citizens*.

43. Tocqueville, *Democracy in America*, Vol. 1, ch. 9, 278.

44. Tocqueville, *Democracy in America*, Vol. 1, ch. 9. On "liberal virtues," see Macedo, *Liberal Virtues*; and Galston, *Liberal Purposes*.

45. Habermas, *Between Facts and Norms*, ch. 8, esp. 373–79.

46. Bickford, "Constructing Inequality," quote on 356.

47. King, "Democratic Hopes in the Polycentric City," 215.

48. Bickford, "Constructing Inequality," 371.

49. Author's analysis of the SCCBS 2000 U.S. Census data. Metropolitan tracts with more than 50 percent of residents living in non-urbanized areas excluded.

50. Jargowsky, "Sprawl, Concentration of Poverty, and Urban Inequality," 57, table 3.2.

51. See Dreier, Mollenkopf, and Swanstrom, *Place Matters*, 36–53, for a helpful overview of central city–suburb income discrepancies between 1960 and 1999.

52. SCCBS and 2000 U.S. Census data. Author's analysis. Metropolitan tracts with more than 50 percent of residents living in non-urbanized areas excluded.

53. Wilson, *When Work Disappears*.

54. Thus, see Wilson, *When Work Disappears*; Kantor and Brenzel, "Urban Education and the Truly Disadvantaged"; and for an overview, powell, "Sprawl, Fragmentation, and the Persistence of Racial Inequality."

55. Powell, "Sprawl, Fragmentation, and the Persistence of Racial Inequality," 89. For a related general discussion, see Ihlanfeldt, "Geography of Economic and Social Opportunity in Metropolitan Areas." Highly influential and still instructive older accounts of the relationship between concentrated poverty, racial segregation, and life outcomes include Massey and Denton, *American Apartheid*, and Jargowsky, *Poverty and Place*. For a recent, methodologically sophisticated demonstration of substantial neighborhood effects on individual outcomes, see Galster, Marcotte, Mandell, Wolman, and Augustine, "Importance of Neighborhood Poverty during Childhood on Fertility, Education, and Earnings Outcomes"; and for a recent theoretical exposition of the idea of a "poverty trap," see Durlauf, "Groups, Social Influences, and Inequality."

56. Rawls, *Theory of Justice*, 63, 92.

57. Orfield, *Metropolitics*, 39.

58. In fiscal year 2007, local government accounted for 43.9 percent of school funding and states for 47.6 percent; the remainder was provided by federal funds. U.S. Department of Education, "Revenues and Expenditure for Public Elementary and Secondary Education: School Year 2006–07 (Fiscal Year 2007)," National Center for Education Statistics, 2009. See also Biddle and Berliner, "Unequal School Funding in the United States."

59. Arroyo, *Funding Gap*.

60. Biddle and Berliner, "Unequal School Funding."

61. See Orfield, *American Metropolitics*.

62. Orfield, *Metropolitics*, 45.

63. Arroyo, *Funding Gap*. Again, there are wide variations among states in the size of this disparity; in Alaska, Minnesota, and New Jersey, per-pupil spending in poorer districts remains substantially higher than in richer districts, even after adjusting for the enhanced needs of poor students.

64. Orfield usefully summarizes an array of factors, each confirmed by a large body of empirical sociological research, that work in depressed neighborhoods to affect life chances: "Whether poor or middle-class, young people who live amid concentrated poverty are far more likely to become pregnant as teenagers, drop out of high school, and remain jobless than their counterparts in socioeconomically mixed neighborhoods. In the social isolation of concentrated poverty, distinctive speech patterns develop that make interaction with mainstream society difficult and complicate educational progress and employment success. Many urban employers believe that the people who live in distressed neighborhoods are an unsuitable work force. In neighborhoods lacking successful middle-class role models, [it is] gang leaders, drug dealers, and other antisocial figures [who] are often the only local residents with money and status. . . . These factors interact with anger, frustration, isolation, boredom and hopelessness and create a synergy of disproportionate levels of crime, violence, and other antisocial behavior" (*American Metropolitics*, 54). On the need to link efforts to equalize educational opportunity with a broader spatial equity and anti-poverty agenda, see Anyon, *Radical Possibilities*.

65. Fishman, *Bourgeois Utopias*.

66. Fishman, *Bourgeois Utopias*.

67. Fogelson, *Bourgeois Nightmares*.

68. On this point, see also Dreier, Mollenkopf, and Swanstrom, *Place Matters*, 36–37.

69. This is not to say that suburbanization in the United States is exclusively an upper-class and upper-middle class affair; as Dolores Hayden has shown, working-class Americans also came to aspire to the idea of the suburban home and by the start of the twentieth century were starting "mail order" and self-built suburbs that took advantage of mass production of housing units and new public transit technologies. See Hayden, *Building Suburbia*.

70. Nivola, *Laws of the Landscape*, 26–27.

71. Orfield, *American Metropolitics*.

72. See Glaeser and Kahn, "Sprawl and Urban Growth" and Kneebone, "Job Sprawl Revisited." See also Williamson, Imbroscio, and Alperovitz, *Making a Place for Community*; and Rae, *City*.

73. Downs, *New Visions for Metropolitan America*, 20.

74. Levine, *Zoned Out*.

75. For elaboration, see Fischel, *Homevoter Hypothesis*, 229–31. Fischel's Tiebout-inspired view of the effects of investing significant powers in localities likely to be dominated by local homeowners is generally positive (particularly with respect to education funding and environmental quality), but he acknowledges that not-in-my-backyard stances against higher-density development exacerbates sprawl. Fischel has recommended making home equity insurance available to suburban homeowners to reduce their incentive to engage in exclusionary zoning; see Fischel, "An Economic History of Zoning and a Cure for Its Exclusionary Effects," esp. 335–36. For an extensive and persuasive critique of Fischel's (and Tiebout's) perspective, see Schragger, "Consuming Government." From the standpoint of egalitarian conceptions of justice, Schragger's most fundamental point contra Fischel is that "the losers in the interlocal competition for low-cost, high-tax-based homeowners—the urban poor, racial minorities, families in search of affordable housing, the elderly—are nowhere to be found in [Fischel's] account of local power" ("Consuming Government," 1826).

76. There have been notable exceptions, particularly challenges in the 1970s to exclusionary zoning in Mount Laurel, New Jersey. As Joseph Singer notes, however, "most states have refused to adopt the Mount Laurel doctrine" (*Introduction to Property*, 627–30).

77. Federal Budget of the United States 2009, Analytical Reports, p. 289, table 19-1; Summary Budget Report.

78. See Williamson et al, *Making a Place for Community*, 74–79; see also Nivola, *Laws of the Landscape*. For an exhaustive analysis of the impact of free parking and parking requirements on travel and residential patterns, see Shoup, *High Cost of Free Parking*.

79. Hoene and Pagano, "Fend-for-Yourself-Federalism," 36–42; Hoene and Pagano, "City Fiscal Conditions in 2009," Figure 3.

80. Katz and Rogers, "Next Urban Agenda," 191.

81. Persky and Wiewel, *When Corporations Leave Town*, 73–97. Note that this estimate of the distribution of externalities is conservative in the sense that it underestimates the proportion of real harm being borne by lower-income households. Persky and Wiewel follow the economist's convention of assigning lower monetary value to externalities

borne by lower-income households than those borne by wealthier households, since such households would not be as willing to pay as much to avoid such externalities as would more-affluent households.

82. Persky and Wiewel (in *When Corporations Leave Town*) find that urban residents bear 96 percent of the total negative externalities created by job sprawl (again, largely because of the spatial mismatch problem).

83. The privileged position of business in the overwhelming majority of cities is one of the best established empirical propositions in U.S. political science. See, among many others, Peterson, *City Limits*; Elkin, *City and Regime in the American Republic*; Stone, *Regime Politics*; Imbroscio, *Reconstructing City Politics*.

84. Buchanan, "Principles of Urban Fiscal Strategy." See Frug, *City Making*, 167–73, for a critical discussion of Buchanan and related thinkers.

85. Helling, "Transportation, Land Use, and the Impact of Sprawl," 130.

86. Raphael and Stoll, "Can Boosting Minority Car-Ownership Rates Narrow Inter-Racial Employment Gaps?"

87. See Stoll, "Spatial Mismatch and Job Sprawl," 127–48.

88. Glaeser and Kahn, "Sprawl and Urban Growth." Quote from article abstract.

89. For a thoughtful discussion about how to increase the access of poor people to cars paratransit, and functional mass transit, see Blumenberg and Waller, "Long Journey to Work," 197–225.

90. Burchell et al., *Costs of Sprawl—2000*, 408.

91. Burchell et al., *Costs of Sprawl—2000*, 425.

92. See Bruegmann, *Sprawl*, 96–98.

93. See Downs's "How Is Suburban Sprawl Related to Urban Decline?" for a clarification of his argument. See also Burchell, Downs, McCann, and Mukherji, *Sprawl Costs*.

94. See Ewing, Pendall, and Chen, "Measuring Sprawl and Its Impact," for a sharp critique of Downs's methodology.

95. Jargowsky, "Sprawl, Concentration of Poverty, and Urban Inequality."

96. Yang and Jargowsky, "Suburban Development and Economic Segregation in the 1990s."

97. Pendall and Carruthers, "Does Density Exacerbate Income Segregation?"

98. Pendall and Carruthers, "Does Density Exacerbate Income Segregation?"

99. Berube, "Two Steps Back."

100. See Downs, *New Visions for Metropolitan America*.

101. For related discussions, see Frug, "Legal Technology of Exclusion"; and powell, "Structural Racism and Spatial Jim Crow," 41–65.

102. Davis, *Planet of Slums*.

103. Basic overviews of the community land trust concept are provided by Finkel, "Affordable Forever," and Fireside, "Burlington Bursts the Affordable Housing Bubble"; see also Williamson, Imbroscio, and Alperovitz, *Making a Place for Community*, 249–63. For interesting critical case studies, see DeFilippis, *Unmaking Goliath*, 87–112, and Bourassa, "Community Land Trust as a Highway Mitigation Tool."

104. Indeed, some scholars have argued that sprawling metropolitan areas can benefit racial minorities by reducing homeownership costs both at the fringe and in urban neighborhoods. See Kahn, "Does Sprawl Reduce the Black-White Housing Consumption Gap?" From the point of view of liberal egalitarianism, the reduction in the black-white

homeownership rate, Kahn reports, is not compelling justification for continuing sprawl as a socio-spatial pattern. (In metropolitan areas with a higher proportion of jobs located at least 10 miles from the geographic core, Kahn finds that the ratio of white-to-black homeownership is roughly 1.4 to 1, compared to 1.5 to 1 in metropolitan areas where employment is more compact.) First, households able to more easily acquire a house in sprawling areas are very likely not the "least well off" in Rawlsian terms. Second, providing low-income or minority households an "exit" option from inner cities is fundamentally different from reducing the place-based inequalities that make central cities relatively undesirable in the first place. If social justice requires ensuring that where you happen to grow up does not inordinately shape one's life chances, then the priority should be on increasing employment and quality of life in those urban neighborhoods that are now the least well off, not on increasing employment and housing on the perimeter. The latter strategy may provide modest benefits likely to be claimed by the relatively well off but does nothing to undercut core inequalities between neighborhoods.

105. See Downs, *Growth Management and Affordable Housing.*

106. See Williamson, Imbroscio, and Alperovitz, *Making a Place for Community*, ch. 11, for discussion. For studies of the impact of the urban-growth boundary on housing prices in Portland, see Phillips and Goodstein, "Growth Management and Housing Prices," and Jun, "Effect of Portland's Urban Growth Boundary on Housing Prices." Jun uses disaggregated data to show that the urban-growth boundary itself has no significant effect on housing prices.

107. Glaeser and Kahn, "Sprawl and Urban Growth"; Gordon and Richardson make the same suggestion in "Are Compact Cities a Desirable Planning Goal?"

Chapter 5

1. Constant, "Liberty of the Ancients Compared with That of the Moderns"; Berlin, "Two Concepts of Liberty."

2. Fishman, *Bourgeois Utopias.*

3. See Popenoe, *Suburban Environment*, ch. 3, for qualitative description of a Swedish suburb in which apartment buildings are the most prominent feature.

4. To be sure, homeownership has its critics as well; writers such as Richard Sennett and Susan Bickford suggest that the private home has been overloaded with unrealistic expectations for all-encompassing fulfillment, at the same time that "public man" has withered. See, e.g., Sennett, *Fall of Public Man.*

5. See Stier, "Liberal Virtue/Communitarian Virtue."

6. Sandel, *Democracy's Discontent*; see also Philip Pettit's useful essay, "Reworking Republicanism."

7. Including Rawls himself; see *Political Liberalism* and *Justice as Fairness.*

8. Dworkin, *Sovereign Virtue*, 233.

9. This example is raised by Peter Berkowitz in his critique of Peter Singer's utilitarianism; see Berkowitz, "Other People's Mothers."

10. Galston, "Political Economy and the Politics of Virtue," 85.

11. Stier, "Liberal Virtue/Communitarian Virtue." See also Macedo, *Liberal Virtues*, and Smith, *Civic Ideals.*

12. Rawls himself states: "In a well-governed state only a small fraction of persons may devote much of their time to politics. There are many other forms of human good" (*Theory of Justice*, 200).

13. While it is correct to state that realizing the difference principle almost certainly would require a robust degree of redistribution, it should be cautioned that Rawls is *not* a defender of the welfare state as traditionally conceived. Rather, he calls for a system of "property-owning democracy," in which widespread initial distributions of wealth and property, not after-the-fact redistribution via the tax system, would play the central role in establishing social equality. See *Justice as Fairness*, 140 ff.

14. Putnam, *Making Democracy Work*.

15. Wirth, "Urbanism as a Way of Life," 143–69.

16. Baumgartner, *Moral Order of a Suburb*, 102–7.

17. These questions pertain to trust of people in general, trust of neighbors, trust of coworkers, trust of fellow congregants, trust of employees in local stores, and trust of the police.

18. However, when employing a fixed-effects model (with controls for each community sample), the proportion of residents driving alone to work in each tract emerges as a positive predictor of higher trust.

19. Ninety-five percent confidence intervals for these estimates are (28.2%, 30.7%) for the shorter commute scenario and (33.7%, 38.0%) for the longer commute scenario.

20. Ninety-five percent confidence intervals for predicted likelihood of being in the high-trust group are (26.2%, 29.1%) for the higher-density, urban setting and (31.3%, 33.5%) for the lower-density, suburban setting.

21. Rahn, Yoon, et al., "Geographies of Trust." Based on analysis of a 2002 survey of 49 communities conducted by the Knight Foundation. Specifically, the researchers measured "sprawl" by tallying the proportion of workers (excluding those using public transit) with commuting times of 45 minutes or longer within each respondent's county, or in some cases, the respondent's city.

22. Bickford, "Constructing Inequality," 358.

23. Young, *Justice and the Politics of Difference*, 238–39.

24. Among nonwhites without a college degree, the sprawl-related variables are not significant predictors of attitudes toward immigrants. For this group, the proportion of Hispanics and the education level in the census tract are the most salient contextual predictors of attitudes toward immigrants, with negative attitudes more prevalent in tracts with fewer college graduates and more Hispanics.

25. Specifically, a resident of a tract built in 1950 with 8,000 persons/square mile is predicted in simulation analysis to have a 18.0 percent (16.7%, 19.3%) likelihood of supporting book censorship, compared to 20.8 percent (19.7%, 21.9%) for a resident of a tract built in 1980 with 1,000 persons/square mile.

26. Bickford, "Constructing Inequality," 356, 362.

27. Bickford, "Constructing Inequality," 356, 362, 363, 369.

28. Bickford, "Constructing Inequality," 363.

29. Kohn, *Brave New Neighborhoods*, 8–9.

30. Low, *Behind the Gates*, 231.

31. Gainsborough, *Fenced Off*.

32. Walks, "Place of Residence, Party Preferences, and Political Attitudes in Canadian Cities and Suburbs." Note that Walks operationalizes what he terms "inner city" residence in terms of the age of neighborhoods, not municipal boundaries, with the oldest, innermost tier of neighborhoods classified as "inner city" and the youngest, outermost tier classified as "outer suburb." In this sense, Walks's approach parallels the measure of "neighborhood age" used in the present study.

33. Question wording is reported in the Social Capital Community Benchmark Survey codebook.

34. This presumption is supported by evidence on how conservatives think differently than liberals about distributive justice presented in Bartels, *Unequal Democracy*, ch. 5.

35. In the multivariate analyses, I convert the five-tier measure of political ideology in the SCCBS into a two-tier variable categorizing respondents as either "liberal" or "not liberal," with respondents calling themselves either moderately or very liberal grouped into the "liberal" category. I then conduct a logit analysis of the resultant variable. This procedure produces similar substantive results as an ordered logit analysis of the original five-tiered variable but is a more efficient estimate; detailed analysis shows that the sprawl-related variables have greater utility in predicting whether someone is a liberal or not than whether one is moderately conservative as opposed to very conservative. Note also that respondents who volunteered "something else" in response to the survey question (just under 1% of the sample) are excluded from this analysis.

36. The findings reported here also hold when including controls for individual quality-of-life evaluations, and also for neighborhood residential stability. I omit quality-of-life evaluation (positive quality-of-life evaluations are correlated with greater conservatism) because its effect on ideology (controlling for other factors) was not found to be statistically significant. Including a measure of neighborhood residential stability in the model reduces the effect associated with neighborhood age, with residential stability appearing as a positive predictor of increased liberalism. Because the theoretical linkage between greater local residential stability (which is generally higher in suburbs) and greater liberalism is not clear, I omit this variable from the reported results.

37. Based on comparing a tract with 65 percent solo drivers that was built in 1950 with a tract of 85 percent solo drivers that was built in 1980.

38. For full discussion, see Williamson, "Sprawl, Spatial Location, and Politics." This basic pattern also held in 2008, with metropolitan counties with older housing stock and less dependence on cars being more likely to support Barack Obama, controlling for other factors. The size of this effect appears to have been smaller than in 2000 and 2004, however. As has been widely noted, Obama did substantially better than John Kerry in numerous suburban counties nationwide.

39. I am indebted to Peter Hall for this example, which has been empirically verified by Lee, Farrell, and Link, "Revisiting the Contact Hypothesis." The authors find that increased exposure to homeless populations is consistently linked to more sympathetic attitudes toward the homeless.

40. 2006 Social Capital Community Survey conducted by the Saguaro Seminar on Civic Engagement at the Kennedy School of Government, Harvard University. Summary results available at http://www.hks.harvard.edu/saguaro/2006sccs.htm.

41. These estimates are based on models excluding controls for county partisan context. For sub-samples of low-income persons and for persons planning to leave their community

(excluding students), neighborhood age and proportion driving alone are jointly significant past the $p < .002$ level as predictors of reduced liberalism; among persons relatively dissatisfied with their neighborhoods, the effect is significant at the $p < .01$ level. In models including controls for county partisan context, the impact of sprawl-related variables on ideology is significant at roughly the $p < .01$ level for low-income residents and for persons planning to move, and (when dropping nonsignificant contextual variables) at the $p < .02$ level for persons dissatisfied with their neighborhood.

42. Among national sample respondents to the 2006 SCCS, 47.1 percent of persons with household income under $30,000 wanted to move, compared to 30.2 percent of persons with income over $75,000; 75.8 percent of persons rating their local quality of life as "fair" or "poor" wished to move, compared to 17.8 percent of those who rated their local quality of life as "excellent"; 73.6 percent of nonstudents planning to move within five years wished to leave, compared to 28.0 percent of those planning to stay (weighted summary statistics). These figures confirm the assumption that income, quality-of-life evaluations, and future plans are reasonable indicators of the likelihood an individual resides in a neighborhood that matches their preferences, in the absence of a direct measure (in the 2000 SCCBS).

43. Further evidence that self-selection is part of the story is provided by the fact that liberals *like* urban areas better than conservatives—or, more precisely, dislike such areas less than conservatives. If we examine the community quality-of-life evaluations of respondents who are "somewhat" or "very" liberal, we find that central city residence, older neighborhoods, and less car-dependent places are all significantly correlated with less community satisfaction. As a descriptive matter, among SCCBS respondents living in a central city neighborhood in which the median housing unit was built prior to 1960 and population density is greater than 8,000 persons/square mile, self-described liberals (n = 1,533) have a 28.3 percent likelihood of rating local community quality of life as "excellent," compared to 22.3 percent for self-described conservatives (n = 994). Conversely, among respondents living in a suburban neighborhood whose median housing unit was built after 1980 and with population density less than 2000 persons/ square mile, 54.2 percent of conservatives (n = 1,127) rate their local quality of life as "excellent," compared to 51.0 percent of liberals (n = 441). Put another way, the gap between quality-of-life evaluations for suburban vis-à-vis urban places, while very substantial regardless of political ideology, is notably larger among conservatives compared to liberals. This might lead us to conclude that part of the evident connection between sprawl and conservatism likely reflects conservatives' stronger preferences for suburban locations.

44. Huckfeldt, "Social Contexts," 117, quoted in Gainsborough, *Fenced Off*, 62.

45. Self-selection also surely plays an important role in explaining Gainsborough's finding that suburban residence was by the 1980s and 1990s strongly correlated with political conservatism, but not in the 1960s. At a minimum, it is unquestionable that white flight from cities is responsible in large measure for the increased relationship between suburban residence and conservatism; the journalist Bill Bishop has recently produced evidence that the proportion of whites living in strong Republican counties increased from under 25 percent in 1970 to 30 percent in 2000, while the proportion of whites living in strong Democratic counties fell from 25 percent to 18 percent over that same time period. See Bishop, *Big Sort*, 53. The focus of Bishop's book is the increasing self-

selection of Americans into neighborhoods of the like-minded and the effect this has on political polarization; see pp. 249–75 for an interesting discussion of how this development has affected political campaigning by the major parties.

But this "big sort" was not simply a measure of individuals making individual decisions to fulfill newfound preferences for suburban living. Rather, this shift was set in motion largely as a result of the epochal conflicts over the racial desegregation of urban public space, public facilities, and public schools in the 1960s. The "new suburban historians" such as Kevin Kruse (in Atlanta), Matthew Lassiter (in Charlotte), and Robert Self (in Oakland) have shown in detail how whites responded to legal gains for African Americans by moving to suburbs, establishing exclusionary barriers, and justifying this arrangement via race-neutral appeals to freedom of association and individual rights. This historical perspective is vital in showing that suburbs were in many cases *created* precisely to provide a venue for the practice of race-based exclusion, in a manner that did not run afoul of federal law mandating integration of public institutions. To speak of white flight as a simple matter of individual preferences being exercised is thus misleading.

On the new suburban history, see Kruse, *White Flight*; Lassiter, *Silent Majority*; Self, *American Babylon*. See also Kruse and Sugrue, *New Suburban History*. I discuss these books and their implications for political scientists further in a recent review essay, "Bringing History Back In? Assessing the New Suburban History."

46. Rawls himself has often been interpreted as a theorist of liberty as noninterference; this is how Pettit characterizes Rawls's view in his *Republicanism*, 50. But as Samuel Freeman stresses, Rawls's conception of liberty does not extend to untrammeled rights to control and use property, own capital, or reshape the landscape, and in this sense is markedly distinct from libertarian accounts of liberty as noninterference. Freeman, *Rawls*. Rawls's own account (in *Justice as Fairness*) of justice as fairness, in which "no priority is assigned to liberty as such, as if the exercise of something called 'liberty' had a preeminent value and were the main, if not the sole, end of social and political justice," is clearly at odds with libertarian accounts of justice. However, the comment (in the following sentence) that "there is a general presumption against imposing legal and other restrictions on conduct without a sufficient reason" might be read as implying a commitment to minimizing interference with liberty to that which is either socially necessary or needed to sustain the principles of justice. Rawls, *Justice as Fairness*.

47. In this sense, the question of suburban preferences—or more broadly, desires to live in a neighborhood insulated from social problems—is analogous to the ambiguities in the difference principle noted by G. A. Cohen. Cohen argues that if the difference principle is simply a public morality and does not also regulate individual choices, the principle will wind up being consistent with very large inequalities, if that is the price necessary to motivate the social contributions of the most talented. One can extend this point to dovetail with the question of sprawl as follows: suppose the most talented will work hard and make a maximal contribution to society (thereby improving the well-being of everyone, including the least well off) only *if* they are rewarded by being allowed to live in tranquil neighborhoods far removed from poverty and other social problems. If that demand is honored, however, the inevitable result will be systemic inequalities correlated with place. Justice as fairness, according to this view, thus *requires* concern with both private ethical stances and public morality if it is to yield results consistent with

substantive egalitarianism. See Cohen, *If You're an Egalitarian, Why Are You So Rich?* For a useful response to Cohen's argument, see J. Cohen, "Taking People as They Are?" In a somewhat different vein, Simone Chambers points out that the problem of selfish preferences within a just order is a problem internal to the ideal theory of justice as fairness; the real political obstacle to the conception, however, are not individual choices but the way the now-dominant "political ethos" justifies sharp inequalities ("Politics of Equality," 87). In the case of sprawl, this manifests itself as widespread approval of, or at least acceptance of, the sorting of income classes into separate neighborhoods.

48. Cohen, "Taking People As They Are," addresses precisely this point, and goes beyond Rawls in acknowledging that egalitarianism sometimes must challenge inegalitarian social norms directly; Rawls's own strategy was to rely on the strong assumption that institutional changes would produce a social ethos supportive of liberal egalitarian norms. As Cohen notes however, this strategy may not always succeed.

49. Samuel Freeman emphasizes that land use regulations are wholly consistent with Rawls's account of liberty. Freeman, *Rawls*, 57.

50. Downs, *New Visions for Metropolitan America*.

51. The question of whether more radical policies aimed at challenging the sorting of rich and poor into different neighborhoods might violate Rawls's commitment to basic liberties merits further exploration. In Rawls's fully developed views, basic liberties are recognized as "basic" by virtue of their crucial role in upholding the two "moral powers," that of having a sense of justice and of having a sense of the good (being reasonable and being rational). Samuel Freeman usefully specifies that Rawls's fully considered view is that basic liberties can only be restricted for the sake of other basic liberties (or in cases where their exercise has no relationship to the relevant moral powers); such basic liberties cannot be restricted for the sake of advancing distributive justice (see Freeman, *Rawls*). Nonbasic liberties, however, can be so regulated, either to advance distributive justice or to realize some "public political" value. What is ruled out is restricting liberty (basic or nonbasic) for the sake of advancing a religious or perfectionist principle, or on sheer aesthetic grounds, or to prevent offense. A key question then is whether the right to live in any residential location the market makes available and that one is willing to pay for is to be considered a basic liberty on which the demands of distributive justice cannot intrude.

Consider first the right to own property, explicitly defended by Rawls. Right to own personal property counts as a basic liberty, because no one could reasonably exercise their moral powers if their living space was subject to invasion by public authorities. But right to use one's land in any way one sees fit regardless of its impact on the environment or neighbors does not similarly count as a basic liberty; the public can reasonably regulate use of property while still respecting property's role in providing individuals space and freedom to exercise their moral powers, provided the regulation is based on a "public reason" (such as environmental protection). Indeed, the analysis here suggests that the case for such policy efforts (from a Rawlsian point of view) is even stronger; regulation of land use and the commercial housing market is required not just to uphold generic public purposes, but the second principle of justice itself.

But consider an alternative defense of sprawl on liberty grounds. We have emphasized here that the sorting of income classes into geographically distinct areas, and the impact this has on equal opportunity, is problematic from an egalitarian perspective.

But what if the defender of this pattern of sorting appeals not to a supposed right to use property free of state regulation, or to a presumption of noninterference with real estate markets, but rather to *freedom of association*? We are free to form families and to choose our own friends and join our own clubs and political parties, freedoms that clearly count as basic liberties for Rawls. Why should we not also be free to choose who we want to live near? Such freedom is clearly very significantly related to the use of our moral powers. It seems objectionable to tell co-religionists they cannot live in proximity with one another, ethnic immigrants that they cannot form local enclaves, or young academics that they cannot congregate in residences within walking distance of taverns and coffeehouses; indeed, it seems objectionable to think that the state should be regulating such choices at all. Why then cannot affluent golfers, or those with a passion for monitoring their stock investments, also congregate near one another? Should not freedom of association protect the rights of the rich to live near one another?

The Rawlsian might respond by saying that individuals should be free to choose where to live within the context of a metropolitan structure that is itself just. But this begs the question of what counts as a just metropolitan structure. If we count freedom of association as a basic liberty, and count freedom to live near who one chooses as part of that freedom of association, and we apply the priority of a scheme of basic liberties over distributive justice, a legislature seeking to apply Rawlsian principles of justice to the construction of a just metropolitan area might reason as follows: Justice requires us to first establish the basic liberties, and this includes freedom of association and the right to live near who one chooses. So the laws must be organized so as to allow people to live near who they want, with no attempt to encourage or discourage the formation of economically (and racially) integrated neighborhoods. After this sorting process has taken place, then we can apply principles of distributive justice to ensure that the impact of neighborhood residence on equal opportunity is minimal. This may take the form of progressive taxation of better-off neighborhoods, providing public goods of equal quality to all neighborhoods, ensuring that no neighborhood employs exclusionary zoning to keep undesirables out (here we assume that in a conflict between freedom of association, which may include freedom to exclude, and individuals' freedom of movement, justice will side with freedom of individual movement). In particular, steps will be taken to ensure that neighborhood schools and police protection are of equal quality across the metropolitan area.

The problem with this line of reasoning is the same as the problem with broader keep-the-sprawl-and-redistribute-the-benefits approaches: it appeals to a veritable sociological impossibility. It is not plausible to think that if the poor and rich are spatially segregated, that schools attended by poor children will afford them the same opportunity as those attended by rich children. (This outcome could be avoided by an extensive system of cross-neighborhood busing, but that solution is only partial, unless we also ban private schooling, which is unlikely.) Other neighborhood effects also may come into play in shaping life expectations and sense of possibility, and hence equality of opportunity, available to children in richer and poorer areas. Beyond this, as we have seen in this chapter, it appears sociologically highly unlikely that residents of richer (suburban) areas segregated from poorer areas will develop the sense of solidarity and fraternity needed to uphold and support politically the demands of egalitarian justice. In short, we may predict that given reasonable assumptions about the motivations and behaviors of privileged groups in real-world settings, permitting the sorting of classes into distinct geographic areas would in time replicate most or all of the sources of inequality now visible in American metropolitan areas—unequal schools, unequal public goods, unequal safety, and limited, ineffective effort to correct those inequalities.

If this account is correct, it presents a problem for Rawlsian approaches to justice: the requirement of freedom of association, if interpreted to include unconditional freedom to live near who one wishes, might seem to place a very significant prior constraint on the ability of legislatures to organize metropolitan areas in such a way as to minimize the impact of place on life opportunities. Rawlsians might respond in one of three ways: by arguing that freedom of association does not include freedom to live near similar or like-minded people and that the state can legitimately aim to prevent the formation of such spatial segregation; by acknowledging that the priority of liberty over distributive justice (at least in some cases) needs to be rethought; or by accepting the prior constraint and seeking to build relatively just metropolitan institutions that take for granted that rich and poor will live in different neighborhoods, often spatially segregated from one another. In theory, it might be possible to construct institutions in such a setting that did ensure that spatial segregation by class had minimal impacts on life chances; but, to reiterate, such schemes would be politically highly implausible given that (a) they would not likely be seen to be in the interest of the most advantaged; (b) the most advantaged will be less likely to exercise solidarity with the least advantaged when they are spatially segregated and live apart; and (c) the most advantaged will have significant, probably disproportionate influence over political affairs.

From an egalitarian point of view, clearly the best response to this conundrum would be to develop the argument that sharp spatial segregation by class and race should not be permitted, and that the individual choices that help produce such segregation should not be classed as a basic liberty. Note that on Rawls's revised account of the basic liberties, the aim is not to maximize liberty; nor is any particular liberty absolutely inviolate (see Freeman, *Rawls*). Rather, the worth of a basic liberty is to be judged by the extent to which it promotes exercise of the two moral powers.

Freedom to live in an exclusive golfing community should not be given the same sanction as freedom to live in an urban commune, insofar as the aim of residence in an exclusive community is not golf but separating one's self from one's fellow citizens in an antidemocratic fashion. To be sure, the Rawlsian, in designing a just metropolitan structure, could take many steps short of directly regulating individual choices to prevent the emergence of economically segregated metropolitan areas. In particular, the organization of local government and the powers assigned such government could be structured so as to prevent the possibility of rich enclaves with exclusionary zoning powers ever emerging; public goods could cease to be distributed as positional goods; and overall narrowing of economic inequality could reduce demand to live in exclusive neighborhoods (see Frug, *City Making*; and Frug, "Legal Technology of Exclusion"). Such steps would reduce much of the privilege now associated with rich, homogeneous communities. But pursuing such an agenda would require the prior judgment that freedom of association is not to be interpreted as covering a "right" for the affluent to spatially separate themselves from other groups in society in ways that have become increasingly common over the past thirty years. Put another way, freedom of association *does* cover the right for golf lovers to live in proximity to golf courses (and one another), but it does not cover the right of golf lovers to also segregate themselves from the rest of society in antidemocratic, antiegalitarian fashion. Those who reside near golf courses should be as likely to also reside near public housing projects, drug rehabilitation clinics, and municipal waste dumps as residents of any other neighborhood.

Such an argument is highly plausible, and it is implicit in the work of (in particular) Loren King, who appeals to a conception of justice as fairness to evaluate the "polycentric city" but also argues that "freedom of association (especially regarding location choices) and jurisdictional autonomy (especially regarding land uses)" are not "unquestionably democratic virtues" and must be balanced with other considerations (King, "Democracy and City Life"). Note also that the term "freedom of association" has historically been employed by white segregationists to defend racial privilege (see Kruse, *White Flight*); not all claims to "freedom of association" should be respected.

It is worth reiterating, however, that direct steps to prevent socioeconomic segregation need not necessarily be the only or even the primary element of an overall strategy to prevent or reduce residential segregation by class. Directly reducing economic inequalities through labor market and tax policies, especially by reducing the exorbitant share of income and wealth now claimed by the top 1 percent of Americans, would likely over time result in a lower degree of economic segregation. Indeed, as noted in the main text, it is difficult to see how *any* socio-spatial arrangement compatible with Rawlsian justice in its ideal form might be adopted in the continued presence of existing large-scale inequalities of income and wealth.

52. Mansfield, *Spirit of Liberalism*, 91. Mansfield is certainly not a majoritarian, but his critique of Rawls focuses on what he sees as the implausible defense of the most disadvantaged against majority interests.

53. See Geuss, *Outside Ethics*, for an interesting discussion of why the Rawlsian paradigm has risen in influence within the academy while remaining politically impotent. Geuss takes the political impotence of Rawls's theory as an indictment of the entire Rawlsian paradigm. For a related view, see Elkin's critique of Rawls in his *Reconstructing the Commercial Republic*.

54. Chambers, "Politics of Equality."

55. A striking exception, pointed out by Perry Anderson, is Rawls's "bitter" judgment, as evidenced in the following statement by Rawls: "Germany between 1870 and 1945 is an example of a country where reasonably favorable conditions existed—economic, technological, and no lack of resources, an educated citizenry and more—but where the political will for a democratic regime was altogether lacking. One might say the same of the United States today, if one decides our constitutional regime is largely democratic in form only." See Rawls, *Justice as Fairness*, 101, n. 23; and Anderson's interesting essay, "Arms and Rights" in *Spectrum*, especially 170–73. I am grateful to David Schweickart for calling my attention to this passage.

56. Another observation of Perry Anderson is pertinent here. Anderson quotes the statement Rawls made in *Political Liberalism*, that his aim is "to work out a conception of political and social justice...congenial to the most deep-seated convictions and traditions of a modern democratic state." Rawls continues, "The point of doing this is to see whether we can resolve the impasse in our recent political history; namely, that there is no agreement on the way basic social institutions should be arranged if they are to conform to the freedom and equality of citizens and persons" (300). Anderson comments,

"If the modern state is as described, deep in its democratic convictions and traditions, how could there possibly be a deadlock over the realization of freedom and equality for its citizens? The two halves of the statement fall apart." Anderson, *Spectrum*, 111–12. In short, Rawls assumes a consensus about substantive commitments to freedom and equality that is in fact yet to be established (within the United States, at least), and seems to believe that philosophy is the proper vehicle for clarifying the meaning of those commitments. But if such commitments are not widely shared, the preeminent task for egalitarian politics must be political struggle and contestation, not philosophical clarification. Chambers reaches a similar conclusion in calling for a new project to "transform public commitments to political equality into public commitments on egalitarian justice." She adds, "Transformation, however, was never on Rawls's agenda. He was an egalitarian and thought that deep down so were we all. Egalitarianism was the reasonable, not revolutionary, conclusion to draw. Would that it were true" (87).

57. For similar argumentation on this point see Flint, *This Land*, 226–27. Compare this judgment, too, with Joshua Cohen's observation that "moral thought is concerned in part with what *I* should do in a world in which other people do not see eye to eye with me, but democratic politics is concerned with what *we* should do when we do not see eye to eye with one another." Cohen notes, "We cannot reasonably demand or even expect a single moral philosophy or doctrine to be embraced in a democratic society even if we think that some specific view would be endorsed by all under idealized conditions. So it is a mistake to defend the plausibility of an assumption of political unanimity by pointing to the role of expectations or unanimity within moral thought. And once we give up on the expectation of moral unanimity in a democracy, we should also give up on the expectation of political unanimity. It is unreasonable to expect all members to accept the same conception of justice and arguably a virtue of democratic politics that they disagree.

"Justice as fairness may be the most reasonable conception of justice for a democratic society. But we cannot expect the most reasonable democratic society to be founded on an agreement about justice" (Cohen, "For a Democratic Society," 130–31). The import of this observation from one of Rawls's most sympathetic commentators is that the egalitarian conception of justice promoted by Rawls will, within a political culture with diverse conceptions of justice, always be controversial and always involve challenges to the rights claims and liberty claims made by relatively privileged persons. Which conception of justice, liberty, and equality prevails will turn not simply on philosophical reasoning, but also on politics.

Chapter 6

1. Sandel, *Democracy's Discontent*; see also Sandel, *Justice*.
2. Sandel, "Reply to Critics."
3. The standard account is Kymlicka, *Liberalism, Community and Culture*. For critical overviews of Sandel's civic republicanism from more sympathetic perspectives, see Beiner, "Introduction," in *Debating Democracy's Discontent*, and Dagger, "Michael Sandel."
4. Rawls, *Political Liberalism*, 205–6.
5. Kymlicka, *Contemporary Political Philosophy*, 300.
6. White, "Rawls, Republicanism, and Property-owning Democracy."

7. Francisco, "Republican Interpretation of the Late Rawls," 288.

8. Kymlicka, "Civic Republicanism and Liberal Egalitarianism," 146.

9. Rawls did address in detail the matter of civil disobedience within "nearly just" regimes, making the important and powerful argument that even reasonably just regimes must accept the legitimacy of citizens registering principled dissent to government actions believed to be unjust (*Theory of Justice*, 308–43). In this case, the dissenters could proceed by making an appeal to widely shared principles of justice and the conscience of the majority. Rawls distinguished this case from situations of more fundamental injustices in which the reigning principles of justice in the public consciousness are themselves unjust (or we might add, in which citizens lack any effective sense of justice at all). Rawls does allow that in *those* more negative circumstances, "one may have no recourse but to oppose the prevailing conception and the institutions it justifies in such ways as promise some success" (*Theory of Justice*, 310), but he does not elaborate upon what this entails, other than to distinguish peaceful civil disobedience from more radical forms (319–23). The clear implication of Rawls's sustained attention to what he terms the "narrow" case of civil disobedience in near-just societies is that he judged the United States (at least at that time) approximated such a near-just society. As discussed at the end of ch. 5, U.S. society has significantly departed from Rawlsian principles of justice since 1970, and Rawls's own view of U.S. democracy appears to have gotten more pessimistic. Consequently, the question of what duties justice requires of citizens in formally democratic regimes that violate the principles of justice in very substantial and pervasive ways, and in which one cannot appeal to the conscience of the majority—i.e., "the commonly shared conception of justice that underlies the political order" (321)—with strong hope of success, particularly with respect to socioeconomic inequalities, remains a major unaddressed area of inquiry within the Rawlsian paradigm, and indeed for all contemporary theories of social justice.

10. Sandel, "Reply to Critics." In a similar vein, Marc Stier argues that efforts by writers such as William Galston and Stephen Macedo to specify "liberal virtues" that liberal states should actively inculcate in its citizens fall short because such "procedural" virtues (tolerance, self-examination) lack motivating force for most citizens; they are not tied closely enough to human happiness and flourishing. Stier goes on to argue that virtues that are more "communitarian" should have a greater motivational capacity (Stier, "Liberal Virtue/Communitarian Virtue").

11. Dagger, *Civic Virtues*.

12. Maynor, *Republicanism in the Modern World*, 75.

13. Francisco, "Republican Interpretation of the Late Rawls," see 271 n. 3. Francisco makes the interesting argument that the Rawlsian conception of social justice *must* take a republican turn if it is to be comprehensible. Francisco argues that while there are important republican tendencies within Rawls's thought, his conceptual separation of "political liberty" from "individual liberty," and "civic virtue" from private virtue, creates problems that a straightforward republican conception of indivisible liberty and virtue can avoid. As Francisco asks, "What guarantee is there for Rawls that private motivations will not conspire against public ones and ruin his entire normative-political edifice? . . . [I]n the eyes of the miscreant and the opportunist, a just society would actually be an obstacle to the realization of his goals and desires and would demand of him (in exchange for fairness and justice), commitments, responsibilities and virtues

that he would surely prefer to spare himself." This line of thought eloquently speaks to the tension between suburban residential preferences and egalitarian social justice identified in ch. 5. Francisco argues that a "republican strategy of continuity—a strategy ensuring that the congruity between the right and the good and between private and public ethics is not merely a lucky coincidence" is needed to rescue justice as fairness as a plausible political doctrine. Francisco notes that Rawls in fact does provide such an argument, by stressing that in the context of a just society, it will be both reasonable *and* rational (i.e., in the citizen's own interest) to endorse principles of justice. In his view, then, Rawls might be described as a closeted republican: the logic of his own theory points in a republican direction, but his appropriation of the "liberal heritages" of dividing liberty and portraying "civic humanism" as a comprehensive doctrine needlessly inhibit and complicate his own arguments for justice.

14. See Macedo et al., *Democracy at Risk*.

15. Here see Geuss, *Outside Ethics*, and Wolin, "Liberal/Democratic Divide."

16. See, especially, Robeyns, "Ideal Theory in Theory and Practice," and other articles in the special July 2008 issue of *Social Theory and Practice*, edited by Robeyns and Swift. See also Mills, "'Ideal Theory' as Ideology"; Sen, "What Do We Want from a Theory of Justice?" and *The Idea of Justice*; and McCarthy, "Political Philosophy and Racial Injustice."

17. Elkin's critique of ideal theory is important, though it may go too far. As Ingrid Robeyns persuasively suggests, there may still be a limited value for ideal theory: she remarks that that ideal theory can play "a rather limited role: it looks like the Paradise Island where we ideally would like to be, but it does not tell us how to get closer to the island." Robeyns argues that ideal theory that avoids "idealizations" of reality can make an important though limited contribution to addressing concrete problems, particularly when the nature of such problems is not immediately obvious. (Robeyns gives the example of gender injustice.) In this book, Rawlsian theory has been applied (in chs. 4 and 5) as an expository device to explain what is unjust about the metropolitan spatial structure of the contemporary United States and to describe how sprawl contributes both to inequalities and to the formation and perpetuation of a political regime that accepts, sustains, and strengthens dramatic inequalities of opportunity (and outcome). But Rawlsian theory, just as Robeyns suggests (and as remarked at the end of ch. 5) tells us very little about how to proceed in correcting those injustices, particularly given the non-ideal circumstances of U.S. politics. See Robeyns, "Ideal Theory in Theory and Practice," quote on 361.

18. Consider the metropolitan-level inequalities described in the previous two chapters and the role of suburbanization and sprawl in constructing and perpetuating a regime of grossly unequal opportunity. Chief among the obstacles to egalitarian reform are the opposition of currently privileged suburban residents. These residents are likely to defend existing arrangements (and their associated privileges) by appeals to (a) the collective self-interest of other suburban residents (b) conceptions of justice (i.e., the claim that existing arrangements are the result of fair choices in the market, or the claim that citizens have "earned" the right to live in a privileged neighborhood) and (c) conceptions of the good life (all I want is life in a quiet neighborhood where I don't have to worry about "urban social problems"). In practical political terms, challenging the status quo requires critical engagement with all three dimensions of this defense.

19. The force of contemporary civic republican critiques of U.S. life was largely anticipated by Tocqueville, who worriedly wrote, "If the citizens continue to shut themselves up more and more narrowly in the little circle of petty domestic interests and keep themselves constantly busy therein, there is a danger that they may in the end become practically out of reach of those great and powerful public emotions which do indeed perturb peoples but which also make them grow and refresh them.... The prospect really does frighten me that they may finally become so engrossed in a cowardly love of immediate pleasures that their interest in their own future and in that of their descendants may vanish, and that they will prefer tamely to follow the course of their destiny rather than make a sudden energetic effort necessary to set things right" Tocqueville, *Democracy in America*, Vol. 2, Part III, ch. 21, 645.

20. Putnam, *Bowling Alone*.

21. The following account pulls together themes from a variety of recent writings in the republican tradition, including especially Sandel, *Democracy's Discontent*, Pettit's *Republicanism*, Dagger's *Civic Virtues*, Honohan's *Civic Republicanism*, Barber's *Strong Democracy*, Maynor's *Republicanism in the Modern World*, Sunstein's "Beyond the Republican Revival," and related writings. For a useful bibliography of important recent writings in the republican tradition, see Laborde and Maynor, *Republicanism and Political Theory*, 22–26. This is not to imply that there exists a unitary republican tradition among contemporary writers, much less historically. Three points of debate within the contemporary republican discourse merit mentioning: the question of whether political participation is to be seen as an intrinsic or an instrumental good (see text); the question of whether politics is to be grounded in an independent moral standard of some kind (i.e., maximizing liberty as non-domination) or whether politics should be seen as the *source* of guiding normative values (as Barber proposes); and the question of whether achieving genuine self-governance requires dramatic changes in the structures of representative democracy. My discussion sets aside these important disputes in order to focus on the practical question at hand; namely, how the civic republican tradition would (in the main) assess suburban sprawl. It should be added that the historical republican tradition is itself very diverse; for a detailed typology of different strands of historic republicanism, see Mouritsen, "Four Models of Republican Liberty and Self-Government."

22. As Richard Dagger remarks, however, "allowing for such differences of emphasis should not obscure two points on which the members of both schools agree: first, that freedom is in some sense freedom *through* government, not complete freedom from it; and second, that anyone who is subject to arbitrary rule cannot be a self-governing citizen" ("Neo-Republicanism and the Civic Economy," 153). The close connection between instrumental and intrinsic conceptions of republican liberty is also a key theme of Maynor, *Republicanism in the Modern World*.

23. See Dagger, "Neo-Republicanism and the Civic Economy," for further discussion. Dagger rightly stresses the overlap between republican strategies for dispersing property and Rawls's concept of a property-owning democracy. Rawls's own reasoning for justice does reflect a concern with maintaining a society of free and equal citizens (see Freeman, *Rawls*). The suggestion here is that in working out appropriate principles of distributive justice, we can proceed not by consulting the apparatus of the original position but rather begin with the question of what resources are needed to produce citizens who are

equally competent and effective in participating in self-governance. For similar argumentation, see Thomas, "Liberalism, Republicanism, and the Idea of an Egalitarian Ethos."

24. Hence Aristotle's observation that "as man is the best of all animals when he has reached his fullest development, so he is worst of all when divorced from law and justice" (*Politics*, Book I, ch. 2, 1253a7–a17, 60).

25. Aristotle, *Politics*.

26. Arendt, *Human Condition*, 54, 52, quoted in Honohan, *Civic Republicanism*, 121–22.

27. The Aristotelian view of political participation as an intrinsic good has been critiqued by some contemporary theorists as (a) unproven and (b) at odds with the common understanding of modern citizens. Point (b) is not in dispute; what is in dispute is whether the reigning understanding of politics as a means to secure private ends is desirable. Argument (a) has some force to it, but civic republicans can contend that the reason political participation is experienced as an indifferent or a negative good has to do with, first, the flawed design of our political institutions and lack of opportunity for truly significant civic participation (a point recognized by Kymlicka in his critique of civic republicanism) and, second, a political economy and larger way of life in which many people feel very harried for time, and time spent participating involves large opportunity costs (a point not acknowledged by Kymlicka). In general, it is correct to say that the notion that participation is an intrinsic human good capable of being widely enjoyed currently carries the status of a hypothesis, or a philosophical assertion, rather than a scientific truth; but it is a hypothesis that by its nature cannot be tested unless institutions are reorganized so as to facilitate meaningful political participation. Kymlicka argues that even if there were dramatic institutional reform aimed at facilitating deliberation and participation, "there would still be many people who would find political life a sacrifice." *Contemporary Political Philosophy*, 297.

This in itself is a plausible (albeit speculative) argument, but it ignores the possibility that citizens' bearing duties they regard as a sacrifice may be a necessary cost for maintaining a robust republican regime. There are also many who find paying taxes a sacrifice, but taxation is still seen as a moral duty. Likewise, while there may indeed be variation among citizens in their taste for participation, this arguably strengthens the case for the state celebrating the virtues and benefits of participation as an intrinsic good, so that as few citizens as possible experience such participation as a net bad. If the belief that participation is not intrinsically worthwhile is widespread among the population, instrumental arguments for encouraging duty-based participation confront a serious motivational problem. On this last point, see Sandel, "Reply to Critics," 325. Importantly, Sandel stresses that "one does not need not to believe that civic virtue constitutes the whole of virtue in order to view it as an intrinsic good, an essential aspect of human flourishing."

28. Barber, *Strong Democracy*.

29. See, among others, Crenson and Ginsberg, *Downsizing Democracy*, for an empirical sketch of U.S. democracy consistent with this judgment.

30. Sandel, *Democracy's Discontent*.

31. For a brief discussion of Dewey's views and how they relate to contemporary questions of sprawl and urbanism, see Leyden and Michelbach, "Democracy and 'Neighborly Communities.' "

32. Elkin, "Citizen and City," 43.

33. We might also add a fifth rationale: the notion that active effort to redress injustices should be regarded as a moral duty of citizens living in imperfect regimes. This last rationale has received perhaps the least development in the recent republican literature, though it is implicit in the accounts of moral reformers at various points in U.S. history provided by Sandel in *Democracy's Discontent*. The idea is simply that under democratic conditions an appropriate interpretation of one's moral duties to humanity (which in turn often derive from a substantive idea of the "good" or one's religious views) is that one should engage in political activity for the purposes of ending injustice. Sandel points out that this set of motivations has played an important part in the history of U.S. social reform, from abolitionists to progressive urban reformers such as Jane Addams; and it continues to play an important role in motivating political engagement of many Americans today, most notably Christian Evangelicals (on the right, and, increasingly, in the center and on the left). To this list we might also add civil rights activists, such as the Student Nonviolent Coordinating Committee, who were moved by Gandhian conceptions of nonviolent resistance to take enormous physical risks in order to challenge segregationist laws and social practices (see Hogan, *Many Minds, One Heart*). Note that this argument for the fundamental importance of political participation is distinct from both the participation as an intrinsic good rationale (derived from Aristotle) and the instrumental emphasis on participation (provided by neo-Roman republicans). More fully developing this line of argument should be regarded as an important priority both for those republicans who, with Sandel, think that substantive religious views should not be bracketed out of public life, and for liberal egalitarians addressing the question of the moral duties of citizens within formally democratic but substantively unjust regimes (see n. 9 above).

34. See, e.g., Verba, Schlozman, and Brady, *Voice and Equality*, 508, and throughout.

35. This is not to say that Arendt thought it was healthy for the majority of society to be utterly uninvolved in politics, to the extent they cannot be bothered to sign a petition or go to a meeting even once a year, or that she would object to the view that it would be beneficial for more Americans to have greater levels of political engagement than they actually do. Rather, her point was that only a minority of citizens at any given time will feel called to devote large amounts of time to extended engagement.

36. For discussion of contemporary local participatory structures, see Fung and Wright, *Deepening Democracy*, and Fung, *Empowered Governance*. It is perhaps noteworthy that the existing literature on institutional innovations in promoting civic participation focuses overwhelmingly on the use of such innovation in central city contexts. See the above, and, e.g., Thomson, *From Neighborhoods to Nation*; and Berry, Portney, and Thomson, *Rebirth of Urban Democracy*.

37. The general doctrine of state neutrality admits of several variations. In its strongest possible formulation, the goal might be neutrality of *effect*; that is, no state actions can have (whatever their justification) the effect of favoring some conceptions of the good over others. This formulation is rejected by Rawls (among others) as simply implausible, given the functions of modern states. A more moderate formulation holds that state policy cannot *aim* at promoting any particular conception of the good, though it might be the case that policies adopted for other reasons have this practical effect. Rawls finds this conception of state neutrality more congenial and adds a further stipulation: the

doctrine of neutrality is to apply only to core constitutional matters, not less "fundamental" questions of policy. Strong objections to each of these formulations of the principle of state neutrality have been raised by a variety of thinkers, perhaps most incisively by Joseph Raz and Richard Arneson. Even if agreement about the good life is impossible, given the fact of moral pluralism, it might be rational for parties in the original position to agree to use *some* conception of the good life as a basis for guiding policy rather than to agree to exclude all considerations of the good from the constitution and policymaking. More generally, such thinkers believe that the neutrality doctrine far overreaches the correct moral intuition that no one should be forced to embrace a conception of the good life with which they do not agree. Non-neutralist (or "perfectionist") policies might take the form of promoting widely (though not universally) valued goods that facilitate human flourishing, or that make it more likely for citizens to make certain kinds of choices rather than others, without resort to direct coercion. Perfectionist policies of this kind would not undercut individuals' ability to choose their own good and take responsibility for those choices; plausibly, they might (in some circumstances) enhance them. See Arneson, "Liberal Neutrality on the Good"; and Raz, *Morality of Freedom*.

38. See West, "Universalism, Liberal Theory, and the Problem of Gay Marriage."

39. Sandel, "What Money Can't Buy."

40. In this sense, civic republicanism coheres quite well with the "capabilities" approach to justice and human flourishing developed by Amartya Sen and Martha Nussbaum, especially Nussbaum's explicitly neo-Aristotelian formulation of ten distinctive capabilities a fully flourishing human being should possess. This is the case even though Nussbaum principally casts her approach as a revision of the basic Rawlsian framework. See Nussbaum, *Women and Human Development*.

41. Honohan, *Civic Republicanism*, 160–62; see also Maynor, *Republicanism in the Modern World*. For further elaboration of virtues related to deliberative engagement that the state should promote (on both deliberative and republican views), see Talisse, *Democracy after Liberalism*.

42. Sandel, *Liberalism and the Limits of Justice*, 141–47.

43. Honohan, *Civic Republicanism*, 156.

44. Honohan, *Civic Republicanism*, 156–57.

45. Dworkin, *Sovereign Virtue*.

46. Jean-Jacques Rousseau, "A Letter from Jean-Jacques Rousseau."

47. It should be stressed that there are other types of public or "common" goods as well—goods that could not exist without the presence of the community. As Charles Taylor has emphasized, human language itself is a prime example of this sort of common good; so, too, are shared cultural meanings and certain kinds of shared experiences that depend on the presence of other people for their very meaning. (A sermon or speech delivered to a completely empty hall is just an individual talking to himself, no matter how brilliant the content of his words.) Numerous types of social recognition—such as the respect afforded to married couples or to parents accompanying very small children in public places—and, arguably, social trust itself, also have this character. Taylor thus suggests that certain kinds of goods are "irreducibly social" and that we ignore the maintenance of such goods at our peril. See Taylor, *Philosophical Arguments*, and Honohan, *Civic Republicanism*, 134–35.

48. See Bickford, "Constructing Inequality," and Kohn, *Brave New Neighborhoods*.

49. Sandel, "What Money Can't Buy."

50. See Marshall, *How Cities Work,* for related argumentation.

51. For related argumentation, see Dagger, "Neo-Republicanism and the Civic Economy," and Pettit, *Republicanism*, 158–67.

52. Honohan, *Civic Republicanism*, 191–92.

53. For an alternative republican account of limited inequality stressing "socio-economic independence" as a counter to domination and dependence, see Pettit, *Republicanism*, 158–63.

54. Mill, *Utilitarianism*.

55. Verba, Schlozman, and Brady, *Voice and Equality*.

56. See Mitchell, *Big-Box Swindle*.

57. See Williamson, Imbroscio, and Alperovitz, *Making a Place for Community*, 89–91.

58. See Frug, *City Making*.

59. Oliver, *Democracy in Suburbia*.

60. See, e.g., Fung, *Empowered Participation*.

61. Elkin, *Reconstructing the Commercial Republic*.

62. Civic republicans, of course, can also avail themselves of the tool of cost–benefit analysis in the broadest sense; that is, they may seek to comprehensively catalogue the likely effects of a given policy before making a practical judgment. Where civic republicans differ from utilitarians, however, is in rejecting the further claim that all relevant goods can be converted to a single quantity of value—utility—and in denying that maximizing such "utility" is the proper way to judge a policy's worth. Instead, the civic republican proposes to proceed by making substantive judgments about the worth of given goods, given the specific context in question. Cutting down an oak tree that helps establishes a small town's identity—or destroying a working-class neighborhood for the sake of an interstate highway or a new factory—might be calculated by utilitarians to maximize long-run utility yet still be fiercely opposed by civic republicans on the grounds that morally important goods—such as the good of local civic identity, or the good of local community stability, or perhaps the capacity of citizens to engage in meaningful self-governance—are being destroyed, and that the loss cannot be compensated for by economic benefit.

63. Knight and Steponaitis, *Archaeology of the Moundville Chiefdom*.

64. Oldenburg, *Great Good Place*.

65. Distinct residential traits identified by Brower include: "clean and well maintained," "quiet," "entirely residential," "has a center," "center of activity," "homes close together," "full of surprises," "need no car," "public transportation," "world-class facilities," "many tourists," "suits newcomers," "meet new people," "active social life," "selection of goods," "easy care of home," "neighbors friendly," "put down roots," "meet people one knows," "neighbors care," "long-lasting relations," "involved in community," "no pressure to join," "residents private," "residents similar," "protected from society," "place for children, "residents diverse," "residents sophisticated," "residents genuine." See Brower, *Good Neighborhoods*, 98–106, 123.

66. Brower, *Good Neighborhoods*, 121.

67. Brower, *Good Neighborhoods*, 129.

68. Brower, *Good Neighborhoods*, 142–45.

69. Brower, *Good Neighborhoods*, 148.

70. Brower, *Good Neighborhoods*, 152.

71. Brower, *Good Neighborhoods*, 157.

72. Kolb, *Sprawling Places*.

73. The rural character of Henry County, Kentucky, where Wendell Berry lives, is increasingly being encroached upon by sprawl from Louisville, and in 2003 the Census classified the county for the first time as part of the Louisville metropolitan statistical area. The moral exemption here given to Mr. Berry does not apply to those Henry County residents who are commuting to Louisville!

74. Arendt also made the converse argument that private life and private spaces become more valuable when complemented by a robust public sphere; the well-lived life, she implies, requires activity in both spheres. Arendt, *Human Condition*.

75. See Sennett, *Uses of Disorder*; see also Bickford, "Constructing Inequality," 356–58, quote from 357.

76. Sandel, *Democracy's Discontent*; Dagger, *Civic Virtues*, 154–55; Barber, "Malled, Mauled, and Overhauled"; Pettit, *Republicanism*, 167.

77. The connection between New Urbanism and civic republicanism is made explicit by David Brain in his "From Good Neighborhoods to Sustainable Cities." Brain likens contemporary zoning practices to the "procedural liberalism" deplored by Michael Sandel, then adds, "The aspiration to good urbanism implies the possibility of a politics that enables citizens to come to some level of substantive agreement about a common good—a civic ideal that requires participation and obligation on the part of the individual."

Chapter 7

1. Oliver, *Democracy in Suburbia*.

2. Freeman, "Effects of Sprawl on Neighborhood Social Ties."

3. Humphries, "Who's Afraid of the Big Bad Firm?"

4. Hopkins, "Discounting Politics." For a more recent analysis focusing on the impact of the presence of a Wal-Mart in one's county on voter turnout and political participation that yields similar findings, see Brown, "Discounting Democracy." Brown draws on several data sets measuring various forms of political participation, including the SCCBS, and finds a consistent negative link between Wal-Mart's presence and political participation. For a related analysis, see also Goetz and Rupasingha, "Wal-Mart and Social Capital."

5. Leyden, "Social Capital and the Built Environment."

6. Among other examples, Lofland cites Nathan Glazer's 1956 statement that "we must root out of our thinking the assumption that the physical form of our communities has social consequences" (*Public Realm*, 180).

7. Lofland distinguishes between the "public realm," a form of public space in which social interactions between strangers predominate, and "public space" itself; in some formally public spaces, social interactions are either primarily intimate or primarily parochial (e.g., a neighborhood bar in an ethnic neighborhood with a regular clientele).

8. Lofland, *Public Realm*, 205.

9. Kohn, *Brave New Neighborhoods*, 4, 6. As noted in ch. 5, Kohn suggests that public space can not only facilitate political participation and communication but can also affect how citizens come to view both themselves and one another:

"Particular spaces...aggregate or exclude; they encourage or inhibit contact between people; and they determine the form and scope of the contact. These effects may be achieved through physical properties, such as accessibility of a courtyard, the arrangement of benches, or the presence of a stage. Public places such as parks and plazas and social spaces such as community centers can encourage a certain kind of civic conversation. Sometimes this dialogue takes place quite literally, for example, when a street preacher or petitioner engages the interest of someone passing by. But this conversation does not necessarily take place with words. Often the dialogue is the internal kind that is motivated by viewing and reflecting upon a range of people and activities. Public space can incite democratic effects when it positions both subject and object together in a shared and contestable world. (16)

10. Brain, "From Good Neighborhoods to Sustainable Cities," quote on 224.

11. Tonkiss, *Space, the City and Social Theory*. Quotes from 59, 60, 61. Tonkiss's discussion is strongly informed by the work of David Harvey, Manuel Castells, and Henri Lefebvre. On the city itself as a site of social and political struggle, see also Mitchell, *Right to the City*.

12. Burchell et al., *Costs of Sprawl—2000*.

13. There is also a positive relationship between longer commuting times and interest in politics bordering on statistical significance (p < .07); in substantive terms, however, this effect is negligible. Since there is no theoretical reason to link longer average commuting times to increased interest in politics, I treat this relationship as an artifact of other spatial characteristics of longer commuting time areas and hence omit the variable. Even when the variable is included, the sprawl-related variables are jointly significant predictors of reduced political interest at the .001 level.

14. The relationship between proportion driving alone in the tract and political knowledge (but not between central city residence and political knowledge) disappears in models adding fixed-effect controls for sample communities, indicating that the relationship between automobile dependence and political knowledge is largely a function of metropolitan-level characteristics.

15. Putnam, *Bowling Alone*; Macedo et al., *Democracy at Risk*.

16. The voting data needs to be treated with particular caution as the rates of voting reported here are far higher than actual voter turnout during the 1996 presidential election. In general this data is subject to a golden-glow effect, with some respondents likely overestimating their rates of social and political participation. We might expect this effect to be markedly more pronounced with respect to voting relative to higher-intensity forms of political participation since the act of voting is so closely tied to widespread normative conceptions of what it means to be a responsible citizen. It is likely more embarrassing for most respondents to admit not voting in the last election than to acknowledge not attending a protest march in the past year.

17. The effect of auto dependence upon voting increases in models that drop a control for residence in the Southern census region. In a model with no regional controls, proportion driving alone to work in the tract is a significant predictor of reduced reported voting at the p < .005 significance level among citizens at least twenty-one years old living in their current community at least five years. Even in this case, however, the substantive effect is negligible; dropping regional controls, it is estimated that a resident of a tract

in which 65 percent of workers drive alone to work has a 88.4 percent (87.3%, 89.3%) likelihood of reporting having voted, compared to 86.7 percent (85.4%, 87.9%) for a resident of a tract in which 85 percent of workers solo commute by car.

18. A resident of a city of 450,000 living in a high-density (8,000 persons/square mile) tract in a neighborhood built in 1950 in which 65 percent of persons drive alone to work is predicted to have a 41.9 percent (40.5%, 43.3%) likelihood of having attended a public meeting in the past year, compared to 41.8 percent (40.3%, 43.1%) for a resident of a city of fewer than 100,000 living in a lower-density (1,000 persons/square mile) tract built in 1980 in which 85 percent of workers drive alone to work.

19. See Cho and Rudolph, "Emanating Political Participation." Cho and Rudolph's analysis focuses on respondents in the SCCBS living in cities with a population greater than 100,000 in which at least 40 cases are present; Cho and Rudolph do not investigate the relationship between specific geographic measures and participation. Their analysis is important in showing "that the spatial structure of political participation is consistent with a diffusion or contagion process." They assert, "Our main contribution lies in establishing the nature of this diffusion process and its *independent* existence from our measures of social network involvement and a wide range of other individual-level and aggregate-level attributes. Collectively, our results point to an important role for casual observation in the diffusion of low-intensity environmental cues in explaining the spatial dependency behind political participation. An important implication of this result is that geographic proximity matters in ways that are not sufficiently accounted for by leading theories of contextual effects" (288). For prominent examples of previous work linking neighborhood context to political participation, see, among others, Huckfeldt, *Politics in Context*; Oliver, *Democracy in Suburbia*; Gimpel, Lay, and Shucknecht, *Cultivating Democracy*; Campbell, *Why We Vote*. For general overviews of the study of political participation in contemporary political science, see review essays by Leighley, "Attitudes, Opportunities and Incentives," and "Commentary on 'Attitudes, Opportunities and Incentives.'"

20. A point stressed by Oliver, *Democracy in Suburbia*.

21. One counterintuitive result also emerges: long commuting times in the census tract emerge as a *positive* predictor of two of these forms of higher-intensity activism (march attendance and attendance at a political rally), though the substantive effect in each case is small. There is no clear reason that longer commuting time should in itself cause increased political participation, and indeed individual-level commuting time has no effect (positive or negative) on higher-intensity activism. Moreover, this positive relationship disappears entirely once we add fixed-effect controls for each community sample, whereas the sprawl-related variables such as neighborhood age and proportion of solo auto commuters remain highly significant. Consequently, I assume here that the observed positive relationship between commuting time and activism is not a causal link and omit average commuting times from the reported models for these variables. Omitting commuting time slightly increases the cumulative substantive effect of the sprawl-related variables.

22. This estimate is based on a binary specification of the activism index in which respondents with zero forms of political participation are coded as zero and all those with one or more are coded as one. Specifying the index instead as an ordinal variable from 0 to

4 (with 4 indicating the respondent participated in each type of political activism), as shown in table 7.10, produces a slightly stronger estimate of the substantive impact of sprawl-related variables on participation.

23. If, for the "proportion of solo drivers" measure, one substitutes variables measuring alternative modes of transportation or alternatives to commuting—carpooling, public transit (bus, rail, or subway), walking and biking, or working at home—further interesting results emerge; high degrees of transit use and of pedestrian friendliness (as measured by walking and biking) are each significant predictors of increased activism, as is the proportion of workers who work at home. High carpooling activity is also positively associated with activism vis-à-vis solo automobile commuting, but the relationship is not statistically significant.

24. These estimates are based on a simplified model that drops the density and neighborhood-age variables, and again are based on binary coding of respondents into two categories: participated in zero or one of these forms of political participation in the past year, or participated in two or more.

25. Based on comparison of a resident of a central city of 450,000 living in a tract in which 65% of workers drive alone to work with a suburban resident living in a tract in which 85% of workers drive alone to work.

26. Based on the author's review of the Web sites of the Industrial Areas Foundation (www.industrialareasfoundation.org), the DART Center (www.thedartcenter.org), and the Gamaliel Foundation (www.gamaliel.org). For informative accounts of urban community organizing, see Warren, *Dry Bones Rattling* and Swarts, *Organizing Urban America*; Swarts's book is particularly relevant as it documents efforts of a St. Louis–based organizing effort to curb sprawl.

27. For a broader analysis of county-level social capital using the County Business Patterns data, see Rupasingha, Goetz, and Freshwater, "Production of Social Capital in U.S. Counties." See also Putnam, "E Pluribus Unum."

28. Data referred to here are 2005 county-level organizational totals for CBP category 8133, "advocacy organizations." These included human rights organizations, environmental organizations, and "other" advocacy groups. Data from the U.S. Census Web site. For a more detailed analysis of this data on advocacy organizations, undertaken at the zip code level, see Knudsen and Clark, "Local Ecology of New Social Movements." In preliminary results, they find a strong link between zip codes with a high number of pedestrian commuters and the presence of advocacy organizations.

29. Analysis based on an unweighted linear regression with robust standard errors, including 844 metropolitan counties (Washington, D.C., excluded). These results are weakened with respect to the neighborhood-age and automobile-dependence variables when the regression is weighted by county population, though the variables remain jointly significant predictors at the $p < .01$ level in the weighted regression.

30. Oliver, *Democracy in Suburbia*, 81–82. An analysis of 2000 census data by Jason Schacter, issued by the Census Bureau, found that the following reasons account for 98.2 percent of all moves: family-related issues, work-related issues, the desire for better housing (roughly 52%), attending college, change of climate, and health. This analysis suggests that no more than 2 percent of all moves could even, in theory, be principally motivated by concern for living in an area that facilitates political participation. Schacter, "Why People Move."

31. Freeman, "Effects of Sprawl on Neighborhood Social Ties."

32. Gainsborough, *Fenced Off*, 60.

33. 2006 Social Capital Community Survey conducted by the Saguaro Seminar on Civic Engagement at the Kennedy School of Government, Harvard University. Summary results available at http://www.hks.harvard.edu/saguaro/2006sccs.htm.

34. These results are based on simplified analyses that drop tract density and neighborhood age as predictors.

35. Altshuler and Luberoff, *Mega-Projects*, ch. 1.

36. See Sellers, "Towards a Comparative Historical Perspective on the Politics of Sprawl."

37. Campbell, *Why We Vote*.

38. Campbell, *Why We Vote*, 65–75.

39. Brain, "From Good Neighborhoods to Sustainable Cities."

40. Indeed, it should be acknowledged that the measures of political participation included in the SCCBS are not exhaustive of the variety of ways citizens engage in politics. Most obviously, they do not include online, electronic forms of political participation (blogging, sending emails to representatives, donating money online), which have become increasingly important since 2000. The relationship, if any, between the organization of space and online participation is a natural area for future research. A particularly interesting question is how online activity interacts with and reinforces face-to-face political engagement. From a specifically civic republican point of view, however, the "traditional' forms of political activity measured here retain importance for their own sake; civic republicans view politics as an activity that is first and foremost *public*; that is, visible to all. The degree to which online communities form or are capable of forming "publics" of this kind remains a very open question. Nor has the importance of traditional political participation declined with the rise of online organizing; indeed, the purpose of Internet use is often to facilitate face-to-face gatherings. It is certainly possible that the rise of online communication may eventually, in interesting and unforeseen ways, alter and complicate the relationships between space and the prevalence of political participation described here. Nonetheless, it is highly likely that those forms of political participation that require face-to-face contact and the gathering of groups into public spaces will continue to be clustered predominantly in traditional urban areas.

41. Thus, see Oliver, *Democracy in Suburbia*; Dreier, Mollenkopf, and Swanstrom, *Place Matters*; Orfield, *Metropolitics*.

42. See Maynor, *Republicanism in the Modern World*, ch. 5, 117–45.

43. Data on voter turnout taken from Michael McDonald's United States Election Project Web site, at http://elections.gmu.edu/voter_turnout.htm. Reported averaged refers to unweighted average turnout in the three elections.

44. Putnam, *Bowling Alone*, 31–47.

45. Elkin, *Reconstructing the Commercial Republic*.

46. Elkin, *Reconstructing the Commercial Republic*.

47. Indeed, Myron Orfield's claim that successful metropolitan political alliances on behalf of regional tax-base sharing and preserving existing communities are possible rests on the possibility that at least some residents of affluent suburbs (especially those with strong religious engagements) will side with residents of central cities and decaying inner suburbs for moral reasons (*Metropolitics*, 1999).

48. For a discussion of part of this tradition, see Guarneri, *Utopian Alternative*.
49. Hayden, *Building Suburbia*, 54–61.
50. See, e.g., the critical discussion in Knox, *Metroburbia USA*, 107–8.
51. On this point, see also Elkin, "Citizen and City."

Chapter 8

1. For a brief but helpful review of the issues, see Kahn, *Green Cities*, 110–29; for a more technical analysis by the same author, see Kahn, "Environmental Impact of Suburbanization." See also Benfield, Ramii, and Chen, *Once There Were Greenfields*, 29–88. On species loss, see Ewing, Kostyacfk, Chen, Stein, and Ernst, *Endangered by Sprawl*. On climate change, see, especially, Ewing, Bartholomew, Winkleman, Walters, and Chen, *Growing Cooler*, and (for a state-level analysis) Pollard, *New Directions*.

2. See Anderson, *Value in Ethics and Economics*; Sagoff, *Price, Principle and the Environment*.

3. Thus, the Sierra Club notes: "The Arctic National Wildlife Refuge is one of America's greatest natural treasures. The 19 million-acre Refuge harbors an unparalleled diversity of wildlife. Encompassing an entire mountain range cross-section, it is the last place in North America where the full spectrum of arctic life is protected in one seamless expanse." See the Sierra Club Web site, www.sierraclub.org/wildlands/arctic.

4. See Ackerman and Heinzerling, *Priceless*, esp. 179–203, for discussion of some of the practical problems with assigning environmental goods monetary value.

5. Opponents of the Disney deal also appealed to the specific historic importance of the area around Manassas. For a recounting of the struggle, see Moe and Wilkie, *Changing Places*, 3–35.

6. See Egan, "Owners of Malibu Mansions Cry, 'This Sand Is My Sand.'"

7. Gillham, *Limitless City*; Glaeser and Kahn, "Sprawl and Urban Growth."

8. This idea is the theme of Louv's *Last Child in the Woods*.

9. Along these lines, see Beatley, *Ethical Land Use*.

10. Benfield, Ramii, and Chen, *Once There Were Greenfields*, 78–84; see also Williamson, Imbroscio, and Alperovitz, *Making a Place for Community*, 82–83.

11. Burchell et al., *Costs of Sprawl—2000*, 8, table ES.8.

12. Benfield, Ramii, and Chen, *Once There Were Greenfields*, 58.

13. For a study of air-pollution trends in California since 1980, see Kahn and Schwarz, "Urban Air Pollution Progress Despite Sprawl." Nationally, levels of ozone, particulates, nitrogen dioxide, carbon monoxide, sulfur dioxide, and lead in the air have all declined since 1980. See United States Environmental Protection Agency, "Latest Findings on National Air Quality—Status and Trends Through 2006."

14. For discussion on this point, see Cannavó, *Working Landscape*.

15. Cannavó, *Working Landscape*, 230–58.

16. Cannavó, *Working Landscape*, 114.

17. Cannavó, *Working Landscape*, 114.

18. See International Council on Clean Transportation, *Passenger Vehicle Greenhouse Gas and Fuel Economy Standards*.

19. Ewing, Bartholomew, Winkleman, Walters, and Chen, *Growing Cooler*, 42. Achieving a 70 percent reduction in 1990 greenhouse-gas emissions levels (5,013 million metric tons of carbon dioxide) would require roughly a 75 percent drop from the 2007 U.S.

level of emissions (5,984 million metric tons). See United States Energy Information Administration, "U.S. Carbon Dioxide Emissions from Energy Sources 2007 Flash Estimate." Estimate of needed annual reduction in greenhouse-gas stabilization from Kasibhatla and Chameides, "G8 Leadership Is Critical." For data on carbon emissions in the United States, see United States Energy Information Administration, "Emissions of Greenhouse Gases in the United States 2008."

20. Glaeser and Kahn, "Greenness of Cities."

21. Brown, Southworth, and Sarzynski, "Shrinking the Carbon Footprint of Metropolitan America," quote on 28. See also Brown, Southworth, and Stovall, "Towards a Climate-friendly Built Environment."

22. Unweighted bivariate correlation. When weighting by population in the metropolitan statistical area, the correlation between proportion driving alone in the MSA and per capita carbon footprint rises to r = .62. Author's calculation based on data reported in Brown, Southworth, and Sarzynski, "Shrinking the Carbon Footprint of Metropolitan America," table A1, and the 2005 American Community Survey of the United States Census.

23. Gonzalez, *Urban Sprawl, Global Warming, and the Empire of Capital*, 16–17. See tables 1.3 and 1.4.

24. Buehler, Pucher, and Kunert, "Making Transportation Sustainable."

25. Buehler, Pucher, and Kunert, "Making Transportation Sustainable."

26. Bruegmann, *Sprawl*, 149–50.

27. For an important discussion of how conceptions of global justice should shape the way responsibilities for addressing global warming are assigned and assumed, see Vanderheiden, *Atmospheric Justice*.

28. This point is well made by Michael Goggin in his "Is It Time for a Change?"

29. This is not to say that prudence requires us to take all possible steps to deal with any possible threat (even a catastrophic threat). Some weighing of the evidence and of the projected costs and benefits of action and inaction, to the extent this is possible, is necessary. This set of issues is thoughtfully discussed by Cass Sunstein in *Worst Case Scenarios*. Sunstein argues that public debate about climate change has not taken enough stock of the possibility of disastrous, worst-case scenarios, a key reason public response to the threat of climate change has been inadequate.

30. See Dunham-Jones and Williamson, *Retrofitting Suburbia*, for a detailed discussion of how existing, car-dependent suburban places can be redeveloped on more urbanist principles.

31. United States Bureau of Transportation Statistics, *National Transportation Statistics 2007*.

32. Brown, Southworth, and Sarzynski, "Shrinking the Carbon Footprint of Metropolitan America," Figures 1, 5.

33. Brown, Southworth and Sarzynski report that "with shared walls and generally smaller square footage, households in buildings with five or more units consume only 38 percent of the energy of households in single family homes" ("Shrinking the Carbon Footprint," 12).

34. Ewing et al., *Growing Cooler*.

35. Ewing et al., *Growing Cooler*, 129. Emphasis in original. Ewing et al. thus recommend that (1) federal policies tying transportation funding to vehicle miles traveled must be altered; (2) highway funding should be subjected to much more critical cost–benefit

scrutiny before being approved; (3) localities should be required to develop comprehensive transportation plans aimed at limiting greenhouse-gas emissions (as opposed to nonexistent plans, or plans predicated on maximizing economic growth); (4) investments should be made in a national passenger-rail system to replace the inadequate, struggling system operated by Amtrak; and (5) a national cap-and-trade emissions system should be implemented. At the state level, the authors recommend using state development funding systematically to promote more-compact communities, eliminating "perverse local fiscal incentives" in which neighboring localities compete with one another for growth, and making all and refurbished streets pedestrian- and bike-friendly. At the regional and local level, governments should (under a systemic plan to reduce greenhouse-gas emissions) direct funding toward (1) supporting existing communities and more-compact growth proposals, (2) developing "nonauto travel modes," (3) establishing transfer of development-rights programs, (4) establishing carbon-emissions-impact fees on new development, (5) removing or revising local zoning ordinances that discourage or forbid high-density development, and (6) encouraging the development of "workforce housing" near employers.

36. See Ewing et al., *Growing Cooler*, 55–89.
37. Kahn, *Green Cities*, 114–15.
38. Bento et al., "Impact of Urban Spatial Structure on Travel Demand in the United States." Cited in Kahn, *Green Cities*, 113.
39. Kahn, *Green Cities*, 116; 2000 U.S. Census.
40. Kahn, *Green Cities*, 119–20.
41. Conlin, "Extreme Commuting"; cited in Lewyn, "Five Myths about Sprawl," 81 ff.
42. See congressional testimony of Anthony Downs to the Subcommittee on Highways and Transit of the Committee on Transportation and Infrastructure in 2000. Downs testified,
   Regarding traffic congestion, I do not believe there is any such thing as a "solution" or a "remedy" that will stop congestion from getting worse. We can and probably should build more roads to accommodate new growth areas, and better repair the roads we already have. We should also develop more effective means of public transit. But the desires of the American public for low-density living served by private transport and the immense flexibility it provides will not be diverted into any huge shift into mass transit. Moreover, all the added public transit we build will not really reduce future traffic congestion much, as our experience to date so clearly demonstrates.
   See also Downs, *Stuck in Traffic*.
43. Kraus, "Gas Prices Send Surge of Riders to Mass Transit."
44. Lee, "Higher Gas Prices and Tolls Cut Congestion."
45. On the gap between the consumer cost of driving and its marginal social cost, see O'Flaherty, *City Economics*, ch. 3.
46. For a preliminary attempt to develop a comprehensive strategy for integrating efforts to create "green jobs" with efforts to stabilize the economic underpinnings of U.S. cities, see Alperovitz and Williamson, "Climate Change, Community Stability, and the Next 150 Million Americans."
47. Nelson, "Leadership in a New Era."
48. Ewing et al., *Growing Cooler*, 155.
49. See Gilbert and Perl, *Transport Revolutions*.

50. In a provocative recent book, George Gonzalez argues that there is a causal connection between the dependence of the American economy on sprawl and related industries and the United States' slow response to global warming. See Gonzalez, *Urban Sprawl, Global Warming, and the Empire of Capital*.

51. Pettit, *Republicanism*, 134–38.

52. For a particularly powerful recent critique of the dominant lifestyle (and mode of politics) in the United States from an environmental perspective, see Speth, *Bridge at the End of the World*.

53. See Sagoff, *Price, Principle and the Environment*; also Smith, *Deliberative Democracy and the Environment*, ch. 2.

54. Smith, *Deliberative Democracy and the Environment*; Eckersley, *Green State*.

55. Eckersley, *Green State*, 85–110. Eckersley provides an extensive green critique of liberalism and of efforts to merge green and liberal thought; see also her critique of Habermas from a green perspective (150–69), and Andrew Dobson's discussion in *Green Political Thought*, 164–72. Prominent efforts to make green politics consistent with Rawlsian liberalism include Wissenburg, *Green Liberalism*, and Hailwood, *How to Be a Green Liberal*.

56. Hence, Eckersley: "Although the primary focus of this book is on the state, my arguments also presuppose active ecological citizens that take responsibility for their state as *their* creation, and bring to life the kinds of green constitutional reforms I have recommended" (*Green State*, 245). On this theme, see also Shutkin, *Land That Could Be*.

57. Cannavó, "'To the Thousandth Generation.'"

58. Hester, *Design for Ecological Democracy*, 7.

59. See Maynor, *Republicanism in the Modern World*, 98 ff., for a useful discussion of John Rawls's telling comment that he "regrets" the fact that political liberalism cannot be truly neutral toward different conceptions of the good.

60. In this vein, see Van Jones's call for a "Green New Deal" in his call to action, *The Green Collar Economy*.

61. Felicity Barringer, "In California, Sprawl Bill Is Heading to Governor"; Kevin Yamamura, "Governor Signs Anti-Sprawl Bill."

Chapter 9

1. Levine, *Zoned Out*.

2. Levine, *Zoned Out*.

3. Fishman, "The Fifth Migration"; Nelson, "Leadership in a New Era."

4. David Rusk, an advocate of annexation and related city expansion strategies, outlines some of the legal obstacles involved in his *Cities without Suburbs*.

5. Frug, "Beyond Regional Government."

6. Frug's proposal and a related proposal by the legal scholar Richard Ford are further discussed in Hayward, "The Difference States Make."

7. Levine, *Zoned Out*.

8. Levine argues that Portland-style boundaries need not be seen as anti-market or anti–property rights, since they increase development rights within the boundary even as they limit them outside the boundary. This argument is persuasive, but hard-core libertarians are not concerned with maximizing the "total" amount of freedom in a society, only with preventing *any* infringement on "freedom" (even if such infringements made

it possible to effect increasing the freedoms of others). Consequently, urban-growth boundaries are bound to invite opposition from libertarians and others who point out that such boundaries do restrict the preferences some individuals may have for living beyond the growth boundary.

9. For a critical evaluation of the success of existing planned suburbs in the United States in fostering an alternative to sprawl, see Forsyth, *Reforming Suburbia*. See also the discussion of planned communities in Talen, *New Urbanism and American Planning*, ch. 6.

10. Mill, *On Liberty*, ch. 5.

11. Peter Gordon and Harry Richardson thus confidently declare that "the sprawl debate, at its most fundamental level, hinges on whether one believes that people have the right to choose where they want to live, what they want to drive, where they want to shop, and soon—if they are willing to pay the full costs involved" ("Sprawl Debate," quote on 149).

12. This is not to say that the state can never have a legitimate coercive claim over individuals: some nations require individuals to serve in the military or in another form of public service, and some nations require citizens to vote. Civic republicans generally might approve of the legitimacy of such measures aimed at directly upholding the security and legitimacy of the state. But measures aimed at coercing individuals into a certain kind of lifestyle undermine the independence of citizens vis-à-vis the state (and thereby the good of non-domination, in Pettit's terms). For a recent discussion of how policymakers can shape desired outcomes without resorting to direct coercion of individuals, see Sunstein and Thaler, *Nudge*.

13. For this observation, I am indebted to comments made by Todd Swanstrom at a workshop on sprawl at the 2004 Urban Affairs Association meetings in Washington, D.C.

14. Other scholars and writers have also offered more positive frameworks for thinking about spatial reform. Important examples include Frug's *City Making*; Calthorpe and Fulton's *Regional City*; and Susan Fainstein's recent work, "Planning and the Just City."

15. Fishman, "The Fifth Migration"; Nelson, "Leadership in a New Era."

16. Haya el Nasser, "Housing Bust Halts Growing Suburbs."

17. The most extensive articulation of how a successful political alliance aimed at reforming growth patterns in metropolitan regions might be formed and held together, that of Myron Orfield, rests heavily on the possibility of religiously minded and other value-motivated suburban residents taking sides, on ethical grounds, with the interests of urban and inner-suburban residents in debates about metropolitan-resource allocation. See Orfield's *Metropolitics* and *American Metropolitics*.

18. This particular virtue is, of course, not unique to civic republicans and has been emphasized by many deliberative democrats who would also classify themselves as Rawlsians. It is of particular importance to civic republicans, however, especially vis-à-vis versions of liberalism that refrain from placing more than modest civic expectations on the citizenry at large.

19. Sandel, *Liberalism and the Limits of Justice*, 183.

BIBLIOGRAPHY

Frank Ackerman and Lisa Heinzerling. *Priceless: On Knowing the Price of Everything and the Value of Nothing.* New York: New Press, 2004.

Daniel Aldrich. *Site Fights: Divisive Facilities and Civil Society in Japan and the West.* Ithaca: Cornell University Press, 2008.

Barbara Alexander. "The U.S. Homebuilding Industry: A Half-Century of Building the American Dream." Dunlop Lecture, Harvard University, Cambridge, MA, October 12, 2000. Available from the Joint Center for Housing Studies, Harvard University.

Kern Alexander and Richard G. Salmon. "Warranting Failure: The 'System' That Breeds Poverty and Starves Public Schools." *Journal of Educational Finance* 33 (2007): 203–21.

Anita Allen and Milton Regan, eds. *Debating Democracy's Discontent: Essays on American Politics, Law, and Public Philosophy.* New York: Oxford University Press, 1998.

Gar Alperovitz and Thad Williamson. "Climate Change, Community Stability, and the Next 150 Million Americans." College Park, MD: The Democracy Collaborative, 2010.

Alan Altshuler. "The Ideo-logics of Urban Land Use Politics." In *Dilemmas of Scale in America's Federal Democracy,* edited by Martha Derthick, 189–226. Cambridge: Cambridge University Press, 1999.

———. *The Urban Transportation System: Politics and Policy Innovation.* Cambridge: MIT Press, 1979.

Alan Altshuler and José Gómez-Ibáñez. *Regulation for Revenue: The Political Economy of Land Use Exactions.* Washington, DC: Brookings Institution Press, 1993.

Alan Altshuler, William Morrill, Harold Wolman, and Faith Mitchell, eds. *Governance and Opportunity in Metropolitan America.* Washington, DC: National Academy Press, 1999.

Elizabeth Anderson. "How Not to Complain About Taxes." *Left2Right* blog, January 2005. http://left2right.typepad.com/main/2005/01/how_not_to_comp.html.

———. *Value in Ethics and Economics.* Cambridge: Harvard University Press, 1993.

Perry Anderson. *Spectrum: From Right to Left in the World of Ideas.* New York: Verso, 2005.

Gustavo Angeles, David Guilkey, and Thomas Mroz. "The Impact of Community Level Variables on Individual Level Outcomes: Theoretical Results and Applications." *Sociological Methods & Research* 34 (2005): 76–121.

Jean Anyon. *Radical Possibilities: Public Policy, Urban Education, and a New Social Movement.* New York: Routledge, 2005.

Hannah Arendt. *The Human Condition.* Chicago: University of Chicago Press, 1958.

Hannah Arendt. *On Revolution.* New York: Penguin Books, 1990.

Aristotle. *The Politics.* Translated by T. A. Sinclair. New York: Penguin, 1962.

Richard Arneson. "Liberal Neutrality on the Good: An Autopsy." In *Perfectionism and Neutrality: Essays in Liberal Theory,* edited by Steven Wall and George Klosko, 191–218. Lanham, MD: Rowman & Littlefield, 2003.

Carmen G. Arroyo. *The Funding Gap.* Washington, DC: The Education Trust, January 2008.

Daniel Attas. *Liberty, Property and Markets: A Critique of Libertarianism.* Burlington, VT: Ashgate, 2005.

James Wood Bailey, *Utilitarianism, Institutions, and Justice.* New York: Oxford University Press, 1997.

Benjamin Barber. "Malled, Mauled, and Overhauled: Arresting Suburban Sprawl by Transforming Suburban Malls into Usable Civic Space." In *Public Space and Democracy,* edited by Marcel Hénaff and Tracy B. Strong, 201–20. Minneapolis: University of Minnesota Press, 2001.

———. *Strong Democracy: Participatory Politics for a New Age.* Berkeley and Los Angeles: University of California Press, 1984.

Felicity Barringer. "In California, Sprawl Bill Is Heading to Governor." *New York Times,* September 1, 2008.

Larry Bartels. *Unequal Democracy: The Political Economy of the New Gilded Age.* Princeton: Princeton University Press, 2008.

M. P. Baumgartner. *The Moral Order of a Suburb.* New York: Oxford University Press, 1988.

Rosalyn Baxandall and Elizabeth Ewen. *Picture Windows: How the Suburbs Happened.* New York: Basic Books, 2000.

Isaac Bayoh, Elena G. Irwin, and Timothy Haab. "Determinants of Residential Location Choice: How Important Are Local Public Goods in Attracting Homeowners to Central City Locations?" *Journal of Regional Science* 46 (2006): 97–120.

Timothy Beatley. *Ethical Land Use: Principles of Policy and Planning.* Baltimore: Johns Hopkins University Press, 1994.

Robert Beauregard. "Federal Policy and Postwar Urban Decline: A Case of Government Complicity?" *Housing Policy Debate* 12 (2001): 129–51.

Robert Beauregard. *When America Became Suburban.* Minneapolis: University of Minnesota Press, 2006.

Ronald Beiner. "Introduction." In *Debating Democracy's Discontent: Essays on American Politics, Law, and Public Philosophy,* edited by Anita Allen and Milton Regan, 1–14. New York: Oxford University Press, 1998.

Kaid Benfield, Matthew Raimi, and Don Chen. *Once There Were Greenfields.* Washington, DC: National Resources Defense Council, 1999.

Seyla Benhabib. *The Rights of Others: Aliens, Residents, and Citizens.* Cambridge: Cambridge University Press, 2004.

Antonio M. Bento, Maureen Cropper, Ahmad Mushfiq Mobarak, and Katja Vinha. "The Impact of Urban Spatial Structure on Travel Demand in the United States." *Review of Economics and Statistics* 87 (2005): 466–78.

Peter Berkowitz. "Other People's Mothers." *New Republic* (January 10, 2000): 27–37.

Isaiah Berlin. "Two Concepts of Liberty." In *Four Essays on Liberty*. New York: Oxford University Press, 1970.

Jeffrey M. Berry, Kent Portney, and Ken Thomson. *The Rebirth of Urban Democracy*. Washington, DC: Brookings Institution Press, 1993.

Alan Berube. "Two Steps Back: City and Suburban Poverty Trends, 1999–2005." Washington, DC: Brookings Institution, December 2006.

Susan Bickford. "Constructing Inequality: City Spaces and the Architecture of Citizenship." *Political Theory* 28 (June 2000): 355–76.

Bruce J. Biddle and David Berliner. "Unequal School Funding in the United States." *Educational Leadership* 59 (2002): 48–59.

Bill Bishop. *The Big Sort: Why the Clustering of Like-Minded America Is Tearing Us Apart*. Boston: Houghton Mifflin, 2008.

John P. Blair. *Local Economic Development: Analysis and Practice*. Thousand Oaks, CA: Sage, 1995.

Evelyn Blumenberg and Margy Waller. "The Long Journey to Work: A Federal Transportation Policy for Working Families." In *Taking the High Road: A Metropolitan Agenda for Transportation Reform,* edited by Bruce Katz and Robert Puentes, 197–225. Washington, DC: Brookings Institution Press, 2005.

William T. Bogart. *Don't Call It Sprawl: Metropolitan Structure in the Twenty-First Century*. Cambridge: Cambridge University Press, 2006.

Steven C. Bourassa. "The Community Land Trust as a Highway Mitigation Tool." *Journal of Urban Affairs* 28 (2006): 399–418.

David Brain. "From Good Neighborhoods to Sustainable Cities: Social Science and the Social Agenda of the New Urbanism." *International Regional Science Review* 28 (2005): 217–38.

David Braybrooke. *Utilitarianism: Restorations; Repairs; Renovations*. Toronto: University of Toronto Press, 2004.

David Braybrooke and Charles E. Lindblom. *A Strategy of Decision: Policy Evaluation as Social Process*. New York: Free Press, 1962.

Barbara Brenzel and Harvey Kantor. "Urban Education and the 'Truly Disadvantaged': The Historical Roots of the Contemporary Crisis, 1945–90." In *The "Underclass" Debate: Views from History,* edited by Michael Katz. Princeton: Princeton University Press, 1993.

Corey Brettschneider. *Democratic Rights: The Substance of Self-Government*. Princeton: Princeton University Press, 2007.

Xavier de Souza Briggs, ed. *The Geography of Opportunity*. Washington, DC: Brookings Institution Press, 2005.

David Brink. "Mill's Deliberative Utilitarianism." In *Mill's Utilitarianism: Critical Essays,* edited by David Lyons. Lanham, MD: Rowman & Littlefield, 1997.

David Brooks. *On Paradise Drive: How We Live Now (and Always Have) in the Future Tense*. New York: Random House, 2004.

Sidney Brower. *Good Neighborhoods*. Westport: Praeger, 1996.

David S. Brown. "Discounting Democracy: Wal-Mart's Impact on Social Capital and Civic Engagement in the U.S." Paper delivered at the annual meeting of the American Political Science Association, Toronto, September 2009.

Marilyn Brown, Frank Southworth, and Andrea Sarzynski. "Shrinking the Carbon Footprint of Metropolitan America." Washington, DC: Brookings Institution, May 2008.

Marilyn Brown, Frank Southworth, and Therese Stovall. "Towards a Climate-Friendly Built Environment." Washington, DC: Pew Center on Global Climate Change, 2005.

Jan Brueckner. "Urban Sprawl: Diagnosis and Remedies." *International Regional Science Review* 23 (2000): 160–71.

Jan Brueckner and Ann Largey. "Social Interaction and Urban Sprawl." *Journal of Urban Economics* 64 (2008): 18–34.

Robert Bruegmann. *Sprawl: A Compact History*. Chicago: University of Chicago Press, 2005.

James Buchanan. "Principles of Urban Fiscal Strategy." *Public Choice* 11 (1971): 1–16.

Ralph Buehler, John Pucher, and Uwe Kunert. "Making Transportation Sustainable: Learning from Germany." Washington, DC: The Brookings Institution, April 2009.

Robert W. Burchell, Anthony Downs, Barbara McCann, and Sahan Mukherji. *Sprawl Costs: Economic Impacts of Unchecked Development*. Washington, DC: Island, 2005.

Robert W. Burchell et al. *The Costs of Sprawl—2000 (Transit Cooperative Research Program Report 74)*. Washington, DC: National Academy Press, 2002.

Marcy Burchfield, Henry G. Overman, Diego Puga, and Matthew Turner. "Causes of Sprawl: A Portrait from Space." *Quarterly Journal of Economics* 121 (2006): 587–633.

Peter Calthorpe and William Fulton. *The Regional City: Planning for the End of Sprawl*. Washington, DC: Island, 2001.

Andrea Campbell. *How Policies Make Citizens: Senior Political Activism and the American Welfare State*. Princeton: Princeton University Press, 2003.

David Campbell. *Why We Vote: How Schools and Communities Shape Our Civic Life*. Princeton: Princeton University Press, 2006.

Heather Campbell and Robert Marshall. "Utilitarianism's Bad Breath? A Re-evaluation of the Public Interest Justification for Planning." *Planning Theory* 1 (2002): 163–87.

Peter Cannavó. " 'To the Thousandth Generation': Timelessness and the Pastoral Nexus between Green Politics and Republicanism." Paper presented at the annual meeting of the American Political Science Association, Chicago, August 2007.

———. *The Working Landscape: Founding, Preservation, and the Politics of Place*. Cambridge, MA: MIT Press, 2007.

Robert Caro. *The Power Broker: Robert Moses and the Fall of New York*. New York: Vintage, 1974.

Simone Chambers. "The Politics of Equality: Rawls On the Barricades." *Perspectives on Politics* 4 (March 2006): 81–89.

Wendy K. Tam Cho and Thomas J. Rudolph. "Emanating Political Participation: Untangling the Spatial Structure Behind Participation." *British Journal of Political Science* 38 (2008): 273–89.

G. A. Cohen. *If You're an Egalitarian, How Come You're So Rich?* Cambridge, MA: Harvard University Press, 2000.

Joshua Cohen. "Choice-Based Libertarianism." Lecture notes available at http://stellar.mit.edu/S/course/17/fa03/17.01j/materials.html.

———. "Deliberation and Democratic Legitimacy." In *Deliberative Democracy: Essays on Reason and Politics*, edited by James Bohman and William Rehg, 67–92. Cambridge, MA: MIT Press, 1997.

———. "For a Democratic Society." In *The Cambridge Companion to Rawls*, edited by Samuel Freeman, 86–138. Cambridge: Cambridge University Press, 2003.

———. "Taking People As They Are?" *Philosophy and Public Affairs* 30 (2002): 363–86.

Lizabeth Cohen. *A Consumer's Republic: The Politics of Consumption in Postwar Suburbia*. New York: Vintage, 2003.

Michelle Conlin. "Extreme Commuting." *Business Week,* February 21, 2005.

Benjamin Constant. "The Liberty of the Ancients Compared with That of the Moderns." In *Political Writings,* translated and edited by Biancamaria Fontana, 309–28. Cambridge: Cambridge University Press, 1988.

Matthew A. Crenson and Benjamin Ginsberg. *Downsizing Democracy.* Baltimore: Johns Hopkins University Press, 2002.

Jackie Cutsinger and George Galster. "There Is No Sprawl Syndrome: A New Typology of Metropolitan Land Use Patterns." *Urban Geography* 27 (2006): 228–52.

Richard Dagger. *Civic Virtues.* New York: Oxford University Press, 1997.

———. "Neo-Republicanism and the Civic Economy." *Politics, Philosophy, and Economics* 5 (2006): 151–73.

———. "Michael Sandel, Public Philosopher." *European Journal of Political Theory* 6 (2007): 219–26.

Herman E. Daly and John B. Cobb, Jr. *For the Common Good: Redirecting the Economy Toward Community, the Environment and a Sustainable Future.* Boston: Beacon, 1989.

Mike Davis. *Planet of Slums.* New York: Verso, 2006.

James DeFilippis. *Unmaking Goliath: Community Control in the Face of Global Capital.* New York: Routledge, 2004.

Mark Delucchi, "Do Motor-Vehicle Users in the United States Pay Their Way?" *Transportation Research* 41 (2007): 982–1003.

Loren Demerath and David Levinger. "The Social Qualities of Being on Foot: A Theoretical Analysis of Pedestrian Activity, Community, and Culture." *City and Community* 2 (2003): 217–37.

Robert D. Dietz. "Local Use of the Mortgage Interest and the Real Estate Tax Deductions," National Association of Home Builders, June 2006. http://www.nahb.org.

Robert D. Dietz and Donald R. Haurin. "The Social and Private Micro-level Consequences of Homeownership." *Journal of Urban Economics* 54 (2003): 401–50.

David Dixon. "The Virtue of Density." *Boston Globe,* July 7, 2003.

Andrew Dobson. *Green Political Thought.* London: Routledge, 2000.

Anthony Downs, ed. *Growth Management and Affordable Housing: Do They Conflict?* Washington, DC: Brookings Institution Press, 2004.

———. "How Is Suburban Sprawl Related to Urban Decline?" March 2, 2000. http://www.anthonydowns.com.

———. *New Visions for Metropolitan America.* Washington, DC: Brookings Institution Press, 1994.

———. *Stuck in Traffic: Coping with Peak-Hour Traffic Congestion.* Washington, DC: Brookings Institution Press, 1992.

———. Testimony to the House Subcommittee on Highways and Transit of the Committee on Transportation and Infrastructure, 107th Congress of the United States, March 21, 2001. http://www.anthonydowns.com/20010322.pdf.

Peter Dreier, John Mollenkopf, and Todd Swanstrom. *Place Matters: Metropolitics for the Twenty-First Century.* Lawrence: University Press of Kansas, 2001.

Andres Duany, Elizabeth Plater-Zyberk, and Jeff Speck. *Suburban Nation: The Rise of Sprawl and the Decline of the American Dream.* New York: North Point, 2000.

Steven N. Durlauf. "Groups, Social Influences, and Inequality." In *Poverty Traps,* edited by Samuel Bowles, Steven N. Durlauf, and Karla Hoff, 141–75. New York: Russell Sage Foundation, 2006.

Ellen Dunham-Jones and June Williamson. *Retrofitting Suburbia: Urban Design Solutions for Redesigning Suburbs*. New York: Wiley, 2009.

Ronald Dworkin. *Sovereign Virtue: The Theory and Practice of Equality*. Cambridge: Harvard University Press, 2000.

Robyn Eckersley. *The Green State: Rethinking Democracy and Sovereignty*. Cambridge, MA: MIT Press, 2004.

Timothy Egan. "Owners of Malibu Mansions Cry, 'This Sand Is My Sand.'" *New York Times*, August 25, 2002.

Stephen Elkin. "Citizen and City: Locality, Public-Spiritedness, and the American Regime." In *Dilemmas of Scale in America's Federal Democracy*, edited by Martha Derthick. Cambridge, UK: Cambridge University Press, 1999.

———. *City and Regime in the American Republic*. Chicago: University of Chicago Press, 1987.

———. *Reconstructing the Commercial Republic*. Chicago: University of Chicago Press, 2006.

Ingrid Ellen. "Spatial Stratification within U.S. Metropolitan Areas." In *Governance and Opportunity in Metropolitan America*, edited by Alan Altshuler, William Morrill, Harold Wolman, and Faith Mitchell, 192–212. Washington, DC: National Academy Press, 1999.

Jon Elster. "Sour Grapes: Utilitarianism and the Genesis of Wants." In *Utilitarianism and Beyond*, edited by Amartya Sen and Bernard Williams. Cambridge: Cambridge University Press, 1982.

James W. Ely, Jr. *The Guardian of Every Other Right: A Constitutional History of Property Rights*. 3rd ed. New York: Oxford University Press, 2008.

Richard A. Epstein. *Takings: Private Property and the Power of Eminent Domain*. Cambridge: Harvard University Press, 1985.

Reid Ewing, Keith Bartholomew, Steve Winkleman, Jerry Walters, and Don Chen. *Growing Cooler: The Evidence on Urban Development and Climate Change*. Washington, DC: Urban Land Institute, 2008.

Reid Ewing, Ross Brownson, and David Berrigan. "Relationship between Sprawl and Weight of United States Youth." *American Journal of Preventive Medicine* 31 (2006): 464–74.

Reid Ewing, John Kostyack, Don Chen, Bruce Stein, and Michelle Ernst. *Endangered by Sprawl: How Runaway Development Threatens American Wildlife*. Washington, DC: National Wildlife Federation, Smart Growth America, and NatureServe, January 2005.

Reid Ewing, Rolf Pendall, and Don Chen, "Measuring Sprawl and Its Impact." Washington, DC: Smart Growth America, 2001.

Reid Ewing, Tom Schmid, Richard Killingsworth, Amy Zlot, and Stephen Raudenbush. "Relationship between Urban Sprawl and Physical Activity, Obesity, and Morbidity." *American Journal of Health Promotion* 18 (2003): 47–57.

Susan Fainstein. "Planning and the Just City." In *Searching for the Just City*, edited by Peter Marcuse et al. 19–39. New York: Routledge, 2009.

Douglas Farr. *Sustainable Urbanism: Urban Design with Nature*. New York: Wiley, 2008.

Federal Budget of the United States 2009. Washington, DC: Government Printing Office, 2008.

Ed Finkel. "Affordable Forever." *Planning* 71 (November 2005): 24–27.

Dan Fireside. "Burlington Busts the Affordable Housing Debate." *Dollars & Sense*, (March/April 2005): 19–29.

William Fischel. "An Economic History of Zoning and a Cure for Its Exclusionary Effects." *Urban Studies* 41 (2004): 317–40.

———. *The Homevoter Hypothesis.* Cambridge, MA: Harvard University Press, 2001.

Robert Fishman. *Bourgeois Utopias: The Rise and Fall of Suburbia.* New York: Basic Books, 1987.

———. "The Fifth Migration." *Journal of the American Planning Association* 71 (2005): 357–66.

Owen Fiss. *A Way Out: America's Ghettos and the Legacy of Racism.* Princeton: Princeton University Press, 2003.

Anthony Flint. *This Land: The Battle over Sprawl and the Future of America.* Baltimore: Johns Hopkins University Press, 2006.

Robert Fogelson. *Bourgeois Nightmares: Suburbia, 1870–1930.* New Haven, CT: Yale University Press, 2005.

Ann Forsyth. *Reforming Suburbia: The Planned Communities of Irvine, Columbia and the Woodlands.* Berkeley and Los Angeles: University of California Press, 2005.

Andres Francisco. "A Republican Interpretation of the Late Rawls." *Journal of Political Philosophy* 14 (2006): 270–88.

Lawrence Frank, Peter Engelke, and Thomas Schmid. *Health and Community Design: The Impact of the Built Environment on Physical Activity.* Washington, DC: Island, 2003.

Robert H. Frank. *Falling Behind: How Rising Inequality Harms the Middle Class.* Berkeley and Los Angeles: University of California Press, 2007.

———. "Why Is Cost–Benefit Analysis So Controversial?" In *Cost–Benefit Analysis: Legal, Economic, and Philosophical Perspectives,* edited by Matthew D. Adler and Eric A. Posner, 77–94. Chicago: University of Chicago Press, 2001.

John W. Frece. "Twenty Lessons from Maryland's Smart Growth Initiative." *Vermont Journal of Environmental Law* 6, no. 3 (2004–5). http://www.vjel.org/journal/pdf/VJEL10023.pdf.

Lance Freeman. "The Effects of Sprawl on Neighborhood Social Ties: An Explanatory Analysis." *Journal of the American Planning Association* 67 (March 2001): 69–77.

Samuel Freeman. *Rawls.* New York: Routledge, 2007.

Eric T. Freyfogle. *The Land We Share: Private Property and the Common Good.* Washington, DC: Island, 2003.

Milton Friedman. *Capitalism and Freedom.* Chicago: University of Chicago Press, 1962.

Gerald Frug. "Beyond Regional Government." *Harvard Law Review* 115 (2002): 1763–836.

———. *City Making: Building Communities without Building Walls.* Princeton: Princeton University Press, 1999.

———. "The Legal Technology of Exclusion in Metropolitan America." In *The New Suburban History,* edited by Michael Kruse and Thomas Sugrue, 205–20. Chicago: University of Chicago Press, 2006.

William Fulton, Rolf Pendall, Mai Nguyen, and Alicia Harrison. "Who Sprawls Most? How Growth Patterns Differ across the U.S." Report of the Center on Urban and Metropolitan Policy, Brookings Institution, Washington, DC, July 2001.

Archon Fung. *Empowered Participation: Reinventing Urban Democracy.* Princeton: Princeton University Press, 2004.

Archon Fung and Erik Olin Wright, eds. *Deepening Democracy: Institutional Innovations in Empowered Participatory Governance.* New York: Verso, 2003.

Juliet Gainsborough. *Fenced Off: The Suburbanization of American Politics.* Washington, DC: Georgetown University Press, 2001.

George Galster, Royce Hanson, Hal Wolman, Stephen Coleman, and Jason Freihage. "Wrestling Sprawl to the Ground: Defining and Measuring an Elusive Concept." *Housing Facts and Findings* 2 (Winter 2000): 3–5.

George Galster, Royce Hanson, Michael Ratcliffe, Hal Wolman, Stephen Coleman, and Jason Freihage. "Wrestling Sprawl to the Ground: Defining and Measuring an Elusive Concept." *Housing Policy Debate* 12 (2001): 681–717.

George Galster, Dave Marcotte, Marv Mandell, Hal Wolman, and Nancy Augustine. "The Importance of Neighborhood Poverty during Childhood on Fertility, Education, and Earnings Outcomes." *Housing Studies* 22 (2007): 723–51.

William Galston. *Liberal Purposes: Goods, Virtues, and Diversity in the Liberal State.* Cambridge: Cambridge University Press, 1991.

———. "Political Economy and the Politics of Virtue: U.S. Public Philosophy at Century's End." In *Debating Democracy's Discontent,* edited by Anita Allen and Milton S. Regan, 63–85. New York: Oxford University Press, 1998.

Herbert Gans. *People and Plans: Essays on Urban Problems and Solutions.* New York: Basic Books, 1968.

Joel Garreau. *Edge City: Life on the New Frontier.* New York: Random House, 1991.

Raymond Geuss. *Outside Ethics.* Princeton: Princeton University Press, 2005.

Richard Gilbert and Anthony Perl. *Transport Revolutions: Moving People and Freight without Oil.* London: Earthscan, 2008.

Oliver Gillham. *The Limitless City.* Washington: Island Press, 2002.

James Gimpel, Celeste Lay, and Jason Shucknecht. *Cultivating Democracy: Civic Environments and Political Socialization in America.* Washington, DC: Brookings Institution Press, 2003.

Edward Glaeser and Joshua Gottlieb. "Urban Resurgence and the Consumer City." *Urban Studies* 43 (2006): 1275–99.

Edward Glaeser and Matthew Kahn. "The Greenness of Cities." Rappaport Institute for Greater Boston Policy Brief, Taubman Center for State and Local Government, Kennedy School of Government, Harvard University, Cambridge, MA, March 2008.

———. "Sprawl and Urban Growth." In *Handbook of Regional and Urban Economics 4,* edited by J. V. Henderson and J. F. Thisse, 2481–527. Amsterdam: Elsevier, 2004.

Stephan J. Goetz and Anil Rupasingha. "Wal-Mart and Social Capital." *American Journal of Agricultural Economics* 88 (2006): 1304–1310.

Michael Goggin. "Is It Time for a Change? Science, Policy, and Climate Change." Harvard College Senior Honors Thesis, 2004.

George A. Gonzalez. *Urban Sprawl, Global Warming, and the Empire of Capital.* Albany: State University of New York Press, 2009.

Robert E. Goodin. *Political Theory and Public Policy.* Chicago: University of Chicago Press, 1982.

———. *Reflective Democracy.* New York: Oxford University Press, 2003.

———. *Utilitarianism as a Public Philosophy.* Cambridge: Cambridge University Press, 1995.

Peter Gordon and Harry W. Richardson. "Are Compact Cities a Desirable Planning Goal?" *Journal of the American Planning Association* 63 (Winter 1997): 95–106.

———. "The Sprawl Debate: Let Markets Plan." *Publius* 31 (2001): 131–49.

Jill Grant. *Planning the Good Community: New Urbanism in Theory and Practice.* New York: Routledge, 2006.

Paul Grogan and Tony Proscio. *Comeback Cities: A Blueprint for Urban Neighborhood Revival.* Boulder, CO: Westview, 2000.

Carl Guarneri. *The Utopian Alternative: Fourierism in Nineteenth-Century America*. Ithaca, NY: Cornell University Press, 1991.

Owen D. Gutfreund. *Twentieth-Century Sprawl: Highways and the Reshaping of the American Landscape*. Oxford: Oxford University Press, 2004.

Amy Gutmann. "What's the Use of Going to School?" In *Utilitarianism and Beyond,* edited by Amartya Sen and Bernard Williams. Cambridge: Cambridge University Press, 1982.

Amy Gutmann and Dennis Thompson. *Democracy and Disagreement*. Cambridge, MA: Harvard University Press, 1996.

Jurgen Habermas. *Between Facts and Norms: Contributions to a Discourse Theory of Law and Democracy*. Translated by William Rehg. Cambridge, MA: MIT Press, 1996.

Jason Hackworth. *The Neoliberal City: Governance, Ideology, and Development in American Urbanism*. Ithaca, NY: Cornell University Press, 2007.

Frank Hahn. "On Some Difficulties of the Utilitarian Economist." In *Utilitarianism and Beyond,* edited by Amartya Sen and Bernard Williams, 187–98. Cambridge: Cambridge University Press, 1982.

Simon Hailwood. *How to Be a Green Liberal: Nature, Value and Liberal Philosophy*. Montreal: McGill-Queens University Press, 2004.

Peter Hall. "Policy Paradigms, Social Learning and the State: The Case of Economic Policy Making in Britain." *Comparative Politics* 25 (1993): 275–97.

Ben Harder. "Weighing In on City Planning." *Science News* (January 20, 2007): 43.

David Harvey. *Justice, Nature, and the Geography of Difference*. Oxford: Blackwell, 1996.

———. *Social Justice and the City*. Baltimore: Johns Hopkins, 1973.

Dolores Hayden. *Building Suburbia: Green Fields and Urban Growth, 1820–2000*. New York: Random House, 2003.

———. "What Is Suburbia? Naming the Layers in the Landscape, 1820–2000." In *Smart Growth: Form and Consequences,* edited by Terry S. Szold and Armando Carbonell. Cambridge, MA: Lincoln Institute, 2003.

Dolores Hayden with Jim Wark. *A Field Guide to Sprawl*. New York: W. W. Norton, 2004.

Clarissa Hayward. "The Difference States Make: Democracy, Identity, and the American City." *American Political Science Review* 97 (2003): 501–14.

Amy Helling. "Transportation, Land Use, and the Impacts of Sprawl on Poor Children and Families." In *Urban Sprawl: Causes, Consequences, and Policy Responses,* edited by Gregory Squires, 119–40. Washington, DC: Urban Institute Press, 2002.

Marcel Hénaff and Tracy B. Strong, eds. *Public Space and Democracy*. Minneapolis: University of Minnesota Press, 2001.

Randolph Héster. *Design for Ecological Democracy*. Cambridge, MA: MIT Press, 2006.

Joel Hirschhorn. *Sprawl Kills: How Blandburbs Steal Your Time, Health and Money*. New York: Sterling & Ross, 2005.

Frank Hobbs and Nicole Stoops. *Demographic Trends in the 20th Century*. (Census 2000 Special Report.) Washington, DC: U.S. Census Bureau, 2002.

Jennifer Hochschild and Nathan Scovronick. *The American Dream and the Public Schools*. New York: Oxford University Press, 2003.

Christopher Hoene and Michael Pagano. "Fend-for-Yourself-Federalism." *Government Finance Review* (October 2003): 36–42.

Wesley Hogan. *Many Minds, One Heart: SNCC's Dream for a New America*. Chapel Hill: University of North Carolina Press, 2007.

Iseult Honohan. *Civic Republicanism*. New York: Routledge, 2002.

Dan Hopkins. "Discounting Politics: The Impact of Large American Retailers on American Communities." Paper prepared for the Harvard Political Psychology and Behavior Workshop, Cambridge, MA. March 11, 2004.

Max Horkheimer and Theodor Adorno. *Dialectic of Enlightenment*. New York: Continuum International Publishing, 1976.

Thomas A. Horne. *Property Rights and Poverty: Political Argument in Britain, 1605–1834*. Chapel Hill: University of North Carolina Press, 1990.

Jeffrey M. Hornstein. *A Nation of Realtors: A Cultural History of the Twentieth-Century American Middle Class*. Durham, NC: Duke University Press, 2005.

Sir Ebenezer Howard. *Garden Cities of To-Morrow* (1898). Cambridge, MA: MIT Press, 1965.

Robert Huckfeldt. "The Social Contexts of Ethnic Politics." *American Politics Quarterly* 11 (1983): 91–123.

———. *Politics in Context: Assimilation and Conflict in Urban Neighborhoods*. New York: Agathon, 1986.

Stan Humphries. "Who's Afraid of the Big Bad Firm." *American Journal of Political Science* 45 (2001): 678–99.

Keith R. Ihlanfeldt. "The Geography of Economic and Social Opportunity in Metropolitan Areas." In *Governance and Opportunity in Metropolitan America*, edited by Alan Altshuler, William Morrill, Harold Wolman and Faith Mitchell, 213–52. Washington, DC: National Academy Press, 1999.

David Imbroscio. "Fighting Poverty with Mobility: A Normative Policy Analysis." *Review of Policy Research* 21 (2008): 447–61.

———. *Reconstructing City Politics: Alternative Economic Development and Urban Regimes*. Thousand Oaks, CA: Sage, 1997.

International Council on Clean Transportation. *Passenger Vehicle Greenhouse Gas and Fuel Economy Standards: A Global Update*. Washington, DC: International Council on Clean Transportation, July 2007.

Kenneth Jackson. *Crabgrass Frontier: The Suburbanization of the United States*. New York: Oxford University Press, 1985.

Hannah Jacobs. "Searching for Balance in the Aftermath of the 2006 Takings Initiatives." *Yale Law Journal* 116 (2007): 1518–1566.

Harvey M. Jacobs. "New Actions or New Arguments over Regulatory Takings." *Yale Law Journal Pocket Part* 65 (2007). http://thepocketpart.org/2007/09/16/jacobs.html.

Jerry Jacobs. *The Mall: An Attempted Escape from Everyday Life*. Prospect Heights, IL: Waveland, 1984.

Paul Jargowsky. *Poverty and Place: Ghettos, Barrios, and the American City*. New York: Russell Sage Foundation, 1997.

———. "Sprawl, Concentration of Poverty, and Urban Inequality." In *Urban Sprawl: Causes, Consequences, and Policy Responses,* edited by Gregory D. Squires. Washington, DC: Urban Institute, 2002.

Van Jones. *The Green Collar Economy: How One Solution Can Fix Our Two Biggest Problems*. New York: HarperCollins, 2008.

Myung-Jin Jun. "The Effects of Portland's Urban Growth Boundary on Housing Prices." *Journal of the American Planning Association* 72 (2006): 239–43.

Matthew Kahn. "Does Sprawl Reduce the Black/White Housing Consumption Gap?" *Housing Policy Debate* 12 (2001): 77–86.

———. "The Environmental Impact of Suburbanization." *Journal of Policy Analysis and Management* 19 (2000): 569–86.

———. *Green Cities*. Washington, DC: Brookings Institution Press, 2006.

Matthew Kahn and Joel Schwarz. "Urban Air Pollution Progress Despite Sprawl: The 'Greening' of the Vehicle Fleet." *Journal of Urban Economics* 63 (2008): 775–87.

Prasad Kasibhatla and William Chameides. "G8 Leadership Is Critical to Curbing Energy-Related CO_2 Emissions." Durham, NC: Nicholas Institute for Environmental Policy Solutions, Duke University, September 2007.

Bruce Katz and Joel Rogers. "The Next Urban Agenda." In *The Next Agenda: Blueprint for a New Progressive Movement,* edited by Robert Borosage and Roger Hickey. Boulder, CO: Westview, 2001.

Gary King, Michael Tomz, and Jason Wittenberg. "Making the Most of Statistical Analyses: Improving Interpretation and Presentation." *American Journal of Political Science* 44 (2000): 347–61.

Loren King. "Democracy and City Life." *Politics, Philosophy, and Economics* 3 (2004): 97–124.

———. "Democratic Hopes in the Polycentric City." *Journal of Politics* 66 (2004): 203–23.

Elizabeth Kneebone. "Job Sprawl Revisited: The Changing Geography of Metropolitan Employment." Washington: Brookings Institution, April 2009.

Vernon J. Knight, Jr. and Vincas P. Steponaitis, eds. *Archaeology of the Moundville Chiefdom.* Tuscaloosa: University of Alabama Press, 2007.

Paul L. Knox. *Metroburbia USA*. New Brunswick, NJ: Rutgers University Press, 2008.

Brian Knudsen and Terry Clark. "The Local Ecology of New Social Movements." Paper delivered at the annual meeting of the American Political Science Association, Toronto, September 2009.

Margaret Kohn. *Brave New Neighborhoods: The Privatization of Public Space*. New York: Routledge, 2004.

Clifford Krauss. "Gas Prices Send Surge of Riders to Mass Transit." *New York Times*, May 10, 2008.

Kevin M. Kruse. *White Flight: Atlanta and the Making of Modern Conservatism*. Princeton: Princeton University Press, 2005.

Kevin M. Kruse and Thomas J. Sugrue, eds. *The New Suburban History*. Chicago: University of Chicago Press, 2006.

David Kolb. *Sprawling Places*. Athens: University of Georgia, 2008

James Howard Kunstler. *The Geography of Nowhere: The Rise and Decline of America's Man-Made Landscape*. New York: Simon & Schuster, 1993.

Will Kymlicka. "Liberal Egalitarianism and Civic Republicanism: Friends or Enemies?" In *Debating Democracy's Discontent: Essays on American Politics, Law, and Public Philosophy,* edited by Anita Allen and Milton Regan, 131–48. New York: Oxford University Press, 1998.

———. *Contemporary Political Philosophy*. 2nd ed. Oxford: Oxford University Press, 2001.

———. *Liberalism, Community and Culture*. New York: Oxford University Press, 1989.

Cécile Laborde and John Maynor, eds. *Republicanism and Political Theory*. Oxford: Blackwell, 2008.

Robert Lang. *Edgeless Cities: Exploring the Elusive Metropolis*. Washington: Brookings Institution Press, 2003.

———. "Office Sprawl: The Evolving Geography of Business." Report of the Center for Urban and Metropolitan Studies, Brookings Institution, Washington, DC, October 2000.

Matthew Lassiter. *The Silent Majority: Suburban Politics in the Sunbelt South*. Princeton: Princeton University Press, 2006.

Barrett A. Lee, Chad R. Farrell, and Bruce G. Link. "Revisiting the Contact Hypothesis: The Case of Public Exposure to Homelessness." *American Sociological Review* 69 (2004): 40–63.

Jennifer Lee. "Higher Gas Prices and Tolls Cut Congestion." *New York Times,* July 3, 2008.

Jan E. Leighley. "Attitudes, Opportunities and Incentives: A Field Essay on Political Participation." *Political Research Quarterly* 48 (1995): 181–209.

———. "Commentary on 'Attitudes, Opportunities and Incentives: A Field Essay on Political Participation.'" *Political Research Quarterly* 61 (2008): 46–49.

Jonathan Levine. *Zoned Out: Regulation, Markets, and Choices in Transportation and Metropolitan Land-Use*. Washington, DC: Resources for the Future, 2006.

Paul G. Lewis. *Shaping Suburbia: How Political Institutions Organize Urban Development*. Pittsburgh: University of Pittsburgh Press, 1996.

Rebecca Lewis, Gerrit-Jan Knaap, and Jungyul Sohn. "Managing Growth with Priority Fund Areas." *Journal of the American Planning Association* 75 (2009): 457–78.

Michael Lewyn. "Five Myths about Sprawl." *Harvard BlackLetter Law Journal* 23 (2007): 81–106.

Kevin Leyden. "Social Capital and the Built Environment." *American Journal of Public Health* 93 (2003): 1546–51.

Kevin Leyden and Philip Michelbach. "Democracy and 'Neighborly Communities': Some Theoretical Considerations on the Built Environment." In *New Urbanism and Beyond: Designing Cities for the Future,* edited by Tigran Haas, 238–43. New York: Rizzoli, 2008.

Charles Lindblom. *Politics and Markets: The World's Political-Economic Systems*. New York: Basic Books, 1977.

Todd Litman. "Policy Implications of Full Social Costing." *Annals of the American Academy of Political and Social Science* 553 (1997): 143–56.

John Locke. *Second Treatise of Government*. Edited by C. B. Macpherson. Indianapolis: Hackett, 1980.

Lyn Lofland. *The Public Realm: Exploring the City's Quintessentially Social Territory*. Hawthorne, NY: Aldine de Gruyter, 1998.

J. Scott Long and Jeremy Freese. *Regression Models for Categorical Dependent Variables Using Stata*. 2nd ed. College Station, TX: StataCorp, 2005.

Russ Lopez and Patricia Hynes. "Sprawl in the 1990s: Measurement, Distribution, and Trends." *Urban Affairs Review* 38 (2003): 325–55.

Glenn Loury. *The Anatomy of Racial Inequality*. Cambridge: Harvard University Press, 2002.

Richard Louv. *Last Child in the Woods: Saving Our Children from Nature-Deficit Disorder*. Chapel Hill, NC: Algonquin, 2005.

Setha Low. *Behind the Gates*. New York: Routledge, 2003.

Kevin Lynch. *Good City Form*. Cambridge: MIT Press, 1981.

Stephen Macedo. *Liberal Virtues: Citizenship, Virtue and Community in Liberal Constitutionalism.*
New York: Oxford University Press, 1990.

Stephen Macedo et al. *Democracy at Risk: How Political Choices Undermine Citizen Participation.*
Washington, DC: Brookings Institution Press, 2005.

Stephen Malpezzi and Wen-Kai Guo. "Measuring 'Sprawl': Alternative Measures of Urban
Form in U.S. Metropolitan Areas." Madison, WI: University of Wisconsin Real Estate
and Urban Land Economics Department, Working Paper, 2001.

Harvey C. Mansfield. *The Spirit of Liberalism.* Cambridge, MA: Harvard University Press, 1978.

Stephen Marglin. *The Dismal Science: How Thinking Like an Economist Undermines Community.*
Cambridge, MA: Harvard University Press, 2008.

Alex Marshall. *How Cities Work: Sprawl, Suburbs, and the Roads Not Taken.* Austin: University
of Texas Press, 2000.

Tom Martinson. *American Dreamscape: The Pursuit of Happiness in Postwar Suburbia.* New York:
Carroll & Graf, 2000.

Karl Marx. "The German Ideology." In *The Marx-Engels Reader*, edited by Robert C. Tucker,
146–202. 2nd ed. New York: W. W. Norton, 1978.

Douglas S. Massey and Nancy A. Denton. *American Apartheid: Segregation and the Making of
the Underclass.* Cambridge, MA: Harvard University Press, 1993.

John Maynor. *Republicanism in the Modern World.* Cambridge, UK: Polity, 2003.

Thomas McCarthy. "Political Philosophy and Racial Injustice: From Normative to Critical
Theory." In *Pragmatism, Judgment, and Critique: Essays for Richard J. Bernstein,* edited by
Seyla Benhabib and Nancy Fraser, 149–70. Cambridge: MIT Press, 2004.

John Stuart Mill. *On Liberty.* London: J. M. Dent, 1993.

——. *Utilitarianism.* London: J. M. Dent, 1993.

David Miller. *Principles of Social Justice.* Cambridge, MA: Harvard University Press, 1999.

Charles Mills. "'Ideal Theory' as Ideology." *Hypatia* 20, no. 3 (2005): 165–84.

Don Mitchell. *The Right to the City: Social Justice and the Fight for Public Space.* New York:
Guilford, 2003.

Stacy Mitchell. *Big-Box Swindle: The True Cost of Mega-Retailers and the Fight for America's
Independent Businesses.* Boston: Beacon, 2006.

Richard Moe and Carter Wilkie. *Changing Places: Rebuilding Community in the Age of Sprawl.*
New York: Henry Holt, 1997.

Charles de Montesquieu. *The Spirit of the Laws.* Translated and edited by Anne M. Cohler,
Basia Carolyn Miller, and Harold Samuel Stone. Cambridge: Cambridge University
Press, 1989.

Per Mouritsen. "Four Models of Republican Liberty and Self-Government." In *Republicanism
in Theory and Practice,* edited by Iseult Honohan and Jeremy Jennings, 17–38. New York:
Routledge, 2006.

Lewis Mumford. *The Culture of Cities.* New York: Harcourt Brace, 1938.

Liam Murphy and Thomas Nagel. *The Myth of Ownership: Taxes and Justice.* New York:
Oxford University Press, 2002.

Jack Nasar. *The Evaluative Image of the City.* Thousand Oaks, CA: Sage, 1998.

Haya el Nasser. "Housing Bust Halts Growing Suburbs." *USA Today,* November 20,
2009.

National Center for Education Statistics. *The Condition of Education 2003.* Washington,
DC: National Center for Education Statistics, 2003.

National Center for Education Statistics. *The Condition of Education 2009*. Washington, DC: National Center for Education Statistics, 2009.

Jennifer Nedelsky. *Private Property and the Limits of American Constitutionalism: The Madisonian Framework and Its Legacy*. Chicago: University of Chicago Press, 1990.

Arthur C. Nelson. "Leadership in a New Era." *Journal of the American Planning Association* 72 (2006): 393–406.

Arthur C. Nelson, Casey J. Dawkins, and Thomas W. Sanchez. *The Social Impacts of Urban Containment*. Burlington, VT: Ashgate, 2007.

Peter Newman, Timothy Beatley, and Heather Boyer. *Resilient Cities: Responding to Peak Oil and Climate Change*. Washington: Island Press, 2009.

Pietro Nivola. *Laws of the Landscape*. Washington, DC: Brookings Institution Press, 1999.

Robert Nozick. *Anarchy, State and Utopia*. New York: Basic Books, 1974.

Martha Nussbaum. *Women and Human Development: The Capabilities Approach*. Cambridge: Cambridge University Press, 2000.

Brendan O'Flaherty. *City Economics*. Cambridge, MA: Harvard University Press, 2005.

Ray Oldenburg. *The Great Good Place*. New York: Marlowe, 1997.

J. Eric Oliver. *Democracy in Suburbia*. Princeton: Princeton University Press, 2001.

———. "Mental Life and the Metropolis in Suburban America: The Psychological Correlates of Metropolitan Place Characteristics." *Urban Affairs Review* 39 (2003): 228–53.

Myron Orfield. *American Metropolitics: The New Suburban Reality*. Washington, DC. Brookings Institution Press, 2002.

———. *Metropolitics: A Regional Agenda for Community and Stability*. Washington, DC: Brookings Institution Press, 1997.

Orlando Patterson. "The American View of Freedom: What We Say, What We Mean." David Riesman Lecture, Harvard University, Cambridge, MA, October 2000. Published in *Society* 38 (May 2001): 37–45.

Rolf Pendall and John Carruthers. "Does Density Exacerbate Income Segregation?" *Housing Policy Debate* 14 (2003): 541–89.

Rolf Pendall, Robert Puentes, and Jonathan Martin. "From Traditional to Reformed: A Review of the Land Use Regulations of the Nation's 50 Largest Metropolitan Areas." Washington, DC: Brookings Institution, August 2006.

Joseph Persky and Haydar Kurban. "Do Federal Spending and Tax Policies Build Cities or Promote Sprawl?" *Regional Science and Urban Economics* 33 (2003): 361–78.

Joseph Persky and Wim Wiewel. *When Corporations Leave Town*. Detroit: Wayne State University Press, 2000.

Paul Peterson. *City Limits*. Chicago: University of Chicago Press, 1981.

Philip Pettit. "Reworking Sandel's Republicanism." In *Debating Democracy's Discontent*, edited by Anita Allen and Milton Regan, 40–61. New York: Oxford University Press, 1998.

———. *Republicanism: A Theory of Freedom and Government*. New York: Oxford University Press, 1998.

Justin Phillips and Eban Goodstein. "Growth Management and Housing Prices: The Case of Portland, Oregon." *Contemporary Economic Policy* 18 (2000): 334–44.

Karl Polanyi. *The Great Transformation: The Political and Economic Origins of Our Time*. Boston: Beacon, 1944.

Trip Pollard. *New Directions: Land Use, Transportation, and Climate Change in Virginia.* Charlottesville: Southern Environmental Law Center, December 2007.

David Popenoe. *The Suburban Environment: Sweden and the United States.* Chicago: University of Chicago Press, 1977.

Michael E. Porter. "New Strategies for Inner City Development." *Economic Development Quarterly* 11 (1997): 11–27.

John powell. "Sprawl, Fragmentation, and the Persistence of Racial Inequality." In *Urban Sprawl: Causes, Consequences, and Policy Responses,* edited by Gregory Squires, 73–117. Washington, DC: Urban Institute Press, 2002.

———. "Structural Racism and Spatial Jim Crow." In *The Black Metropolis in the Twenty-first Century: Race, Power, and Politics of Place,* edited by Robert D. Bullard, 41–65. Lanham: Rowman & Littlefield, 2007.

David Primo, Matthew Jacobsmeier, and Jeffrey Milyo. "Estimating the Impact of State Policies and Institutions with Mixed-Level Data." *State Politics and Policy Quarterly* 7 (2007): 446–59.

Robert D. Putnam. *Bowling Alone: The Collapse and Revival of American Community.* New York: Simon & Schuster, 2000.

———. "E Pluribus Unum: Diversity and Community in the 21st Century." *Scandinavian Political Studies* 30 (2007): 137–74.

———. *Making Democracy Work: Civic Traditions in Modern Italy.* Princeton: Princeton University Press, 1993.

Margaret Jane Radin. *Reinterpreting Property.* Chicago: University of Chicago, 1993.

Douglas Rae. *City: Urbanism and Its End.* New Haven, CT: Yale University Press, 2003.

Wendy Rahn, Kwang Suk Yoon, Michael Garet, Stephen Lipson, and Katherine Loflin. "Geographies of Trust." *American Behavioral Scientist* 52 (2009): 1666–1683.

Steven Raphael and Michael Stoll. "Can Boosting Minority Car-Ownership Rates Narrow Inter-Racial Employment Gaps?" *The Brookings-Wharton Papers on Economic Affairs* (June 2000): 99–145.

John Rawls. *Justice as Fairness: A Restatement.* Cambridge: Harvard University Press, 2001.

———. *Political Liberalism.* New York: Columbia University Press, 1993.

———. *A Theory of Justice.* Cambridge, MA: Harvard University Press, 1971, revised 1999.

Joseph Raz. *The Morality of Freedom.* New York: Oxford University Press, 1986.

Henry S. Richardson. *Democratic Autonomy: Public Reasoning about the Ends of Policy.* New York: Oxford University Press, 2002.

———. "The Stupidity of the Cost–Benefit Standard." In *Cost-Benefit Analysis: Legal, Economic, and Philosophical Perspectives,* edited by M. D. Adler and E. A. Posner, 135–67. Chicago: University of Chicago Press, 2001.

Ingrid Robeyns. "Ideal Theory in Theory and Practice." *Social Theory and Practice* 34 (2008): 341–62.

Willard Rodgers. "Residential Satisfaction in Relationship to Size of Place." *Social Psychology Quarterly* 43 (1980): 436–41.

Jean-Jacques Rousseau. "Discourse on the Origins of Inequality." In *Rousseau: The Discourses and Other Early Political Writings,* edited by Victor Gourevitch, 111–88. Cambridge: Cambridge University Press, 1997.

———. "A Letter from Jean-Jacques Rousseau." 1757. Translated by Arthur Goldhammer. *New York Review of Books,* May 15, 2003.

————. *The Social Contract*. In *Rousseau: The Social Contract and Other Later Political Writings,* edited by Victor Gourevitch, 39–152. Cambridge: Cambridge University Press, 1997.

Anil Rupasingha, Stephan Goetz, and David Freshwater. "The Production of Social Capital in U.S. Counties." *Journal of Socio-Economics* 35 (2006): 83–101.

David Rusk. *Cities without Suburbs.* 2nd ed. Washington, DC: Woodrow Wilson Center Press, 1995.

Mark Sagoff. *Price, Principle and the Environment.* Cambridge: Cambridge University Press, 2004.

Michael J. Sandel. *Democracy's Discontent: America in Search of a Public Philosophy.* Cambridge, MA: Harvard University, 1996.

————. *Justice: What's the Right Thing to Do?* New York: Farrar, Straus and Giroux, 2009.

————. *Liberalism and the Limits of Justice.* Cambridge: Cambridge University Press, 1982.

————. "Reply to Critics." In *Debating Democracy's Discontent: Essays on American Politics, Law, and Public Philosophy,* edited by Anita Allen and Milton Regan, 319–335. New York: Oxford University Press, 1998.

————. "What Money Can't Buy: The Moral Limits of Markets." The Tanner Lectures, Brasenose College, Oxford, England, 1998.

Jason Schacter. "Why People Move: Exploring the March 2000 Current Population Survey." Washington, DC: United States Census Bureau, 2001.

Juliet Schor. *Born to Buy: The Commercialized Child and the New Consumer Culture.* New York: Scribner, 2004.

————. *The Overspent American.* New York: Basic Books, 1998.

Richard Schragger. "Consuming Government." *Michigan Law Review* 101 (2003): 1824–57.

Robert O. Self. *American Babylon: Race and the Struggle of Postwar Oakland.* Princeton: Princeton University Press, 2003.

Jefferey M. Sellers. "Toward a Comparative Historical Perspective on the Politics of Sprawl: California and Oregon Compared." Paper prepared for the annual meeting of the Urban Affairs Association, Detroit, Michigan, March 2001.

Amartya Sen. "The Discipline of Cost-Benefit Analysis." In Matthew D. Adler and Eric A. Posner, eds. *Cost-Benefit Analysis: Legal, Economic, and Philosophical Perspectives.* Chicago: University of Chicago Press, 2001, 95–116.

————. *The Idea of Justice.* Cambridge: Harvard University Press, 2009.

————. *On Ethics and Economics.* Oxford: Blackwell, 1987.

————. "What Do We Want from a Theory of Justice?" *Journal of Philosophy* 103 (2006): 215–38.

Amartya Sen and Bernard Williams, eds. *Utilitarianism and Beyond.* Cambridge: Cambridge University Press, 1982.

Richard Sennett. *The Fall of Public Man.* New York: Knopf, 1977.

————. *Flesh and Stone: The Body and the City in Western Civilization.* New York: W. W. Norton, 1994.

————. *The Uses of Disorder: Personal Identity and City Life.* New York: Knopf, 1970.

Tommie Shelby. "Justice, Deviance, and the Dark Ghetto." *Philosophy and Public Affairs* 35 (2007): 126–60.

Donald Shoup. *The High Cost of Free Parking.* Chicago: American Planning Association, 2005.

William Shutkin. *The Land That Could Be: Environmentalism and Democracy in the Twenty-first Century.* Cambridge, MA: MIT Press, 2000.

Georg Simmel. "The Metropolis and Mental Life." 1905. In *Classic Essays on the Culture of Cities*, edited by Richard Sennett, 47–60. Englewood Cliffs, NJ: Prentice Hall, 1969.

Joseph W. Singer. *The Edges of the Field: Lessons on the Obligations of Ownership.* Boston: Beacon, 2000.

———. *Entitlement: The Paradoxes of Property.* New Haven, CT: Yale University Press, 2000.

———. *Introduction to Property.* 2nd ed. New York: Aspen, 2005.

David Smith. *Geography and Social Justice.* Oxford, MA: Blackwell, 1994.

Graham Smith. *Deliberative Democracy and the Environment.* New York: Routledge, 2003.

Kevin B. Smith. "Economic Techniques." In *The Oxford Handbook of Public Policy,* edited by Michael Moran, Martin Rein, and Robert E. Goodin, 729–45. New York: Oxford University Press, 2006.

Rogers Smith. *Civic Ideals: Conflicting Ideals of Citizenship in U.S. History.* New Haven, CT: Yale University Press, 1997.

Tom A. B. Snijders and Roel J. Bosker. *Multilevel Analysis: An Introduction to Basic and Advanced Multilevel Modeling.* London: Sage, 1999.

James Gustave Speth. *The Bridge at the End of the World: Capitalism, the Environment, and Crossing from Crisis to Sustainability.* New Haven, CT: Yale University Press, 2008.

Lynn A. Staeheli and Don Mitchell. "USA's Destiny? Regulating Space and Creating Community in American Shopping Malls." *Urban Studies* 43 (2006): 977–92.

StataCorp. *Stata User's Guide Release 9.* College Station, TX: StataCorp, 2005.

Marc Stier. "Liberal Virtue/Communitarian Virtue." Paper delivered at the annual meeting of the American Political Science Association, Boston, August 2002.

Michael Stoll. "Spatial Mismatch and Job Sprawl." In *The Black Metropolis in the Twenty-first Century: Race, Power, and Politics of Place,* edited by Robert D. Bullard, 127–48. Lanham: Rowman & Littlefield, 2007.

Clarence Stone. *Regime Politics: Governing Atlanta, 1946–88.* Lawrence: University Press of Kansas, 1989.

Thomas Sugrue. *The Origins of the Urban Crisis: Race and Inequality in Postwar Detroit.* Princeton: Princeton University Press, 1996.

Cass Sunstein. "Beyond the Republican Revival." *Yale Law Journal* 97 (1988): 1539–90.

———. *Worst Case Scenarios.* Cambridge, MA: Harvard University Press, 2007.

Cass Sunstein and Richard Thaler. *Nudge: Improving Decisions about Health, Wealth, and Happiness.* New Haven, CT: Yale University Press, 2008.

Heidi Swarts. *Organizing Urban America: Secular and Faith-Based Progressive Movements.* Minneapolis: University of Minnesota Press, 2008.

Emily Talen. *New Urbanism and American Planning: The Conflict of Cultures.* New York: Routledge, 2005.

Robert Talisse. *Democracy after Liberalism: Pragmatism and Deliberative Politics.* New York: Routledge, 2005.

Charles Taylor. "The Diversity of Goods." In *Utilitarianism and Beyond,* edited by Amartya Sen and Bernard Williams, 129–44. Cambridge: Cambridge University Press, 1982.

———. *Philosophical Arguments.* Cambridge, MA: Harvard University Press, 1995.

———. *Sources of the Self: The Making of the Modern Identity.* Cambridge, MA: Harvard University Press, 1992.

Texas Transportation Institute. 2009 *Urban Mobility Report.* http://mobility.tamu.edu/ums.

Alan Thomas. "Liberalism, Republicanism, and the Idea of an Egalitarian Ethos." In *Property-Owning Democracy: Rawls and Beyond*, edited by Martin O'Neill and Thad Williamson. Cambridge: Wiley-Blackwell, 2010.

G. Scott Thomas. *The United States of Suburbia*. Amherst, NY: Prometheus Books, 1998.

Ken Thomson. *From Neighborhood to Nation: The Democratic Foundations of Civil Society*. Hanover, NH: University Press of New England, 2001.

Ann R. Tickamyer. "Space Matters! Spatial Inequality in Future Sociology." *Contemporary Sociology* 29 (2000): 805–13.

Charles Tiebout. "A Pure Theory of Local Expenditures." *Journal of Political Economy* 64 (1956): 416–424.

Alexis de Tocqueville, *Democracy in America*. New York: HarperCollins, 2000. Translated by George Lawrence.

Michael Tomz, Jason Wittenberg, and Gary King (2001). *CLARIFY: Software for Interpreting and Presenting Statistical Results*. Version 2.0. Cambridge, MA: Harvard University, June 1. http://gking.harvard.edu.

Fran Tonkiss. *Space, the City and Social Theory*. Malden: Polity Press, 2005.

Transit Cooperative Research Program, *Costs of Sprawl—2000*. Washington: National Academy Press, 2002.

United States Bureau of Transportation Statistics. *National Transportation Statistics 2007*. Washington: Bureau of Transportation Statistics, 2007.

United States Census. *County and City Data Book 2000*. Washington, DC: U.S. Census Bureau, 2002.

———. 2008 National Population Projections, released August 14, 2008. http://www
.census.gov/population/www/projections/2008projections.html.

United States Energy Information Administration. "Emissions of Greenhouse Gases in the United States 2008." Washington, DC: U.S. Department of Energy. ftp://ftp.eia.doe.gov/
pub/oiaf/1605/cdrom/pdf/ggrpt/057308.pdf.

———. "U.S. Carbon Dioxide Emissions from Energy Sources 2007 Flash Estimate."
Washington, DC: U.S. Department of Energy. http://www.eia.doe.gov/oiaf/1605/flash/
flash.html.

United States Environmental Protection Agency. EPA report "Latest Findings on National Air Quality—Status and Trends Through 2006." http://www.epa.gov/air/airtrends/2007.

Steve Vanderheiden. *Atmospheric Justice: A Political Theory of Climate Change*. New York: Oxford University Press, 2008.

Sidney Verba, Kay Schlozman, and Henry Brady. *Voice and Equality: Civic Voluntarism in American Politics*. Cambridge: Harvard University Press, 1995.

Jeremy Waldron. *The Right to Private Property*. New York: Oxford University Press, 1988.

Alan Walks. "Place of Residence, Party Preferences, and Political Attitudes in Canadian Cities and Suburbs." *Journal of Urban Affairs* 26 (2004): 269–295.

Mark R. Warren. *Dry Bones Rattling: Community Building to Revitalize American Democracy*. Princeton: Princeton University Press, 2001.

Michael Walzer. *Spheres of Justice*. New York Basic Books, 1983.

Robin West. "Universalism, Liberal Theory, and the Problem of Gay Marriage." *Florida State University Law Review* 25 (1998): 705–730.

Stuart White. "Rawls, Republicanism, and Property-Owning Democracy." In *Property-Owning Democracy: Rawls and Beyond*, edited by Martin O'Neill and Thad Williamson. London: Wiley-Blackwell, 2010.

Wim Wiewel and Joseph J. Persky, eds., *Suburban Sprawl: Private Decisions and Public Policy.* Armonk, NY: M. E. Sharpe, 2002.

Wim Wiewel, Joseph Persky, and Mark Sendzik. "Private Benefits and Public Costs: Policies to Address Suburban Sprawl." *Policy Studies Journal* 27 (1999): 96–114.

Thad Williamson. "Bringing History Back In? Assessing the New Suburban History," presented at the annual meeting of the American Political Science Association, Boston, August 2008.

———. "Sprawl, Spatial Location, and Politics: How Ideological Identification Tracks the Built Environment." *American Politics Research* 36 (2008): 903–33.

Thad Williamson, David Imbroscio, and Gar Alperovitz. *Making a Place for Community: Local Democracy in a Global Era.* New York: Routledge Press, 2002.

William Julius Wilson. *When Work Disappears: The World of the New Urban Poor.* New York: Vintage Books, 1996.

Christopher Winship and Larry Radbill. "Sampling Weights and Regression Analysis." *Sociological Methods & Research* 23 (1994): 230–57.

Louis Wirth. "Urbanism as a Way of Life." *American Journal of Sociology* 44 (1938): 1–24.

Marcel Wissenburg. *Green Liberalism: The Free and the Green Society.* London: UCL Press, 1998.

Jonathan Wolff. *Robert Nozick: Property, Justice, and the Minimal State.* Stanford: Stanford University Press, 1991.

Jonathan Wolff and Dirk Haubrich. "Economism and Its Limits." In *The Oxford Handbook of Public Policy*, edited by Michael Moran, Martin Rein, and Robert E. Goodin, 746–70. New York: Oxford University Press, 2006.

Sheldon Wolin. "The Liberal/Democratic Divide: On Rawls's *Political Liberalism*." *Political Theory* 24 (1996): 97–119.

Harold Wolman, George Galster, Royce Hanson, Michael Ratcliffe, Kimberly Furdell, and Andrea Sarzynski. "The Fundamental Challenge in Measuring Sprawl: Which Land Should Be Considered?" *Professional Geographer* 57 (2005): 94–105.

Jeffrey Wooldridge. *Econometric Analysis of Cross-Section and Panel Data.* Cambridge: MIT Press, 2002.

Kevin Yamamura. "Governor Signs Anti-Sprawl Bill." *Sacramento Bee*, October 1, 2008.

Rebecca Yang and Paul Jargowsky. "Suburban Development and Economic Segregation in the 1990s." *Journal of Urban Affairs*, 28 (2006): 253–273.

Iris Marion Young. *Inclusion and Democracy.* New York: Oxford University Press, 2000.

———. *Justice and the Politics of Difference.* Princeton: Princeton University Press, 1990.

Karen Zivi. "Cultivating Character: John Stuart Mill and the Subject of Rights." *American Journal of Political Science* 50 (2006): 49–61.

censoring books, support for, 164–65

central city residence
  and community satisfaction, 349n43
  as sprawl measure, 45–46
  trust, negative predictor of, 160

central city schools, 132

central city status, in community life, 86

centrality, sprawl dimension of, 24

civic cost of sprawl, 4

civic decline in United States, 187

civic engagement, 217

civic life, and sprawl-related spatial features,
  240–41

civic participation's influence on sprawl,
  future of, 240

civic republicanism, 361n40
  Aristotelian propositions, 187
  central claim of, 203
  and common goods, 187
  and concerns on sprawl, 203
  citizens' active involvement under,
    181, 182
  critique of sprawl under, 196–97
  critiques of U.S. life, 358n19
  debate on sprawl, scope for, 284–85
  on democratic citizenship, 179
  distinctive values of, 269
  fundamental claims of, 188
  and green political orientation, 263–64
  and increased political participation, 192
  and liberalism, 180–86
  and maximizing economic growth, 80
  and misplaced commodification, 200–202
  neo-Roman or neo-Aristotelian form of,
    186
  and non-domination, 183
  objections to corporate conglomerates,
    204–6
  observations on built environment,
    212–13
  private lives and public good, 199
  private space, objections to, 214
  public deliberation about social practices,
    193
  public deliberation and neighborhood
    choices, 201
  regime, meaning of, 198
  republican virtues' list, 195–96
  self-governance and freedom, 206, 215
  and socio-spatial arrangements, 208–9
  strands of thoughts on, 190–91

themes of, 186

civic virtue, 179–80
  applying civic republicanism, 207–16
  contemporary civic republicanism,
    186–88
  debating good life, 193–95
  egalitarianism and equal citizenship
    requirements, 202–3
  effects of socio-spatial patterns on, 208
  freedom as self-governance, centrality of
    participation in self-rule, 188–93
  and neutral state, 154
  and personal interests, 195
  and political economy of citizenship,
    203–7
  and private virtue, 356–57n13
  and public goods, 198–200
  and relationship between liberalism and
    republicanism, 180–86
  republican virtue, and state promotion of,
    195–98
  and spatial organization, 155–56

civil disobedience, 356n9

Clarify (computer program), 89, 90

climate change
  public understanding of, 256
  stemming, suggestions on, 257–59
  structure of built environment on,
    264–65

Clinton administration, urban policy, 175

collective identity and built environment,
  200–201

commercialism, 26

common-interest developments (CIDS)
  seclusion and control in, 165

communities' spatial layout, and human
  violation of, 127

commuting time, 328–29n78
  and higher-intensity activism, 365n21
  importance of, for social capital, 94–96
  and quality of life, 91
  and well-being, 88, 90, 96, 98, 107

compact growth scenario
  quality of life in, 101
  urban-growth, 65–66

compactness, sprawl dimension of, 24

concentrated poverty areas
  economic and racial diversity in,
    142–45
  and equality of opportunity, 119
  ill effects of, 132

normative behavior, and spatial location, 40–41

nuclearity, sprawl dimension of, 24

oil consumption
    limitation of, 258, 262
older neighborhoods
    approachability of strangers in, 165
    and community satisfaction, 349n43
organization of built environment
    applying civic republicanism to, 207–8
    impact on way of life, 186
    levels of public deliberation on, 202

Pareto optimality, 63, 69, 271
personal happiness, in contemporary
    metropolis, 88
petition signing and sprawl, 226
place, reason for attraction, 42
policies on new development, 254
policy alternatives to sprawl, 147–48
policy diversity and normative arguments,
    7–10
policy learning, 9, 318n16
policy reform, and sprawl, 267, 271–79
political awareness, 224–25
political consciousness, effects of space on,
    165
political deliberation, in society with equal
    concern, 154–55
political discourse, in United States, 186
political engagement
    boundedness and increased activity in,
        219
    intensity of, 225–29
    and local contexts, 218
    and spatial design, 220
    and sprawl, 239
    sprawl-related variables, 222, 232, 233
political ideology, 169, 170
    measure of, 348n35
    SCCBS's data on, 167
    and sprawl-related factors, 168, 171, 172
"political liberty" and "individual liberty,"
    356–57n13
political orientation and sprawl, 165–72
political participation, 190
    achieving freedom in self-governance by,
        202
    Aristotelian view of, 359n27
    common forms of, 225

contribution of neighborhood, 212
desirability of, 191–92
high-intensity participation, 228, 230,
    231
long-established predictors of, 218
low-intensity participation, 225–27
measures of, 367n40
spatial policies aimed at boosting, 247
and sprawl, link between, 227–232
political will, correction of sprawl-related
    inequalities, 176
poor urban residents, interests in well-being
    of, 171
Portland-style growth boundaries, 371n8
"positive" freedoms, 21
power politics in civic life, concept of, 247
preference satisfaction, in housing
    development, 77–84
preference satisfaction, public policy
    making, 85
private decisions, liberals' interventions
    into, 153
private housing market, 278–79
private ideo-logics, 60–61
    versus public ideo-logics, 13–14
private personal space, 152
private space
    and automobiles, 36–37
    civic republican objection, 214
    spatial development, 75
privatistic preferences, 214–15
    in residential partnership, 213
    and sprawling, cause and effect of, 238
procedural liberalism, 363n77
property, 15
property claims, 16
property law, 20
property-owning democracy, 347n13,
    358–59n23
property rights
    theory of, 15–18
    history and practice, 18–20
"property rights" movement, 20
prototypical sprawling community, 64
proximity, sprawl dimension of, 24
public deliberation process, individuals'
    preferences, 83
public good, 198, 199
public ideo-logics, 15
    versus private ideo-logics, 13–14
public life in United States, nature of, 186

private space and automobiles, affluence
and preference for, 36–37
technological shifts and industry
deconcentration, 31
urban decline and metropolitan
fragmentation, 31–32
sprawl, measures of
automobile dependence, 46
central city/suburban residence, 44–46
density, 46
neighborhood age, 46–47
sprawl, related measures, 48–49
city size, 49
commuting times, 49
demographic contextual variables, 50–51
residential stability, 50
sprawl-related individual variables, 50
sprawl debate, 9–10, 98, 372n11
sprawl growth scenario, 65–66
and quality of life, 101
sprawl-containment policy, 9
state neutrality
and best way of life, 194
general doctrine of, 360–61n37
stay-cation trend, implications of, 262
stewardship, concept of, 198
Student Nonviolent Coordinating
Committee, 360n33
subjective quality-of-life ratings, 91, 92
suburban affluence
and central city decay, 128
and the poorest residents in urban areas,
130
school education, public funding
disparities, 131–32
and urban poverty, 134–38
suburban areas, facilitating civility, 220
suburban communities, 25–26
suburban growth, U.S. economic policy, 3–4
suburbanization, 152–53, 172
Americans' preference for, 76
Americans' view on, 178
benefits of, 65
and causal connection between urban
stress, 134
and conservative political outlook,
167, 168
critique on, 214
debates on, 63
distributional consequences of job sprawl,
137

economic dependence of cities in, 138
effects of, 128
environmental concerns of, 71
federal and local policies accelerating,
32–36
history of, 268
and homeownership, 34–35
impacts of automobile dependency in,
146
inequalities in, 134
inequities generated by, 68
and middle-class people, 151
nature of neighborhoods, 134
plausible alternatives to, 64
poverty rate under, 139
public costs associated with, 65
reasons for existence of, 75
share of public subsidies, disparities, 136
and sprawl, distinction made between,
145–46
in the United States, 344n69
and urban decline, causal connection
between, 134–40
utilitarian analyses of, 70–71
zoning practices in, 135–36
suburban living
and newfound preferences, 350n46
questions of, 350–51n47
suburban municipalities, urban annexation
of, 272
suburban residence, measure of sprawl,
45–46
suburban sprawl, see sprawl
supply-side mechanisms, 233–35
Supreme Court rulings, on land use, 320n44
systemic unfairness, and sprawl
existence of urban black ghettoes, 116
harms associated with socio-spatial
patterns, 119
possible cause and a possible effect
of, 111

taxation and regulation, 19
telecommuting, future of, 261
thin democracy, 190, 191
Tocquevillian claim, concerning political
participation, 190
tolerance and spatial context, 157, 158
tract-level racial diversity, predictor of
dissatisfaction, 94
trading off goods, 100